The Jo Anne Stolaroff Cotsen Prize Imprint
honors outstanding studies in archaeology
to commemorate a special person whose
appreciation for scholarship was recognized
by all whose lives she touched.

The Early Iron Age Cemetery at Torone

Volume 2: Illustrations

COTSEN INSTITUTE OF
ARCHAEOLOGY AT UCLA

The Early Iron Age Cemetery at Torone

Excavations Conducted by the
Australian Archaeological Institute at Athens
in Collaboration with the
Athens Archaeological Society

Volume 2: Illustrations

John K. Papadopoulos

With contributions by
Jonathan H. Musgrave
Sandor Bökönyi [†]
Deborah Ruscillo
Ferenc Gyulai and Kristina Kelertas
R. E. Jones
I. K. Whitbread

Monumenta Archaeologica 24
Cotsen Institute of Archaeology at UCLA
University of California, Los Angeles
2005

COTSEN INSTITUTE OF
ARCHAEOLOGY AT UCLA

Production by Leyba Associates, Villanueva, New Mexico
Copy editing by Catherine Chambers
Cover design by William Morosi
Index by Robert Swanson

The publication of this volume was made possible by a grant from the Institute for Aegean Prehistory and the Steinmetz Chair Endowment in Classical Archaeology and Material Culture at UCLA.

Library of Congress Cataloging-in-Publication Data
Papadopoulos, John K., 1958-
  The early Iron Age cemetery at Torone / John K. Papadopoulos.
    p. cm. -- (Monumenta archaeologica ; 24)
  Includes bibliographical references and index.
  ISBN 1-931745-16-1
  1. Torone (Extinct city) 2. Excavations (Archaeology)--Greece--Torone Region. 3. Iron age--Greece--Torone (Extinct city) 4. Tombs--Greece--Torone (Extinct city) 5. Torone Region (Greece)--Antiquities. I. Title. II. Monumenta archaeologica (Cotsen Institute of Archaeology at UCLA) ; v. 24.
    DF261.T75P36 2005
    938'.1--dc22
                                                                                    2005022875

Contents

FIGURES

TOMB CONTENTS

MORTUARY PRACTICES

PLATES

FIGURE 1. Map of Greece showing some of the main Early Iron Age sites. (Robert Finnerty)

711

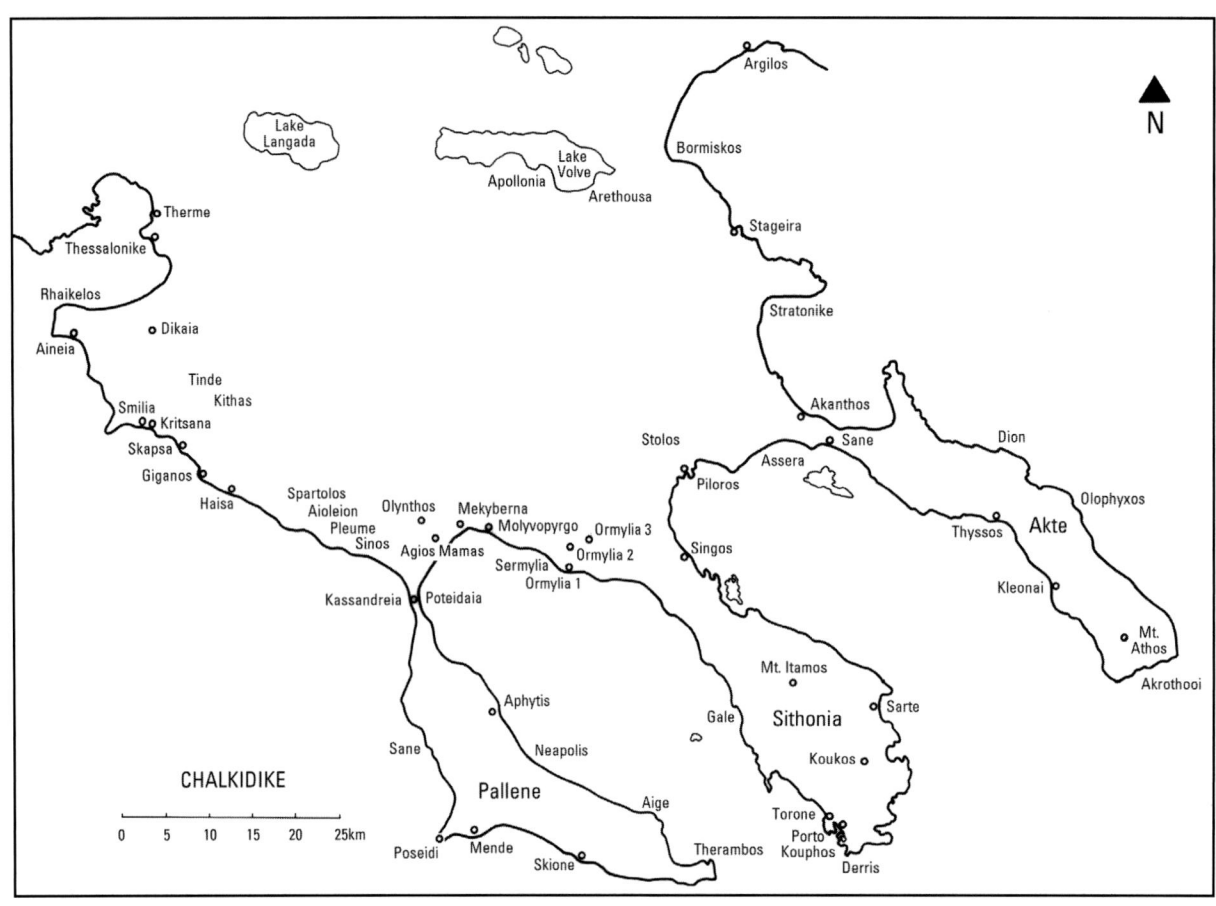

FIGURE 2. Chalkidike. Map showing principal sites, in part following Zahrnt 1971. (Anne Hooton)

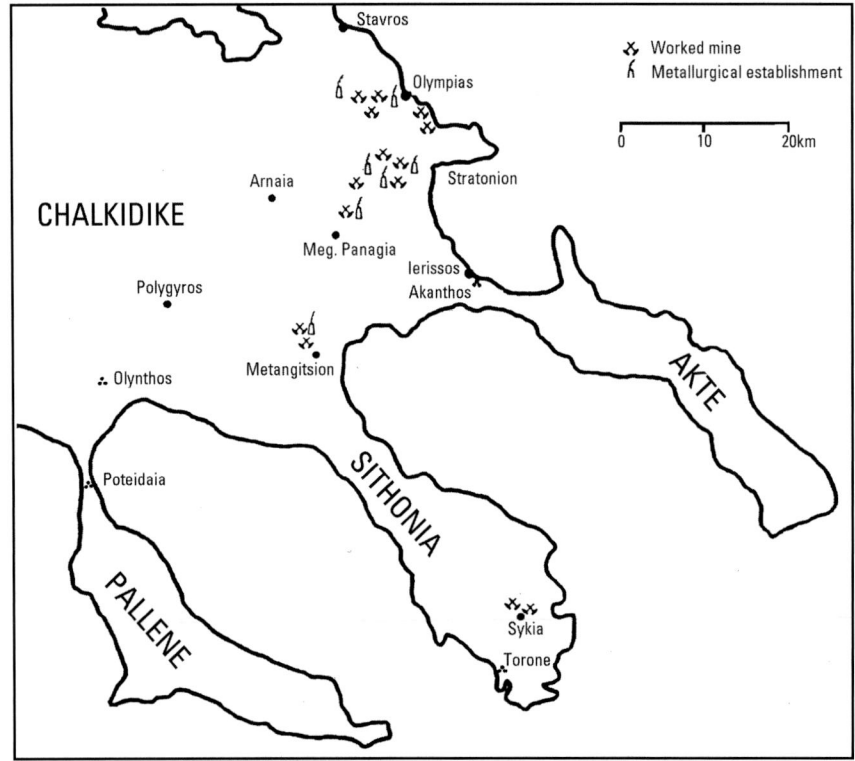

FIGURE 3. Chalkidike. Map showing worked mines and metallurgical establishments (after Wagner, Pernicka, Vavelides, Baranyi, and Bassiakos 1986 [= Pernicka 1987:655, fig. 23]).

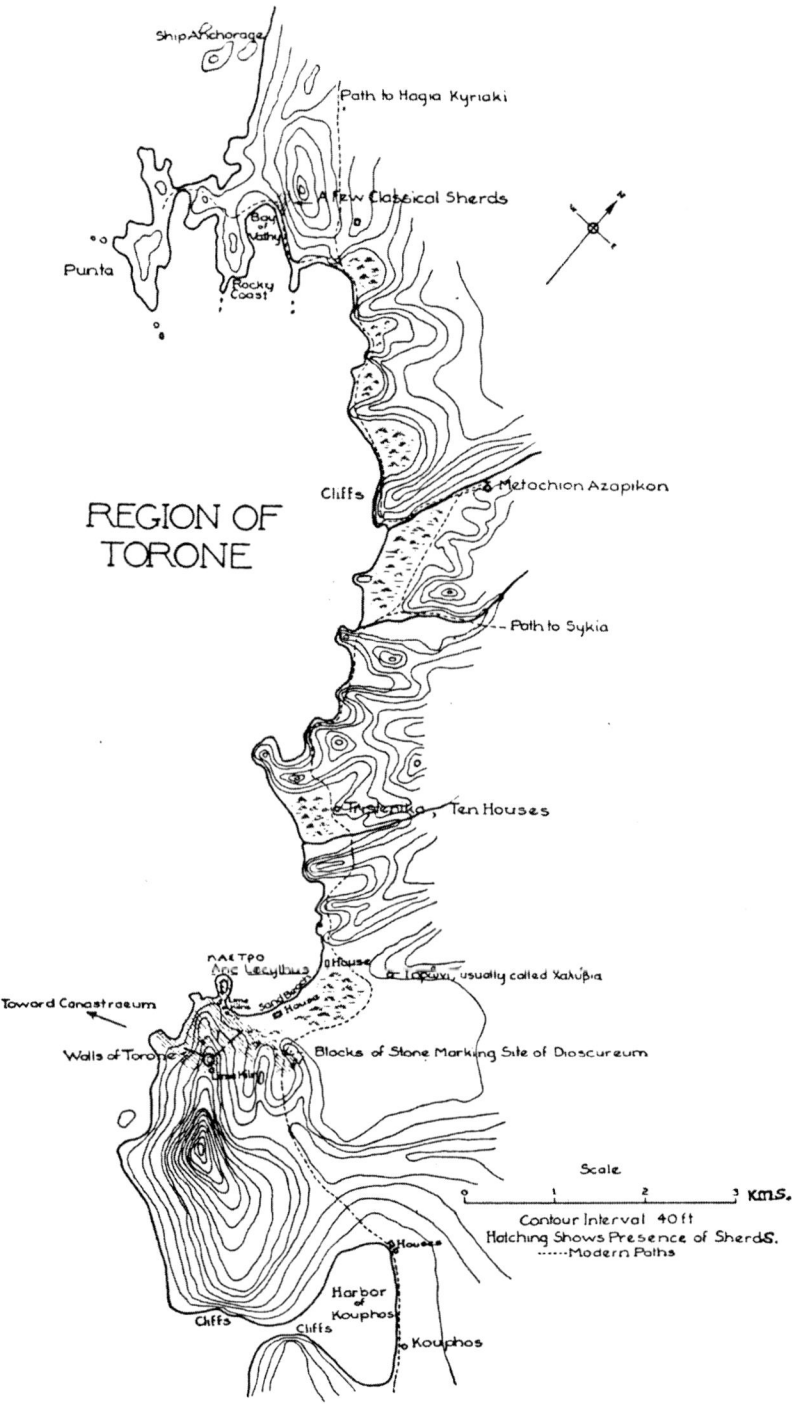

FIGURE 4. Benjamin Meritt's sketch map of Torone and vicinity published in 1923.

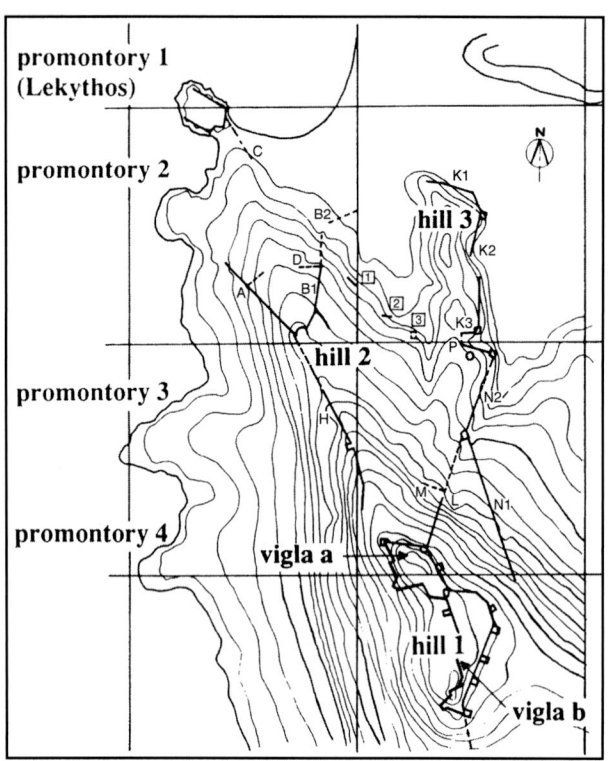

FIGURE 5. Torone. Sketch plan of the site showing Classical, Hellenistic, and later fortifications.

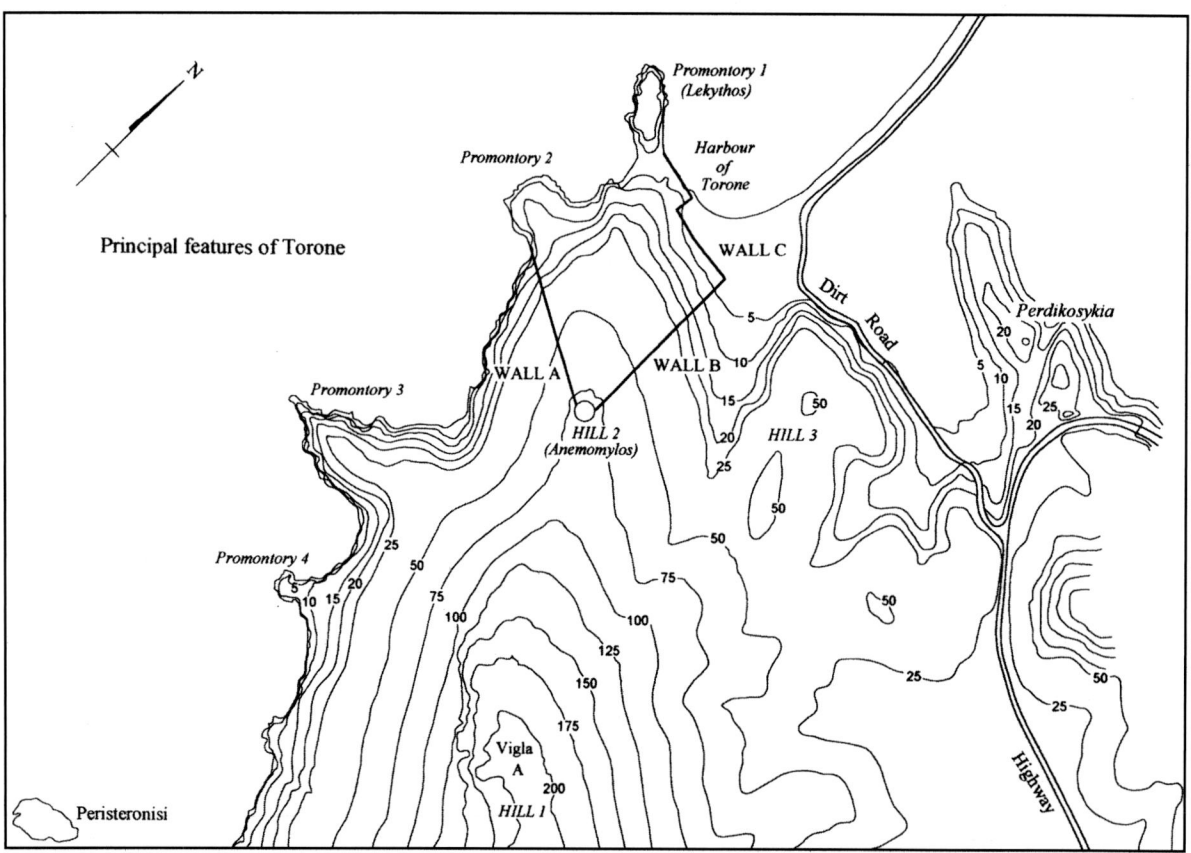

FIGURE 6. Torone. Plan of the northern part of the site showing the reconstructed trace of the Classical fortification, together with the hills and promontories that constitute the site.

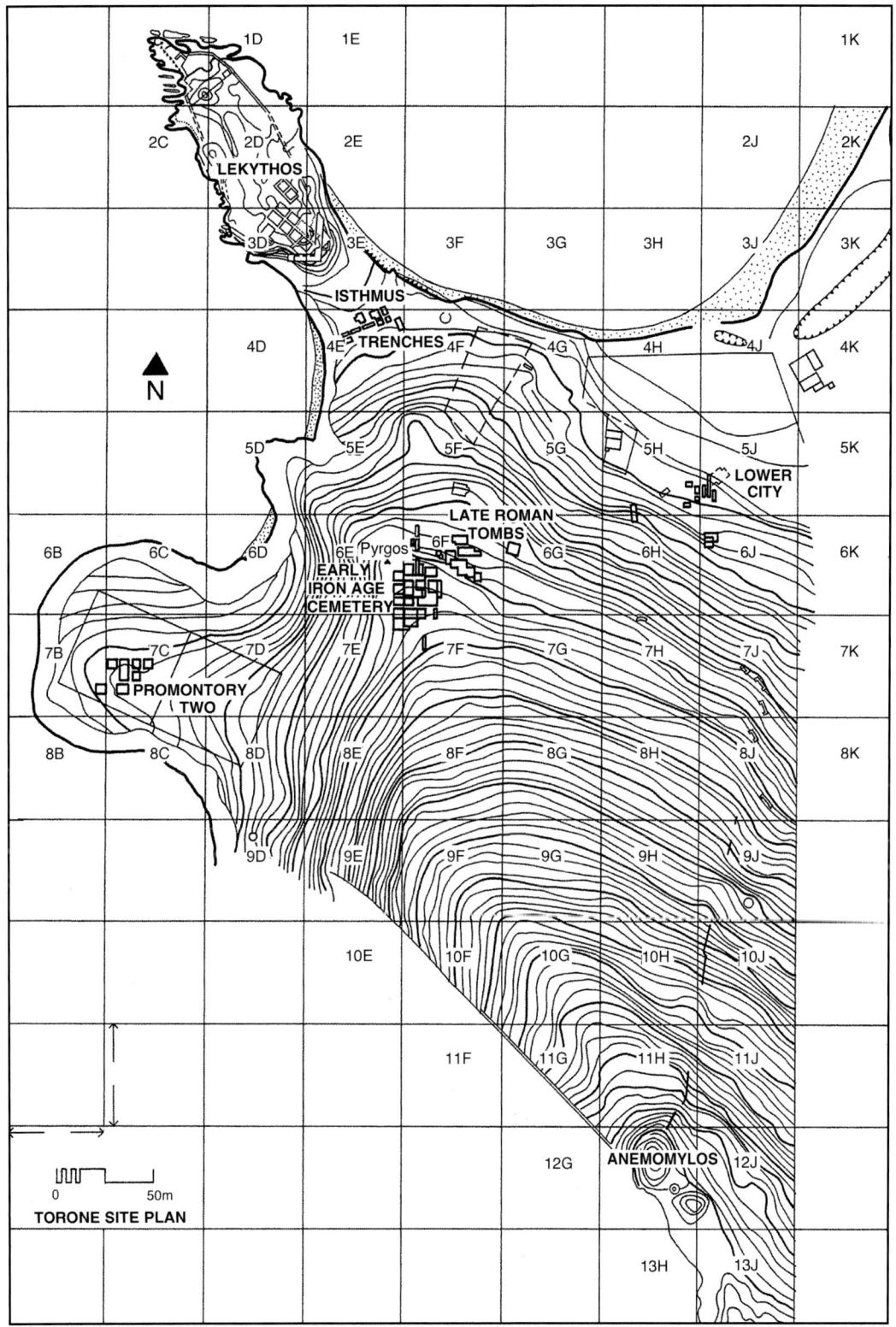

FIGURE 7. Torone. Grid plan of the NW part of the site, including the fortified Classical city, showing location of the Early Iron Age cemetery.

FIGURE 8. Vincenzo Coronelli's 1659 view of Torone, labeled Toron.

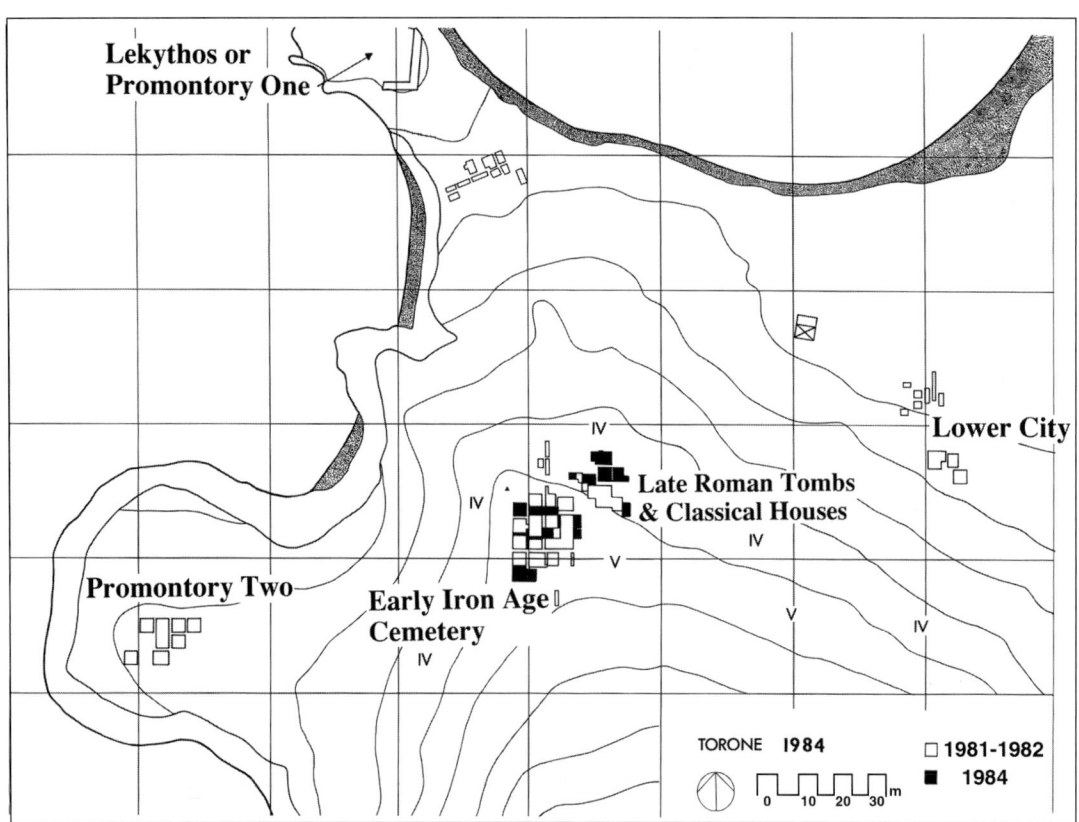

FIGURE 9. Torone. Plan of lower site showing location of the Early Iron Age cemetery and locations of the 1981–1982 and 1984 trenches.

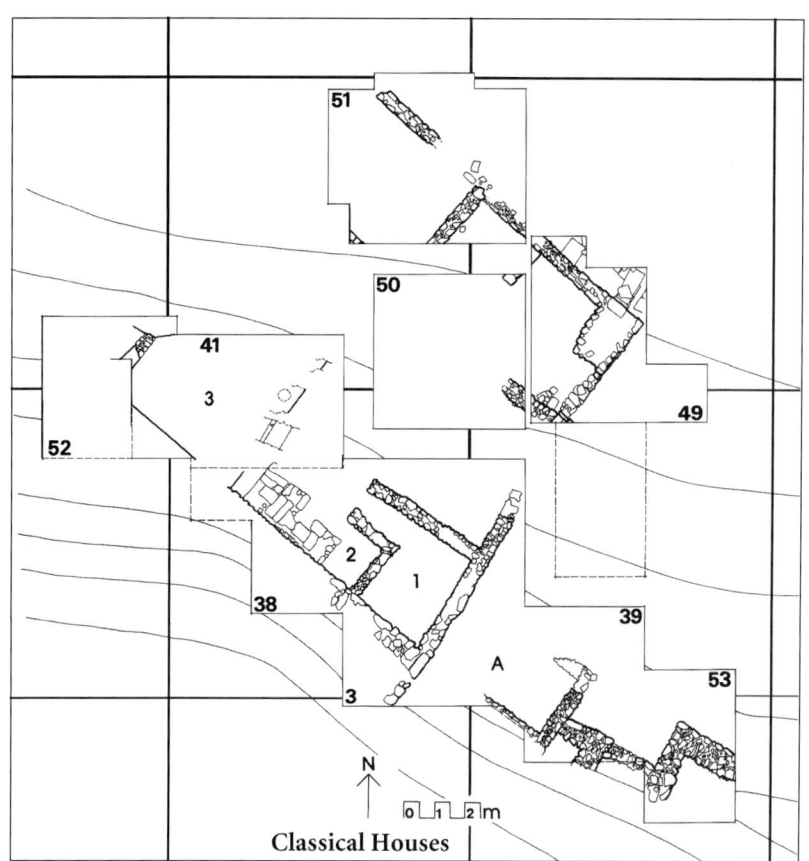

FIGURE 10. Terrace IV. Plan of Classical domestic architecture (numbers refer to trenches, except for architectural units 1, 2, and 3).

Classical Houses

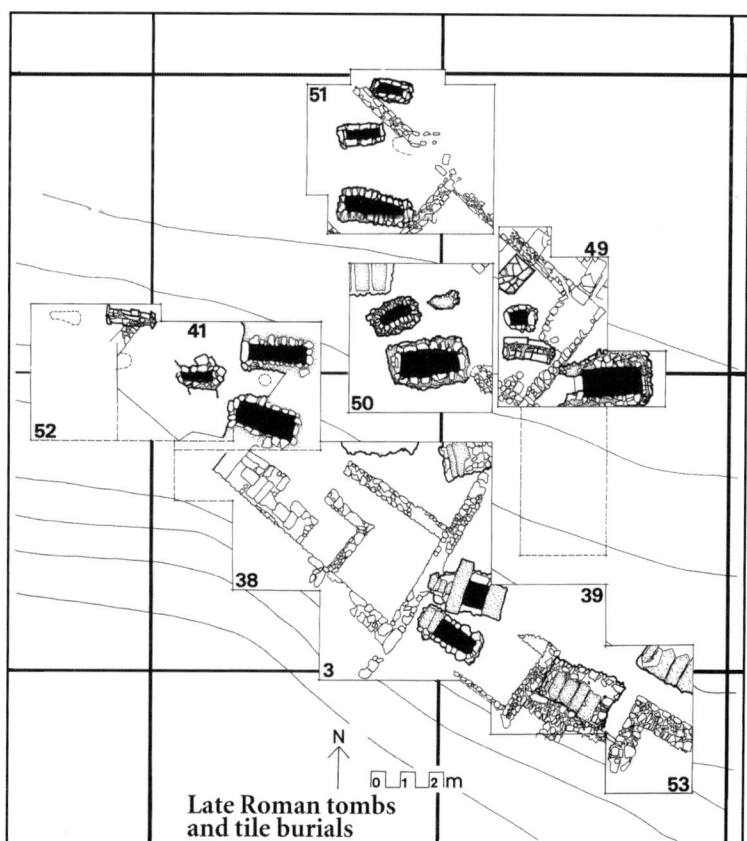

FIGURE 11. Terrace IV. Plan of Late Roman tombs.

Late Roman tombs and tile burials

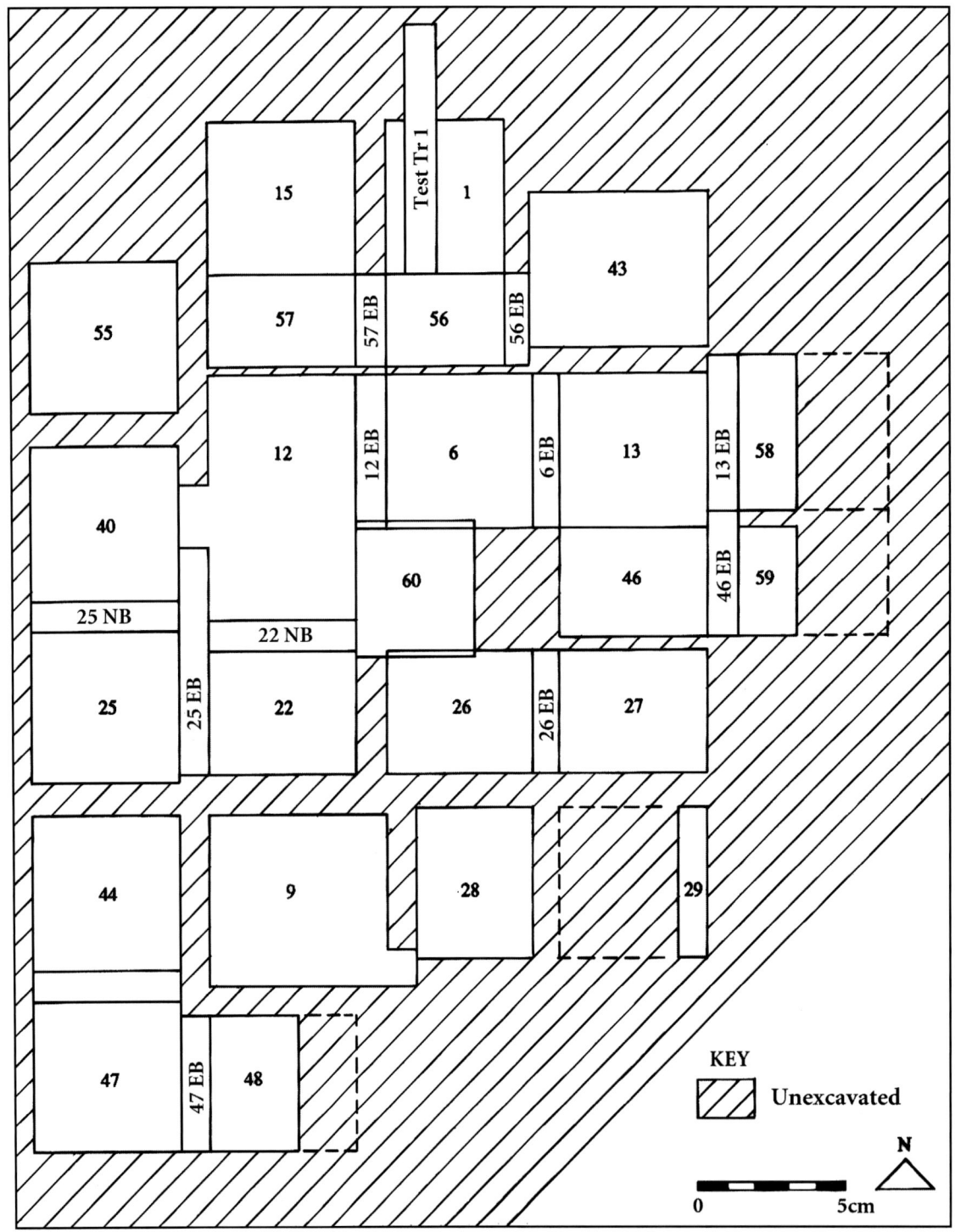

FIGURE 12. Terrace V. Plan showing layout of excavated trenches and baulks.

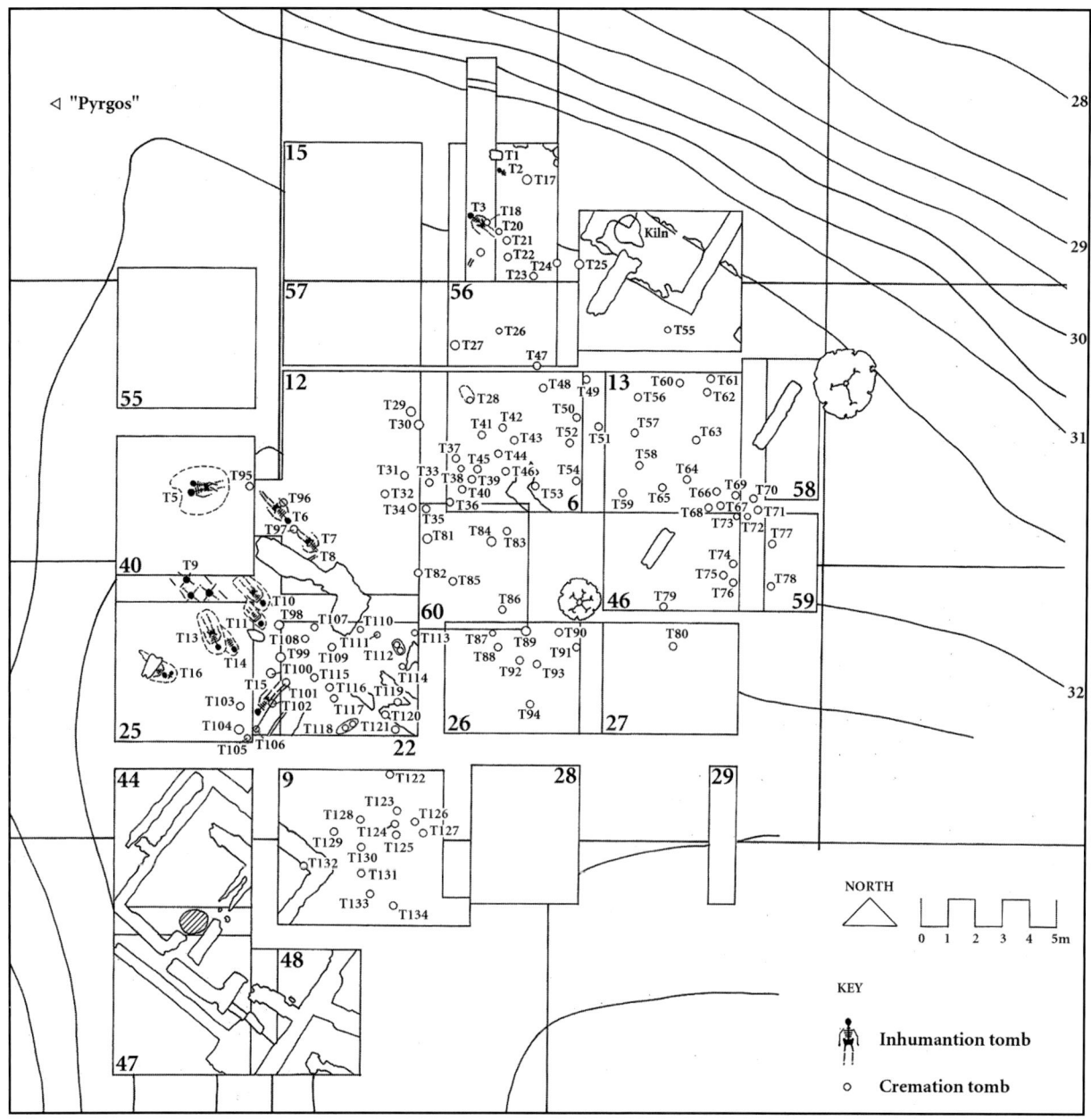

FIGURE 13. Terrace V. Plan of Early Iron Age cemetery and kiln, as well as Classical domestic architecture as preserved.

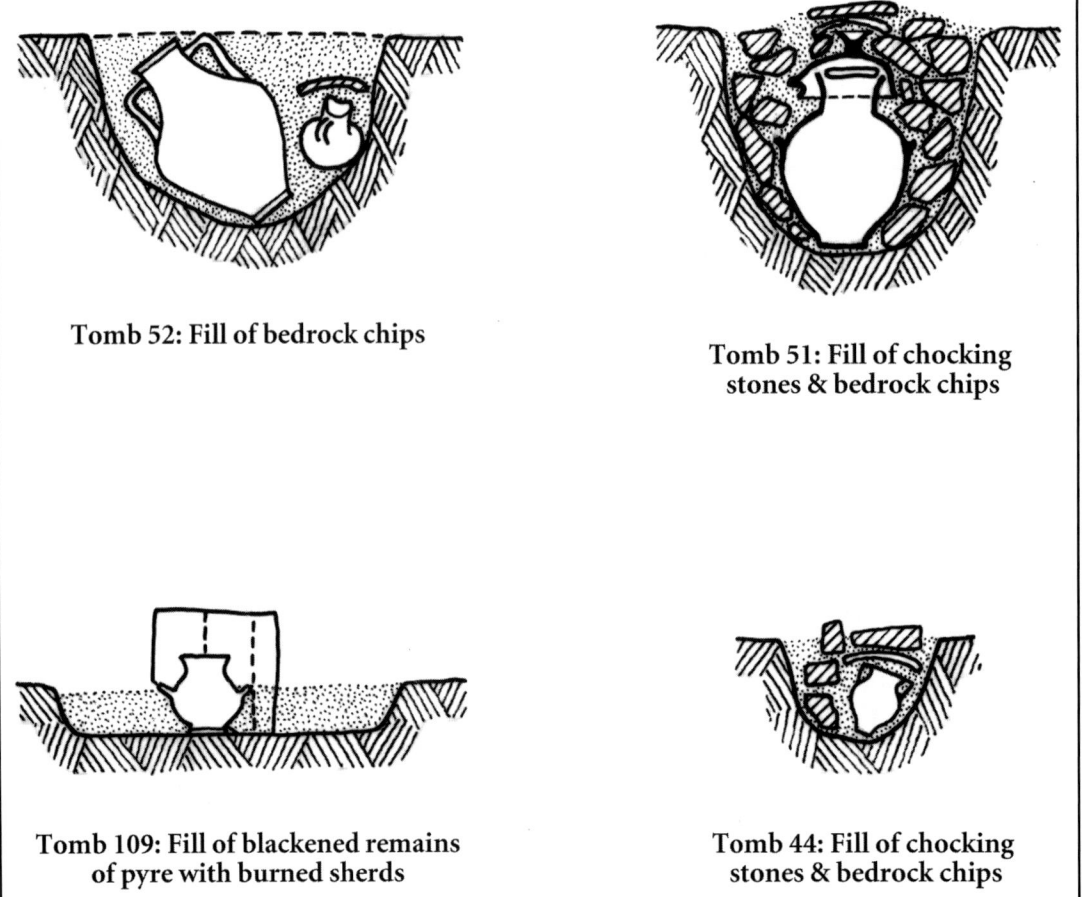

Tomb 52: Fill of bedrock chips

Tomb 51: Fill of chocking
stones & bedrock chips

Tomb 109: Fill of blackened remains
of pyre with burned sherds

Tomb 44: Fill of chocking
stones & bedrock chips

FIGURE 14 (on facing page). Sketch sections of some typical cremation tombs (not to scale).

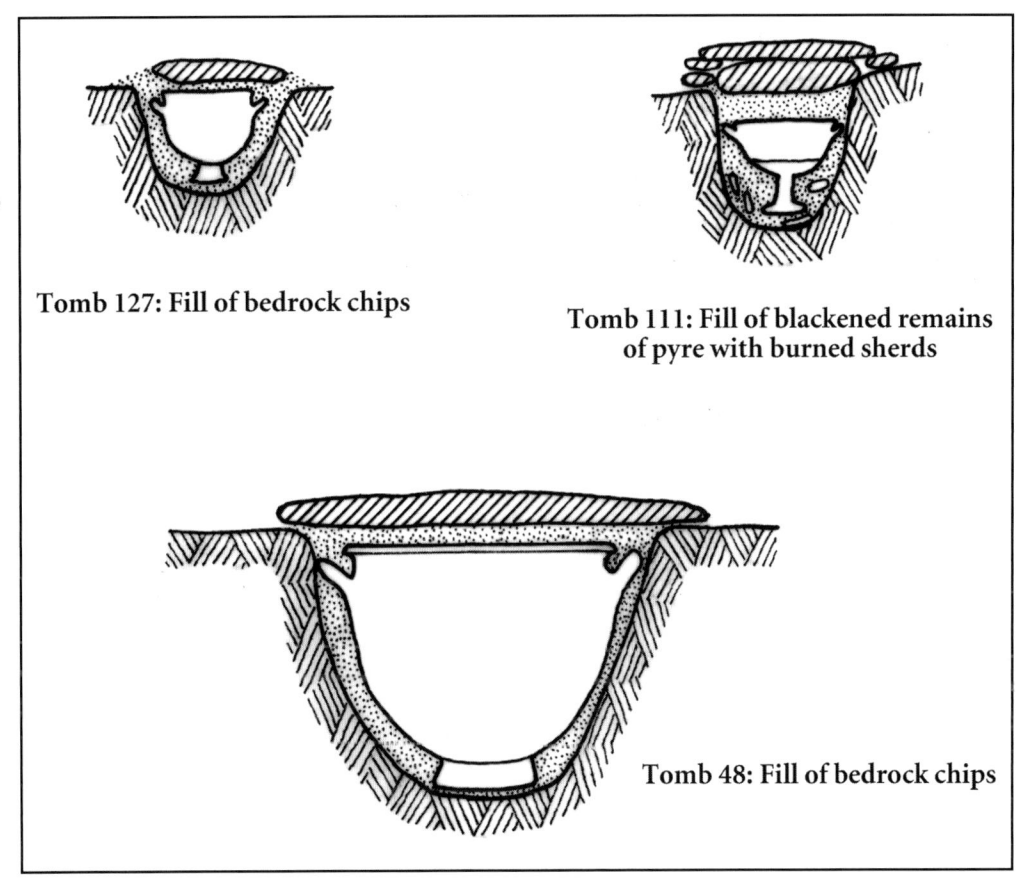

FIGURE 14 (continued). Sketch sections of some typical cremation tombs (not to scale).

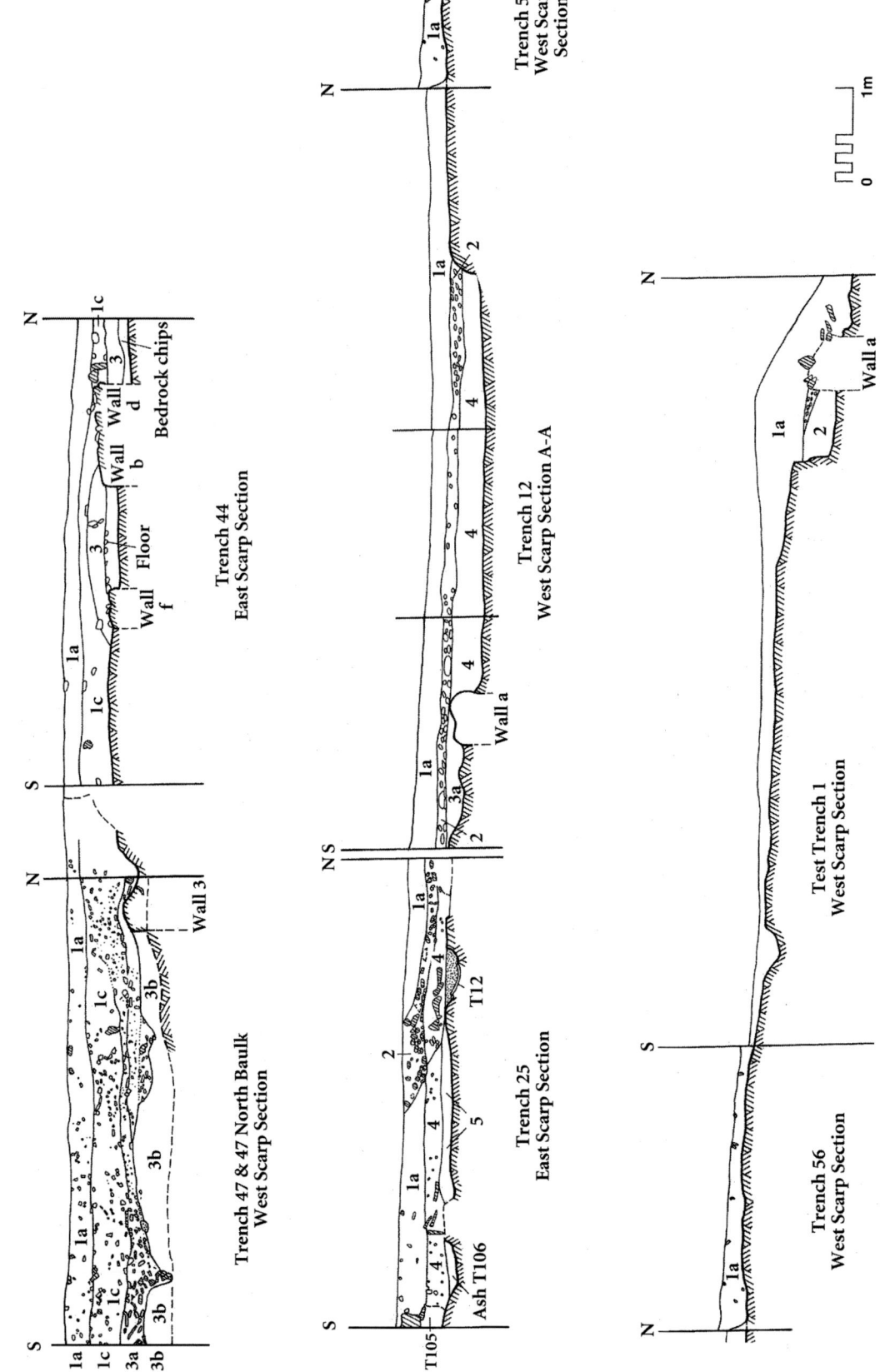

FIGURE 15 (on facing page). Terrace V. Sections through the terrace as excavated. (*a*) North–south section through west and central portion of excavated area.

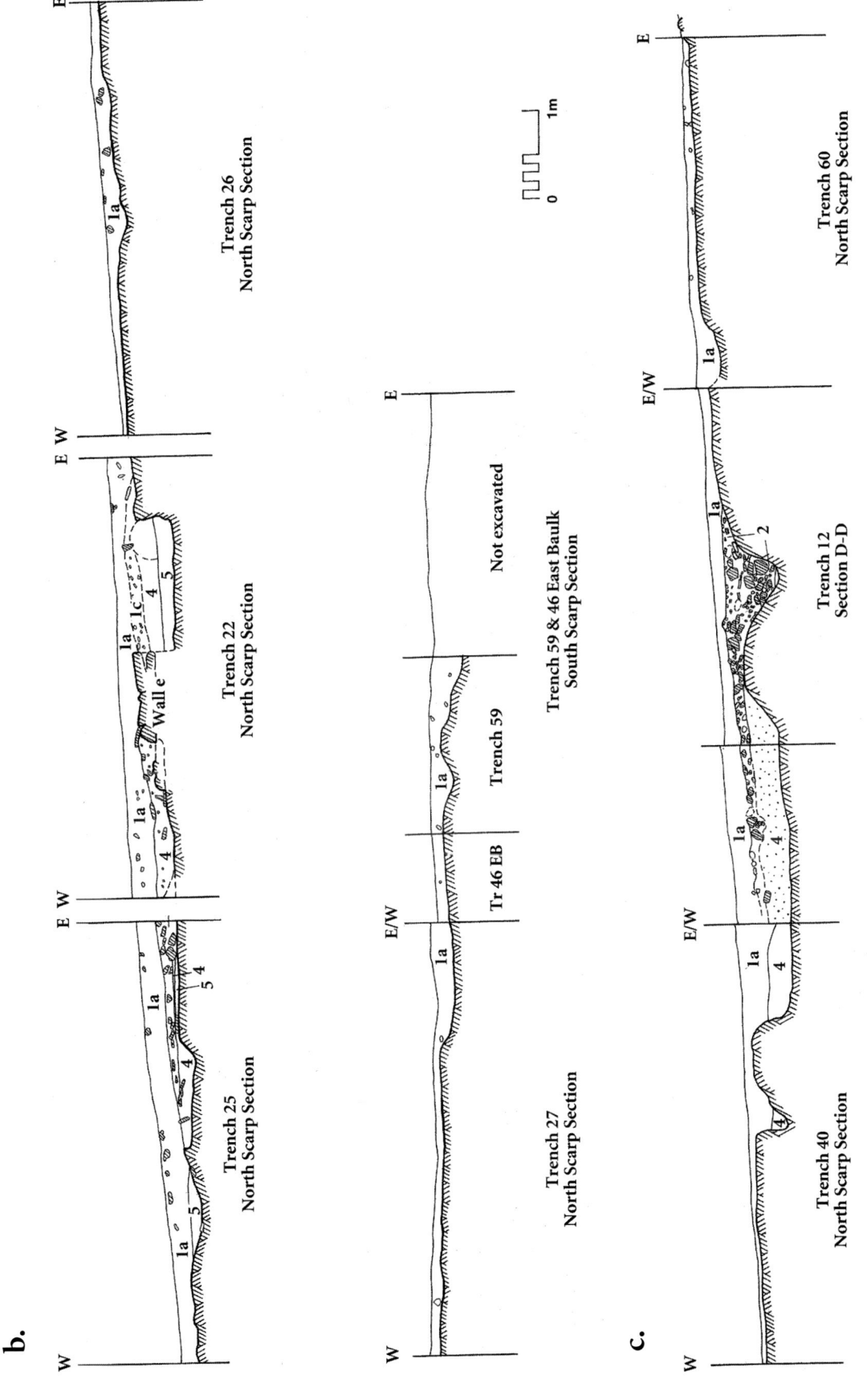

b.

Trench 26
North Scarp Section

Trench 22
North Scarp Section

Trench 25
North Scarp Section

Trench 59 & 46 East Baulk
South Scarp Section

Not excavated

Trench 59

Tr 46 EB

Trench 27
North Scarp Section

c.

Trench 60
North Scarp Section

Trench 12
Section D-D

Trench 40
North Scarp Section

FIGURE 15 (continued). Terrace V. Sections through the terrace as excavated. (*b*): *Top two rows*. East–west section through south-central portion of excavated area. (*c*) East–west section through central portion of excavated area.

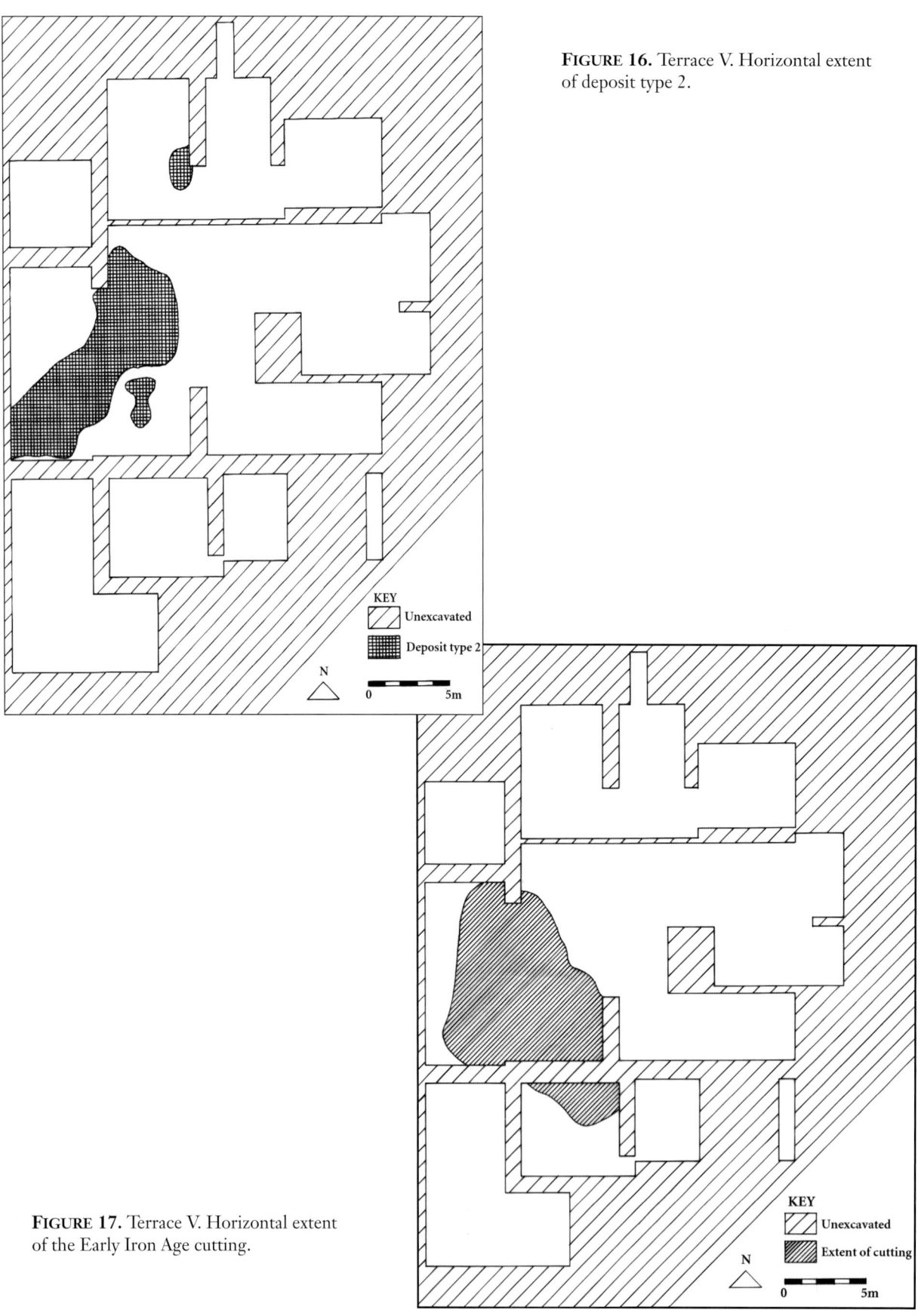

FIGURE 16. Terrace V. Horizontal extent of deposit type 2.

KEY

Unexcavated

Deposit type 2

N

0   5m

FIGURE 17. Terrace V. Horizontal extent of the Early Iron Age cutting.

KEY

Unexcavated

Extent of cutting

N

0   5m

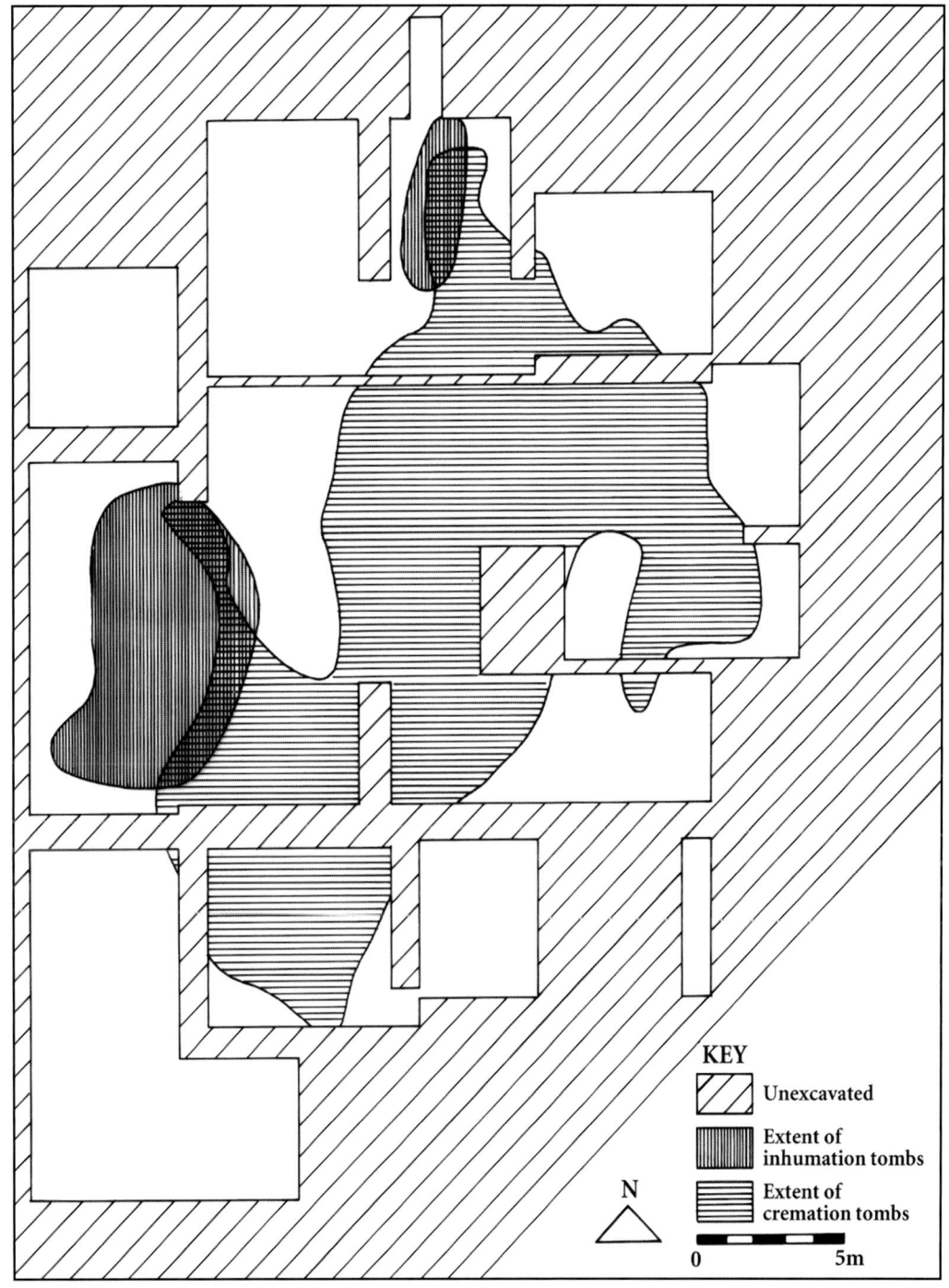

FIGURE 18. Terrace V. Horizontal extent of inhumation and cremation tombs.

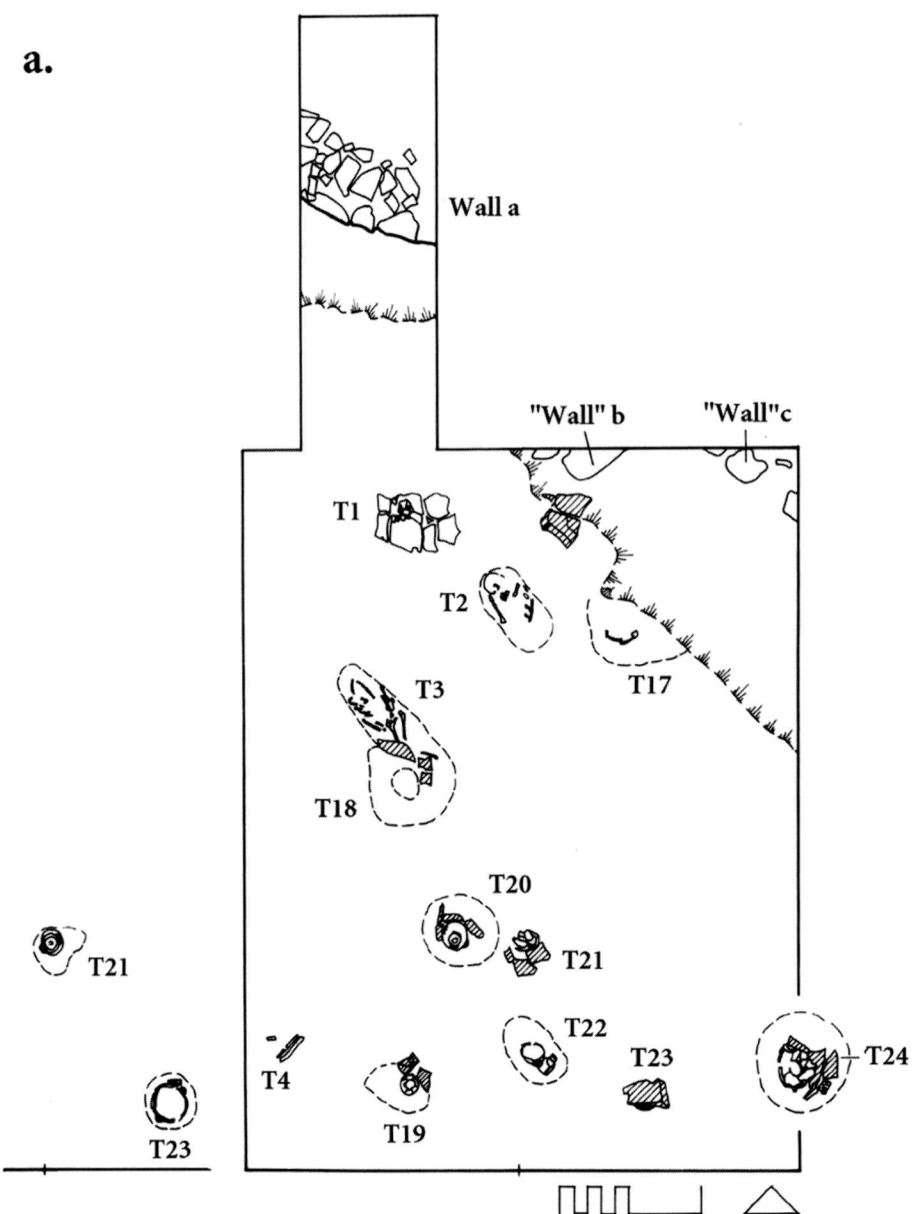

a.

Wall a

"Wall" b   "Wall" c

T1

T2

T17

T3

T18

T20

T21

T21

T22

T4   T23   T24

T23   T19

FIGURE 19 (on facing page). Trench 1, incorporating Test Trench 1. (*a*) Plan.

b.

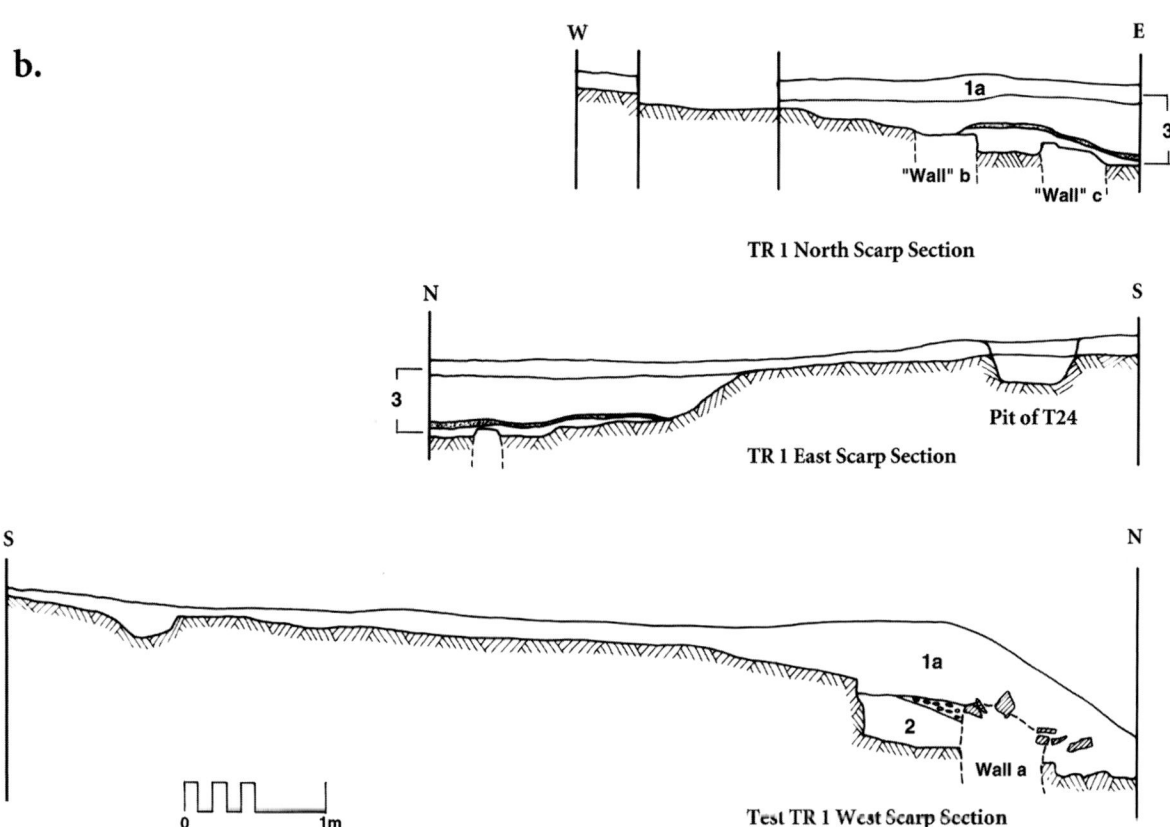

FIGURE 19 (continued). Trench 1, incorporating Test Trench 1. (*b*) Sections.

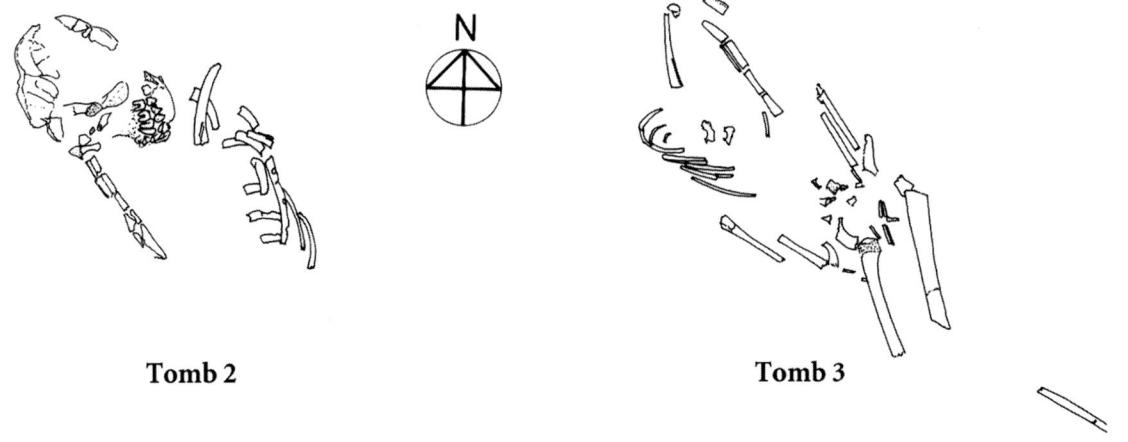

FIGURE 20. Plans of skeletons of Inhumation Tombs 2 and 3 as preserved (scale 1:10).

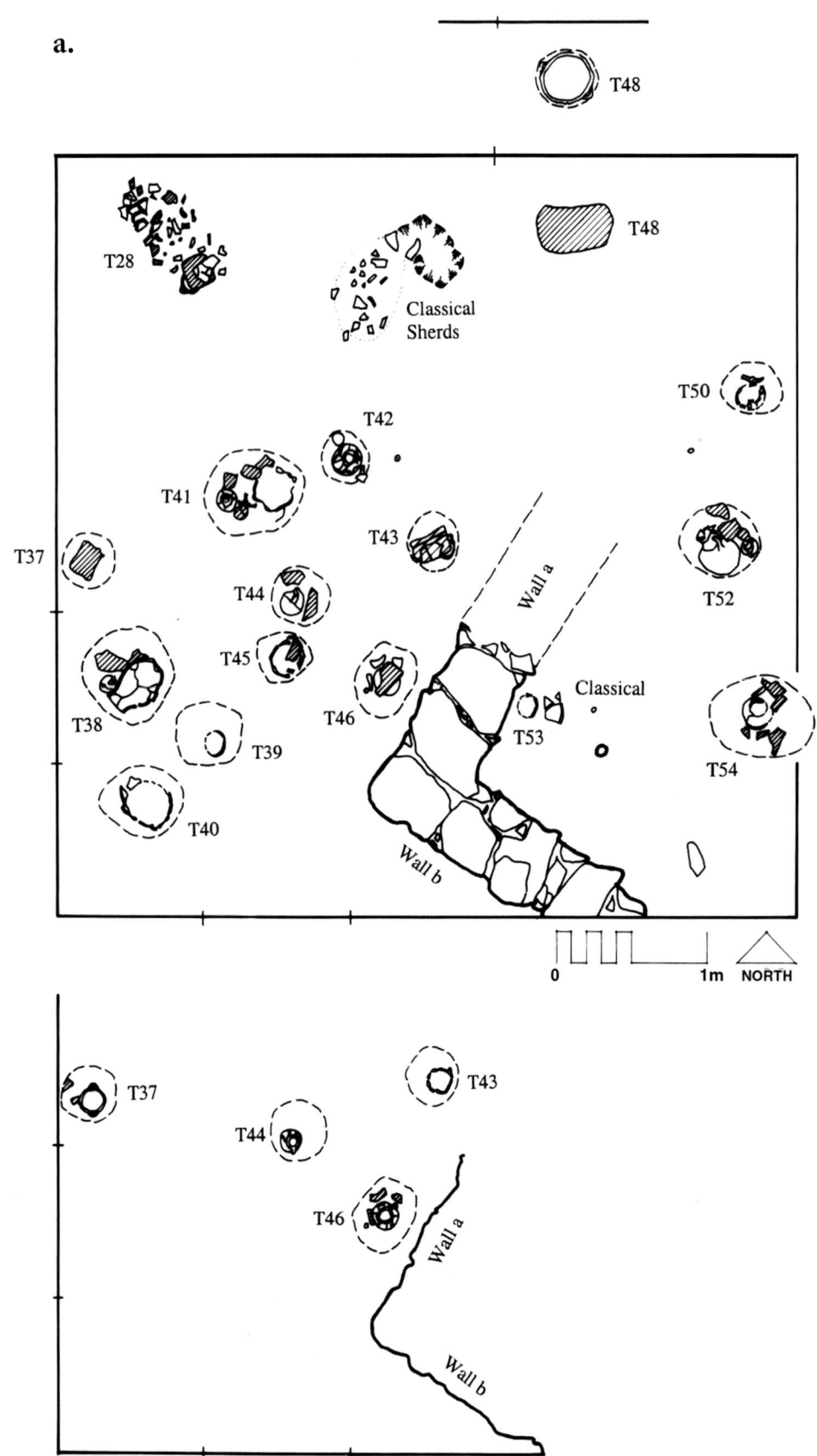

FIGURE 21 (on facing page). Trench 6. (*a*) Plan of tombs, covered and uncovered.

b.

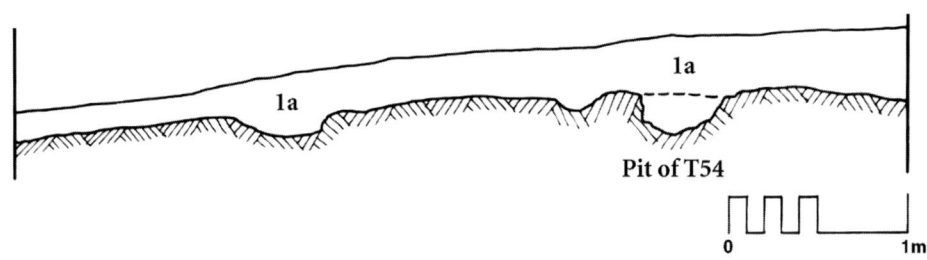

FIGURE 21 (continued). Trench 6. (*b*) East scarp section.

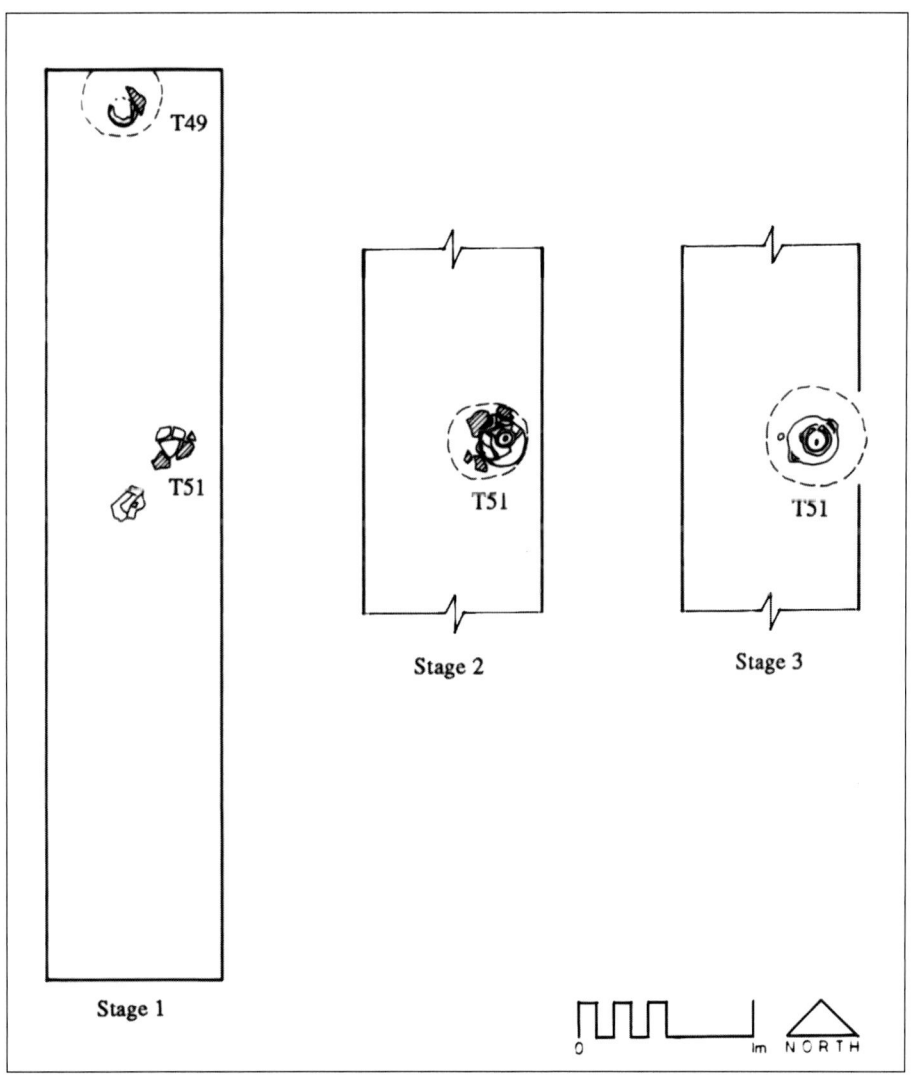

FIGURE 22. Trench 6 East Baulk. Plan, including various stages of the excavation of Tomb 51.

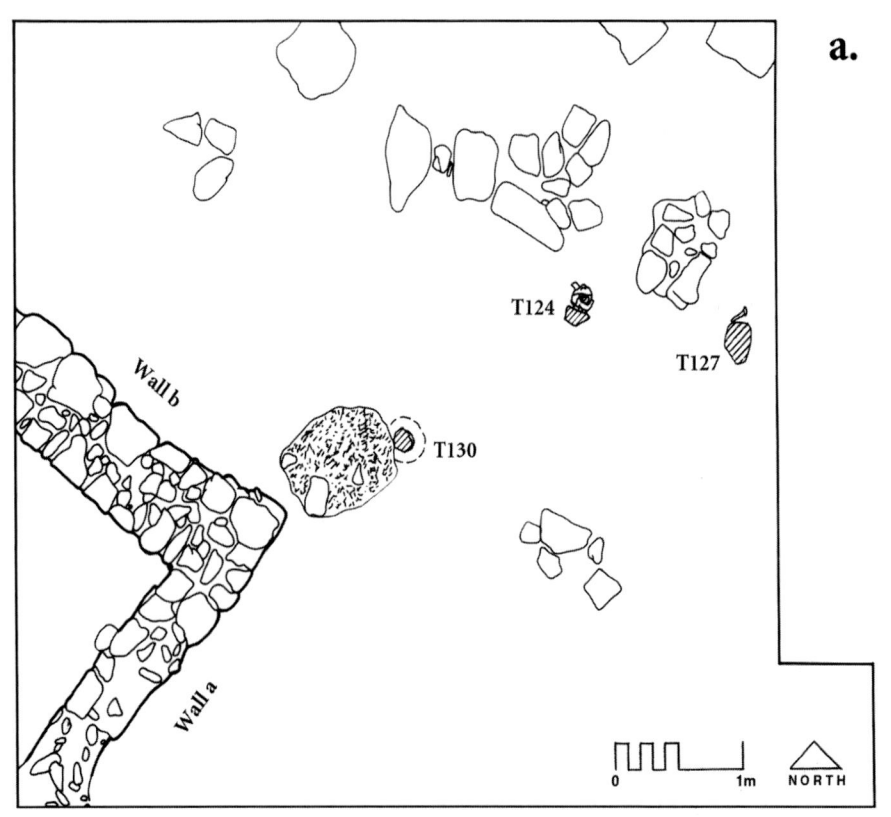

a.

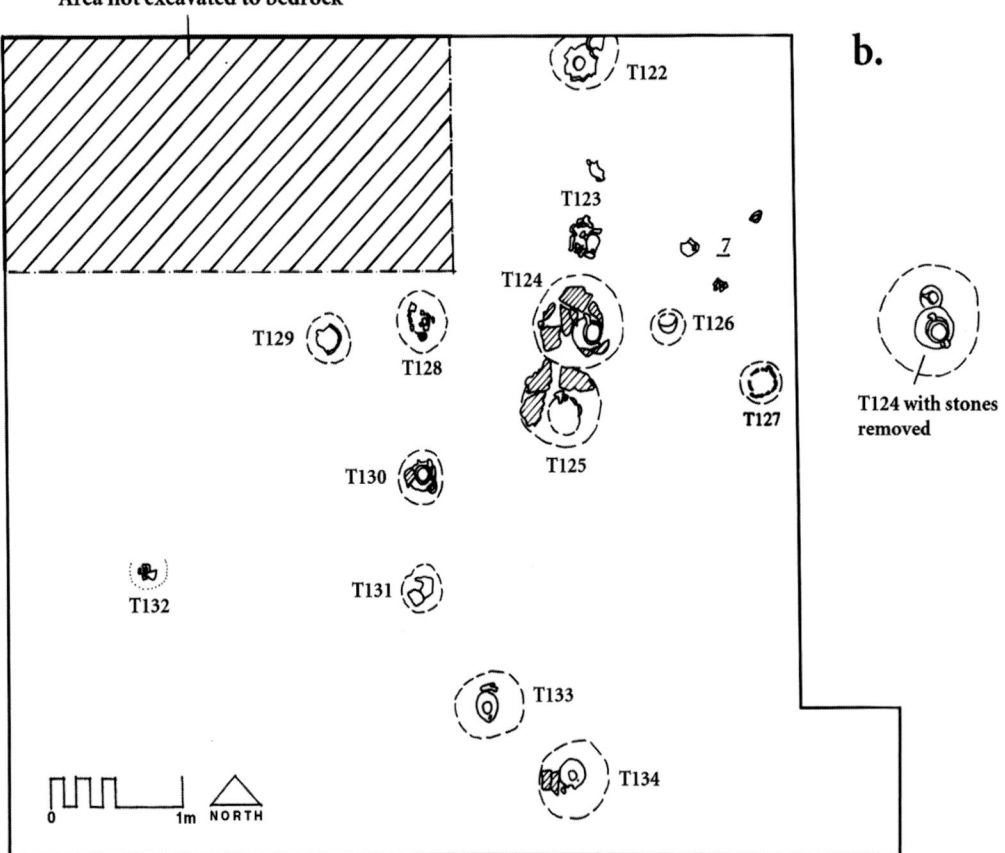

b.

FIGURE 23 (on facing page). Trench 9. (*a*) Plan (Stage 1) showing covered tombs and Classical walls, paving stones, and tumble. (*b*) Plan (Stage 2) showing Early Iron Age tombs uncovered.

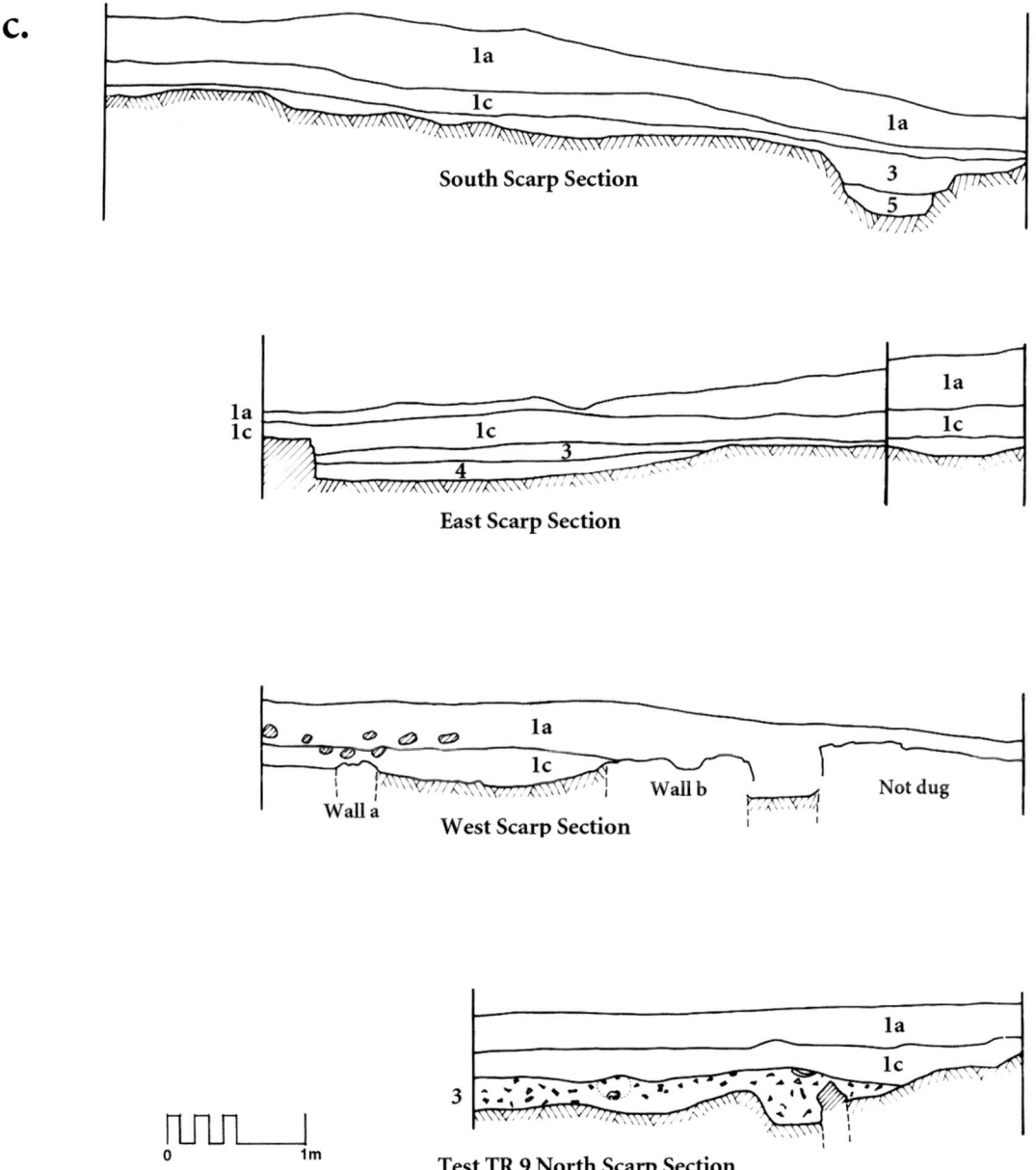

c.

South Scarp Section

East Scarp Section

West Scarp Section

Test TR 9 North Scarp Section

0   1m

FIGURE 23 (continued). Trench 9. (*c*) Sections.

a.

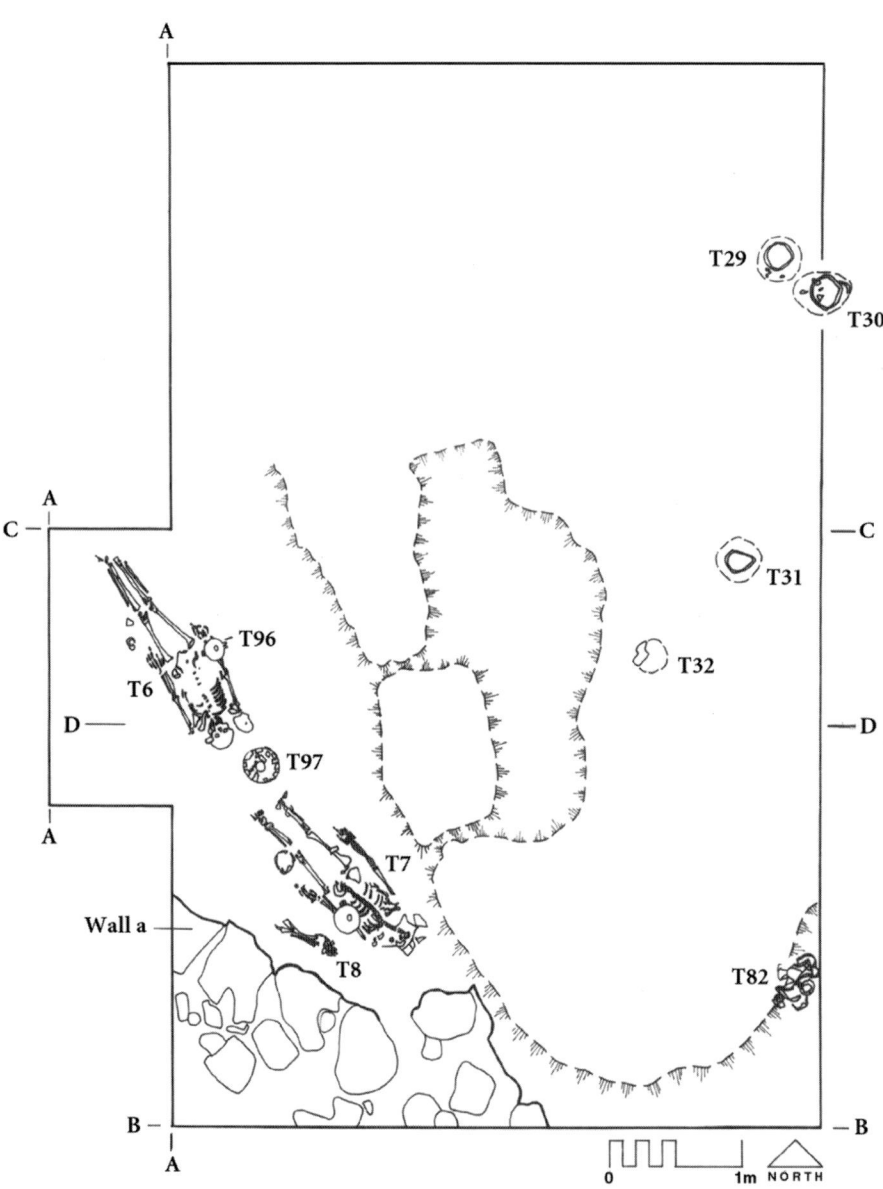

FIGURE 24 (on pages 732–735). Trench 12. (*a*) Plan.

b.

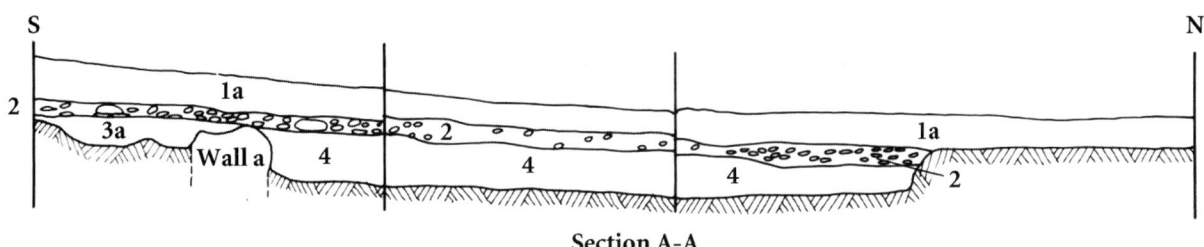

Section A-A

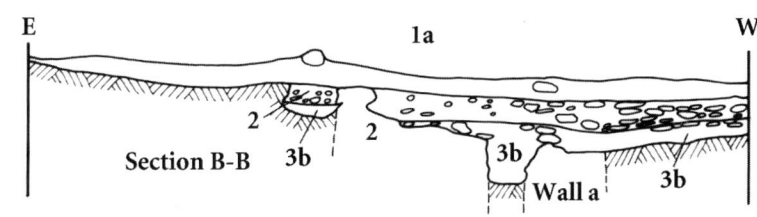

Section B-B

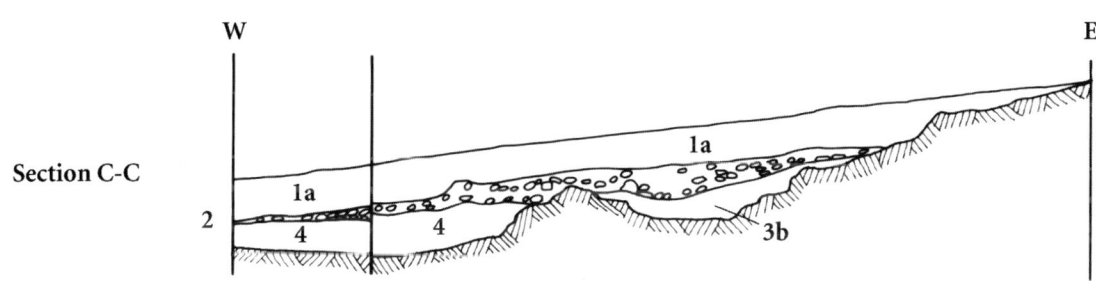

Section C-C

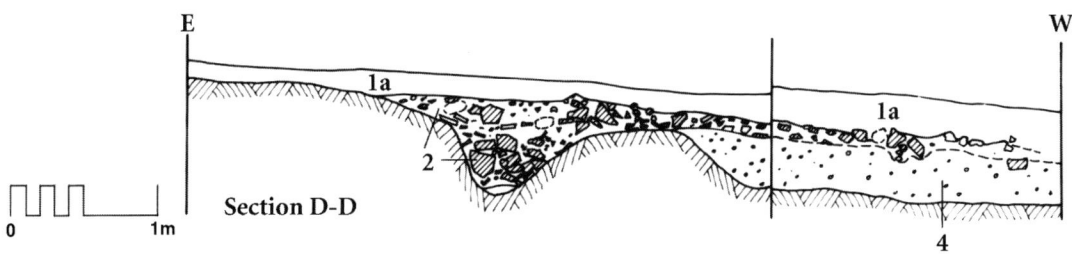

Section D-D

FIGURE 24 (continued). Trench 12. (*b*) Sections.

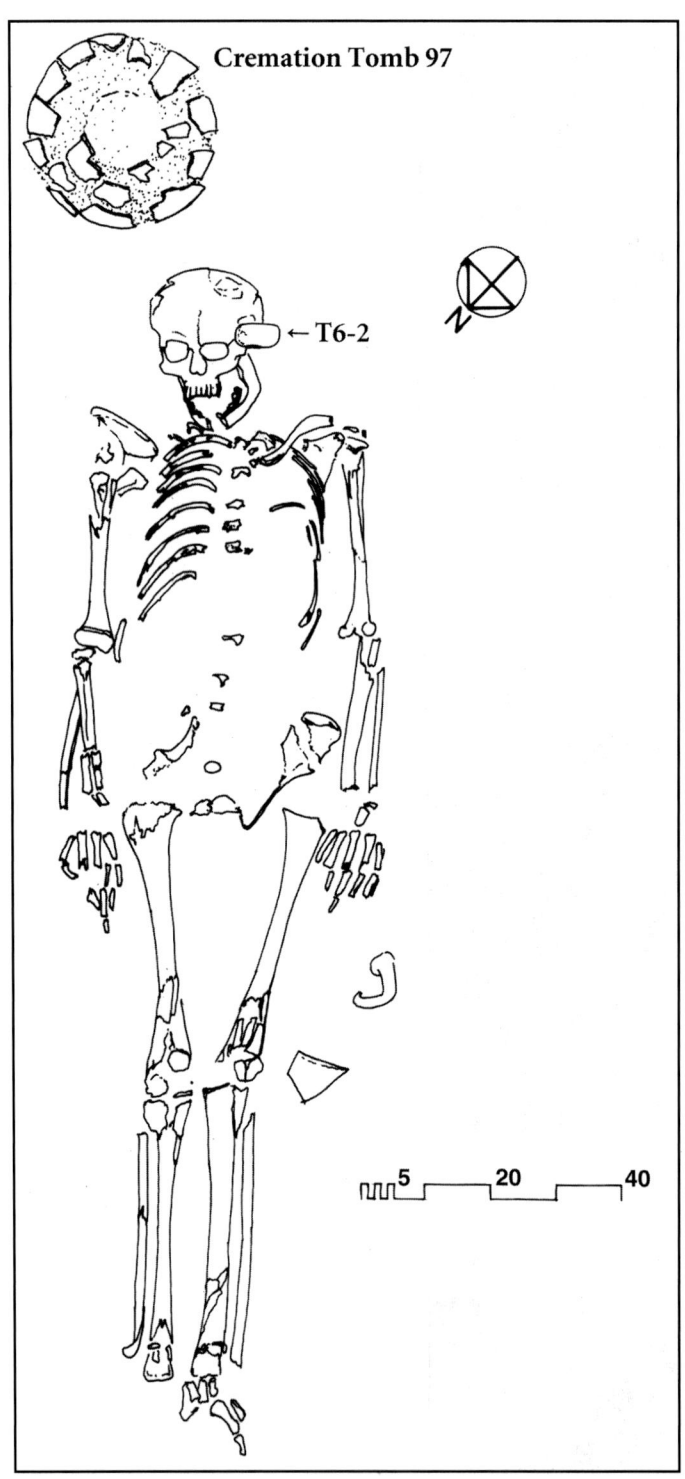

FIGURE 24 (continued). Trench 12. (*c*) Plan of skeleton of Inhumation Tomb 6 as preserved and its relationship to Cremation Tomb 97.

d.

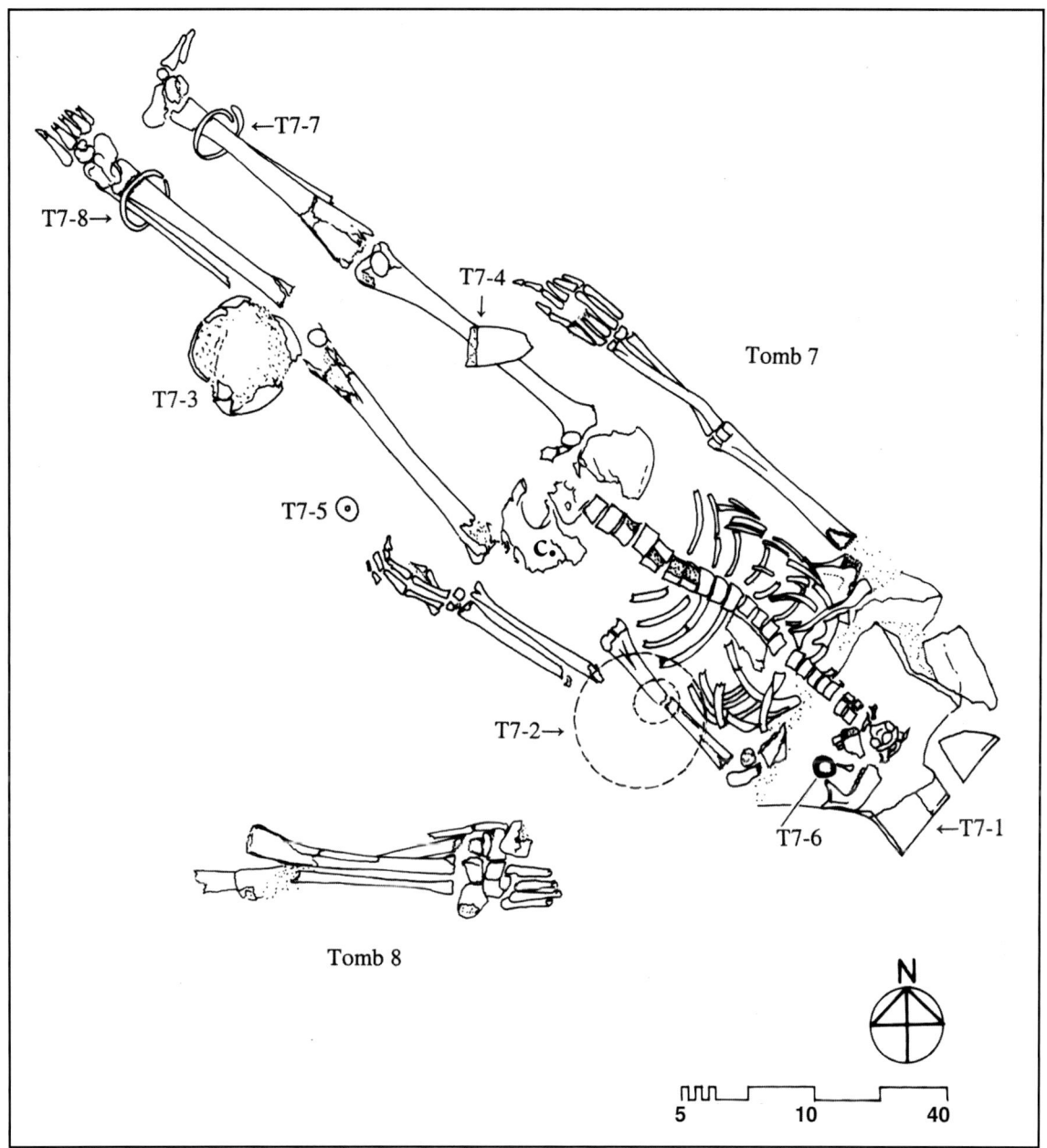

FIGURE 24 (continued). Trench 12. (*d*) Plan of skeletons of Inhumation Tombs 7 and 8 as preserved.

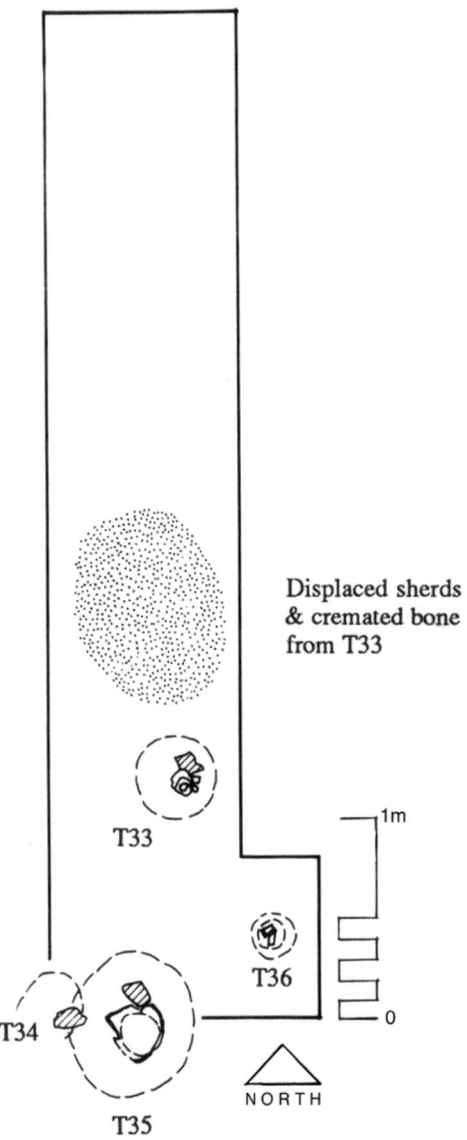

Displaced sherds
& cremated bone
from T33

FIGURE 25. Trench 12 East Baulk. Plan.

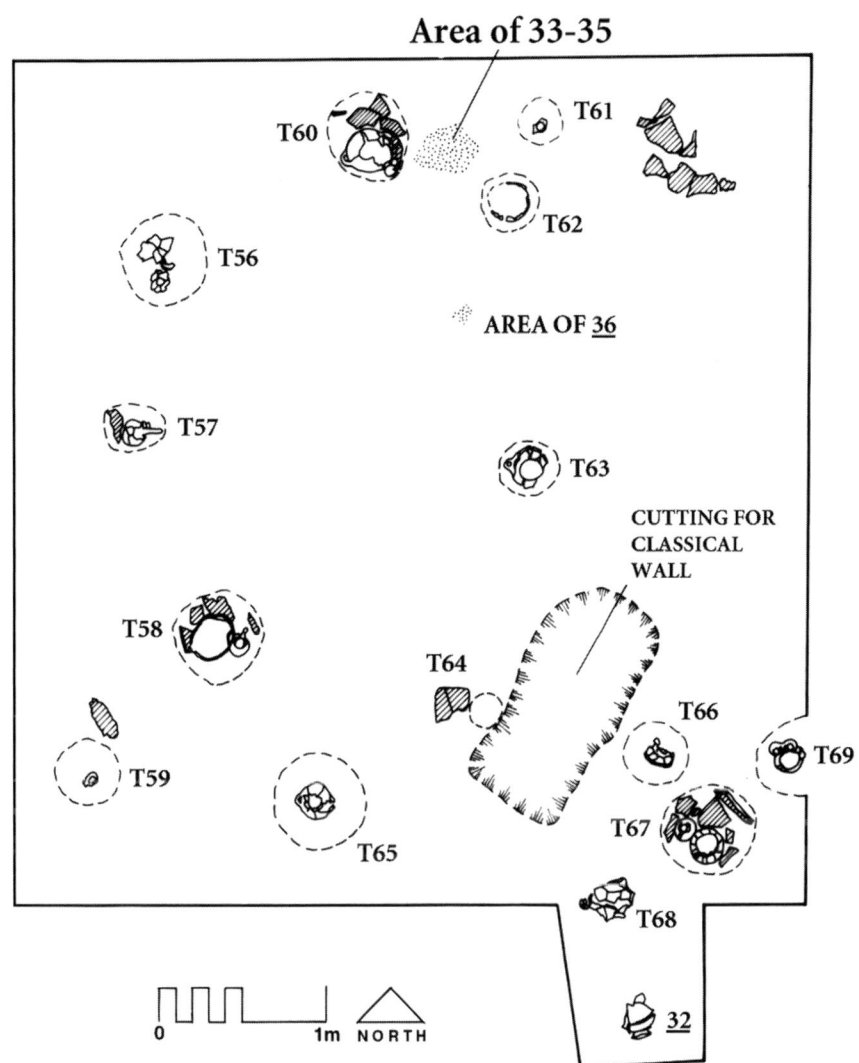

FIGURE 26. Trench 13. Plan.

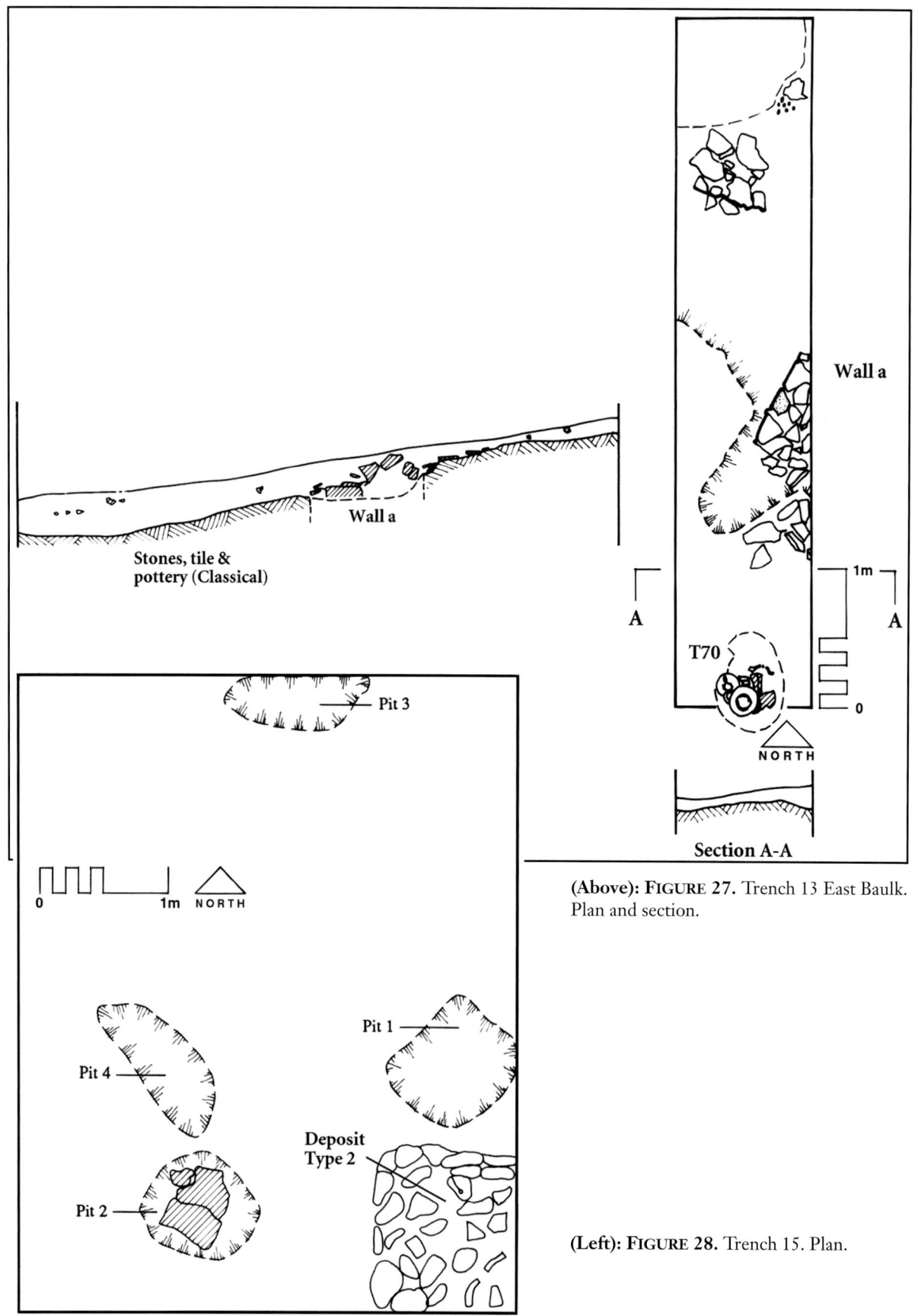

Stones, tile &
pottery (Classical)

Wall a

Wall a

T70

NORTH

Section A-A

(Above): FIGURE 27. Trench 13 East Baulk.
Plan and section.

Pit 3

0   1m   NORTH

Pit 1

Pit 4

Deposit
Type 2

Pit 2

(Left): FIGURE 28. Trench 15. Plan.

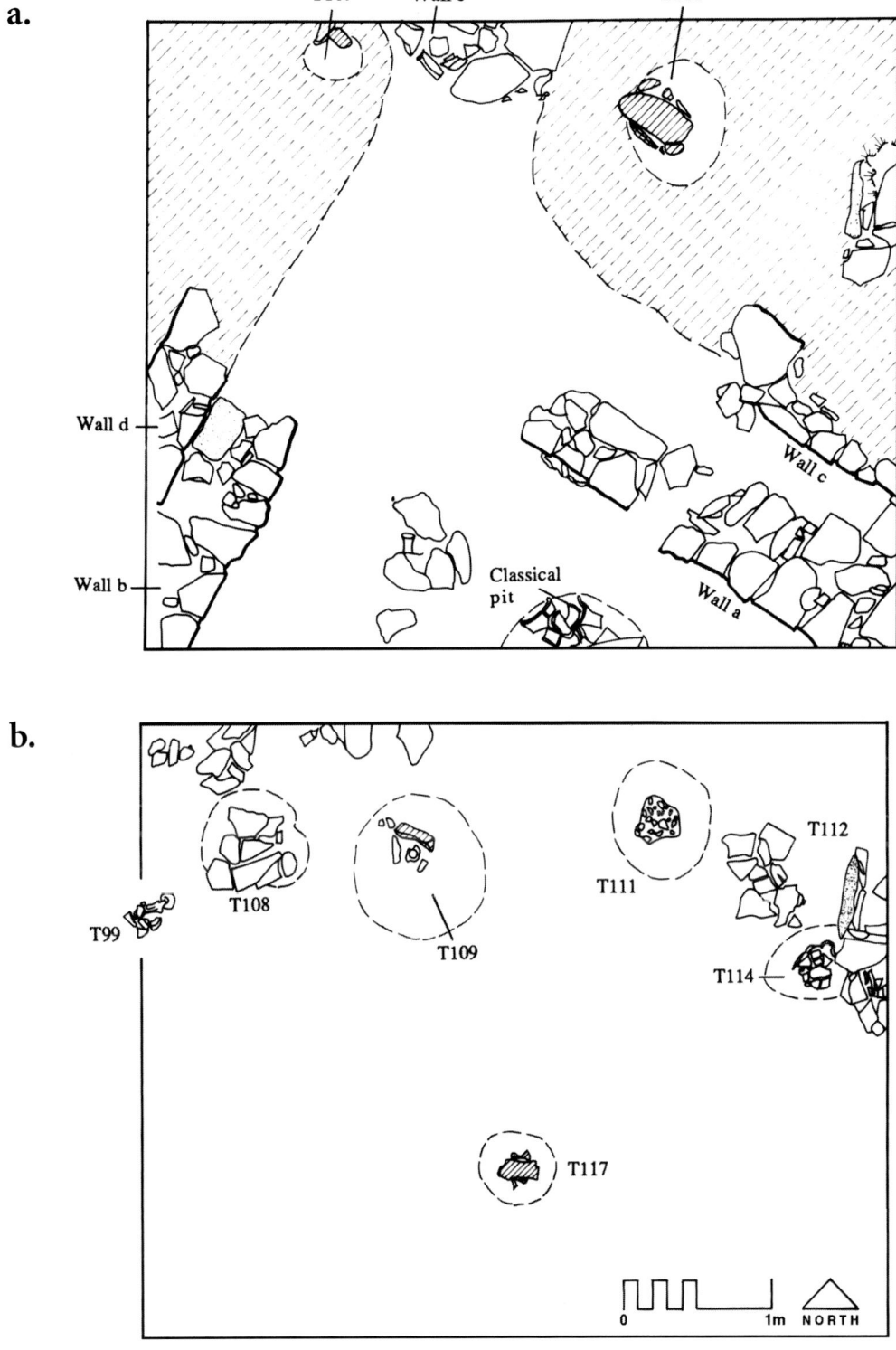

FIGURE 29 Trench 22 (**on following page**). (*a*) Plan (Stage 1). (*b*) Plan (Stage 2).

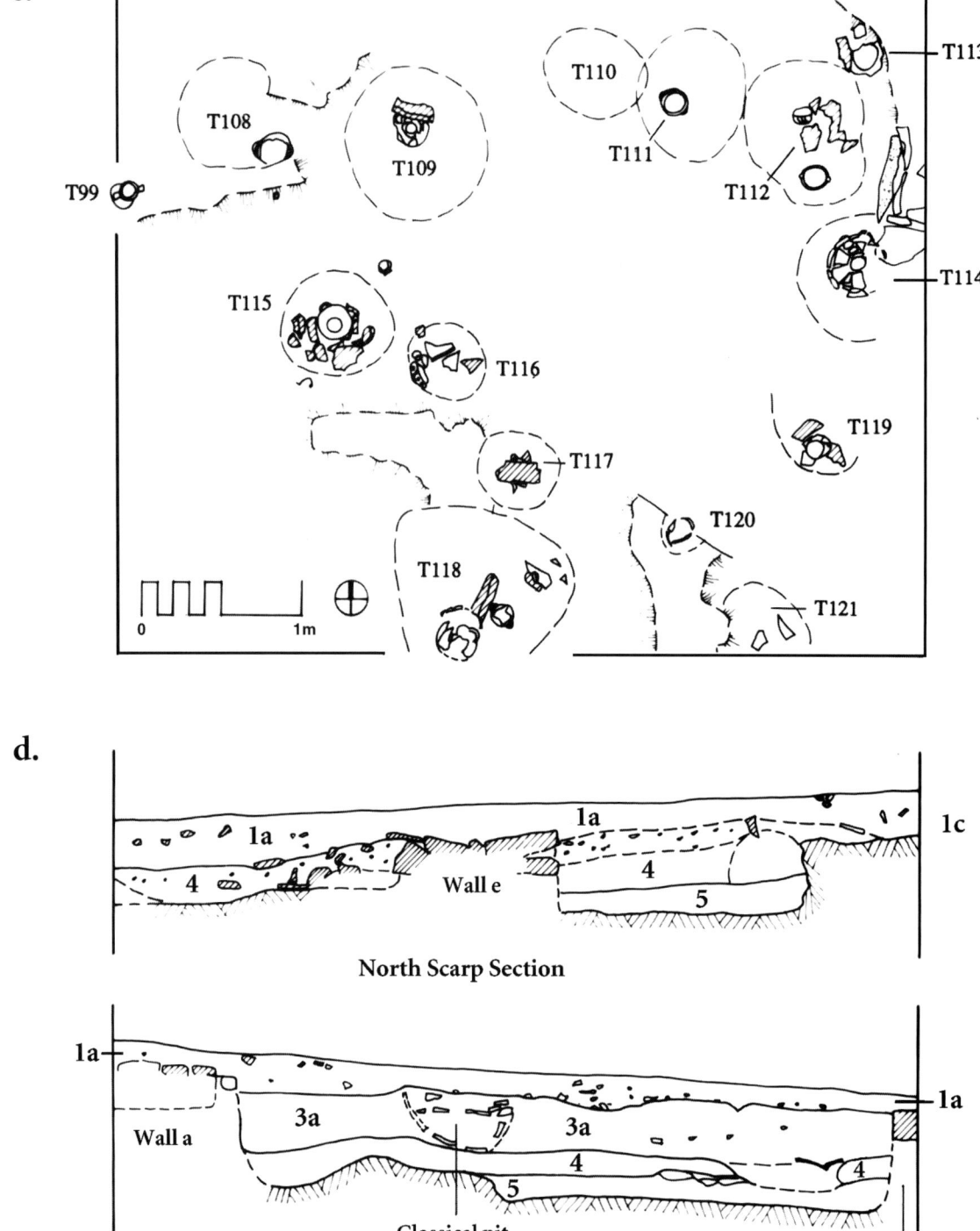

c.

T99

T108

T109

T110

T111

T112

T113

T114

T115

T116

T117

T119

T120

T118

T121

0   1m

d.

1a   1a   1c

Wall e

4   4

5

North Scarp Section

1a   1a

Wall a

3a   3a

4   4

5

Classical pit

South Scarp Section   Wall b

FIGURE 29 (**continued**). Trench 22. (*c*) Plan (Stage 3). (*d*) Sections.

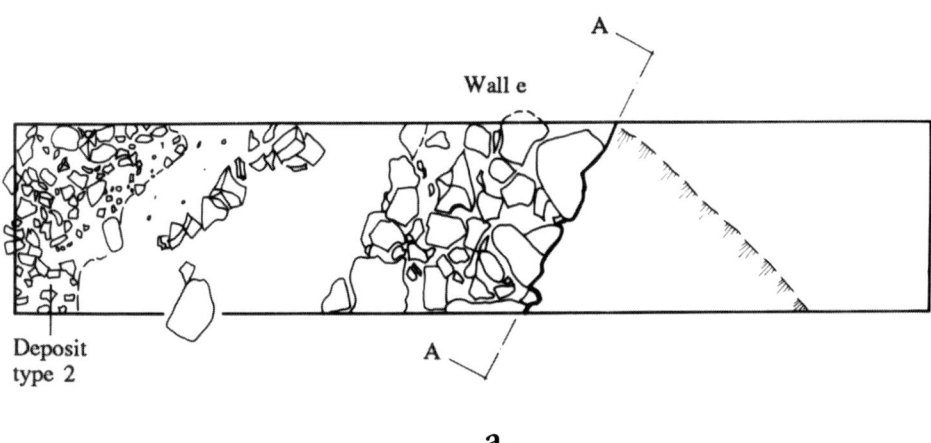

a.

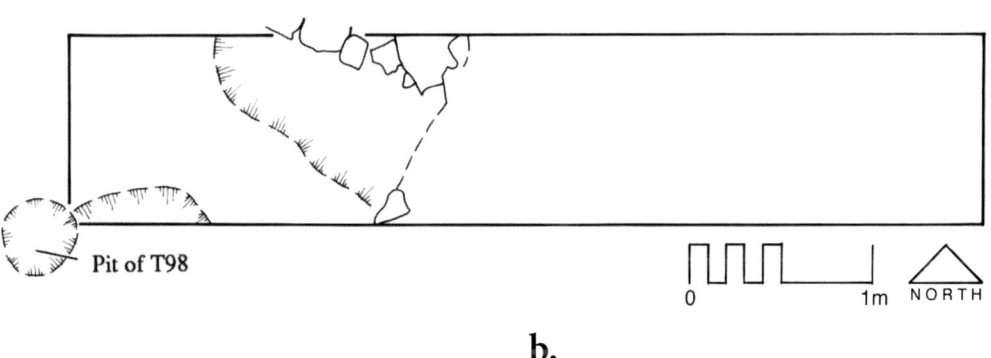

b.

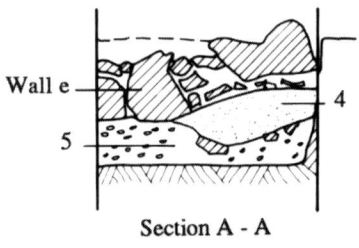

c.

FIGURE 30. Trench 22 North Baulk. (*a*) Plan (Stage 1). (*b*) Plan (Stage 2). (*c*) Section.

a.

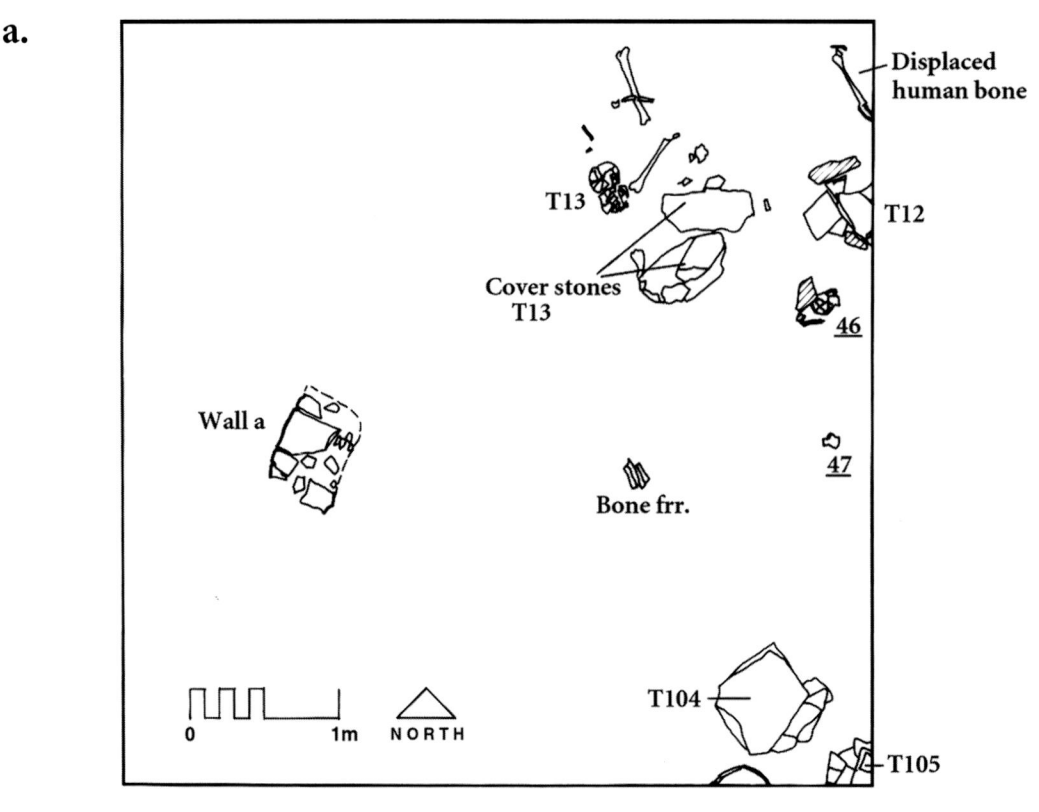

b.

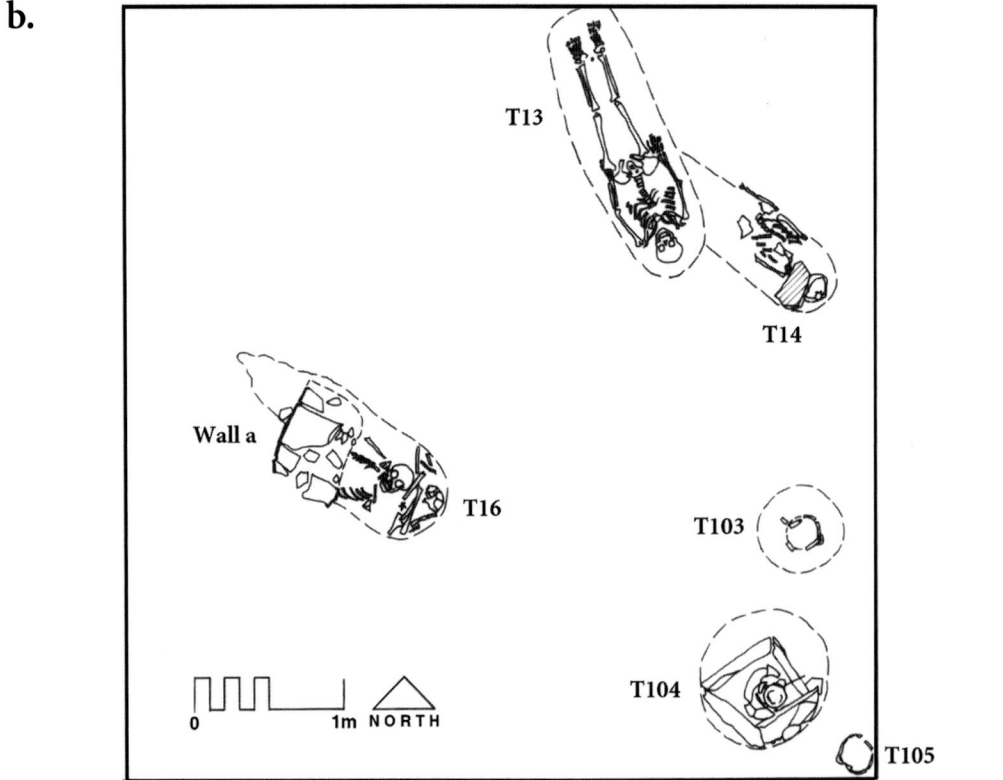

FIGURE 31 (on pages 742–744). Trench 25. (*a*) Plan (Stage 1) showing Classical wall *a* and upper parts of Early Iron Age tombs as preserved. (*b*) Plan (Stage 2) showing Classical wall *a* and upper parts of Early Iron Age tombs uncovered.

c.

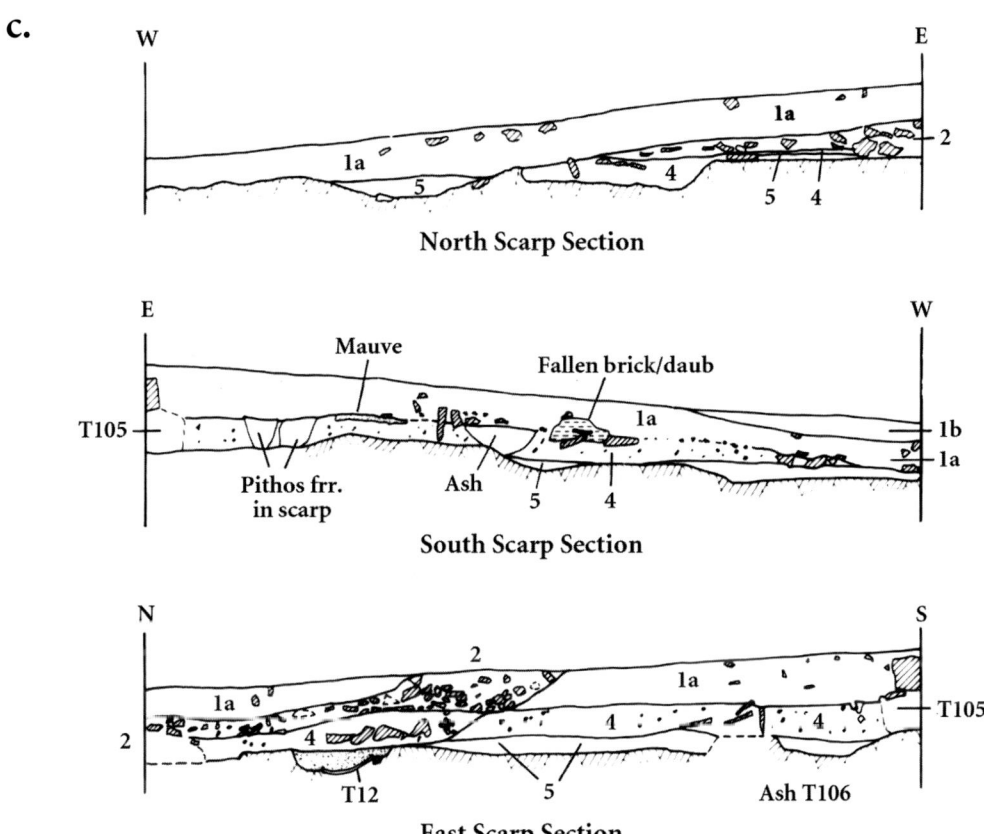

North Scarp Section

South Scarp Section

East Scarp Section

FIGURE 31 (continued). Trench 25. (*c*) Sections.

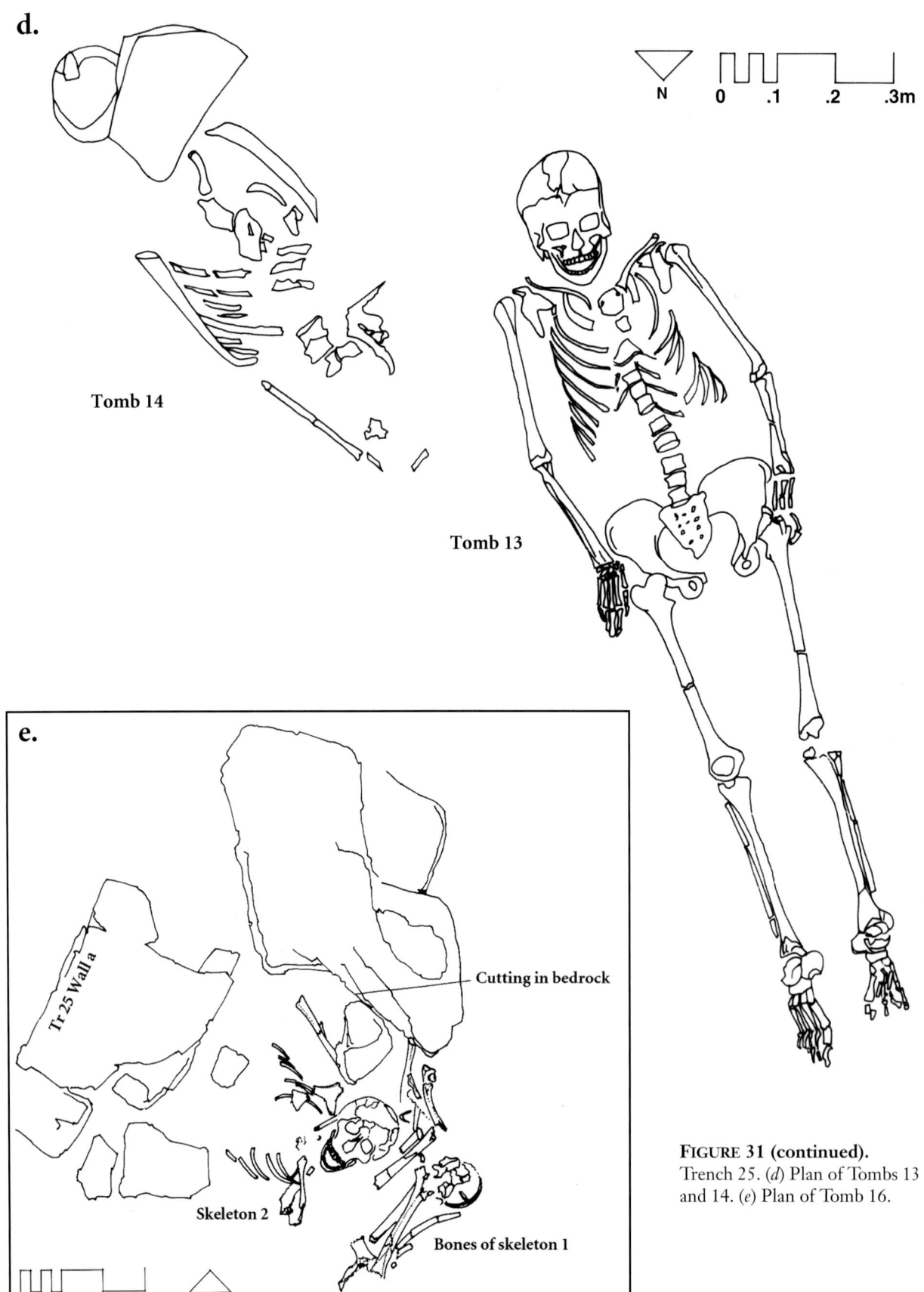

d.

N   0   .1   .2   .3m

Tomb 14

Tomb 13

e.

Tr 25 Wall a

Cutting in bedrock

Skeleton 2

Bones of skeleton 1

0   .1   .2   .3m   NORTH

FIGURE 31 (continued).
Trench 25. (*d*) Plan of Tombs 13
and 14. (*e*) Plan of Tomb 16.

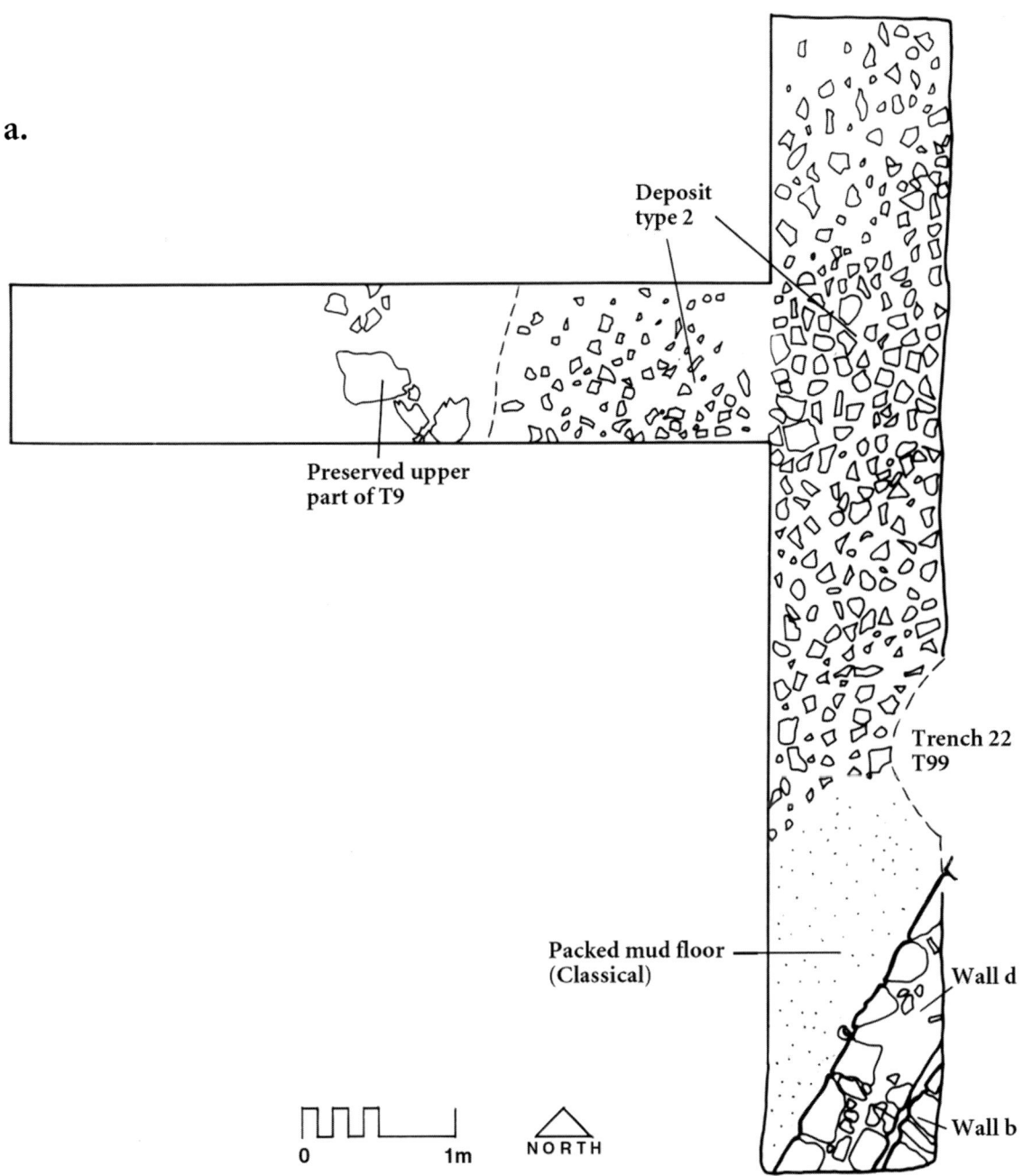

a.

Deposit
type 2

Preserved upper
part of T9

Trench 22
T99

Packed mud floor
(Classical)

Wall d

Wall b

0   1m   NORTH

FIGURE 32 (on pages 745–752). Trench 25 North and East Baulks. (*a*) Plan (Stage 1).

b.

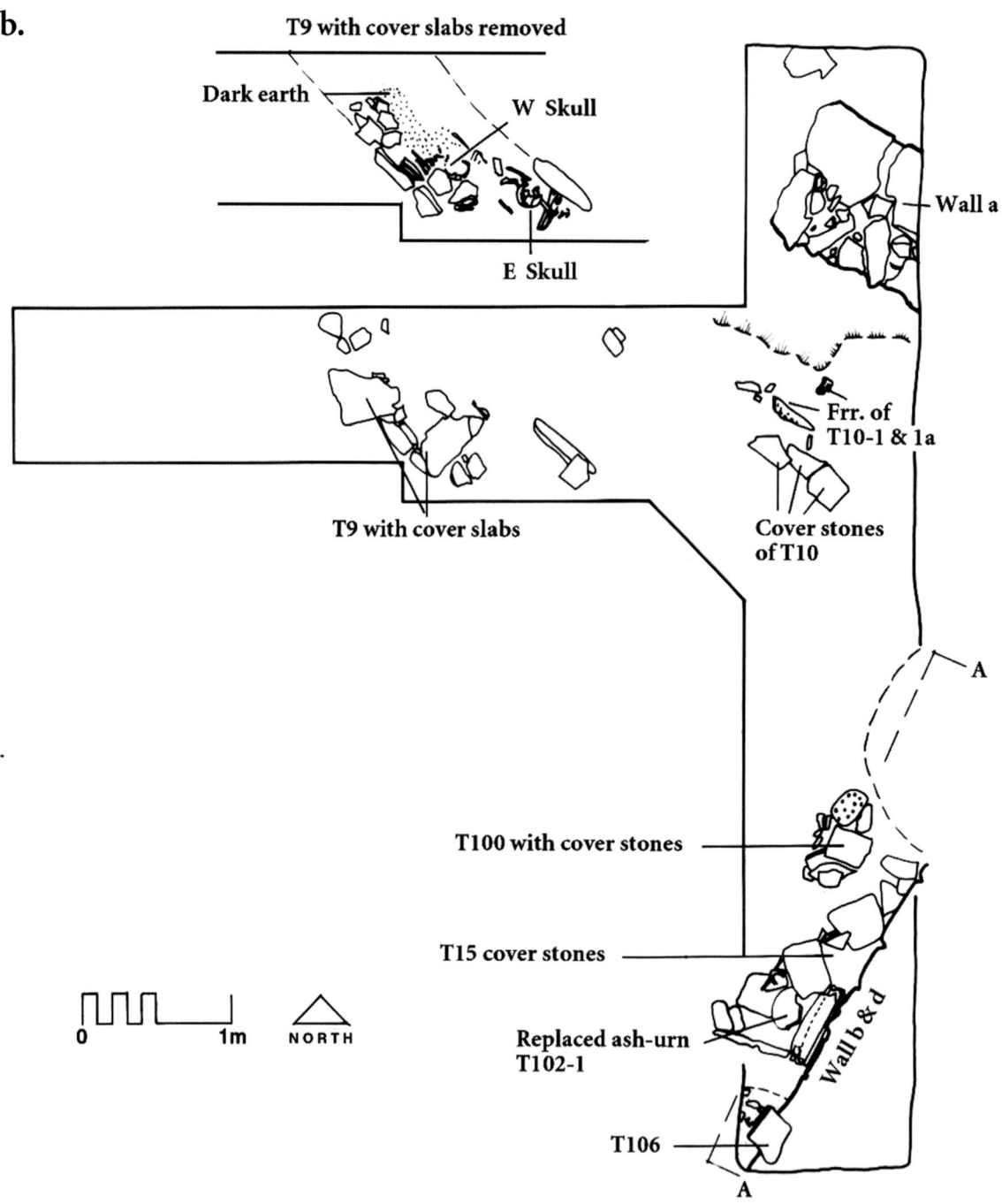

T9 with cover slabs removed

Dark earth

W Skull

E Skull

Wall a

Frr. of
T10-1 & 1a

Cover stones
of T10

A

T9 with cover slabs

0   1m   NORTH

T100 with cover stones

T15 cover stones

Wall b & d

Replaced ash-urn
T102-1

T106

A

FIGURE 32 (continued). Trench 25 North and East Baulks. (*b*) Plan (Stage 2).

C.

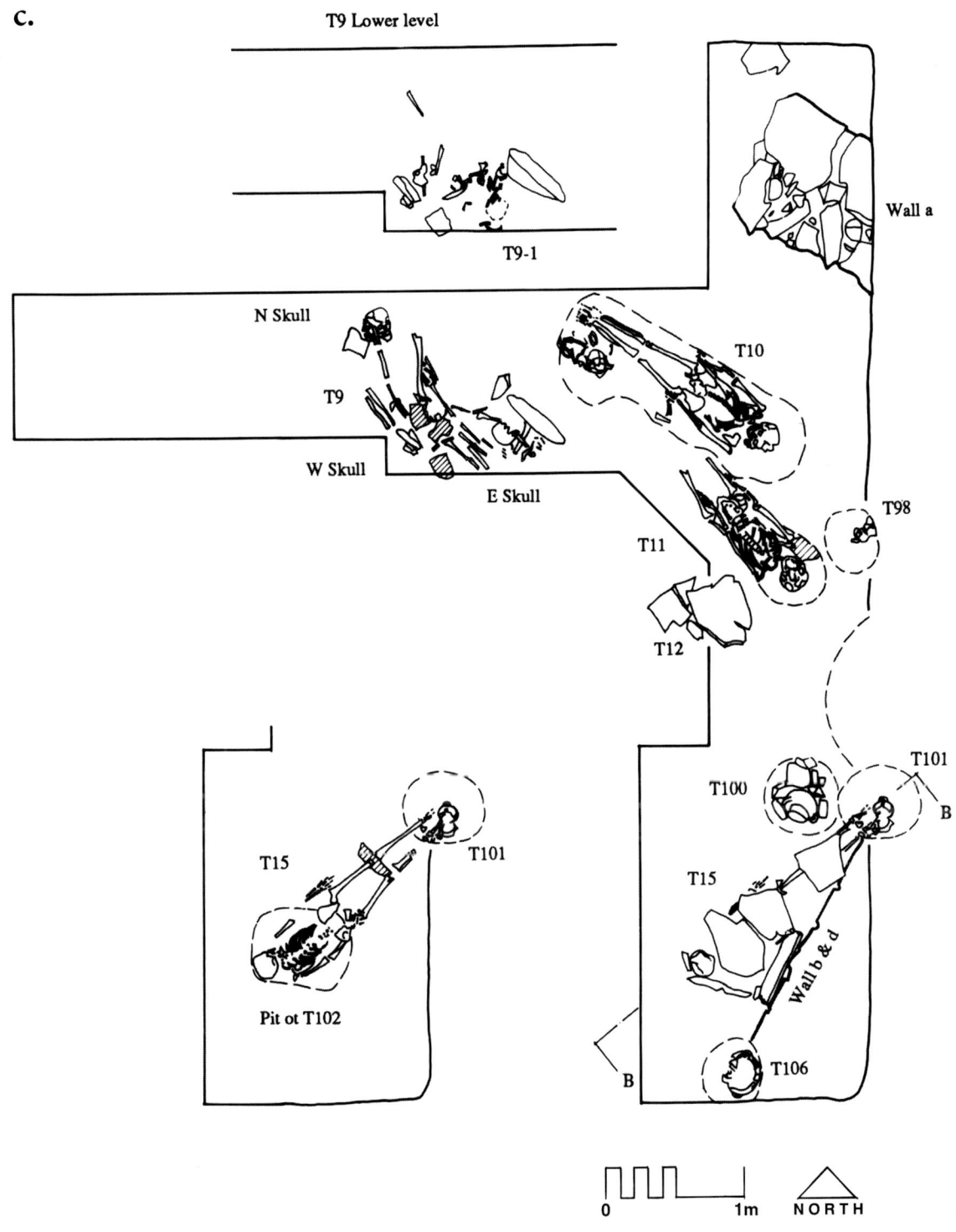

T9 Lower level

T9-1

Wall a

N Skull

T9

T10

W Skull

E Skull

T98

T11

T12

T100

T101

B

T15

T101

T15

Wall b & d

Pit ot T102

B

T106

0   1m   NORTH

FIGURE 32 (continued). Trench 25 North and East Baulks. (*c*) Plan (Stage 3).

d.

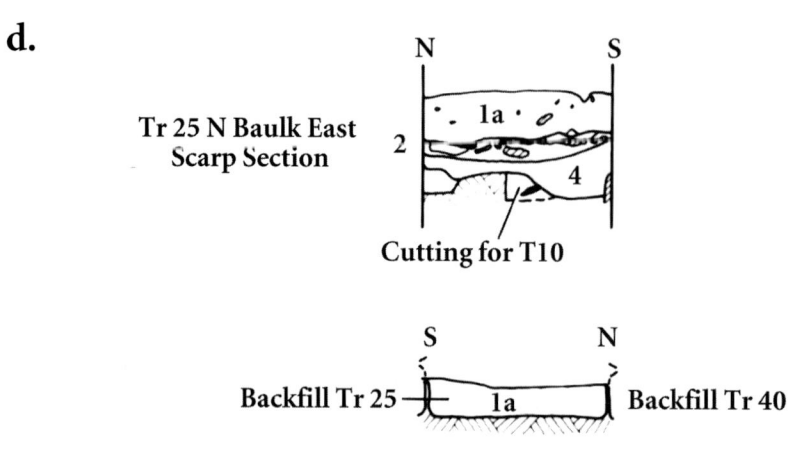

Tr 25 N Baulk East
Scarp Section

Cutting for T10

Backfill Tr 25

Backfill Tr 40

Tr 25 N Baulk
West Scarp Section

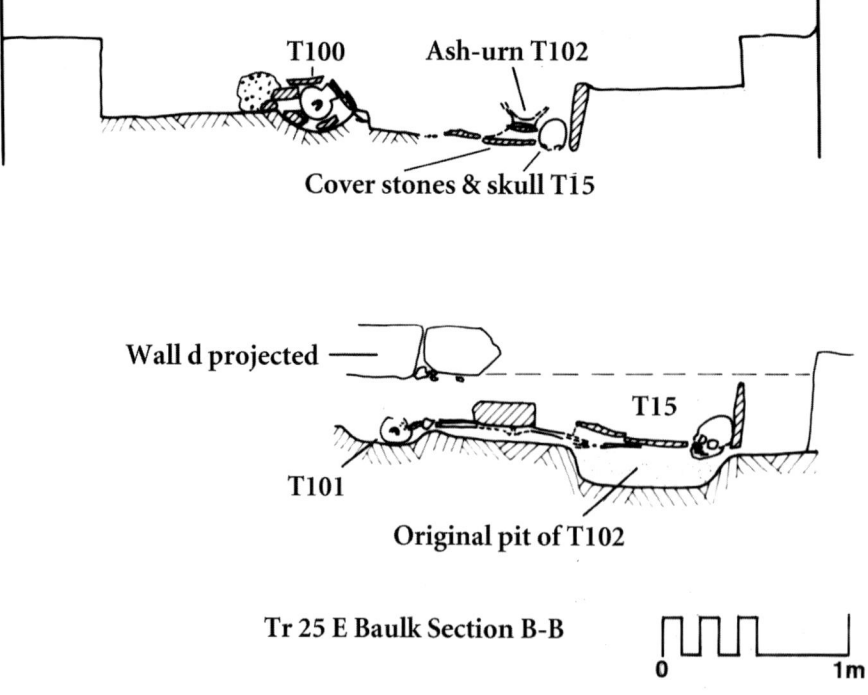

FIGURE 32 (continued). Trench 25 North and East Baulks. (*d*) Sections.

e.

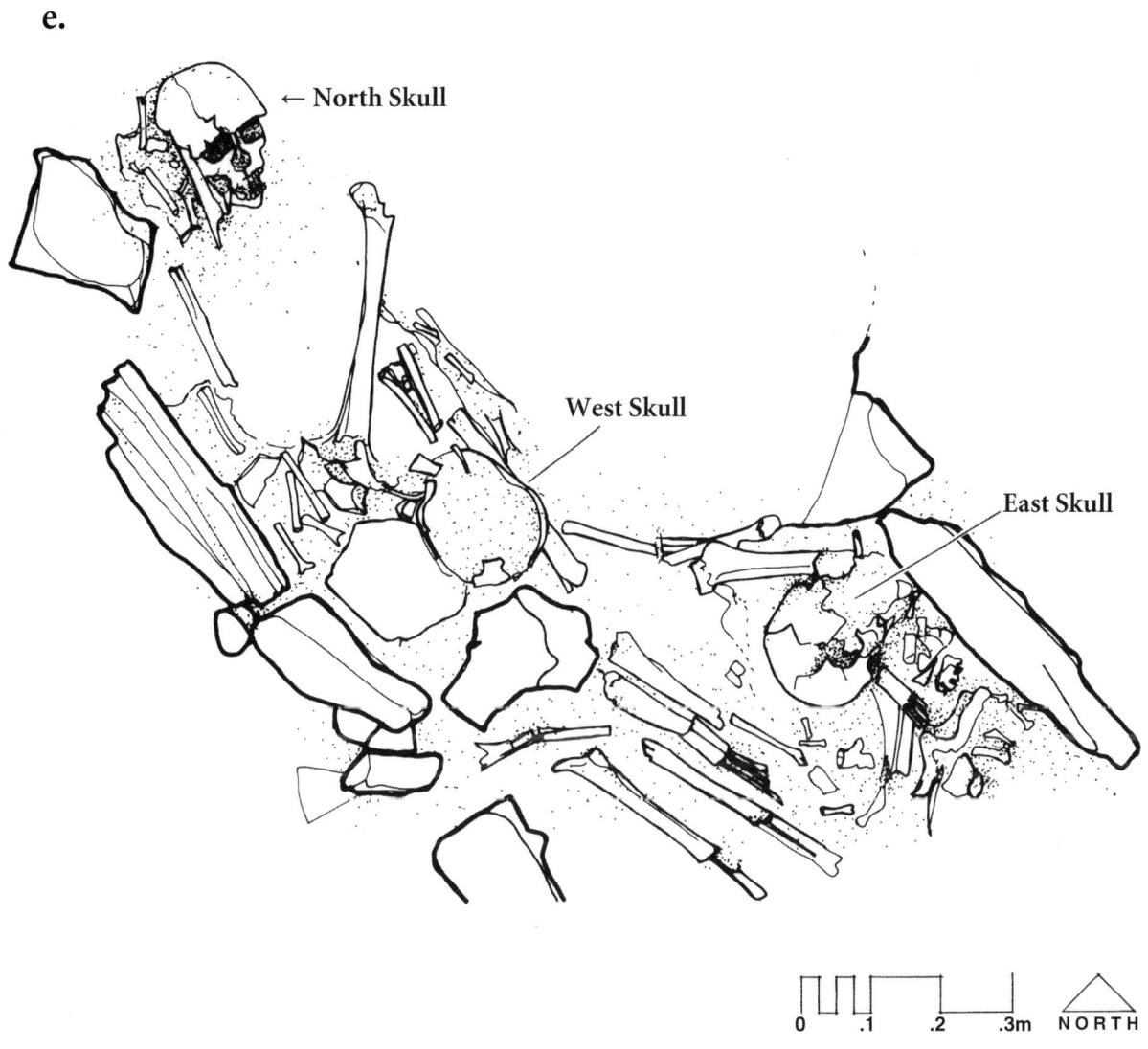

← **North Skull**

West Skull

East Skull

0   .1   .2   .3m   NORTH

FIGURE 32 (continued). Trench 25 North and East Baulks. (*e*) Plan of Inhumation Tomb 9 as preserved.

f.

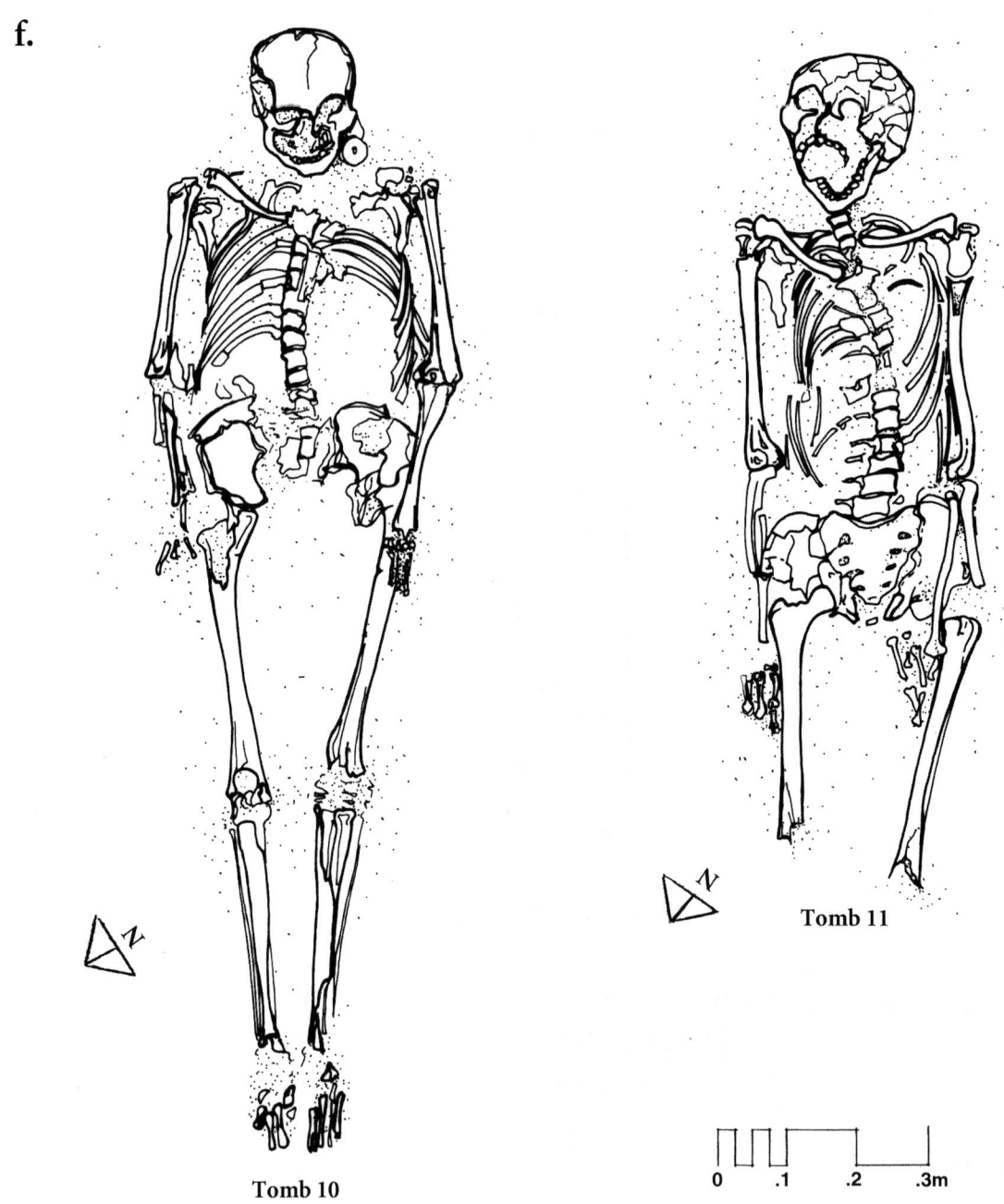

Tomb 10

Tomb 11

FIGURE 32 (continued). Trench 25 North and East Baulks. (*f*) Plan of skeletons of Inhumation Tombs 10 and 11; for their relationship to each other see (*c*).

g.

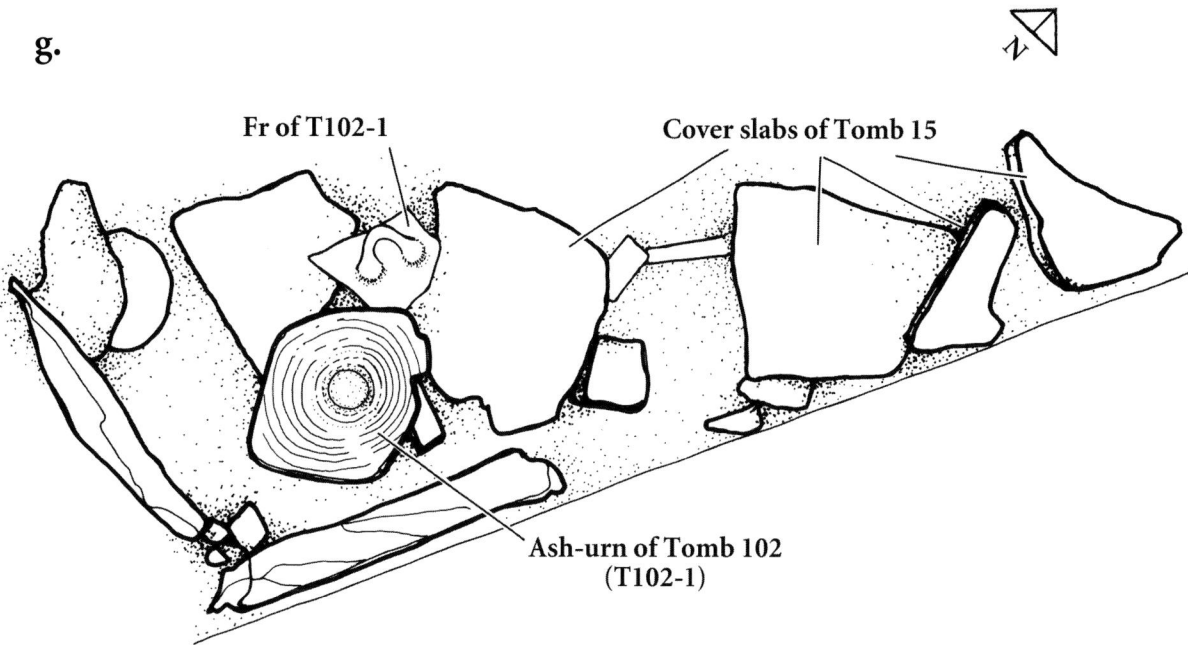

Fr of T102-1

Cover slabs of Tomb 15

Ash-urn of Tomb 102
(T102-1)

h.

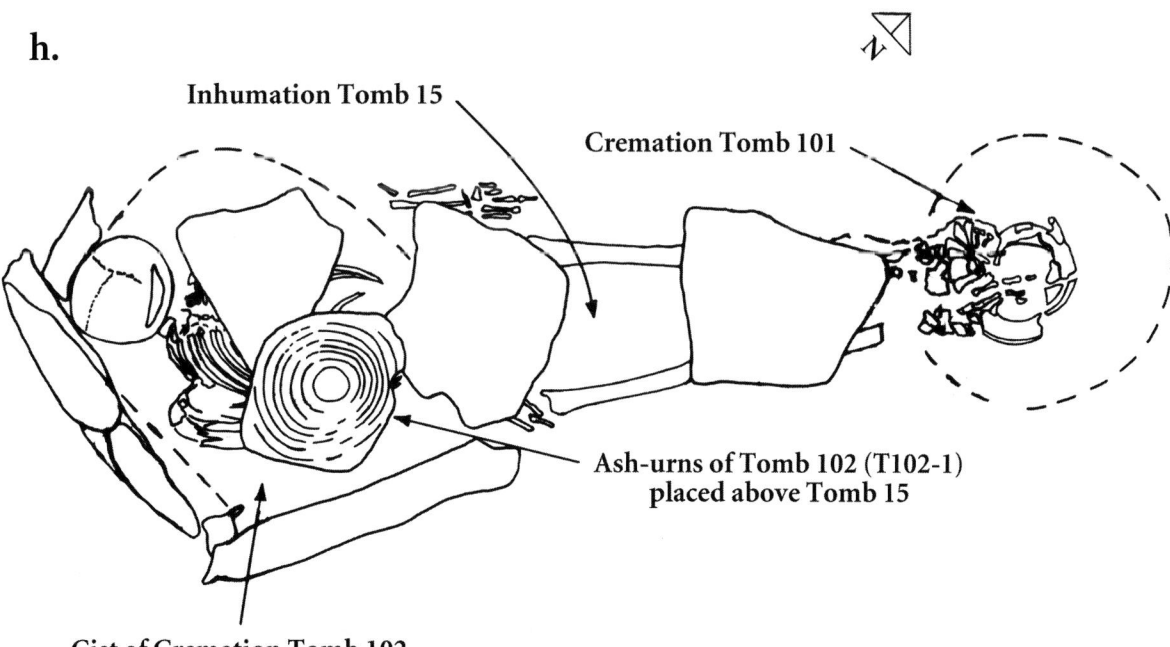

Inhumation Tomb 15

Cremation Tomb 101

Ash-urns of Tomb 102 (T102-1)
placed above Tomb 15

Cist of Cremation Tomb 102

FIGURE 32 (continued). Trench 25 North and East Baulks. (*g*) Plan of Tombs 15, 101, and 102 (Stage 1).
(*h*) Plan of Tombs 15, 101, and 102 (Stage 2).

i.

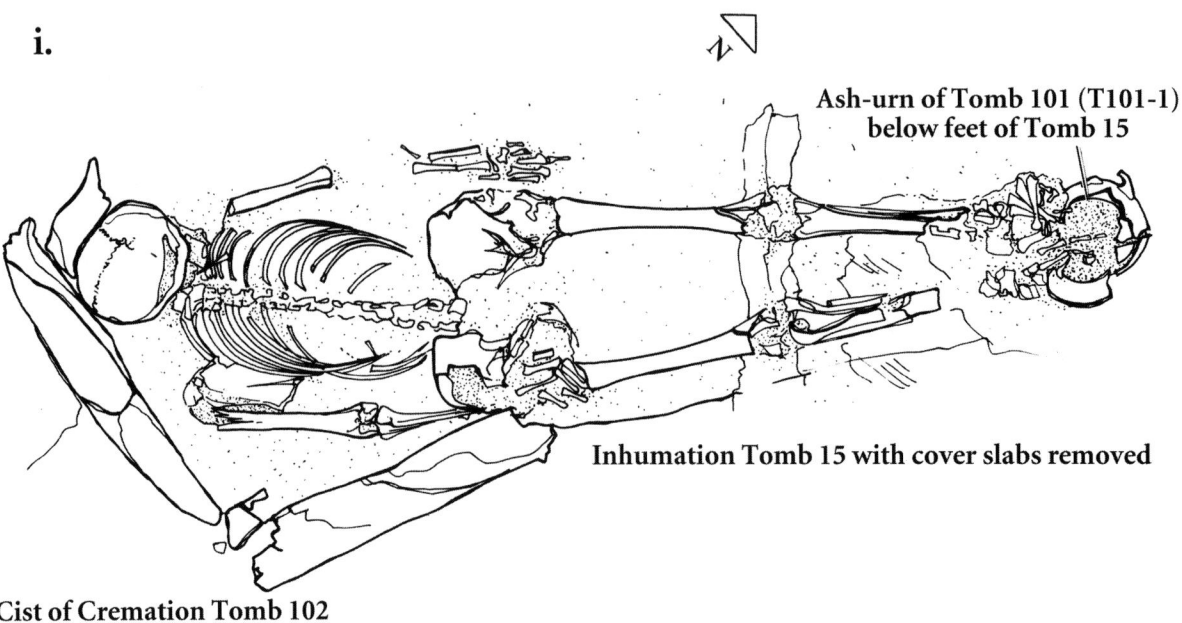

**Ash-urn of Tomb 101 (T101-1)
below feet of Tomb 15**

Inhumation Tomb 15 with cover slabs removed

Cist of Cremation Tomb 102

FIGURE 32 (continued). Trench 25 North and East Baulks. (*i*) Plan of Tombs 15, 101, and 102 (Stage 3).

a.

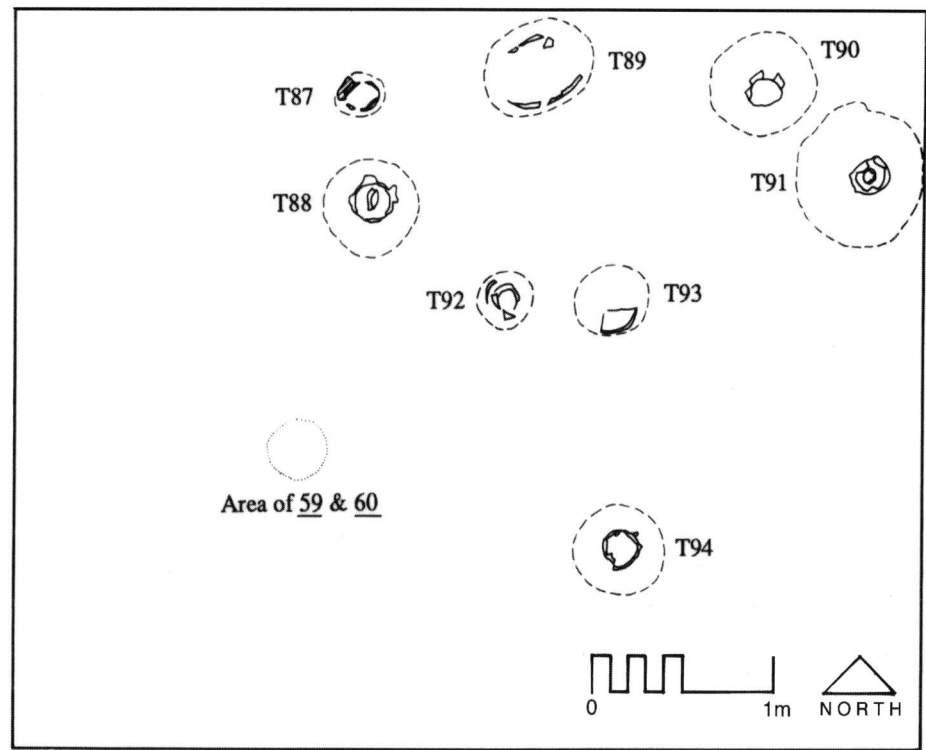

b.

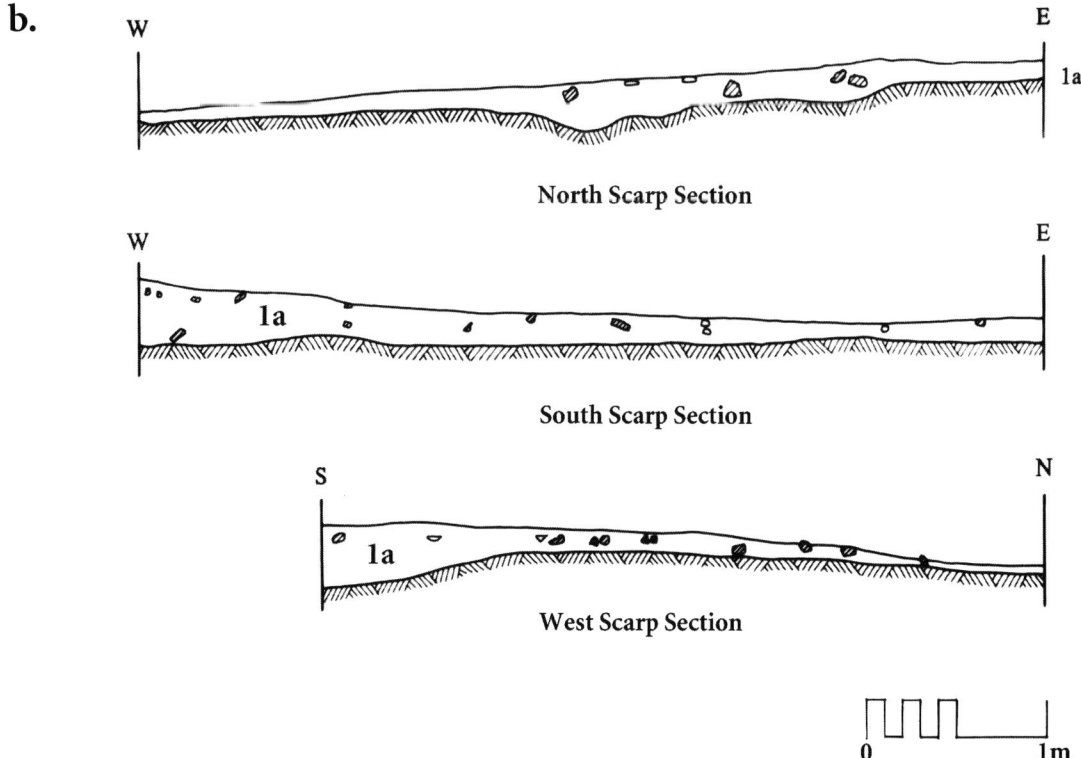

FIGURE 33. Trench 26. (*a*) Plan. (*b*) Sections.

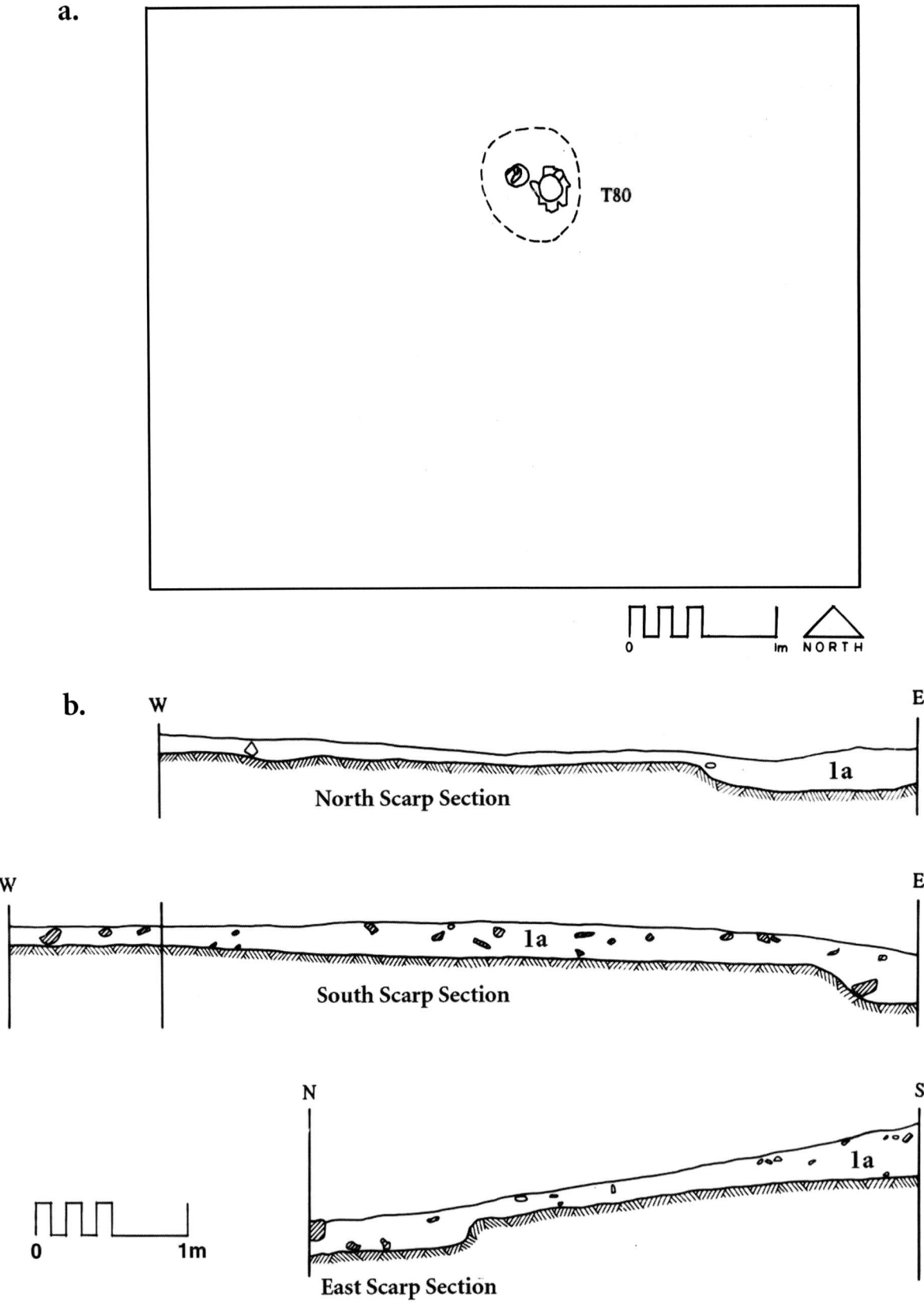

FIGURE 34. Trench 27. (*a*) Plan. (*b*) Sections.

a.

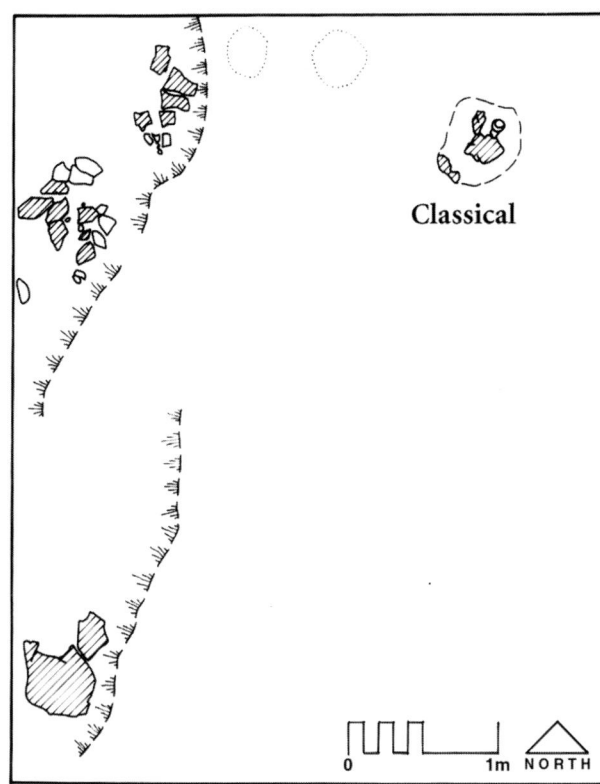

Classical

0 1m NORTH

b.

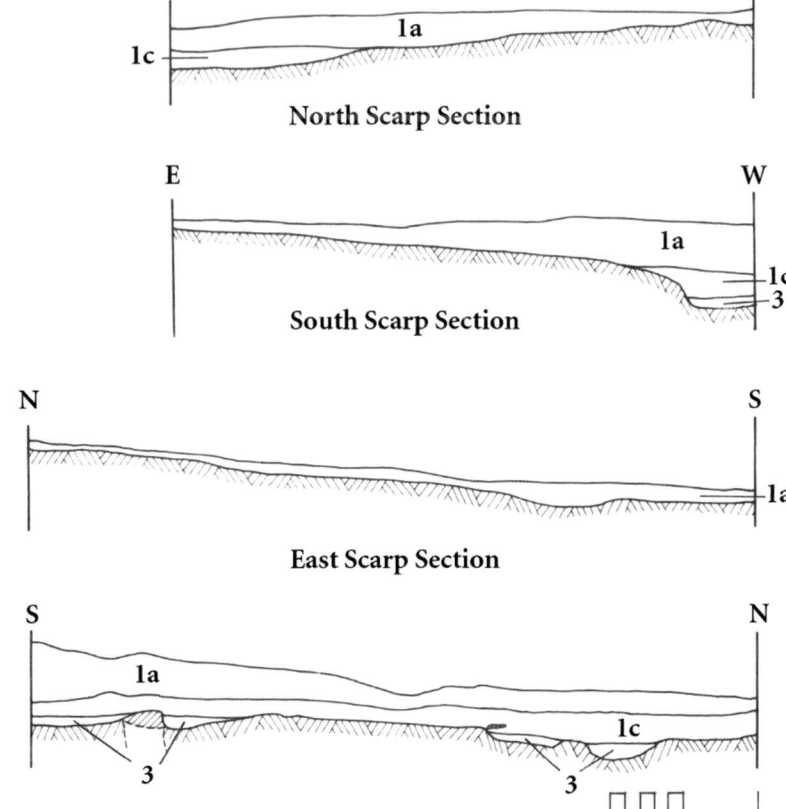

W 1a E
1c
North Scarp Section

E W
1a
1c
3
South Scarp Section

N S
1a
East Scarp Section

S N
1a
1c
3 3
West Scarp Section

0 1m

FIGURE 35. Trench 28. (*a*) Plan. (*b*) Sections.

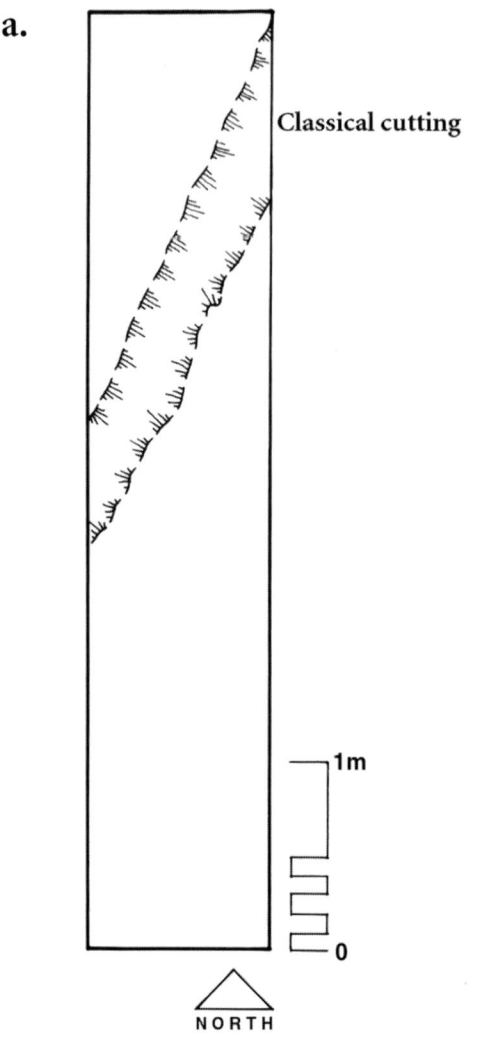

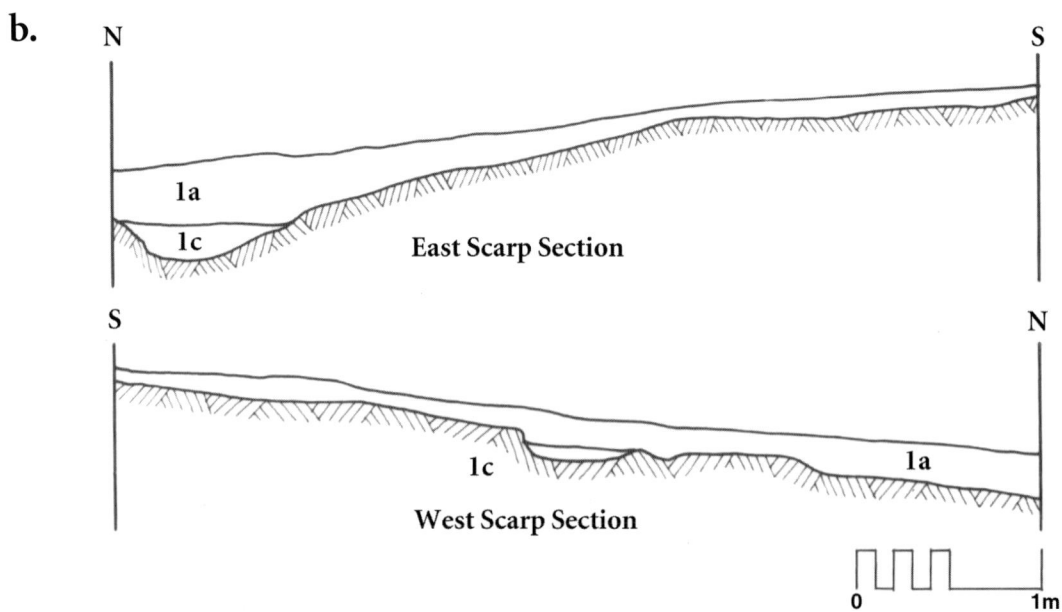

FIGURE 36. Trench 29. (*a*) Plan. (*b*) Sections.

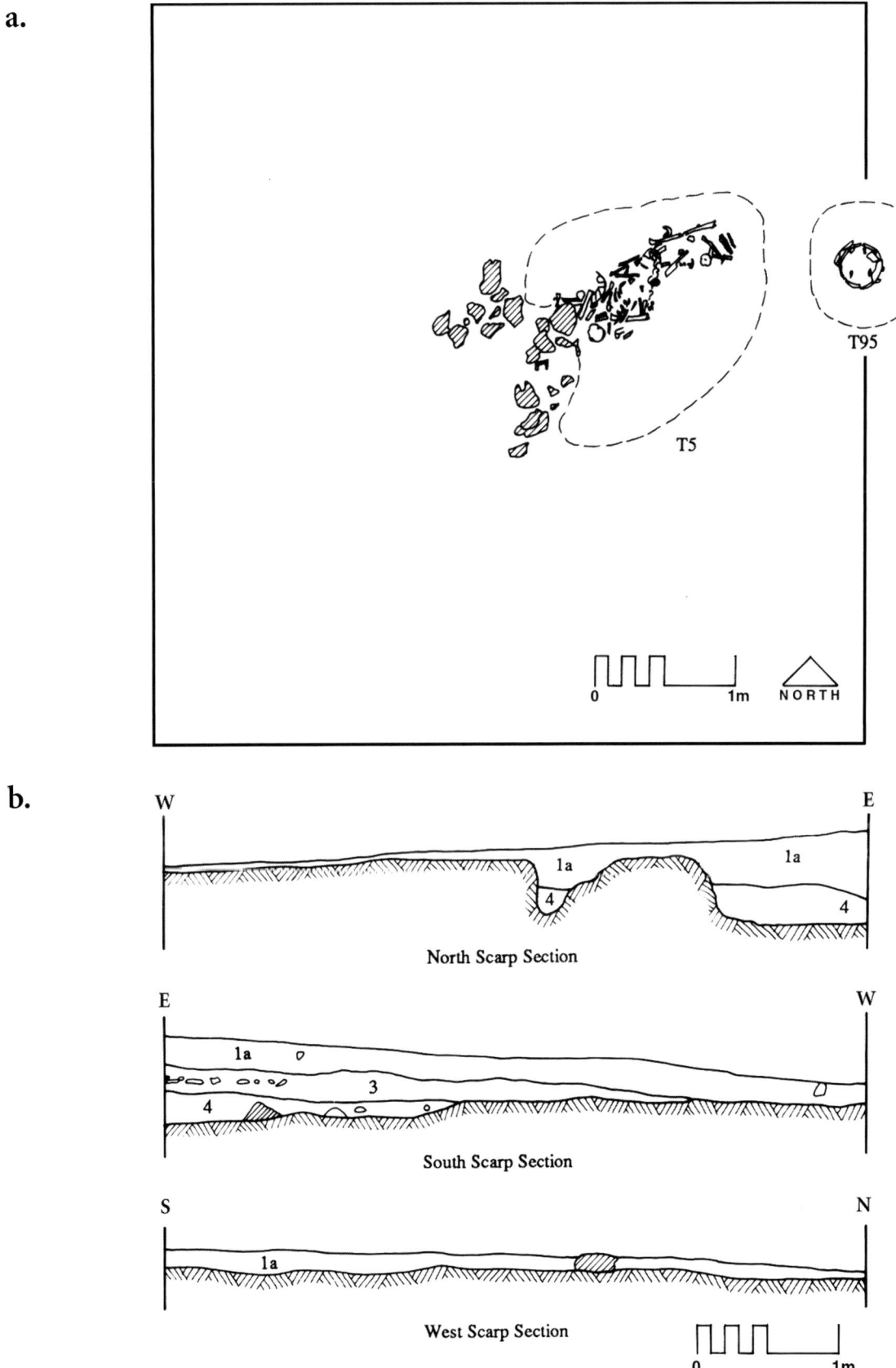

a.

T95

T5

0   1m   NORTH

b.

W   E

1a   1a

4   4

North Scarp Section

E   W

1a

3

4

South Scarp Section

S   N

1a

West Scarp Section

0   1m

FIGURE 37 (on following page). Trench 40. (*a*) Plan (*b*) Sections.

c.

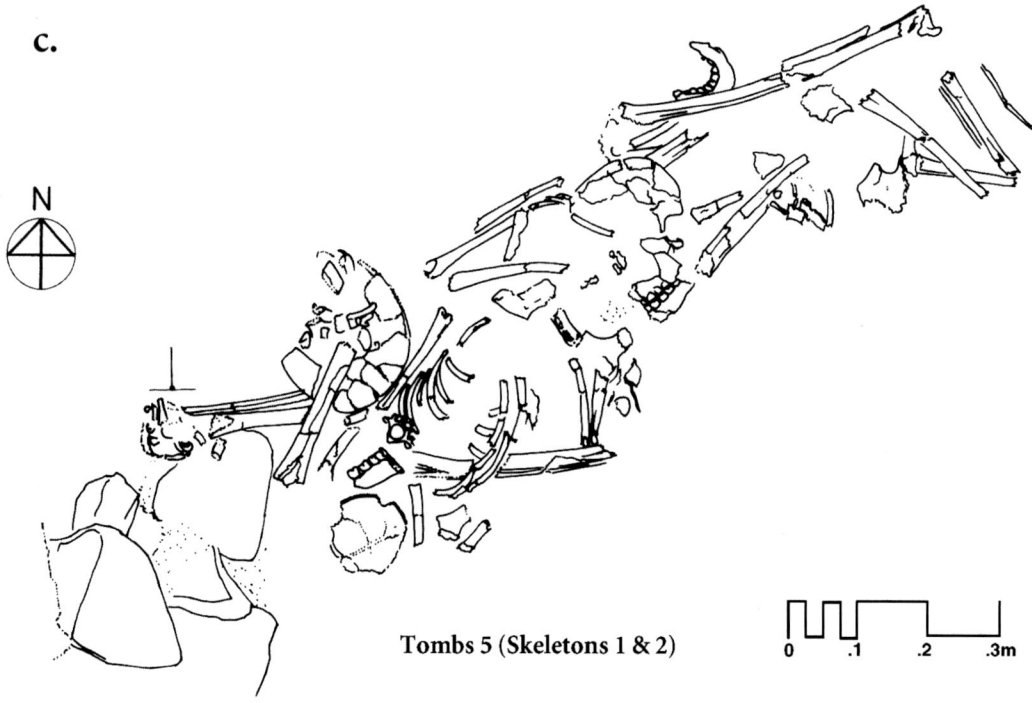

Tombs 5 (Skeletons 1 & 2)

FIGURE 37 (continued). Trench 40. (*c*) Plan of skeleton of Inhumation Tomb 5.

a.

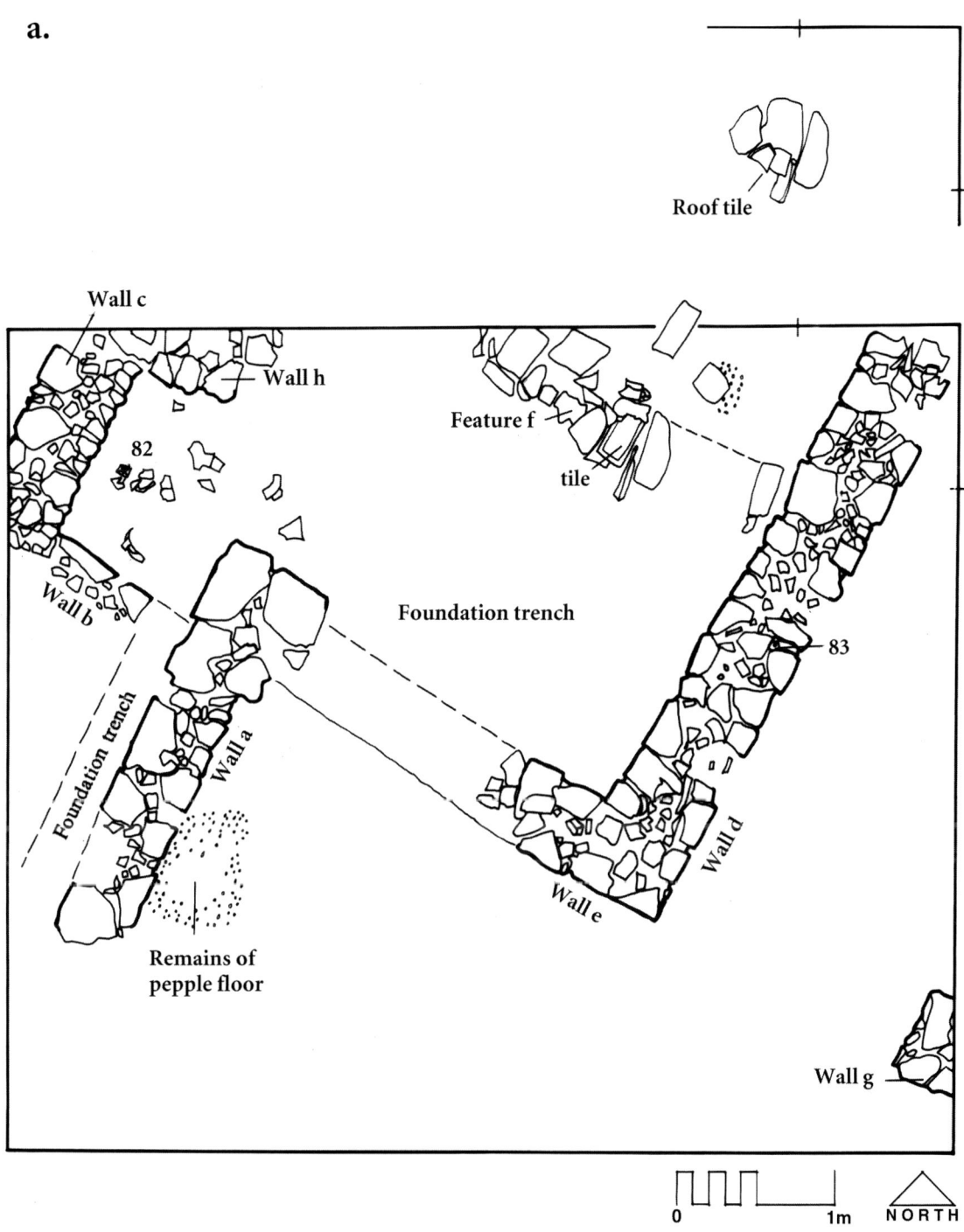

Roof tile

Wall c

Wall h

Feature f

tile

82

Wall b

Foundation trench

Foundation trench

Wall a

83

Remains of
pepple floor

Wall e

Wall d

Wall g

0   1m   NORTH

FIGURE 38 (on pages 759–761). Trench 43. (*a*) Plan (Stage 1), showing later phases of Classical domestic architecture and locations of Early Iron Age loomweights (82, 83).

b.

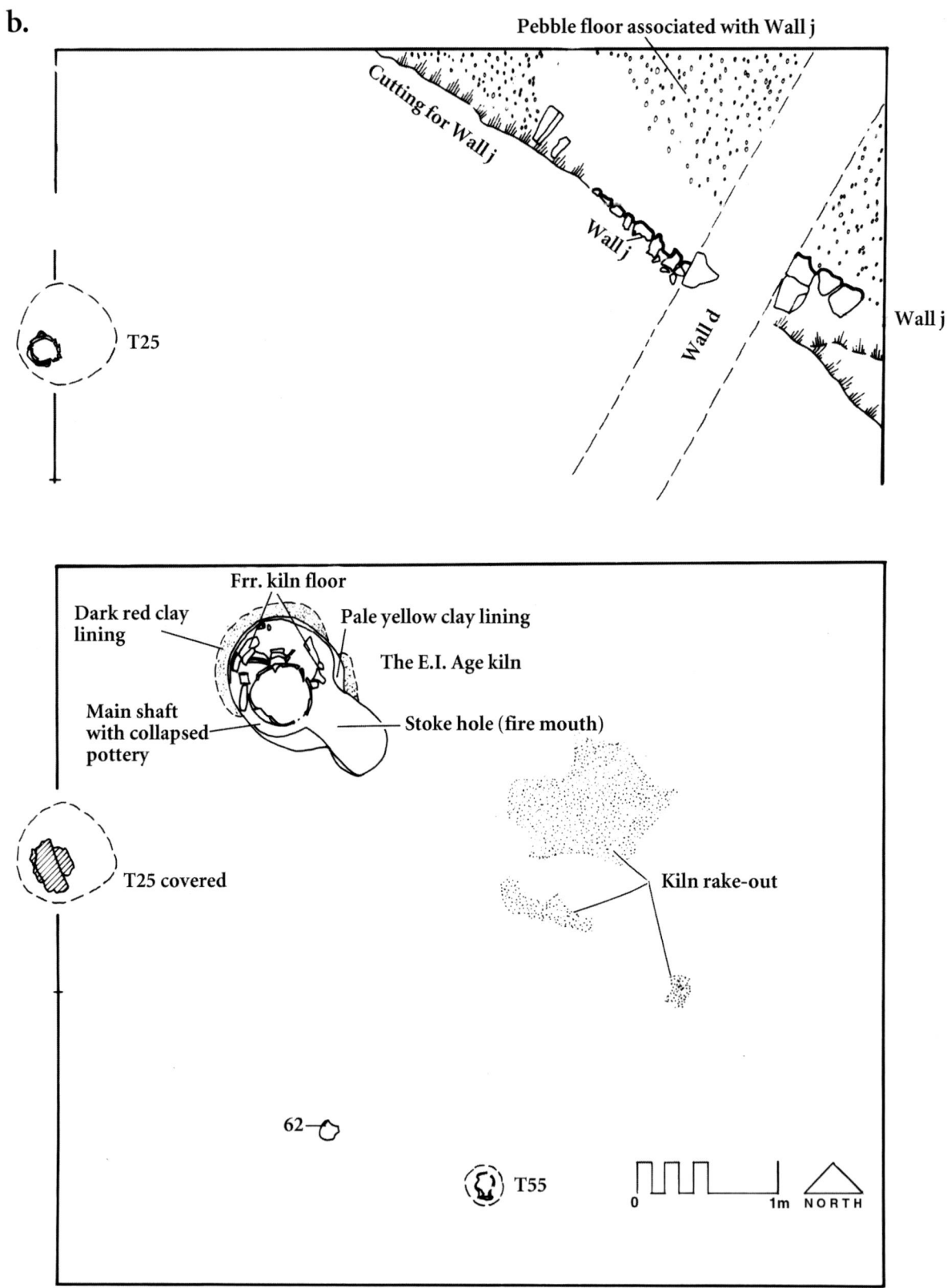

FIGURE 38 (continued). Trench 43. (*b*) Plan (Stage 2), showing Early Iron Age kiln and tombs, as well as the preserved remains of the earlier phase of Classical domestic architecture.

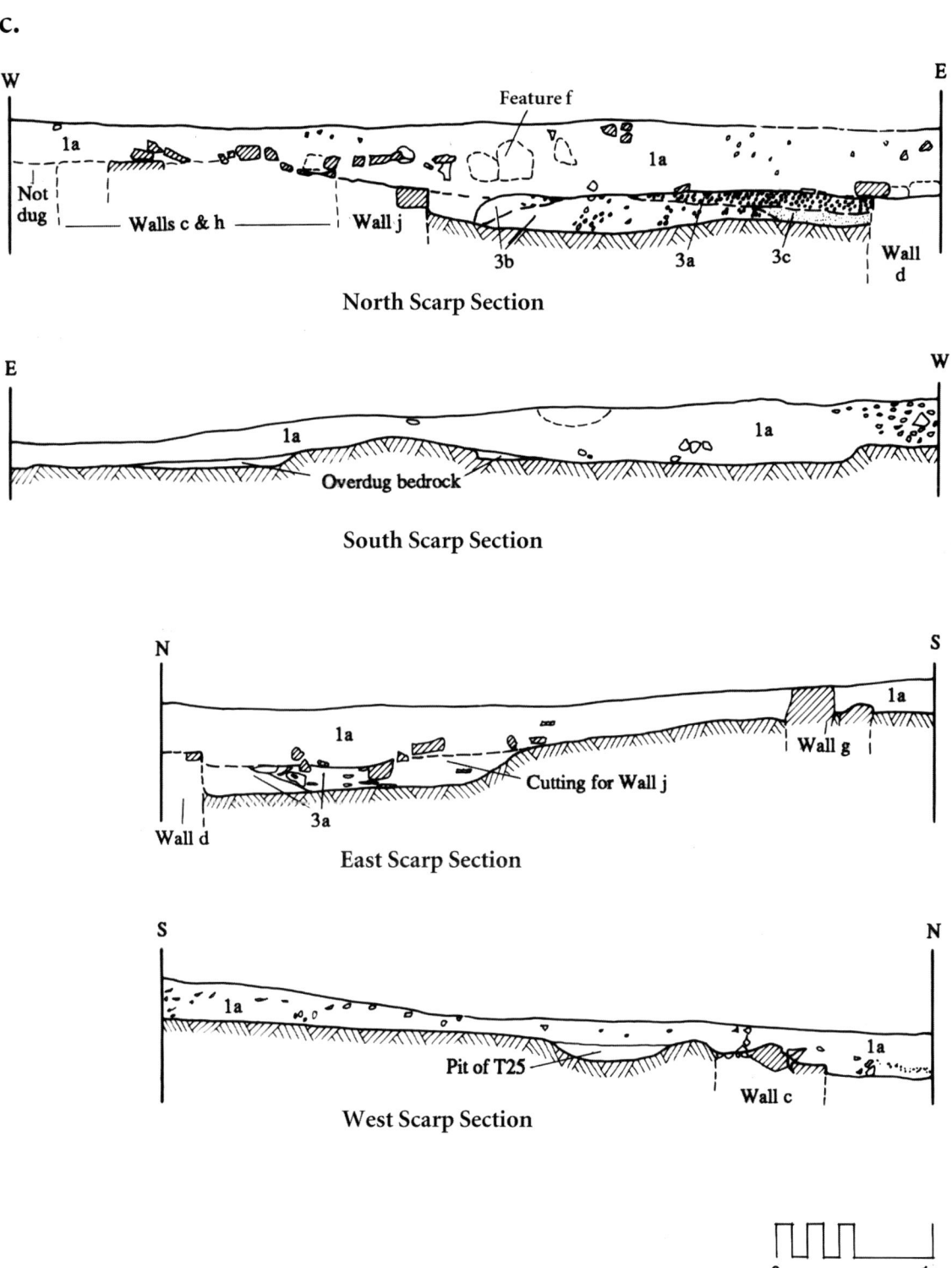

c.

W   E

Feature f

1a

Not
dug

Walls c & h   Wall j

3b   3a   3c   Wall d

1a

North Scarp Section

E   W

1a   1a

Overdug bedrock

South Scarp Section

N   S

1a   1a

Wall g

Cutting for Wall j

3a

Wall d

East Scarp Section

S   N

1a   1a

Pit of T25

Wall c

West Scarp Section

0   1m

FIGURE 38 (continued). Trench 43. (c) Sections.

a.

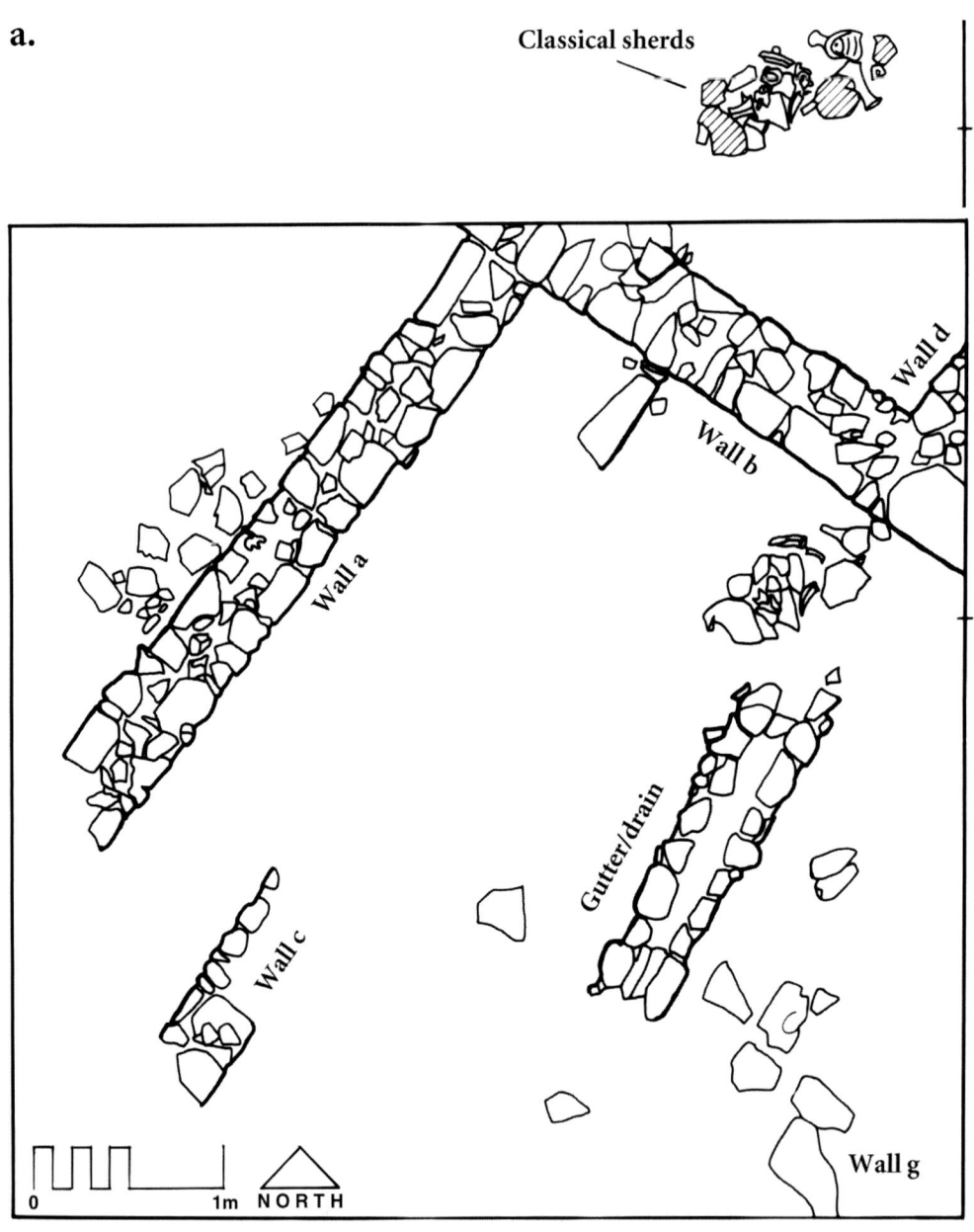

Classical sherds

Wall d

Wall b

Wall a

Gutter/drain

Wall c

Wall g

0 1m NORTH

FIGURE 39 (on pages 762–764). Trench 44. (*a*) Plan (Stage 1).

b.

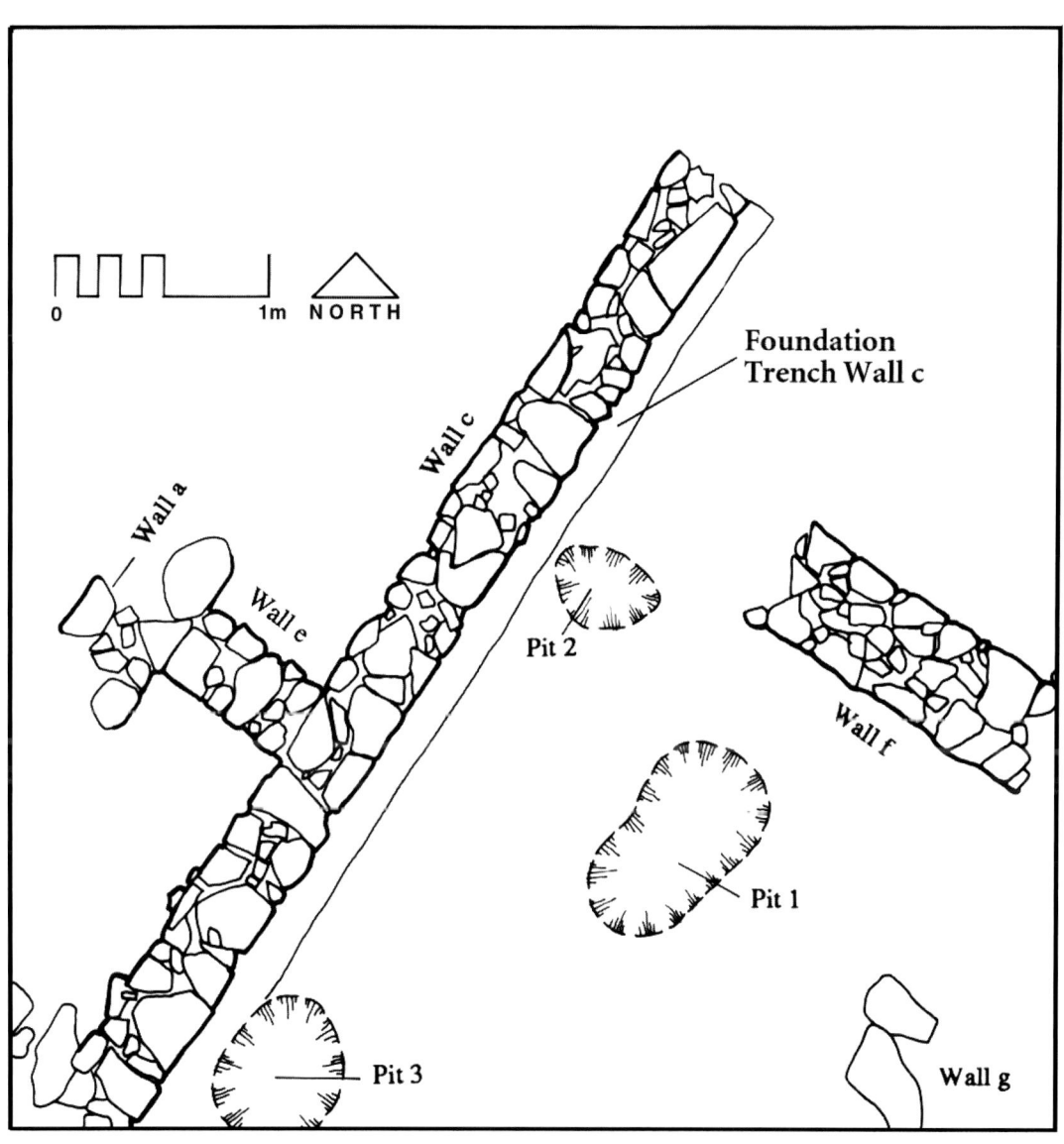

Wall c

Foundation
Trench Wall c

Wall a

Wall e

Pit 2

Wall f

Pit 1

Pit 3

Wall g

0   1m   NORTH

FIGURE 39 (continued). Trench 44. (*b*) Plan (Stage 2).

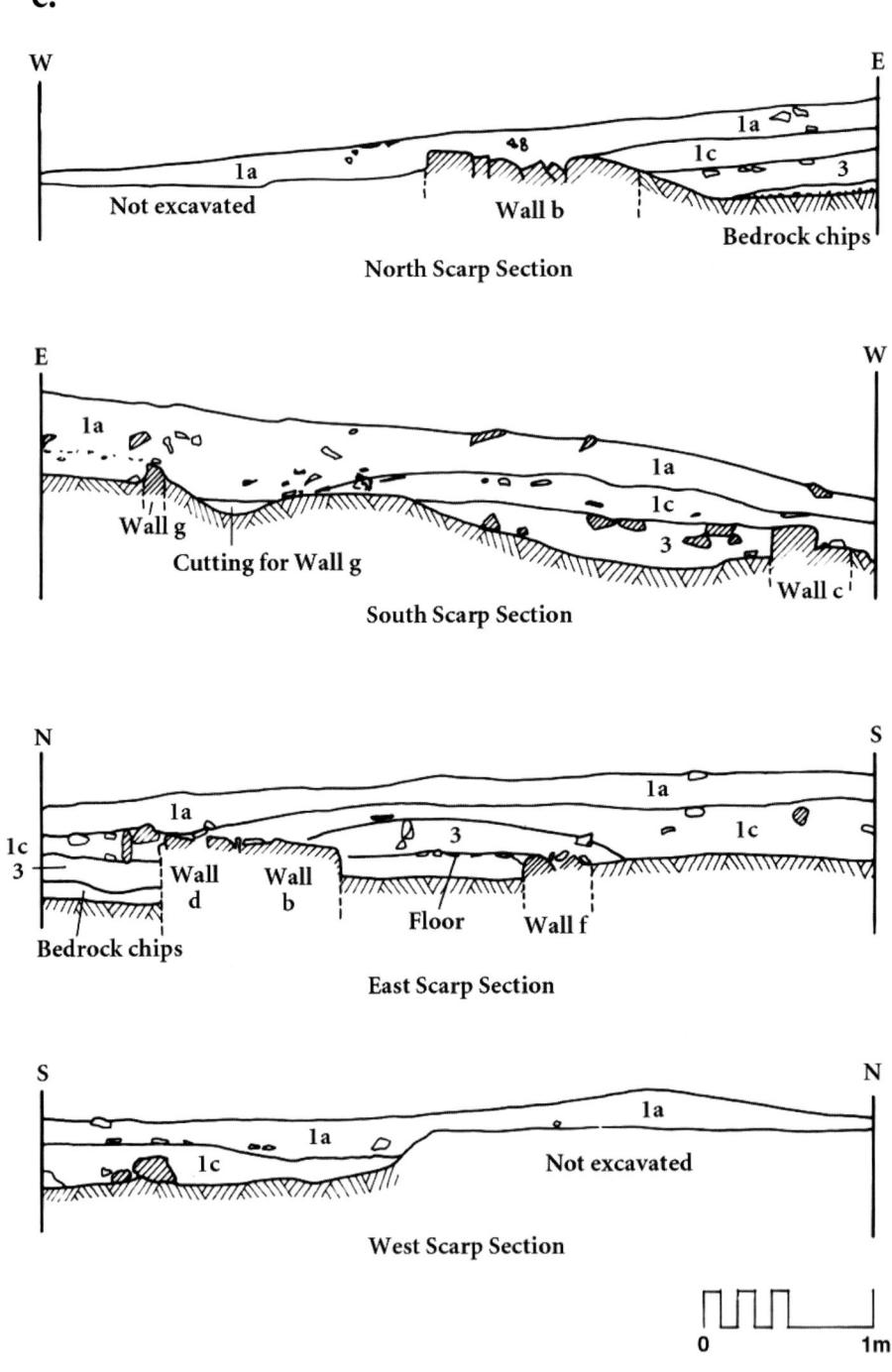

FIGURE 39 (continued). Trench 44. (*c*) Sections.

a.

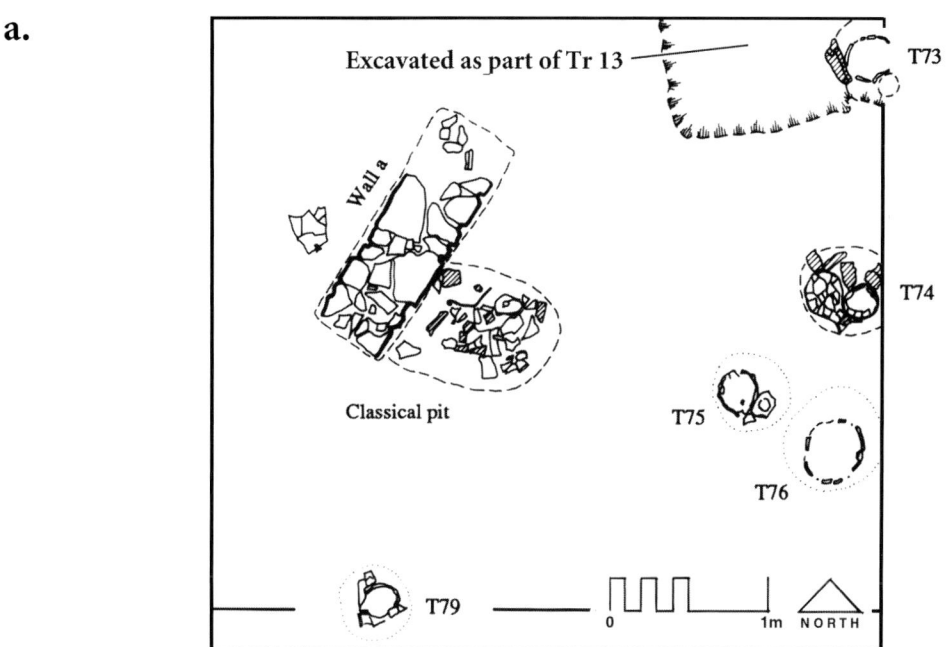

b.

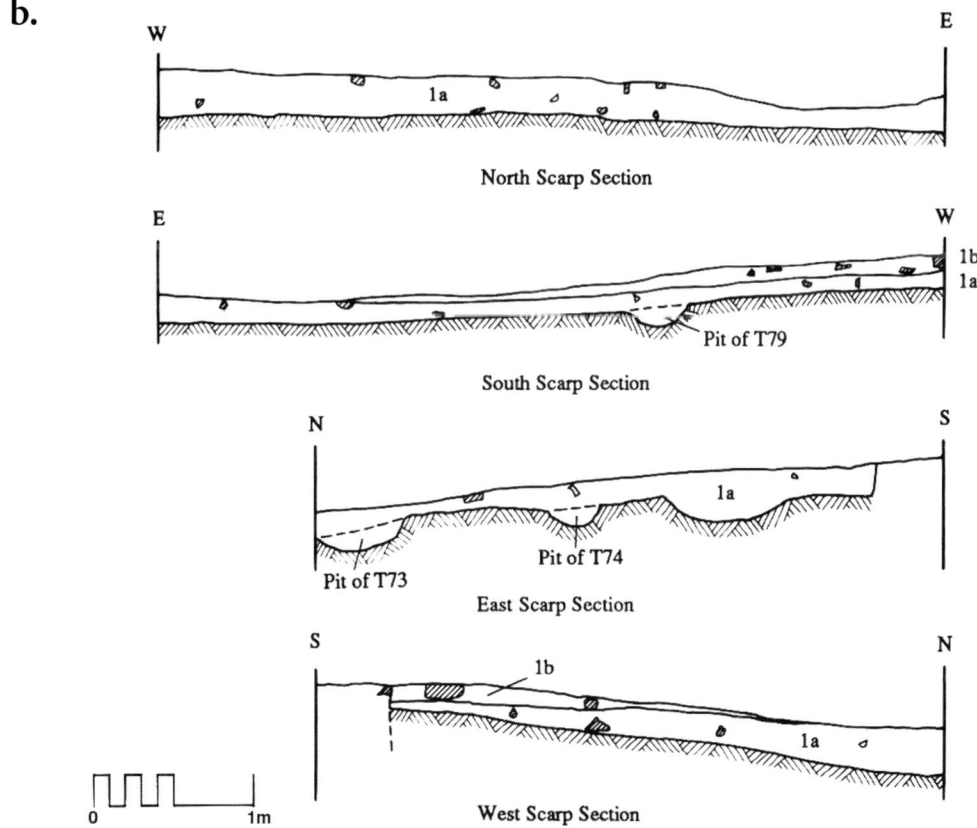

FIGURE 40. Trench 46. (*a*) Plan. (*b*) Sections.

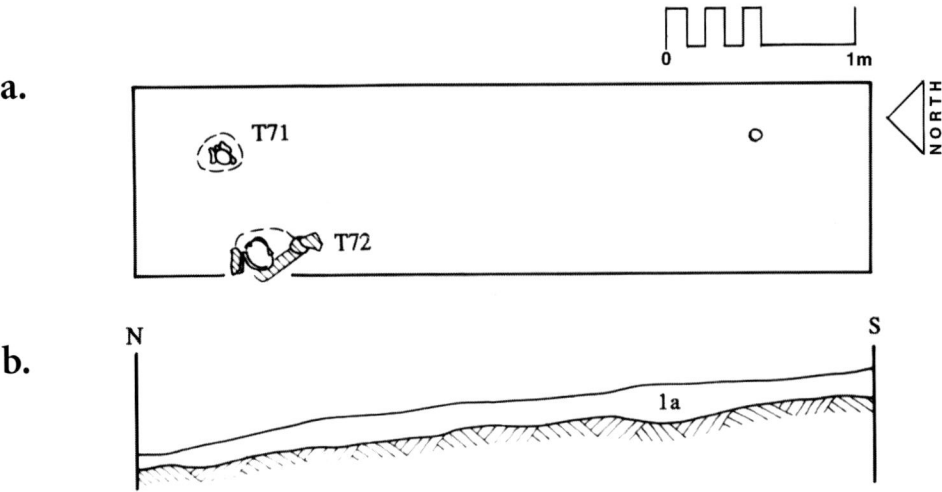

FIGURE 41. Trench 46 East Baulk. (*a*) Plan. (*b*) Section.

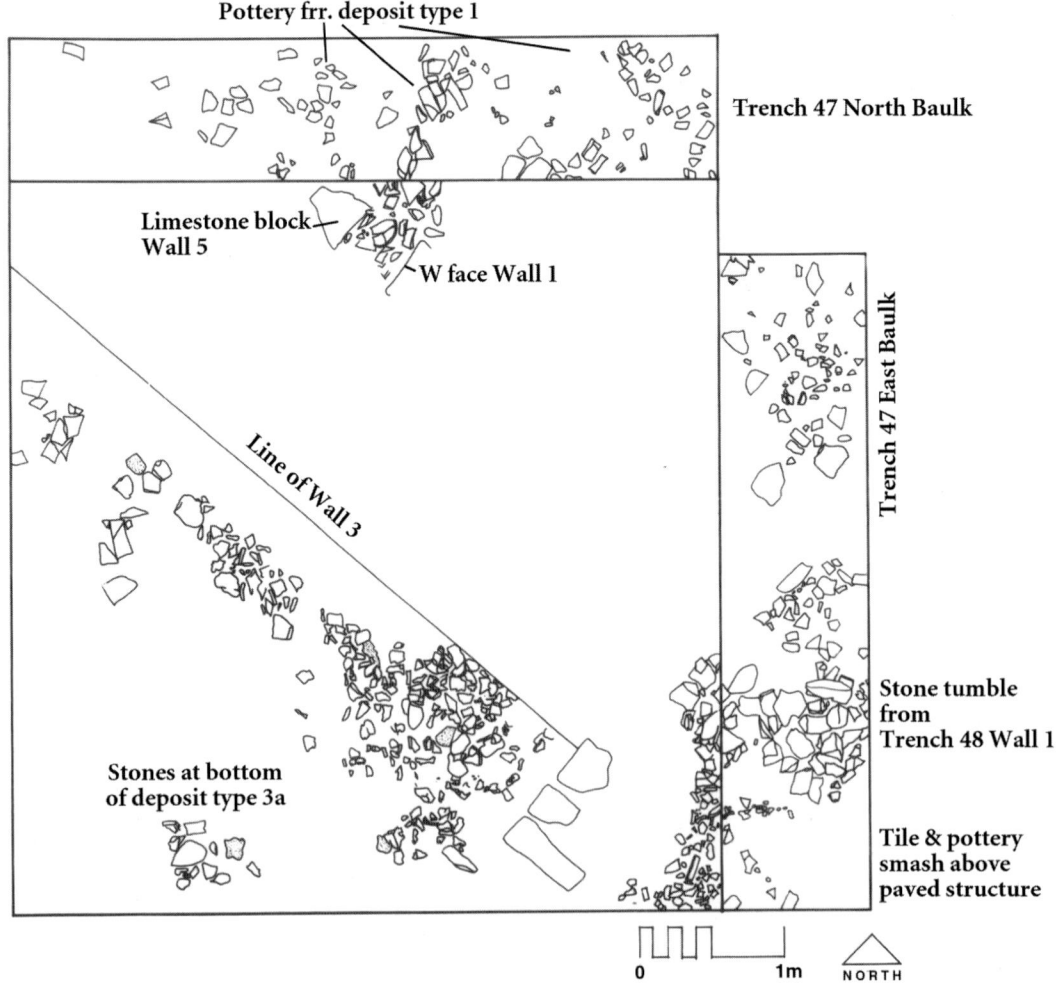

FIGURE 42. Trenches 47 and 47 North and East Baulks. Plan (Stage 1).

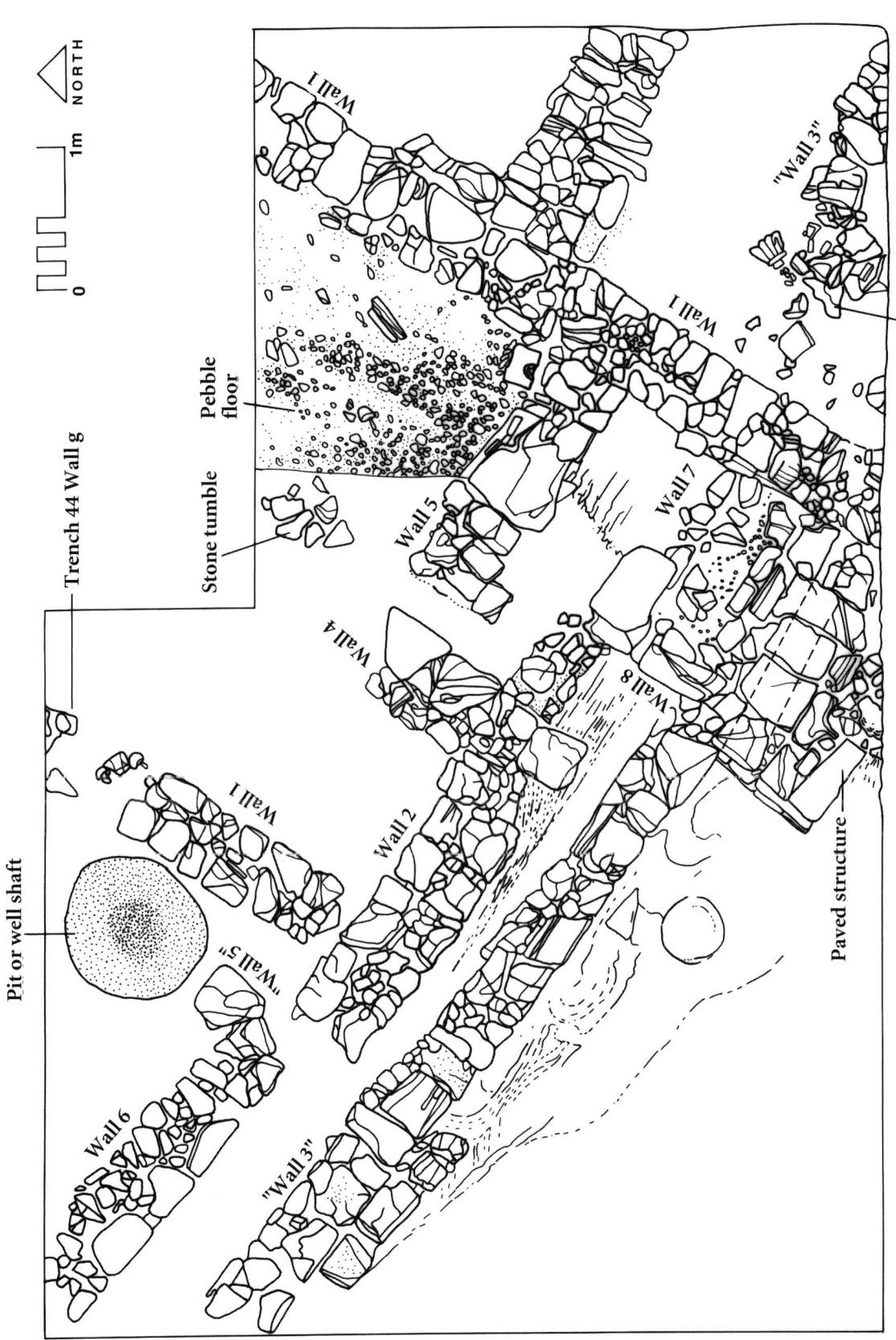

Pit or well shaft

Trench 44 Wall g

Stone tumble

Pebble floor

"Wall" 3"

"Wall" 2

Wall 1

Wall 5

Wall 7

Wall 4

Wall 8

Wall 2

Wall 1

"Wall" 5"

Wall 6

"Wall" 3"

Paved structure

0 1m

NORTH

FIGURE 43. Trenches 47, 47 North and East Baulks, and 48. Plan (Stage 2).

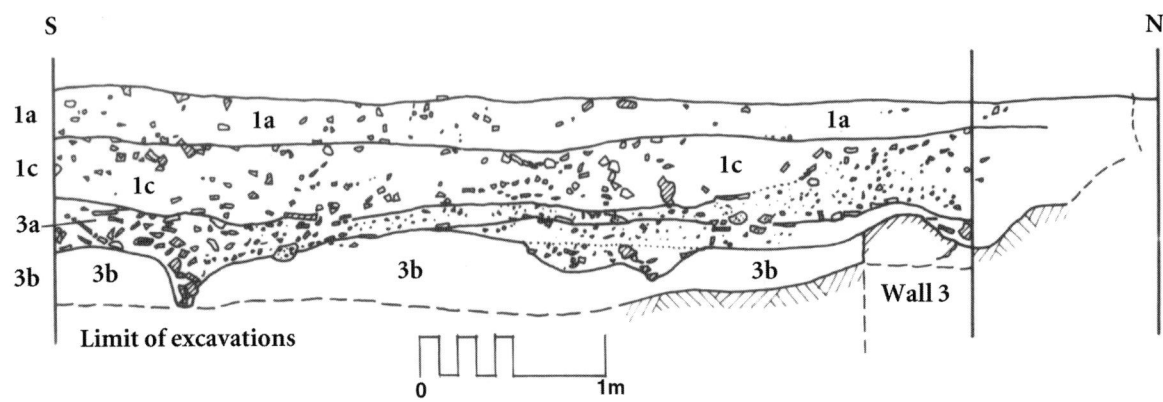

FIGURE 44. Trench 47 and 47 North Baulk. Section (west scarp).

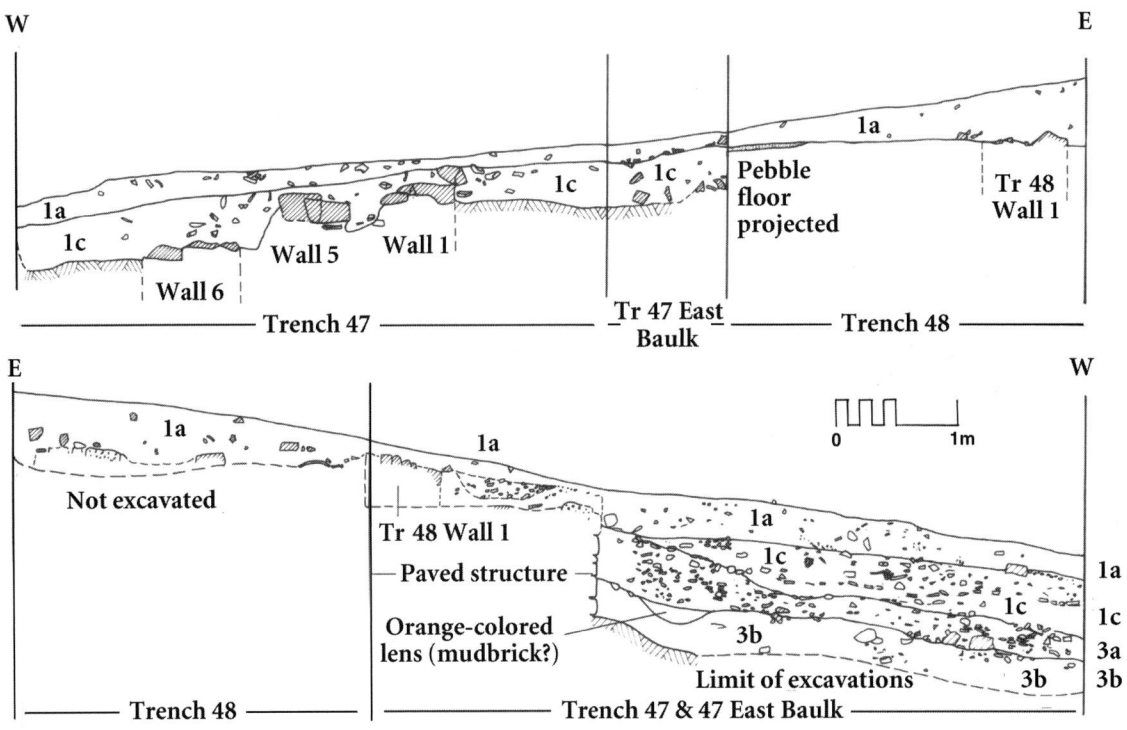

FIGURE 45. Trenches 47, 47 East Baulk, and 48. Sections (north and south scarps).

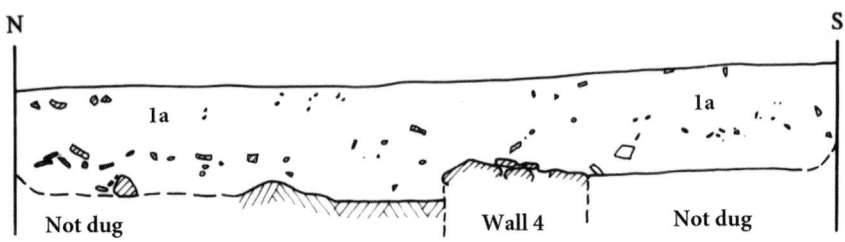

FIGURE 46. Trench 48. Section (east scarp).

a.

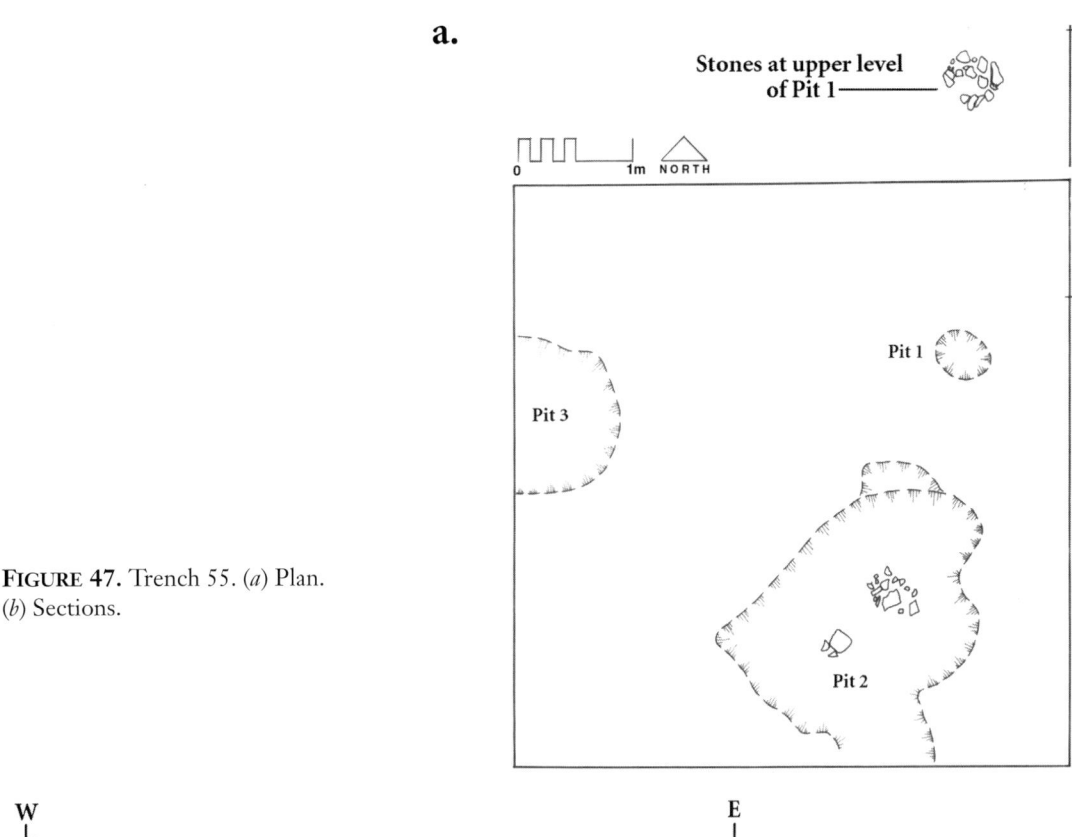

FIGURE 47. Trench 55. (*a*) Plan.
(*b*) Sections.

b.

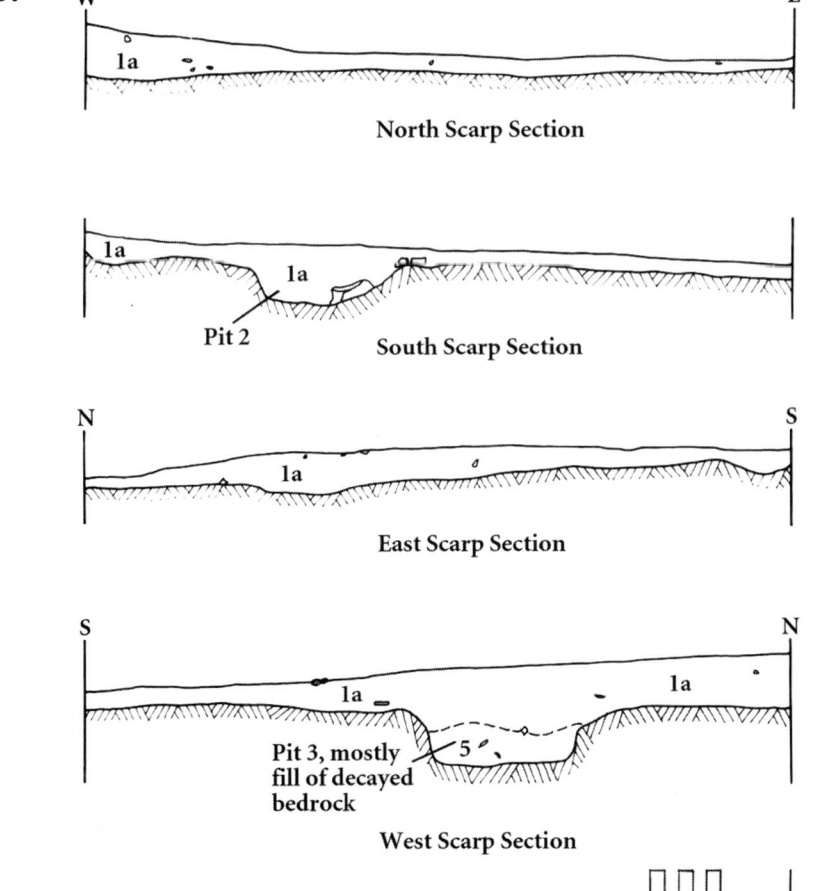

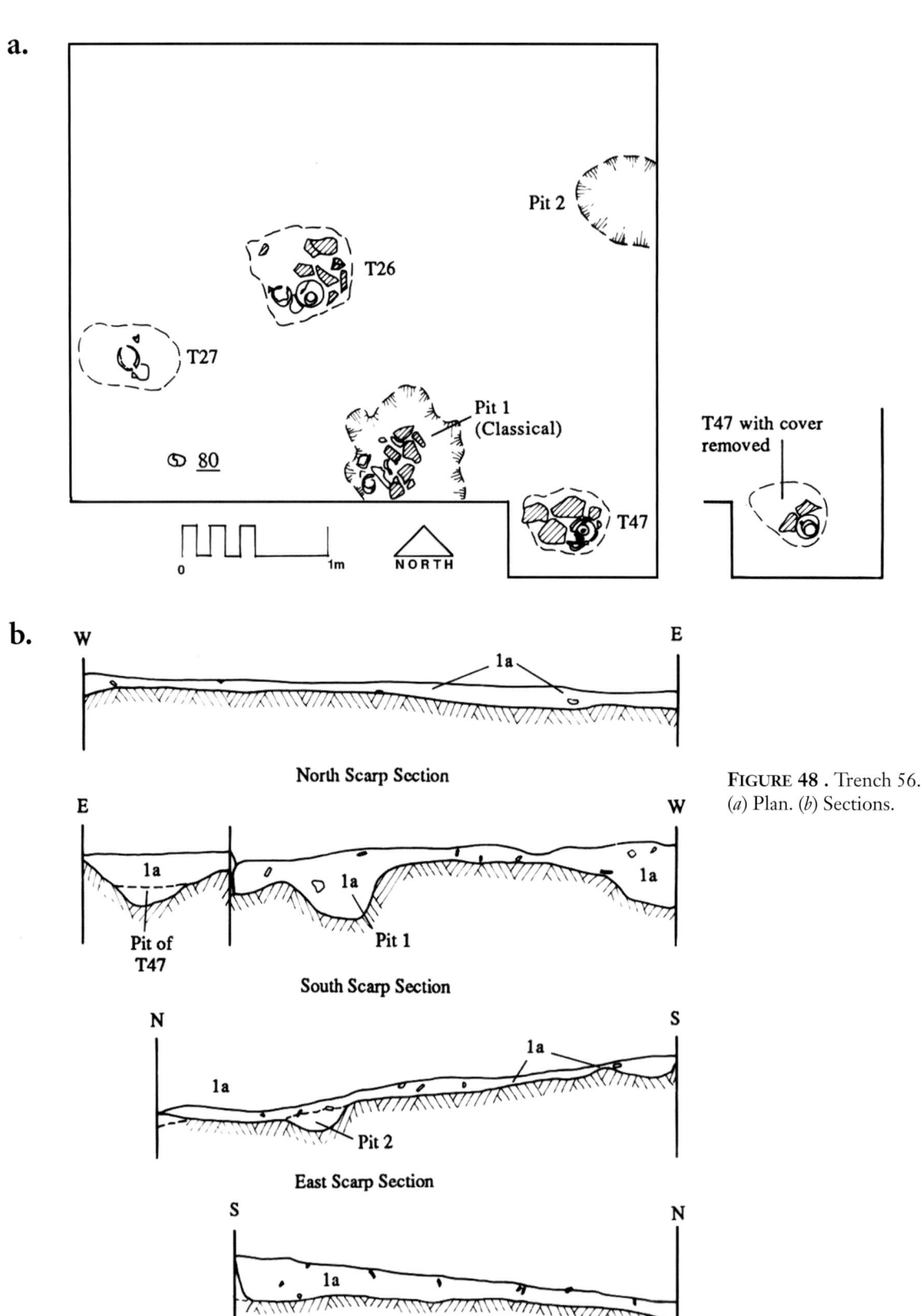

a.

Pit 2

T26

T27

⊙ <u>80</u>

Pit 1
(Classical)

T47

0   1m

NORTH

T47 with cover
removed

b.

W   E

1a

North Scarp Section

E   W

1a

1a   1a

Pit of
T47

Pit 1

South Scarp Section

N   S

1a

1a

Pit 2

East Scarp Section

S   N

1a

West Scarp Section

0   1m

FIGURE 48 . Trench 56.
(*a*) Plan. (*b*) Sections.

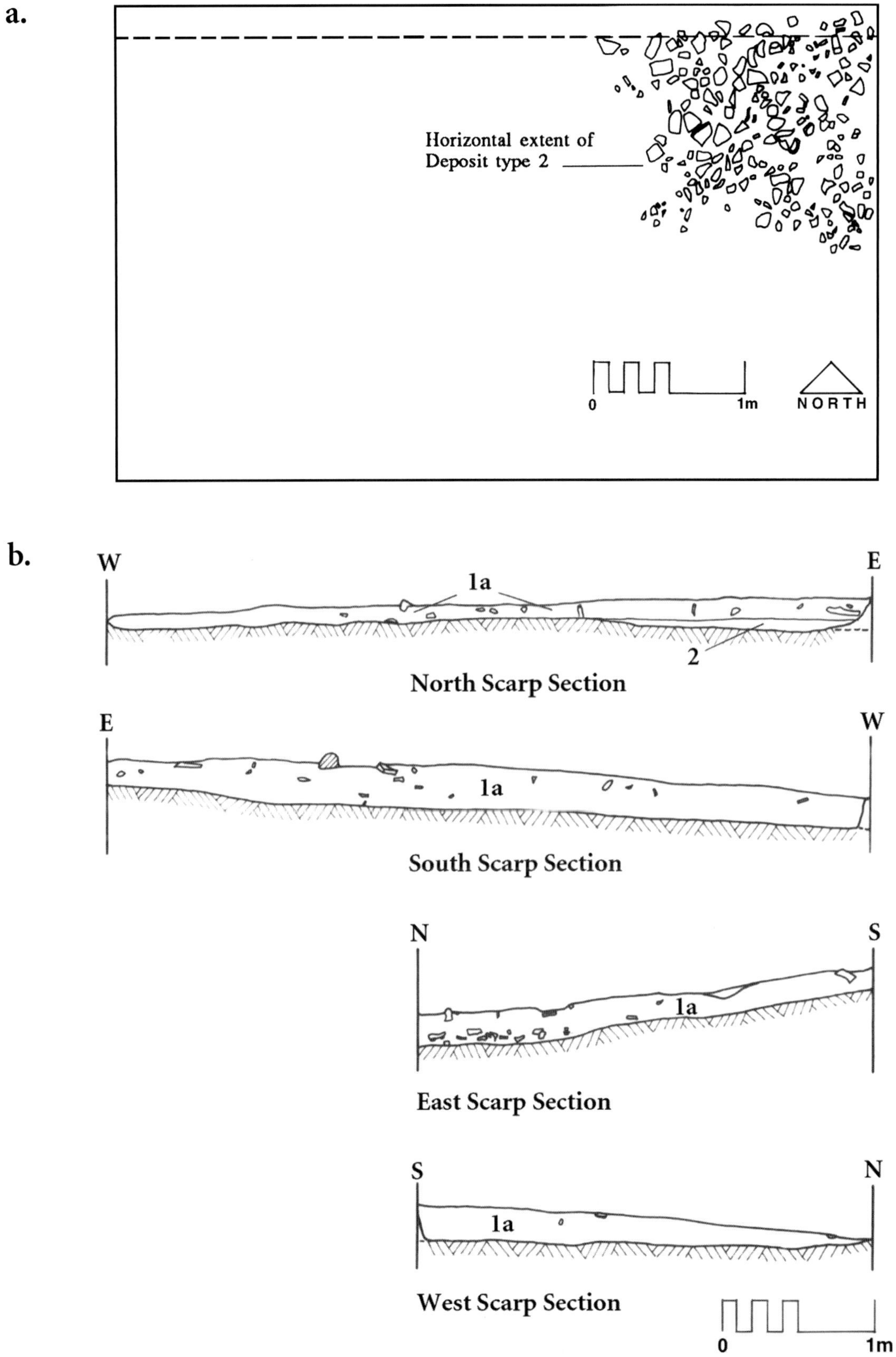

a.

Horizontal extent of
Deposit type 2

0   1m   NORTH

b.

W   1a   E

2

North Scarp Section

E   W

1a

South Scarp Section

N   S

1a

East Scarp Section

S   N

1a

West Scarp Section

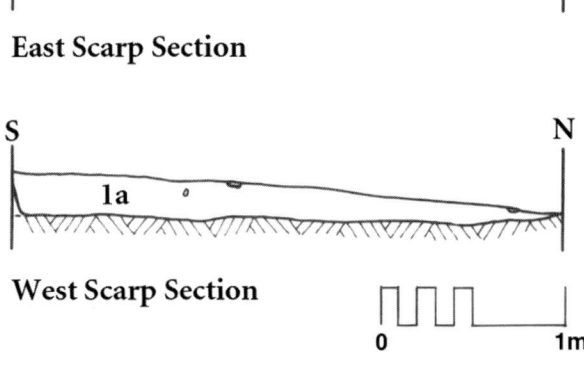

0   1m

FIGURE 49. Trench 57. (*a*) Plan (*b*) Sections.

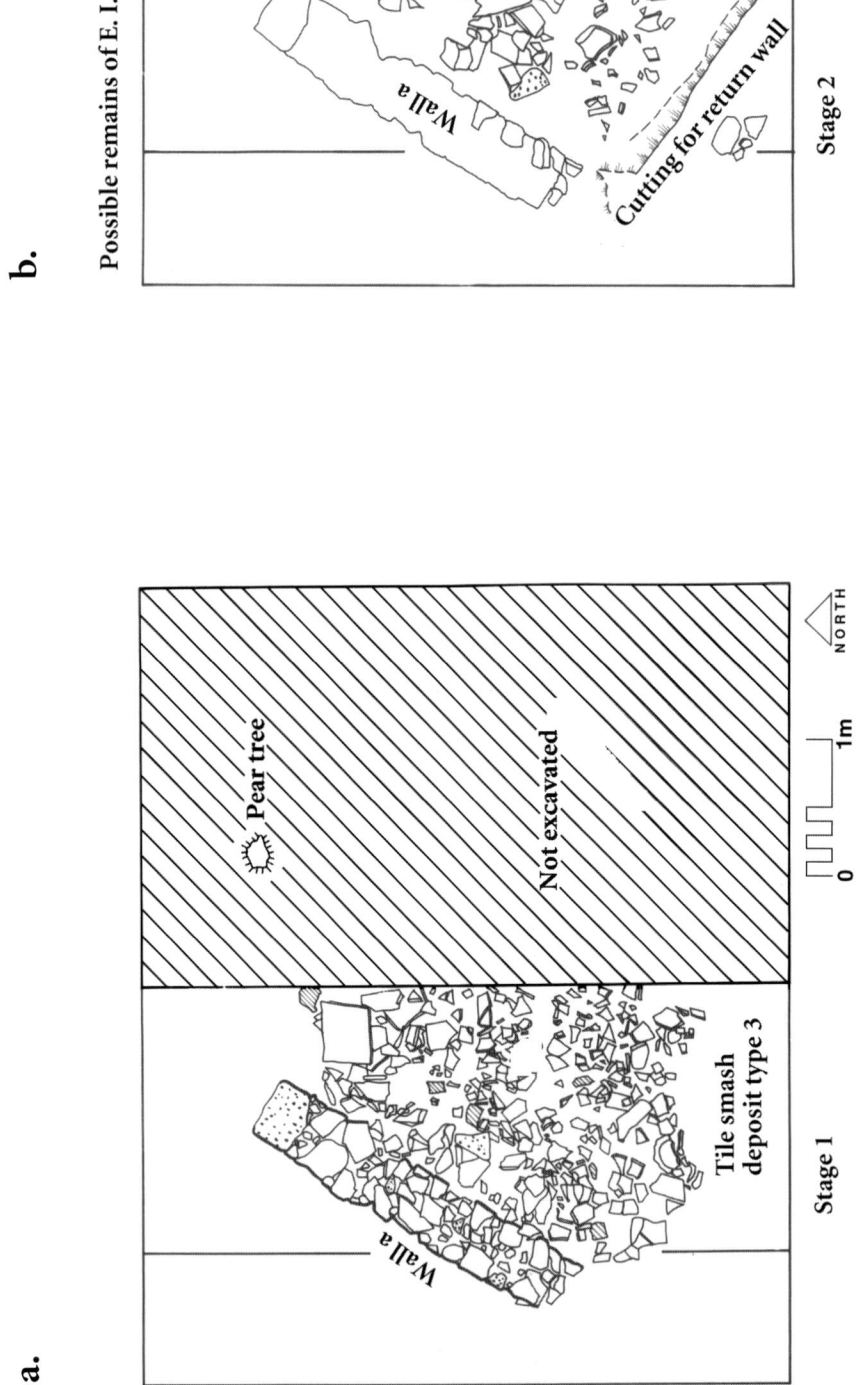

FIGURE 50. Trenches 58 and 13 East Baulk. (*a*) Plan (Stage 1). (*b*) Plan (Stage 2).

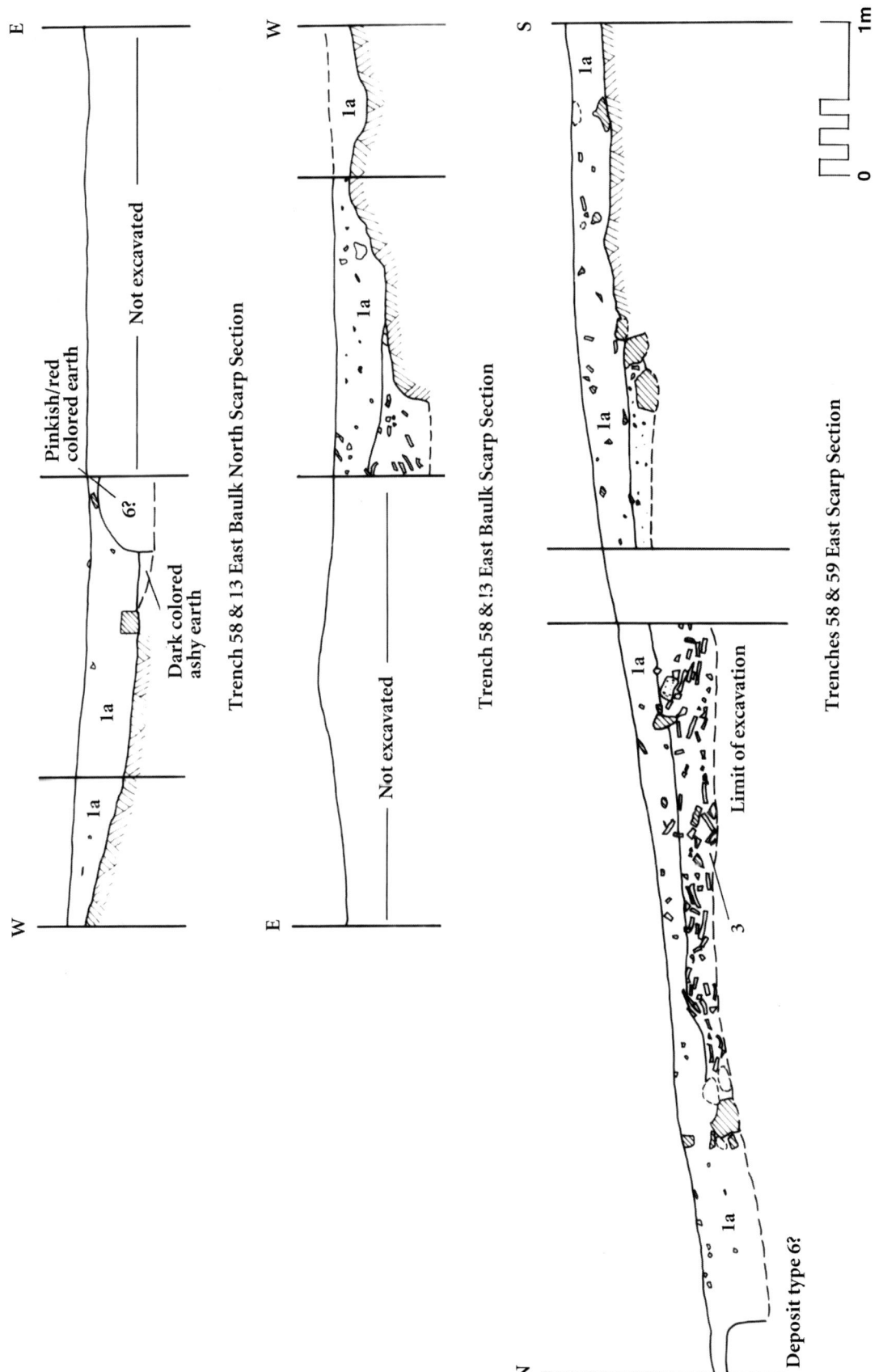

Trench 58 & 13 East Baulk North Scarp Section

Trench 58 & 13 East Baulk Scarp Section

Trenches 58 & 59 East Scarp Section

FIGURE 51. Trenches 58, 59, and 13 East Baulk. Sections.

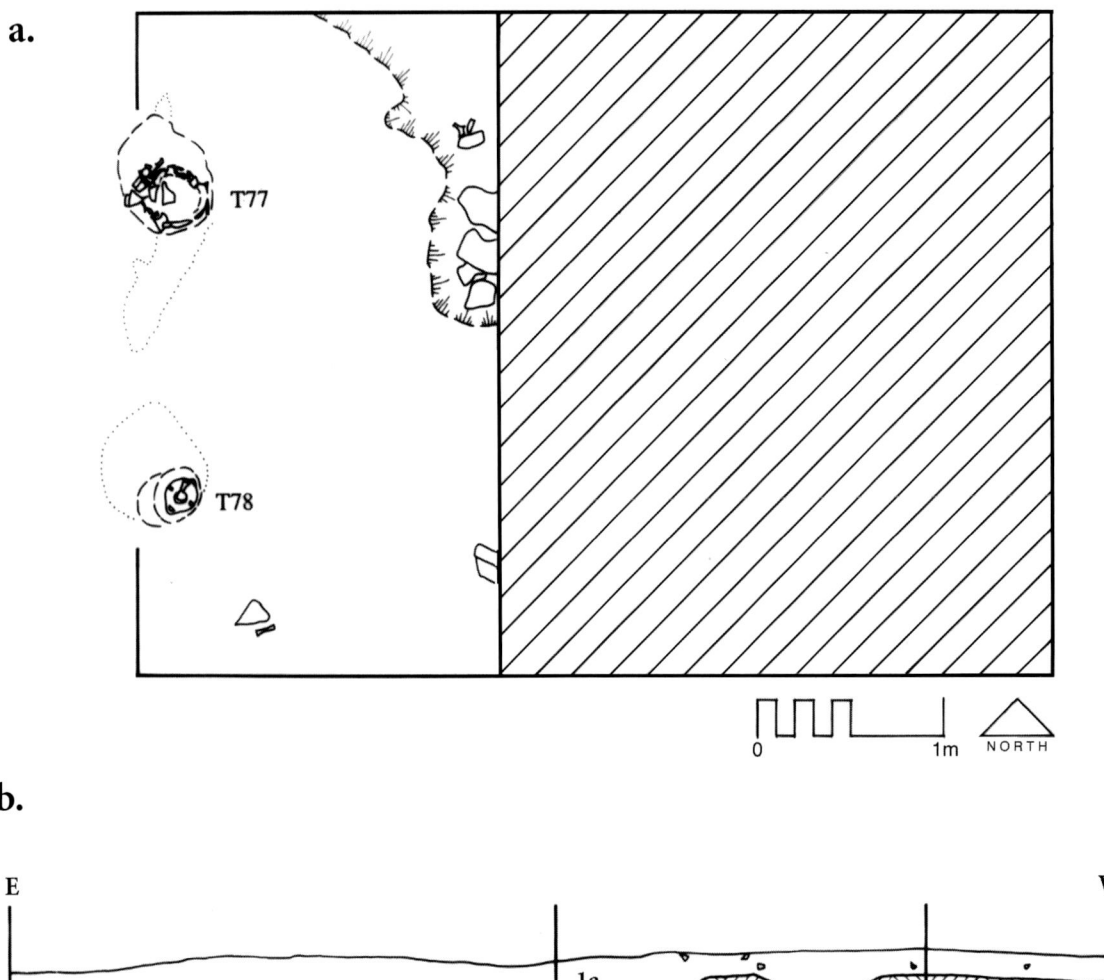

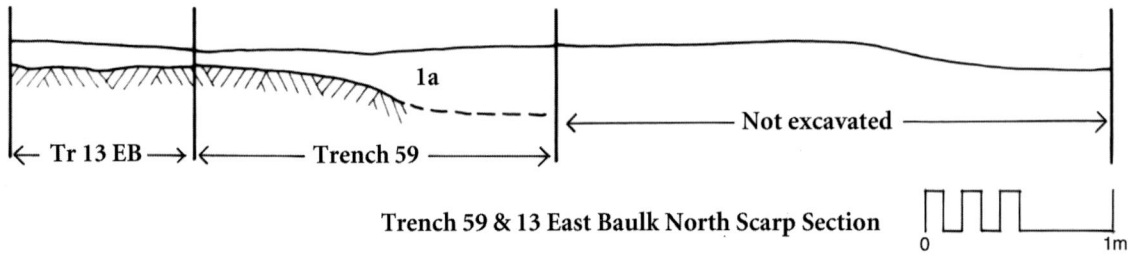

FIGURE 52. Trench 59. (*a*) Plan. (*b*) Sections.

a.

Area dug in 1981 associated with
tomb pits of T35 and T34

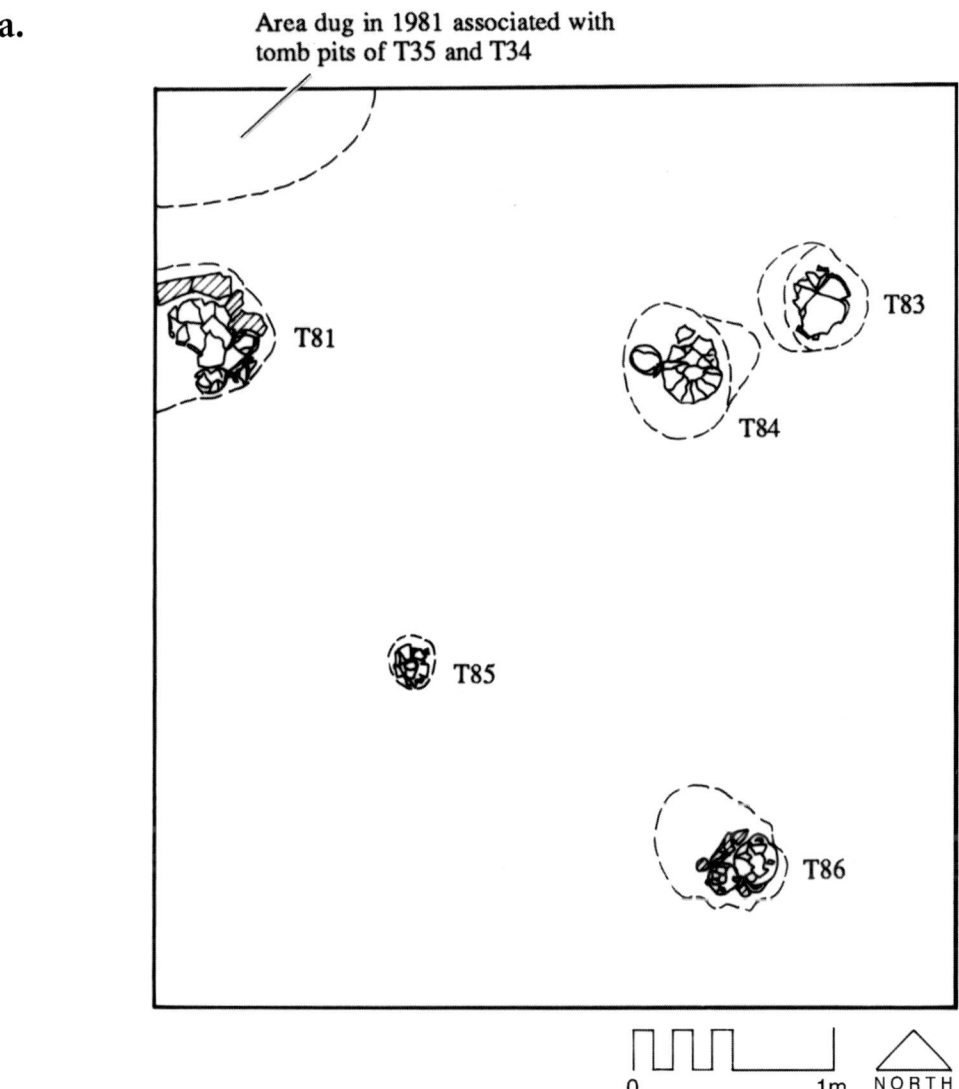

FIGURE 53 (on following page). Trench 60. (*a*) Plan.

b.

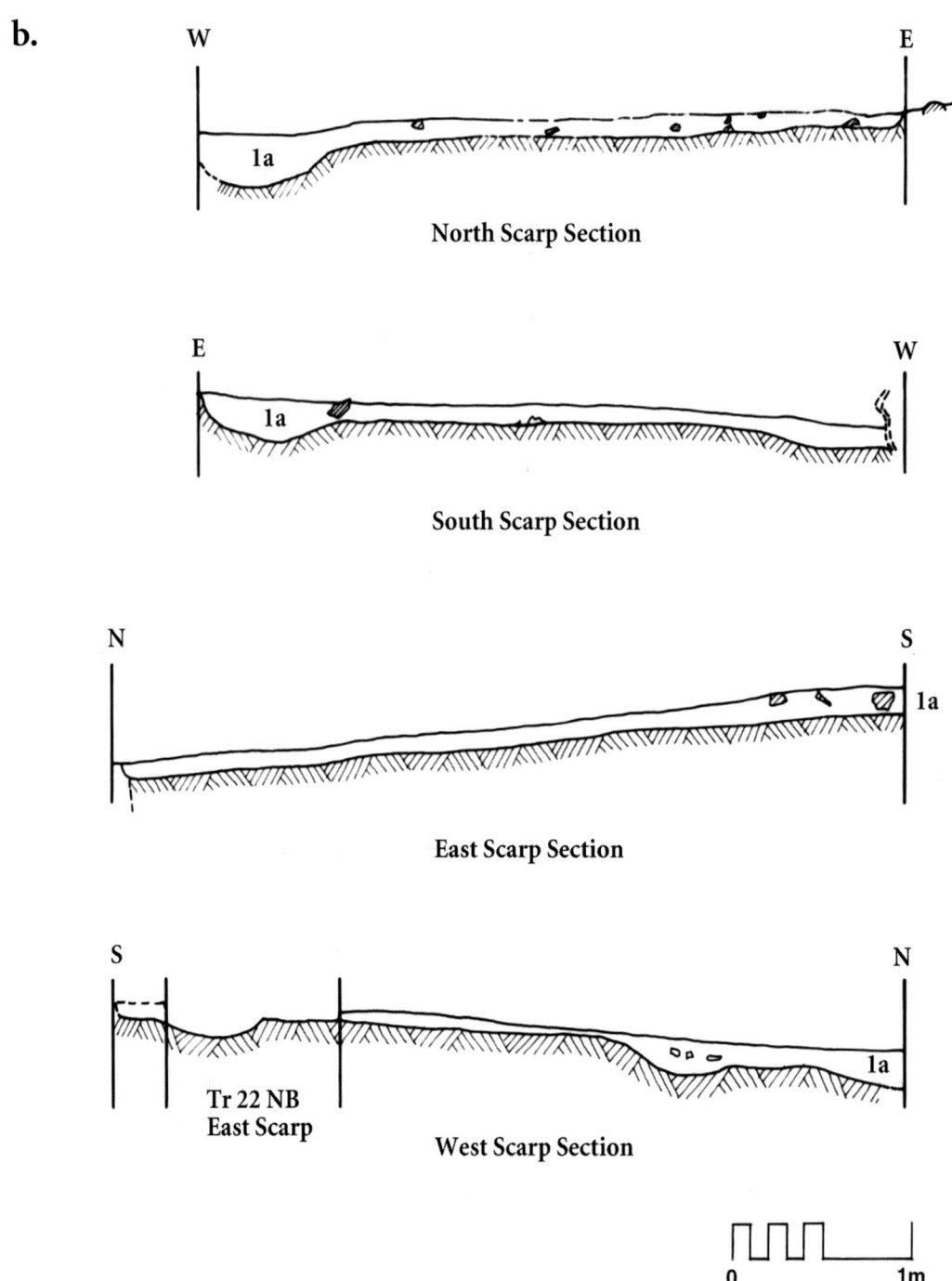

North Scarp Section

South Scarp Section

East Scarp Section

West Scarp Section

Tr 22 NB
East Scarp

0   1m

FIGURE 53 (continued). Trench 60. (*b*) Sections.

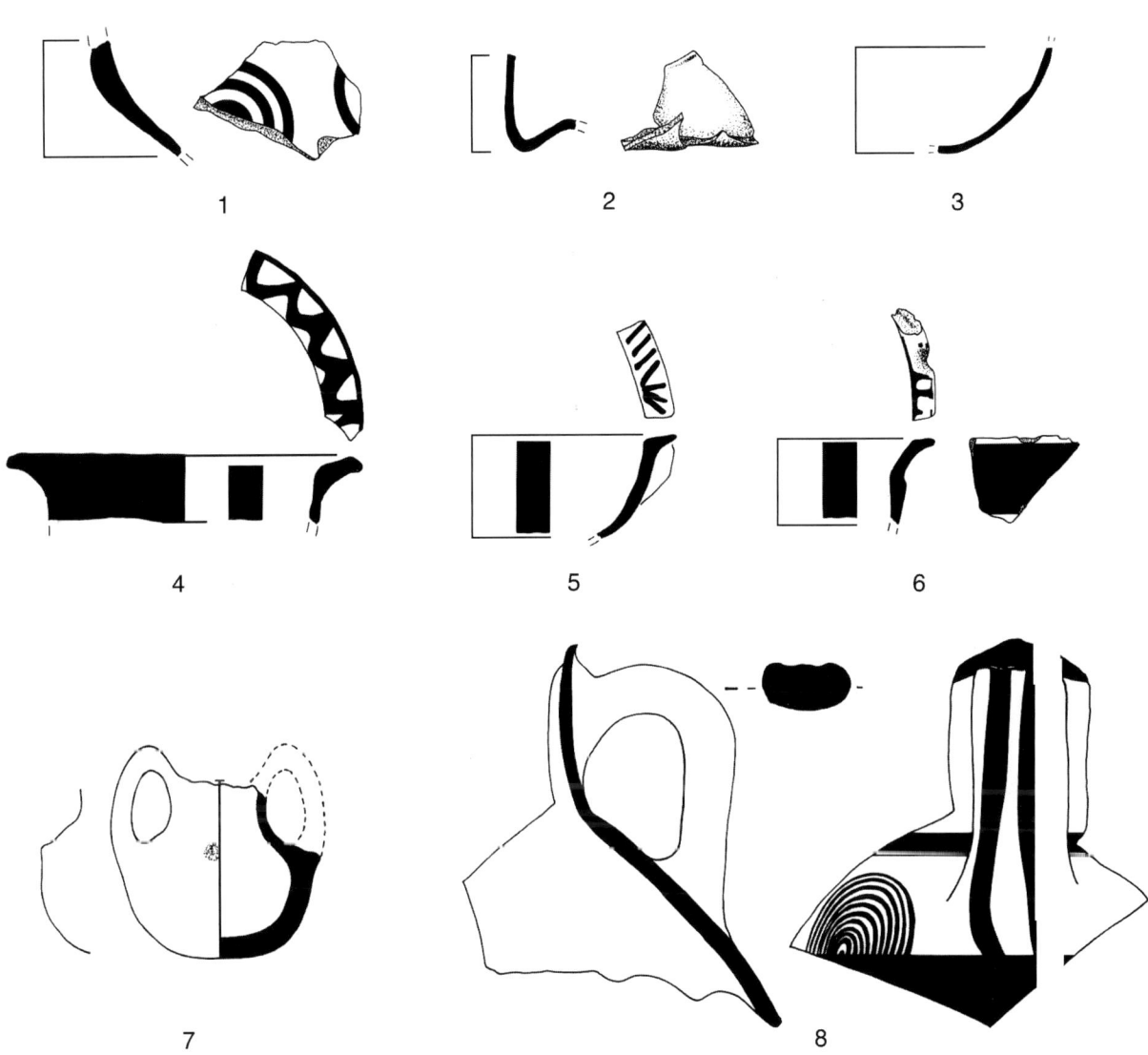

FIGURE 54. 1–8.

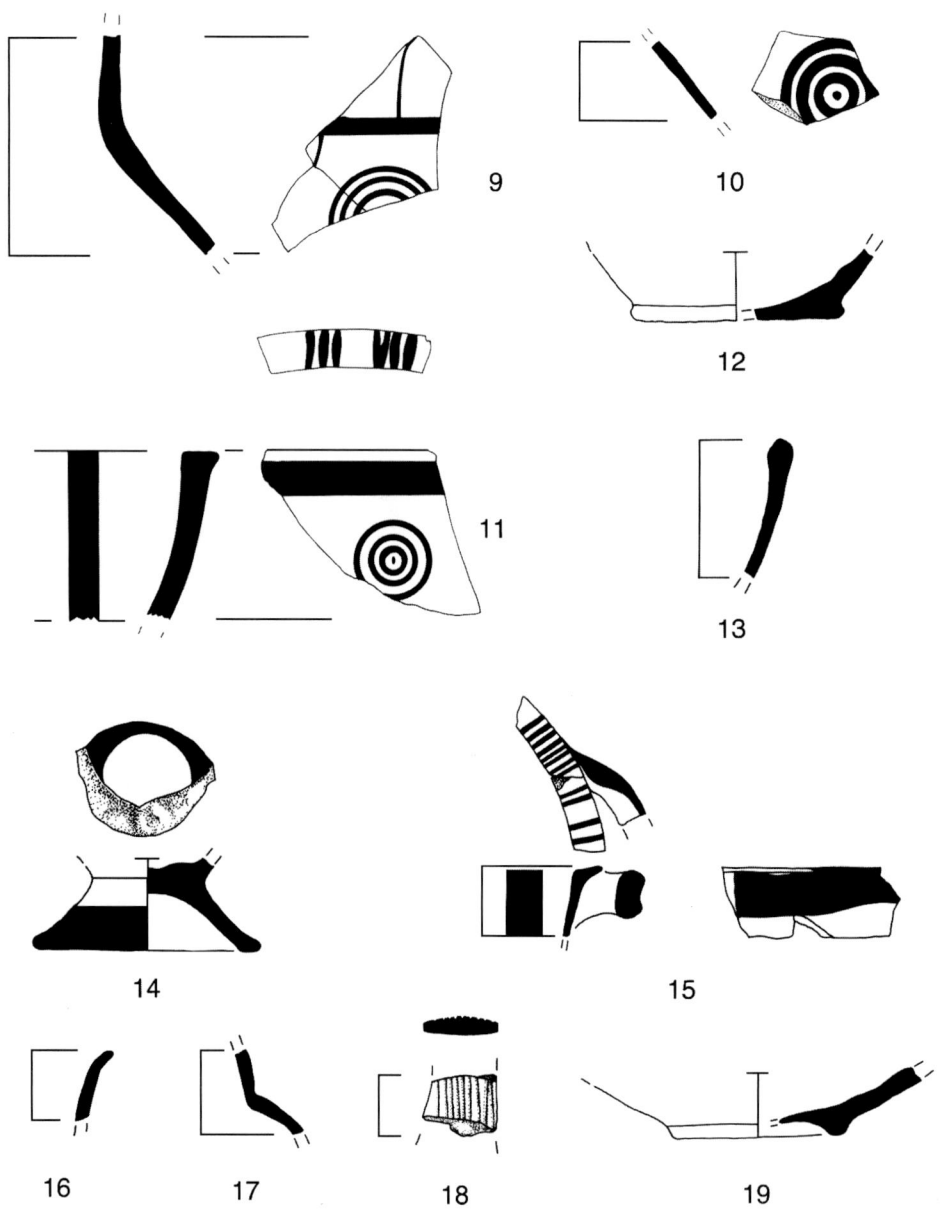

FIGURE 55. 9–19.

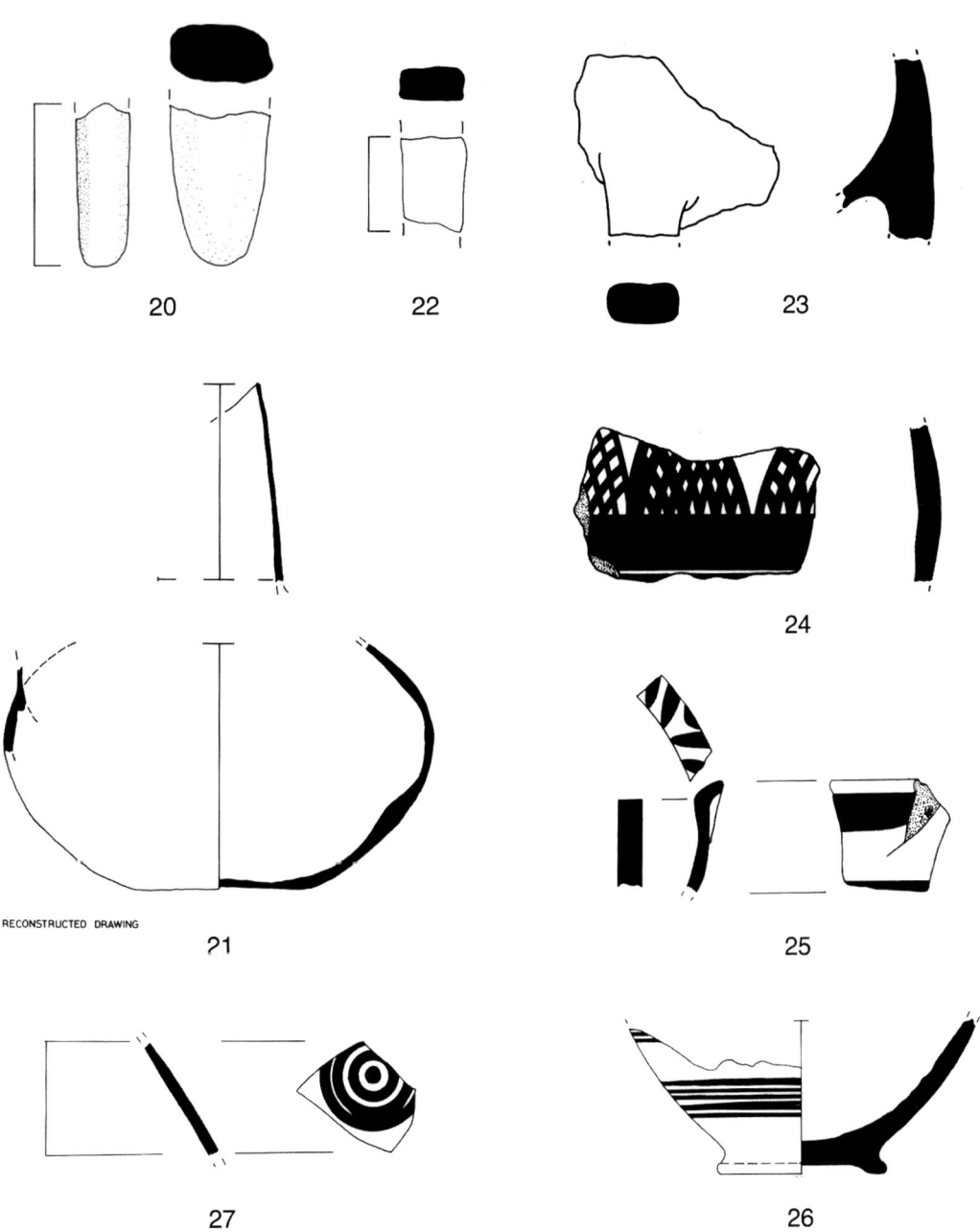

FIGURE 56. 20–27.

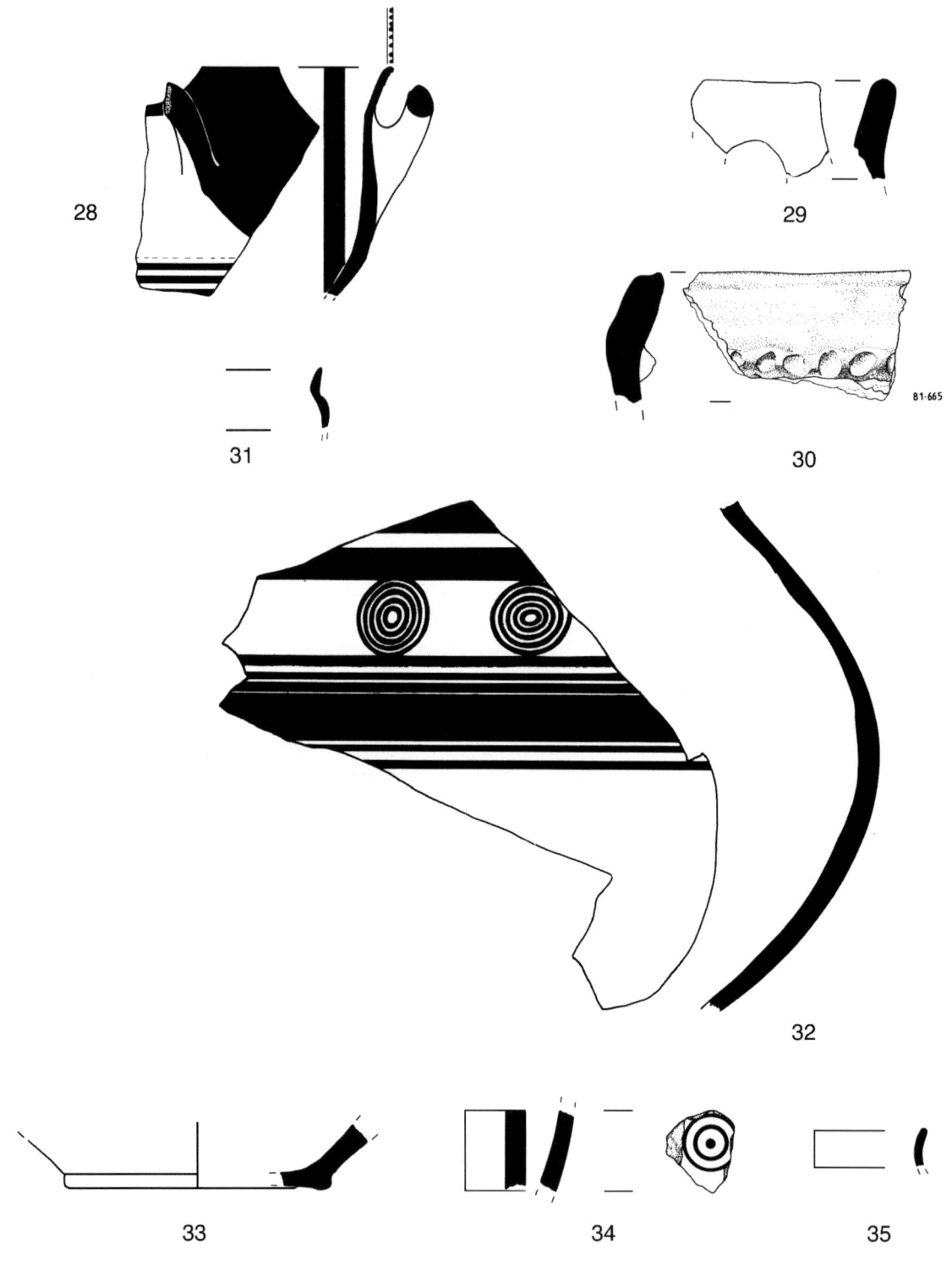

FIGURE 57. 28–35.

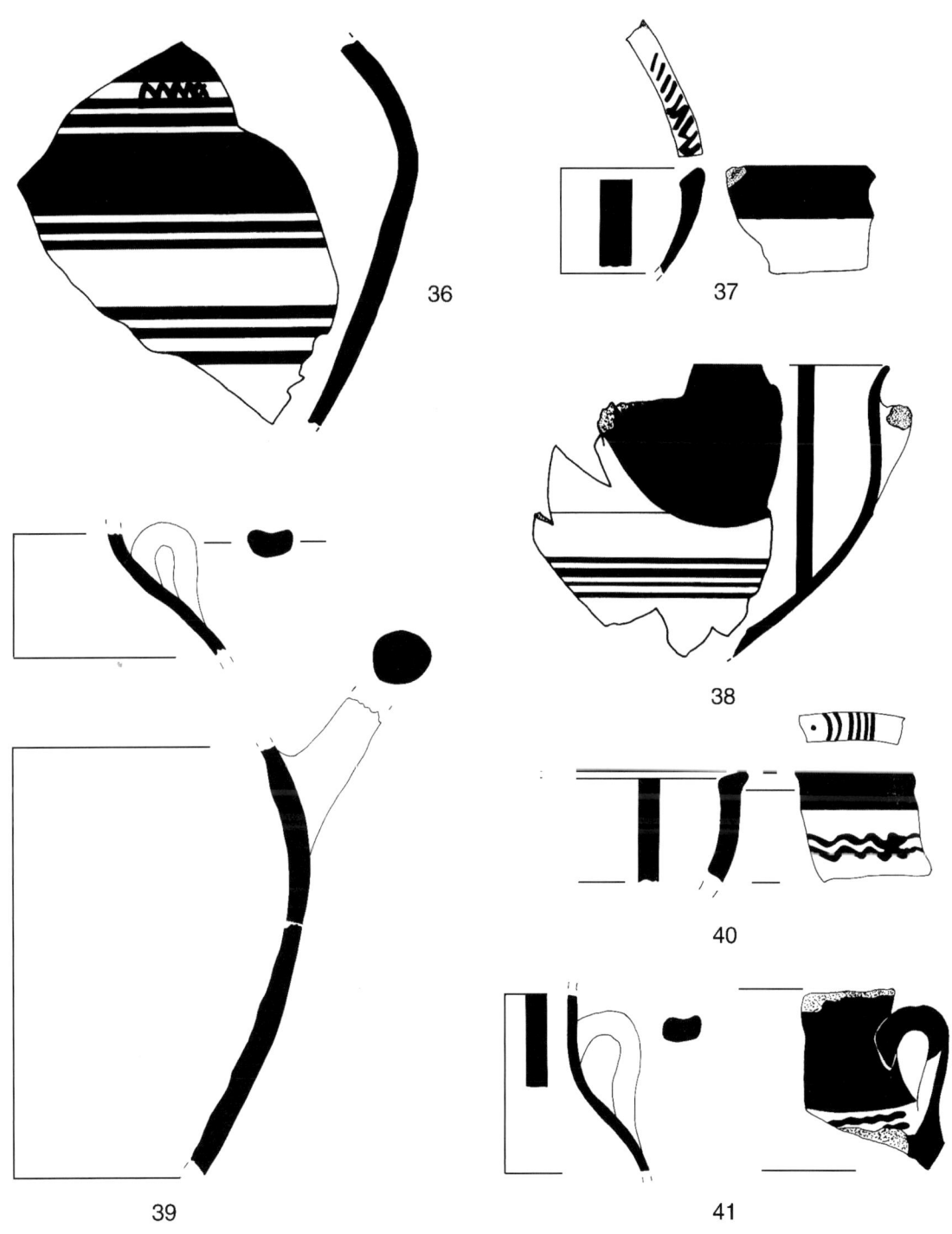

FIGURE 58. 36–41.

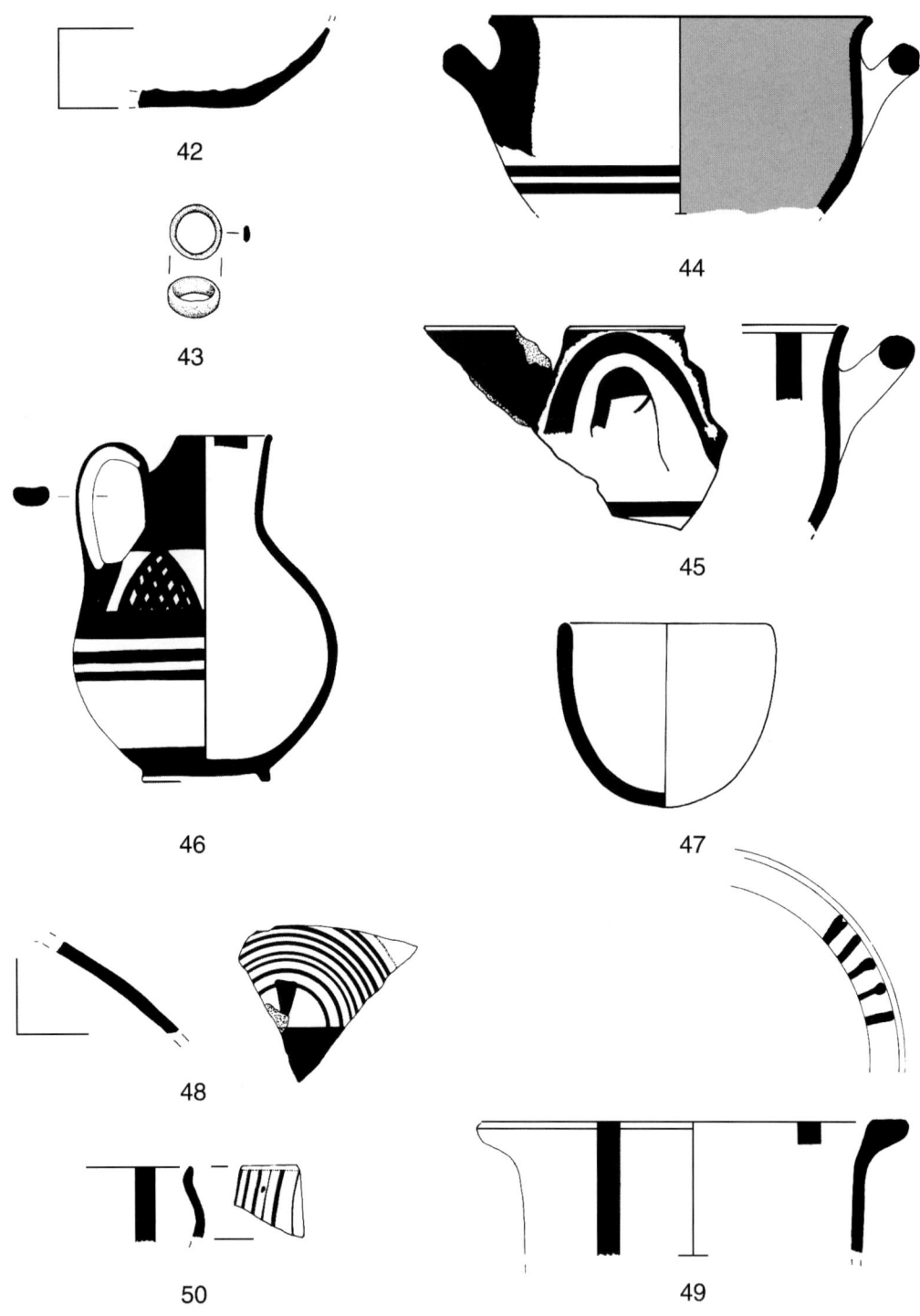

FIGURE 59. 42–50.

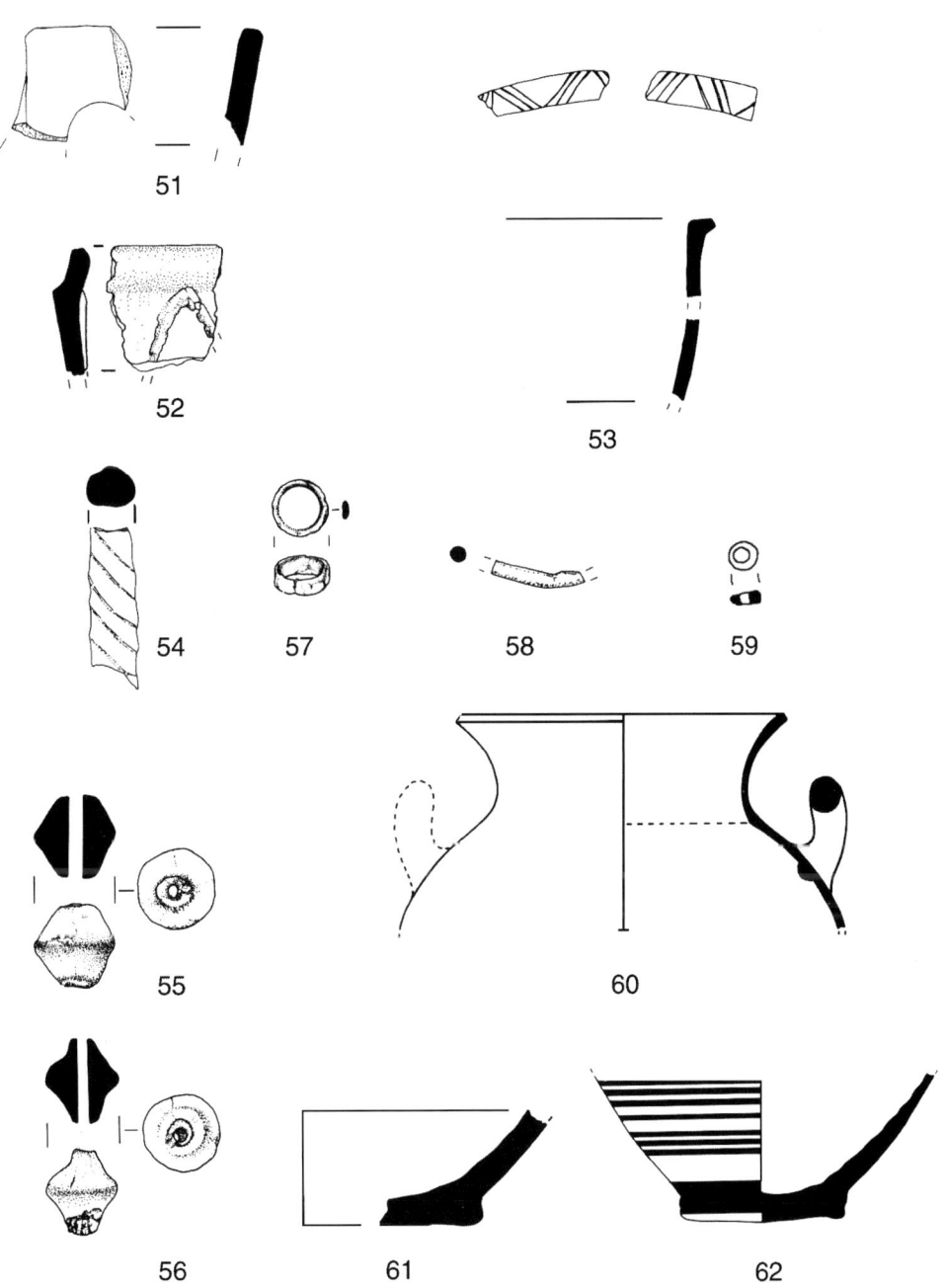

Figure 60. 51–62.

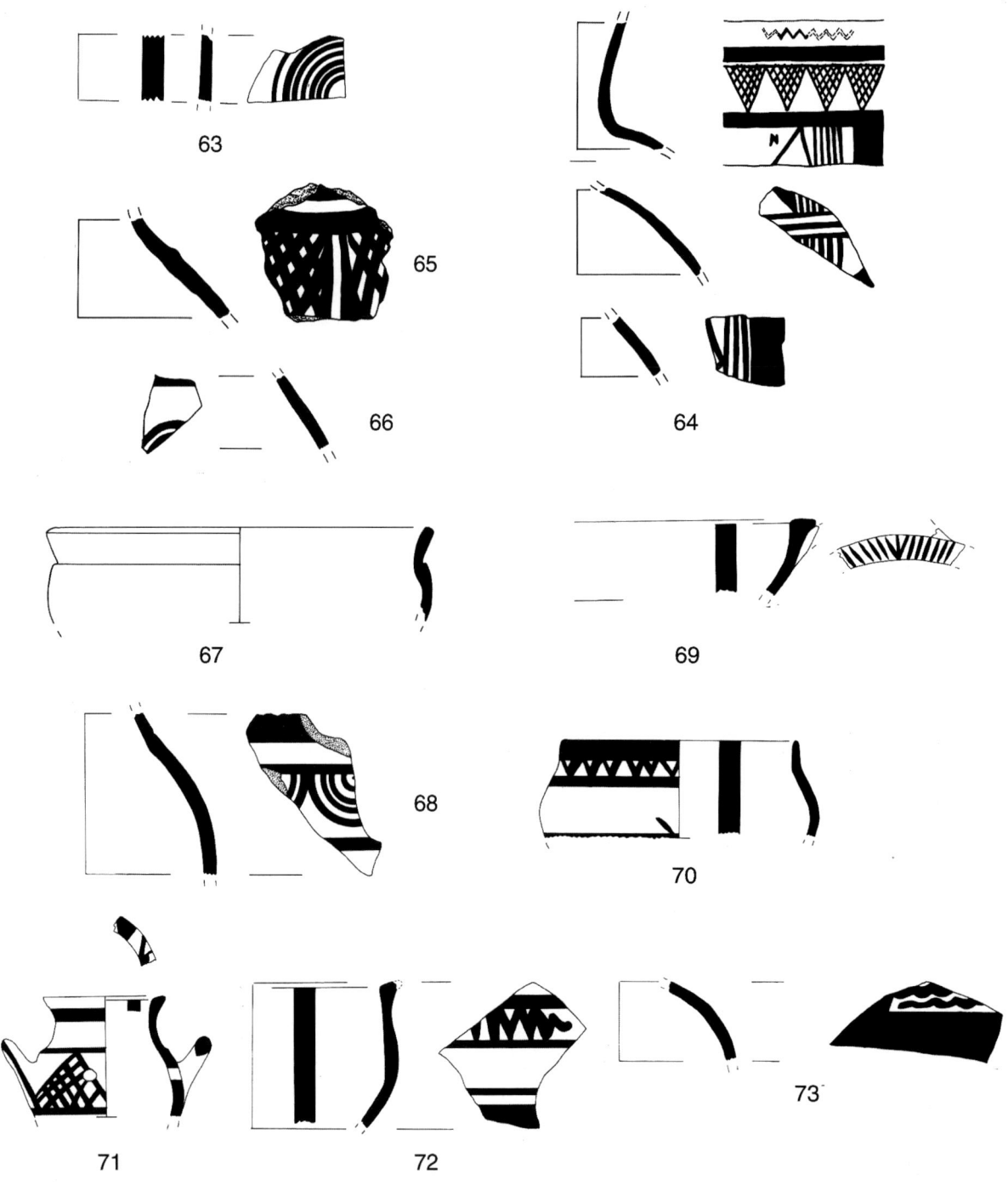

FIGURE 61. 63–73.

FIGURE 62. 74–81.

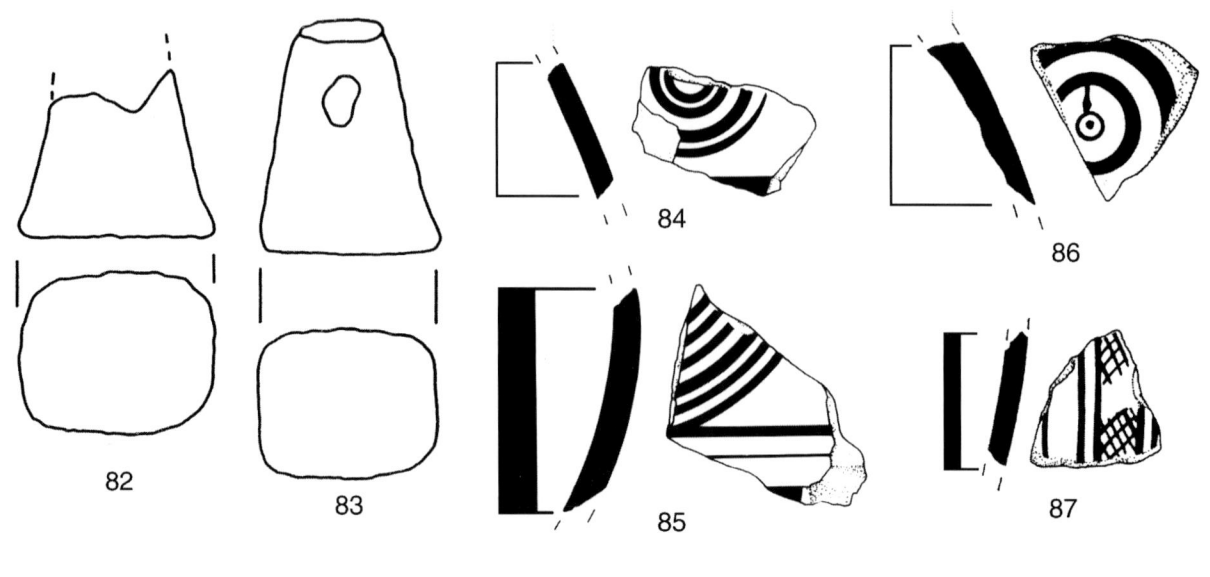

FIGURE 63. 82–87.

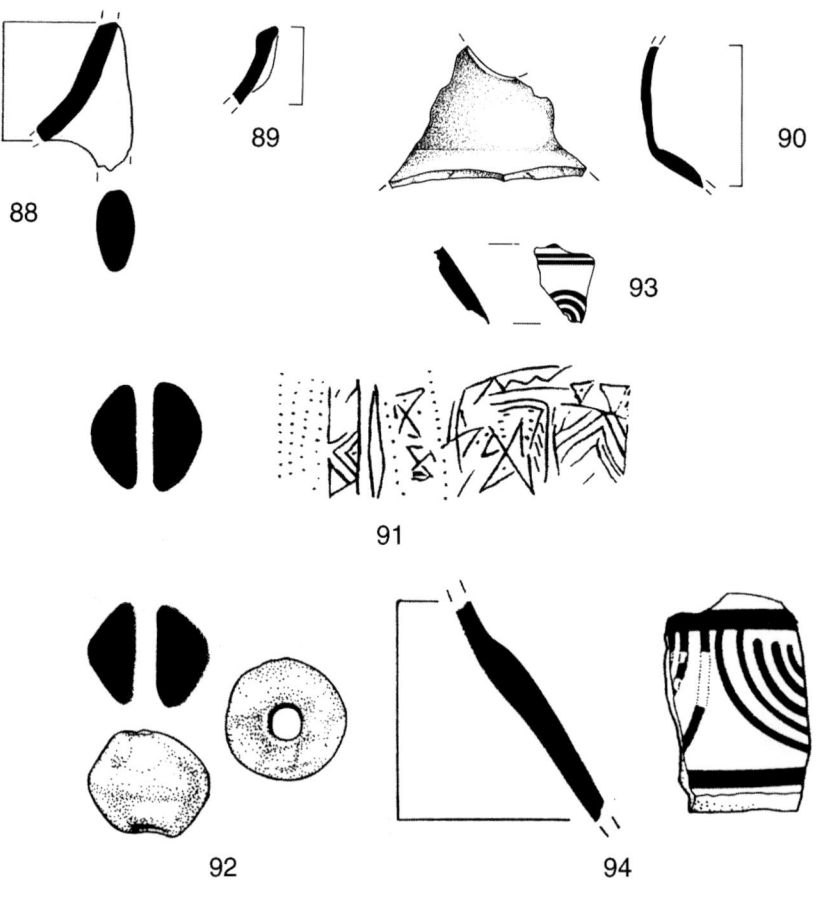

FIGURE 64. 88–94.

a.

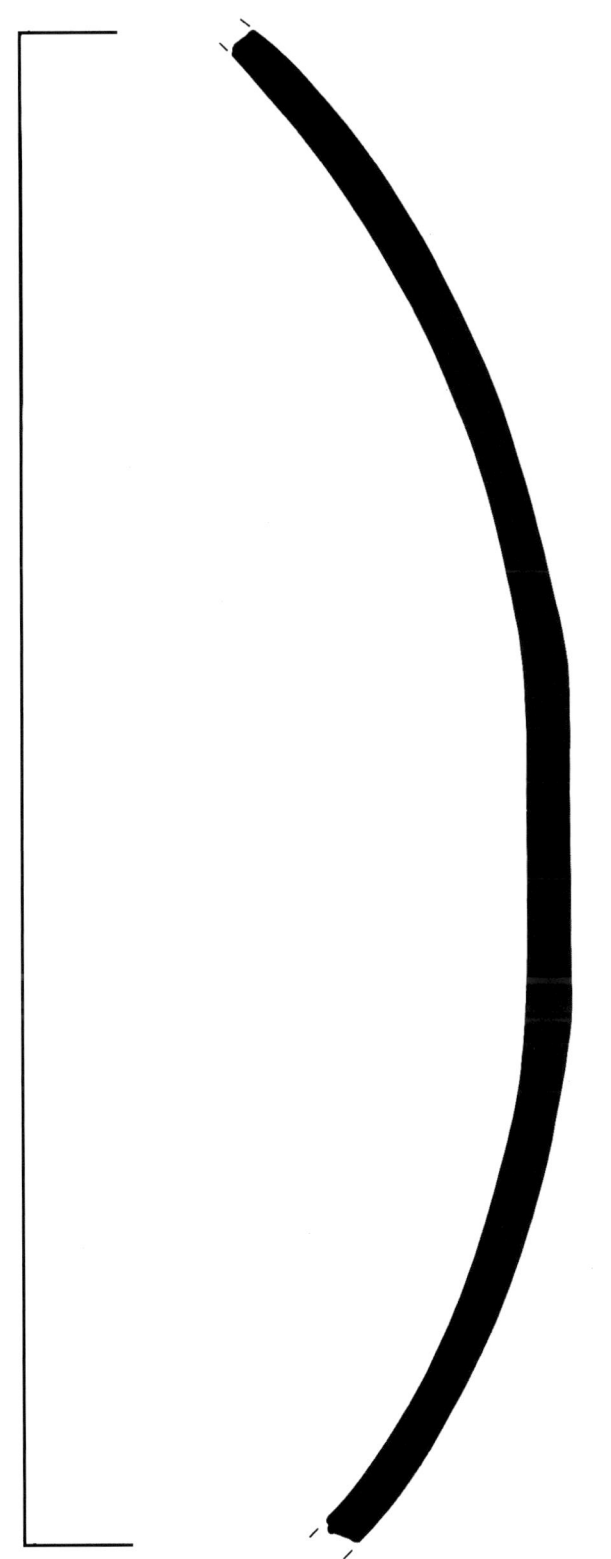

b.

Figure 65. Tomb 1. (*a*) **T1-1.**
(*b*) **T1-2.**

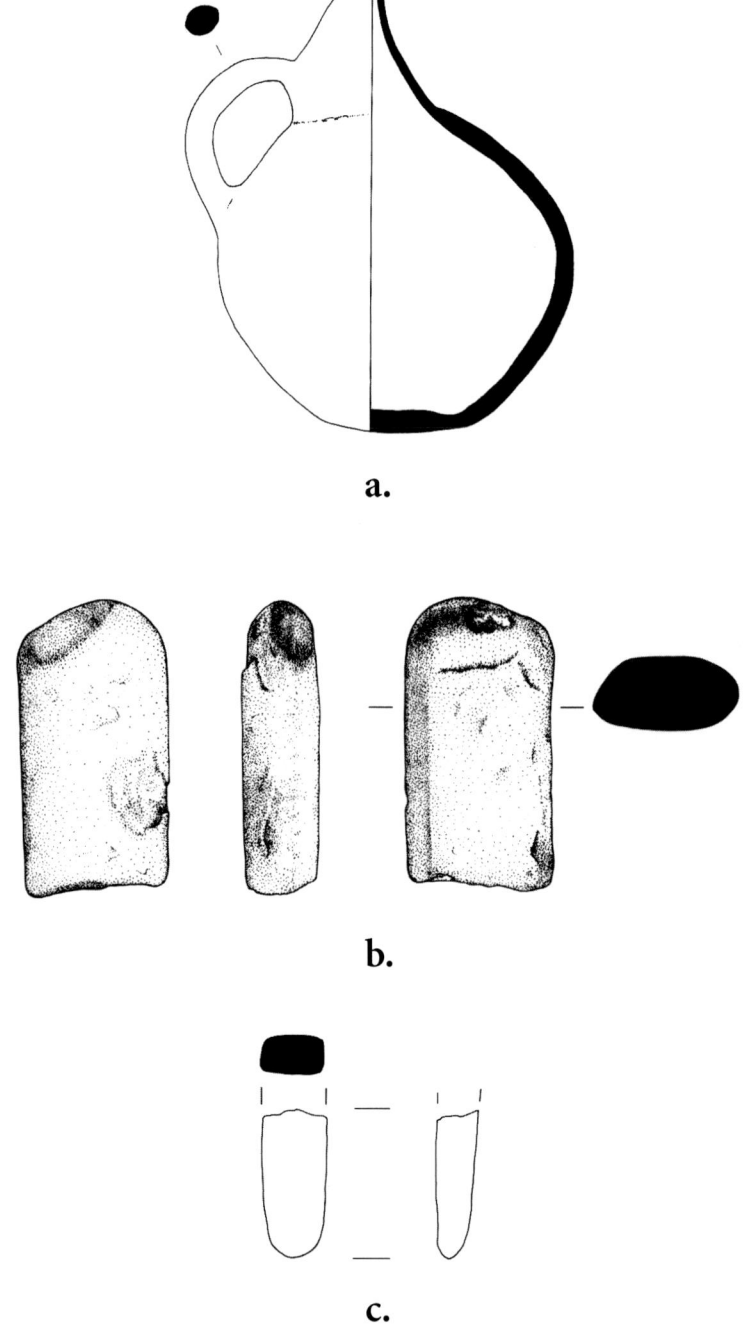

FIGURE 66. Tomb 6. (*a*) **T6-1.** (*b*) **T6-2.** (*c*) **T6-3.**

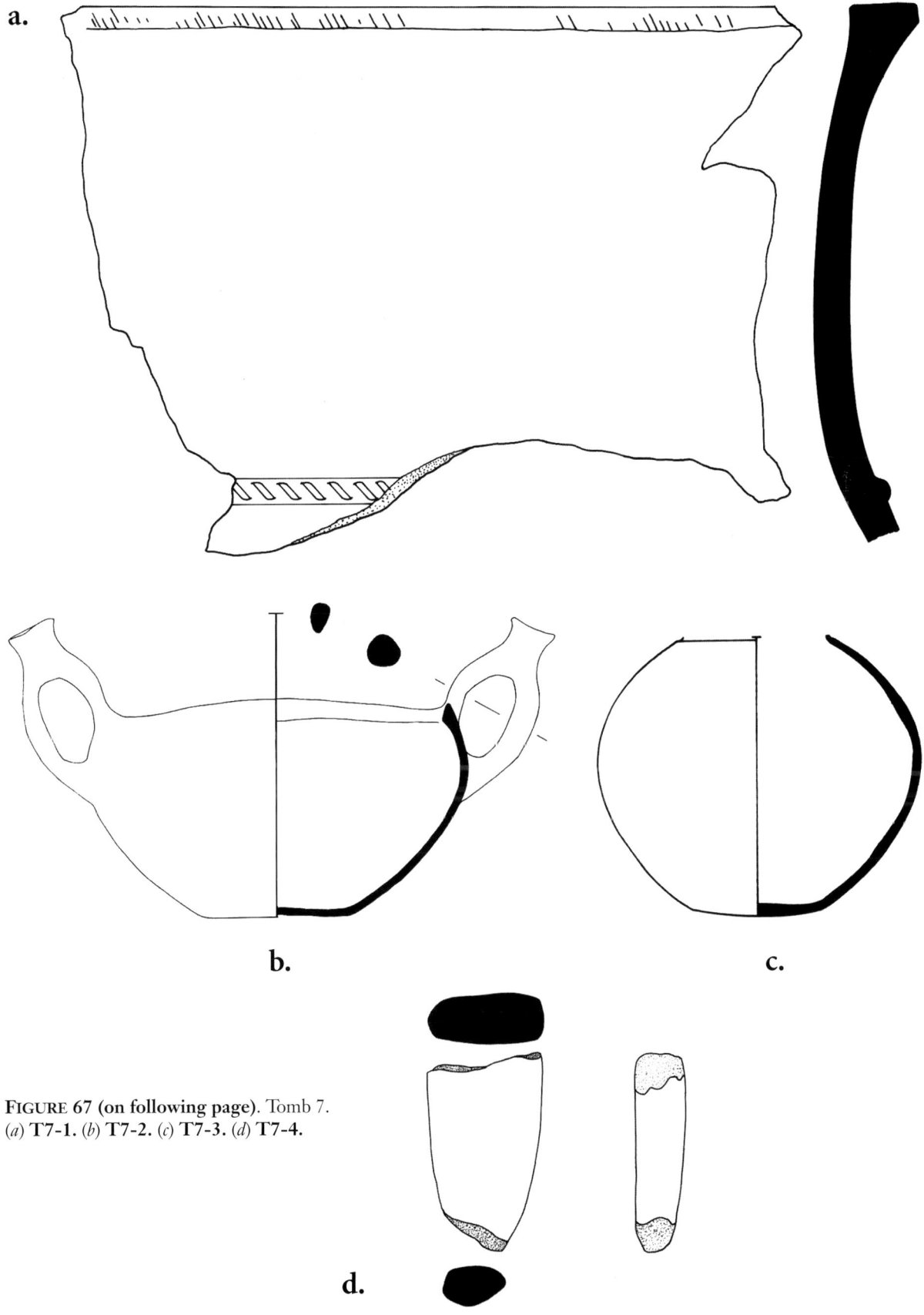

FIGURE 67 (on following page). Tomb 7.
(*a*) **T7-1.** (*b*) **T7-2.** (*c*) **T7-3.** (*d*) **T7-4.**

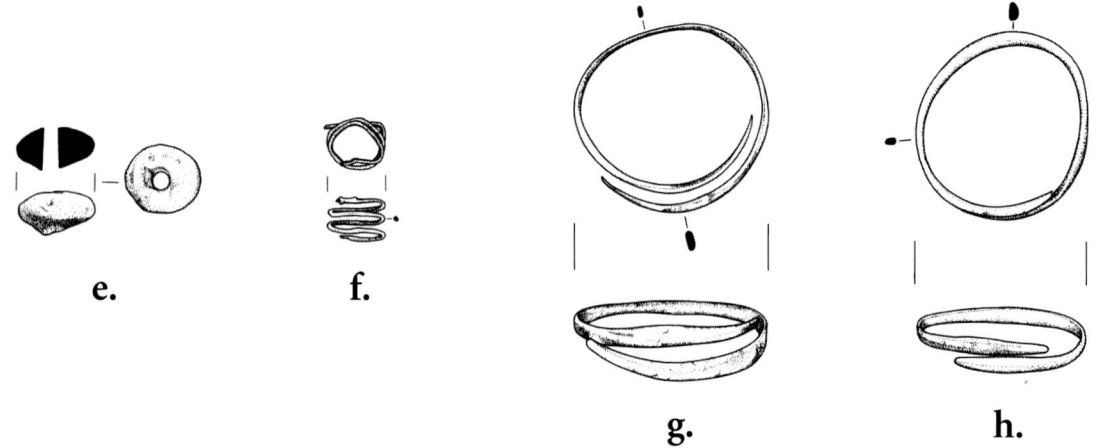

FIGURE 67 (continued). Tomb 7. (*e*) **T7-5.** (*f*) **T7-6.** (*g*) **T7-7.** (*h*) **T7-8.**

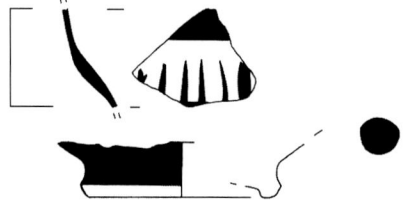

FIGURE 68. Tomb 9. **T9-1.**

a.

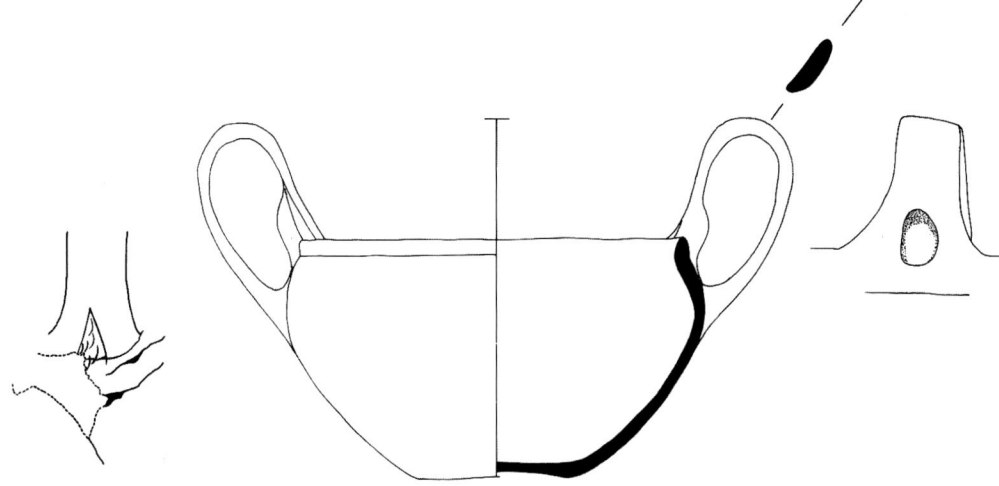

b.

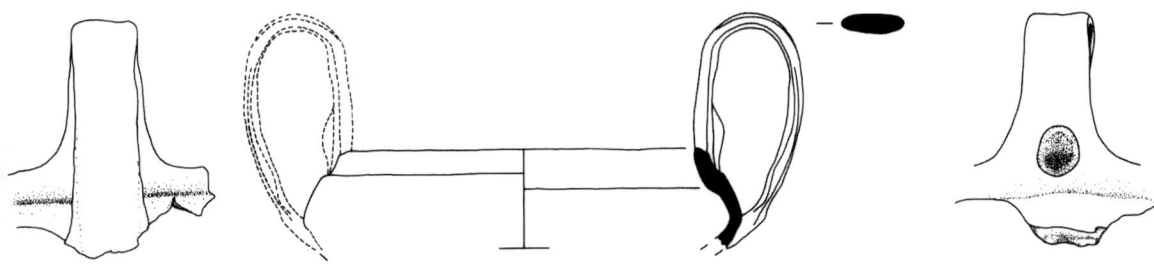

FIGURE 69 (on following page). Tomb 10.
(*a*) T10-1. (*b*) T10-1a. (*c*) T10-2.

c.

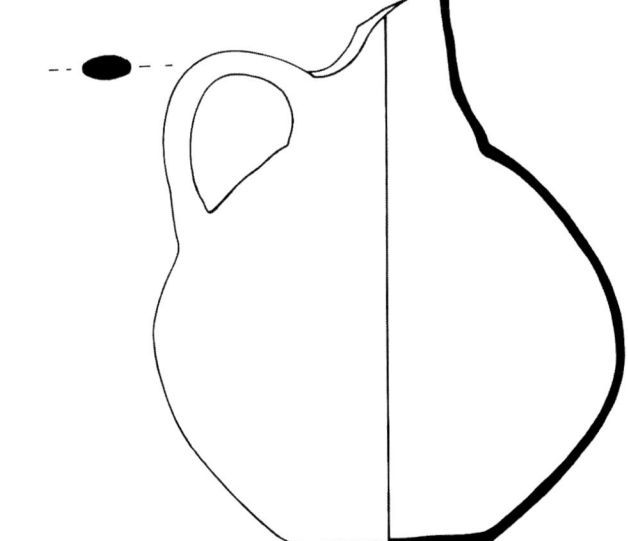

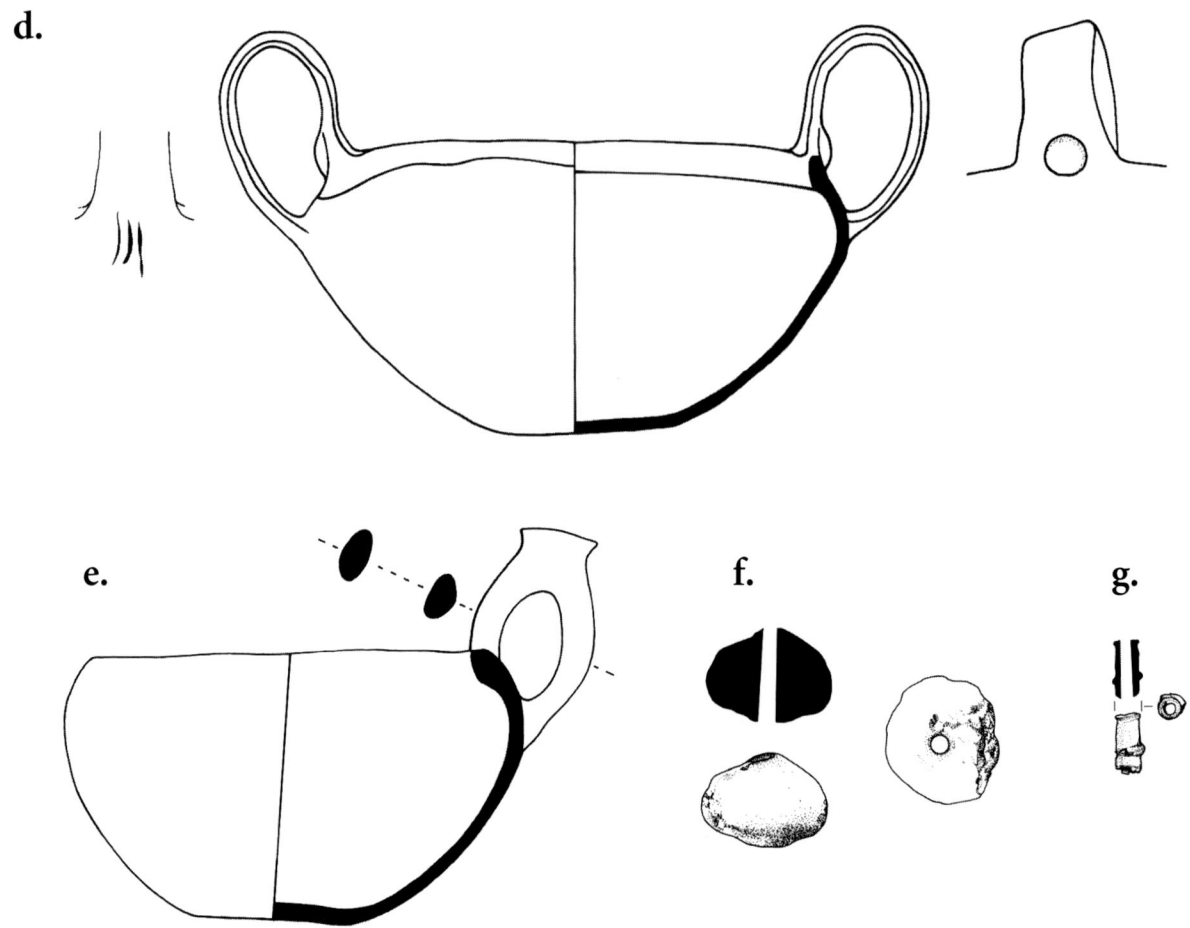

FIGURE 69 (continued). Tomb 10. (*d*) **T10-3.** (*e*) **T10-4.** (*f*) **T10-5.** (*g*) **T10-7.**

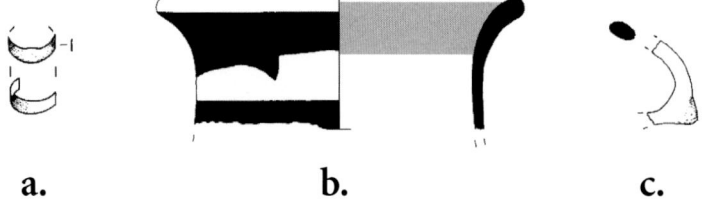

FIGURE 70. Tomb 11. (*a*) **T11-1.** (*b*) **T11-2.** (*c*) **T11-3.**

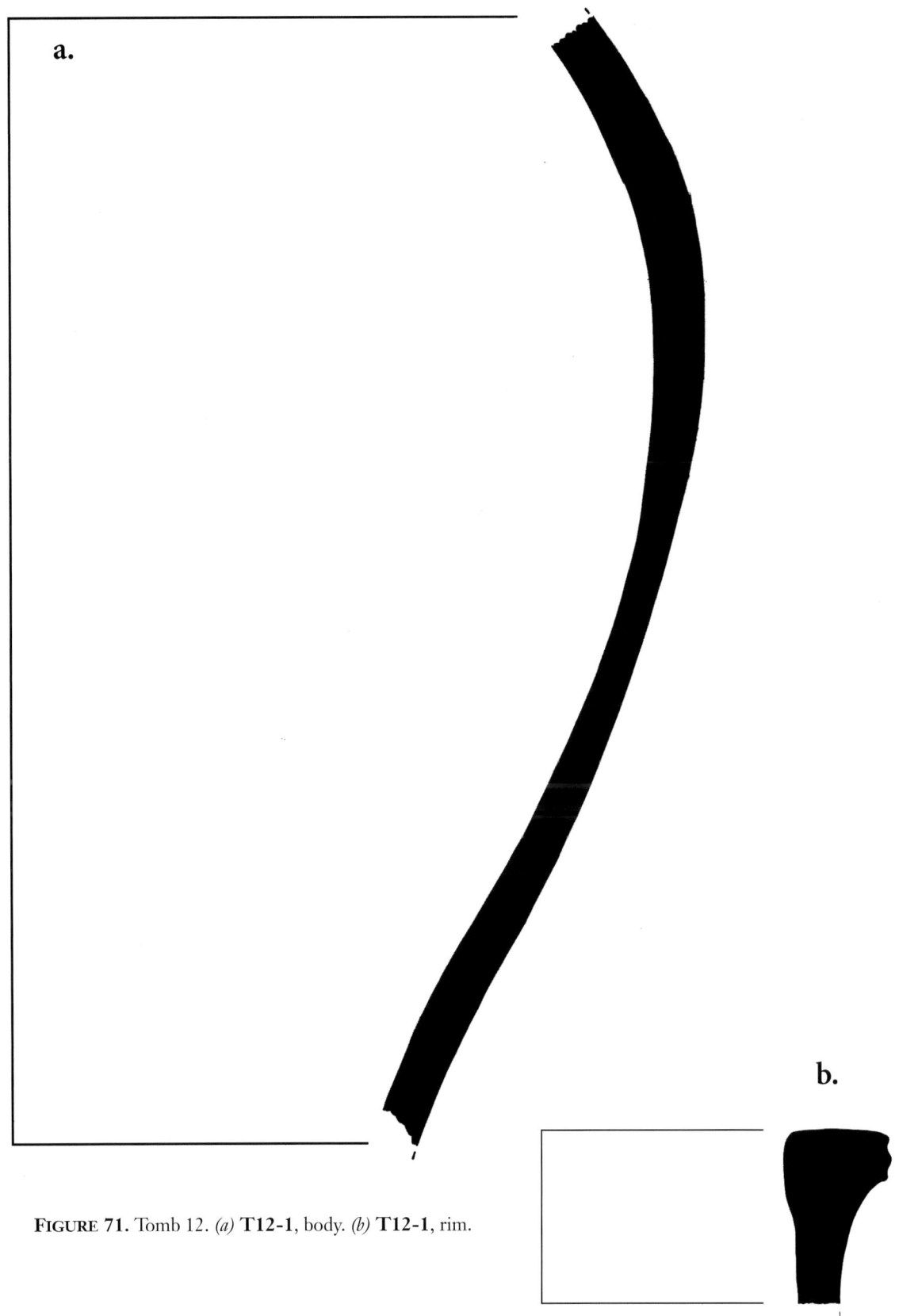

FIGURE 71. Tomb 12. *(a)* **T12-1**, body. *(b)* **T12-1**, rim.

a.

b.

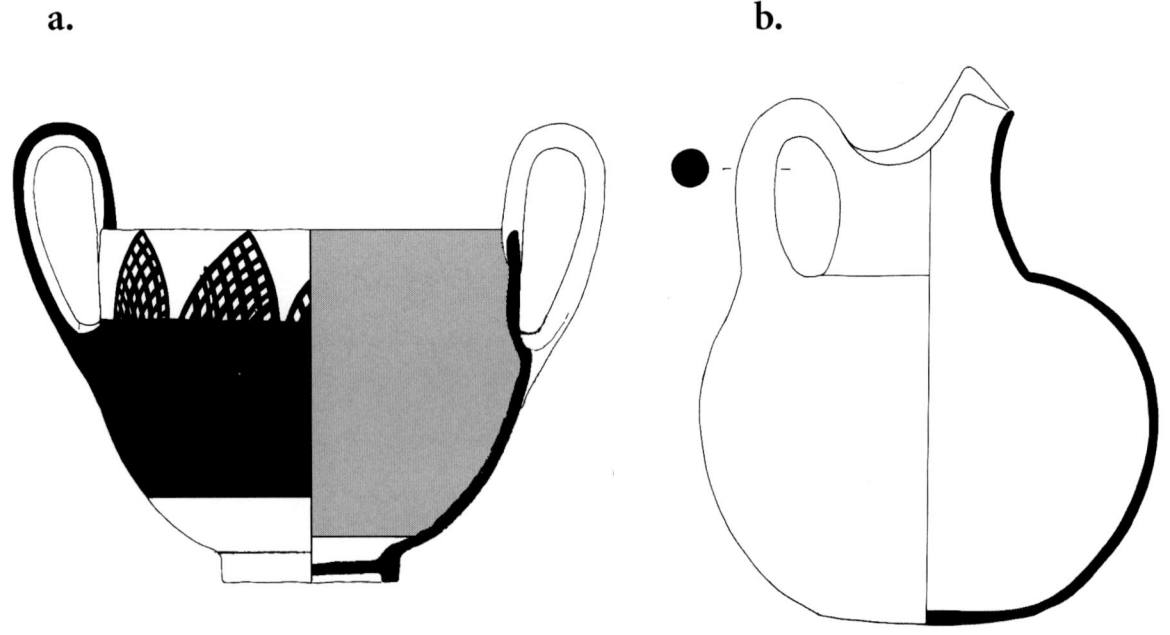

FIGURE 72. Tomb 13. (*a*) **T13-1.** (*b*) **T13-2.**

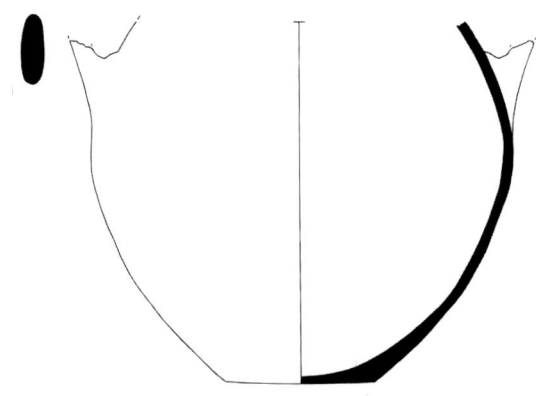

FIGURE 73. Tomb 17. **T17-1.**

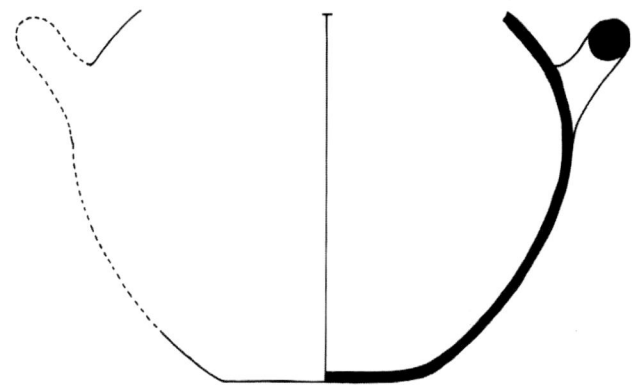

FIGURE 74. Tomb 18. **T18-1.**

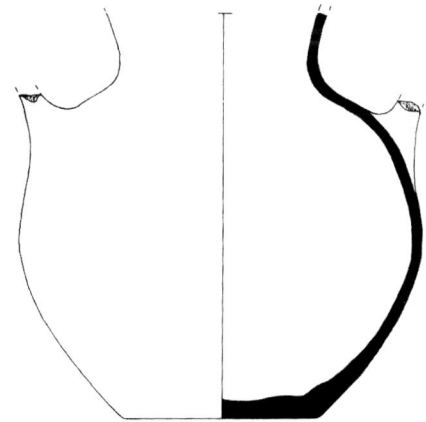

FIGURE 75. Tomb 19. **T19-1.**

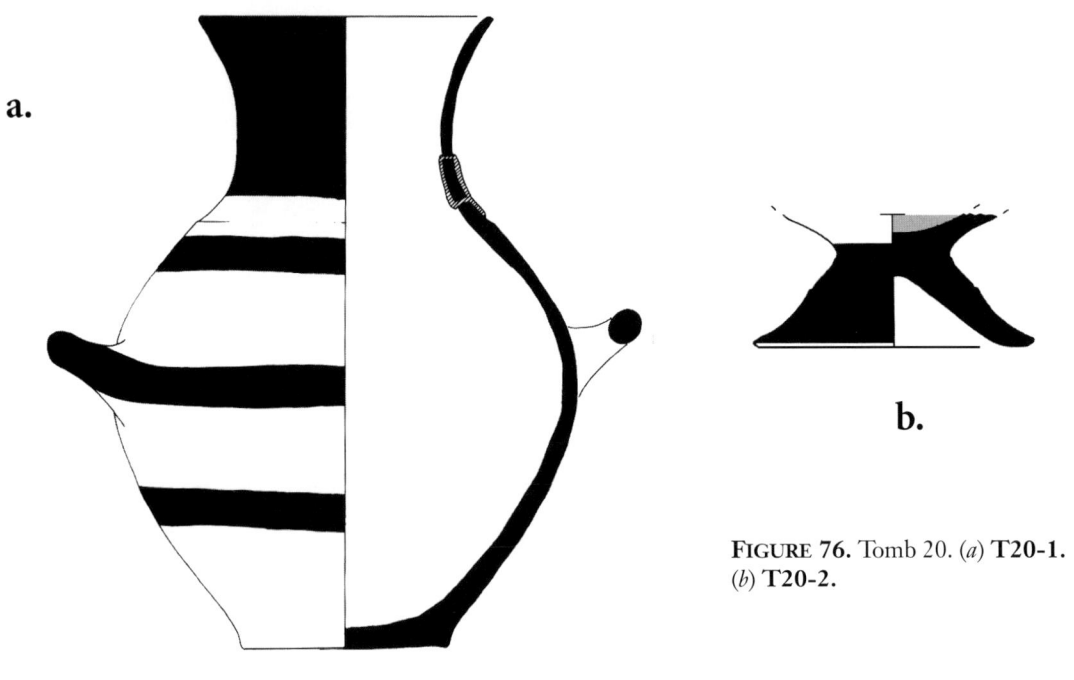

FIGURE 76. Tomb 20. (*a*) **T20-1.**
(*b*) **T20-2.**

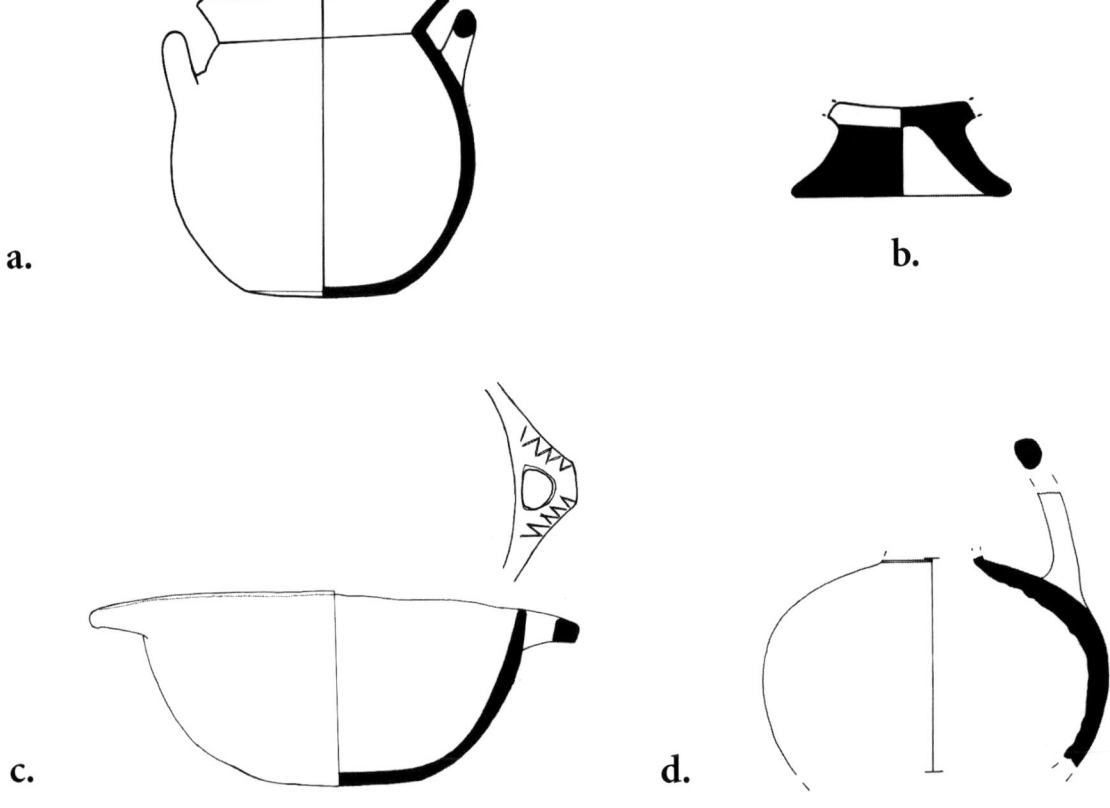

FIGURE 77. Tomb 21. (*a*) **T21-1.** (*b*) **T21-2.** (*c*) **T21-3.** (*d*) **T21-4.**

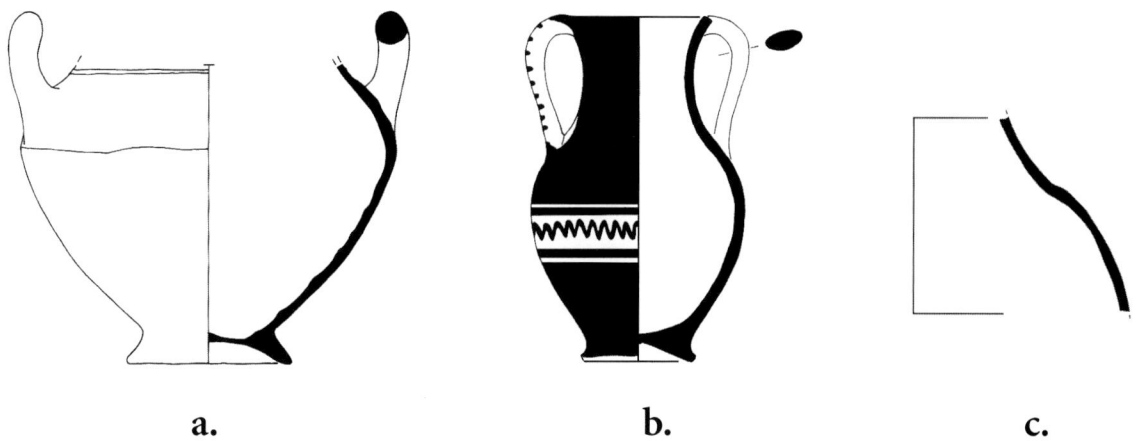

FIGURE 78. Tomb 22. (*a*) **T22-1**. (*b*) **T22-2**. (*c*) **T22-3**.

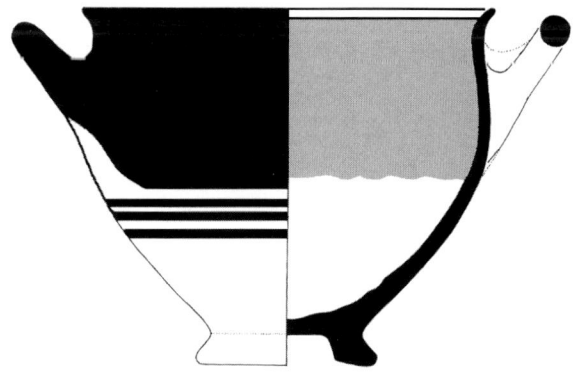

FIGURE 79. Tomb 23. **T23-1**.

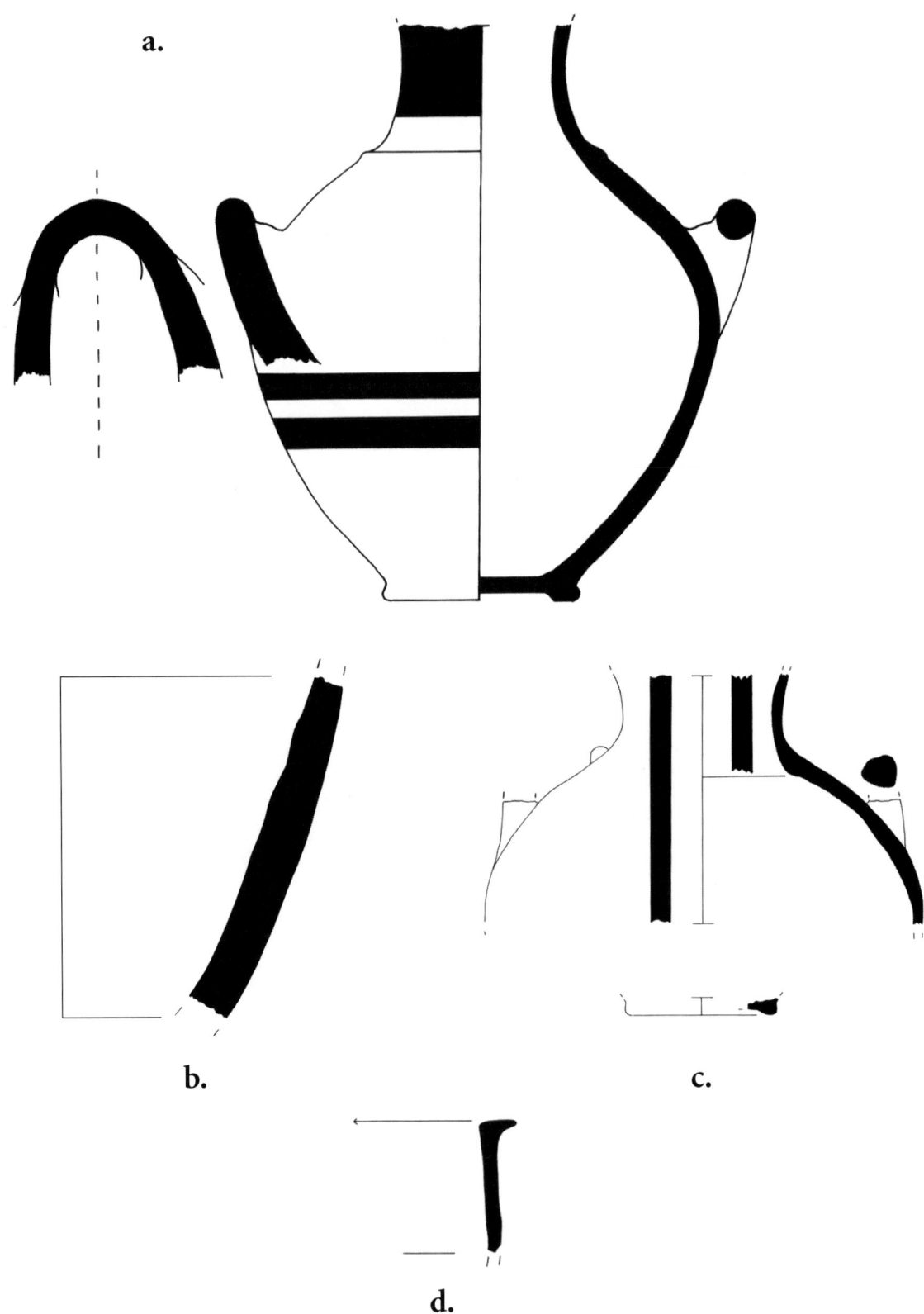

FIGURE 80. Tomb 24. (*a*) **T24-1**. (*b*) **T24-2**. (*c*) **T24-3**. (*d*) **T24-4**.

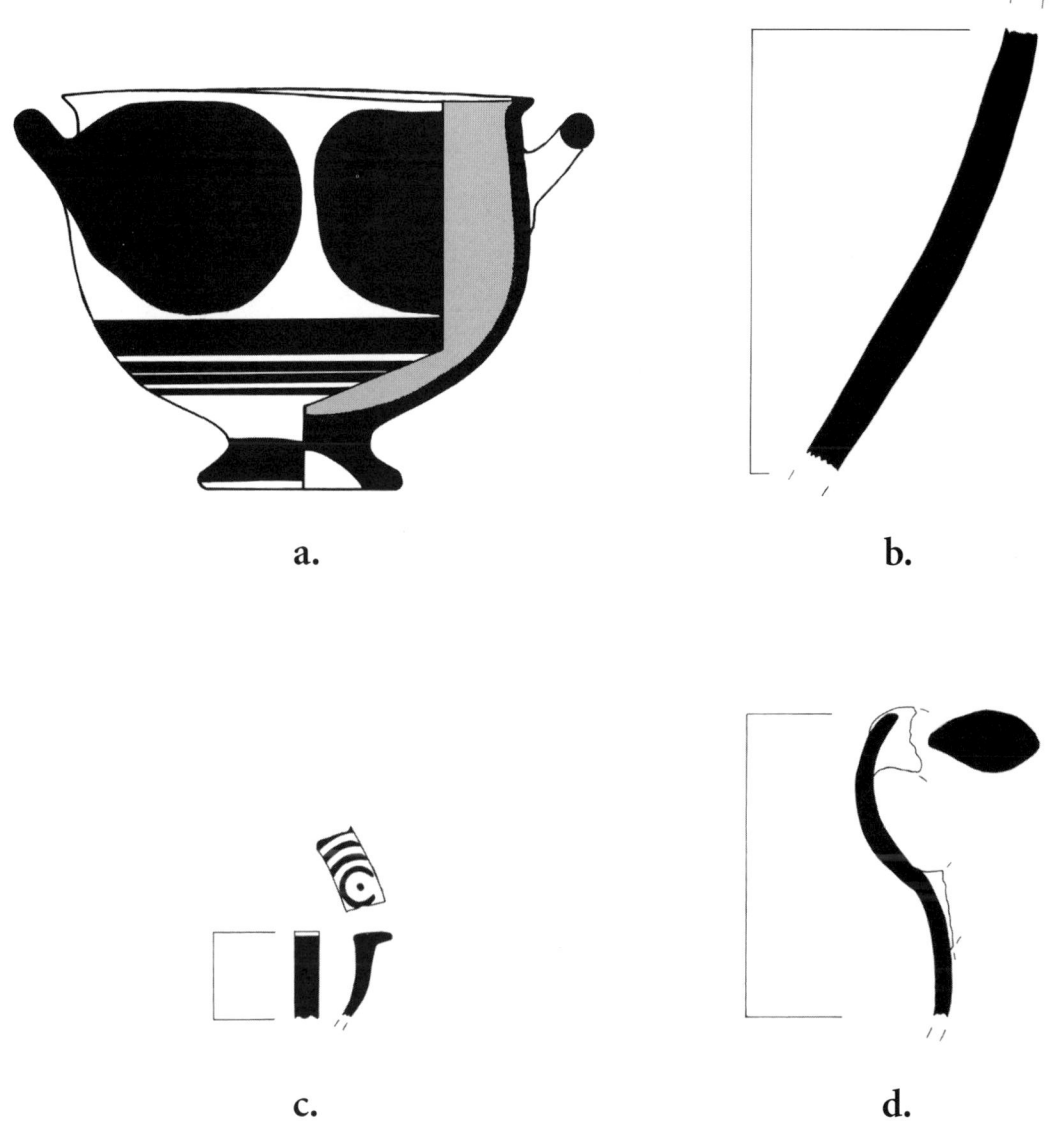

FIGURE 81. Tomb 25. (*a*) **T25-1**. (*b*) **T25-2**. (*c*) **T25-3**. (*d*) **T25-4**.

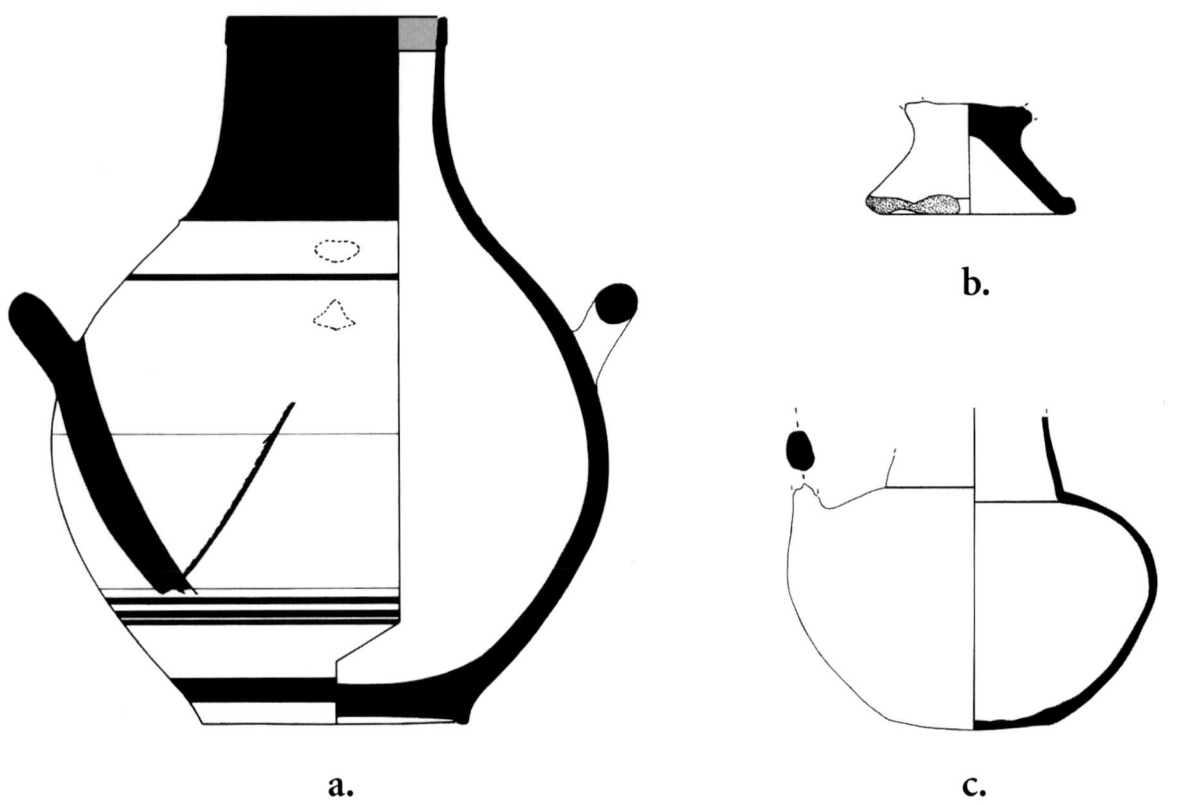

FIGURE 82. Tomb 26. (*a*) **T26-1**. (*b*) **T26-2**. (*c*)**T26-3**.

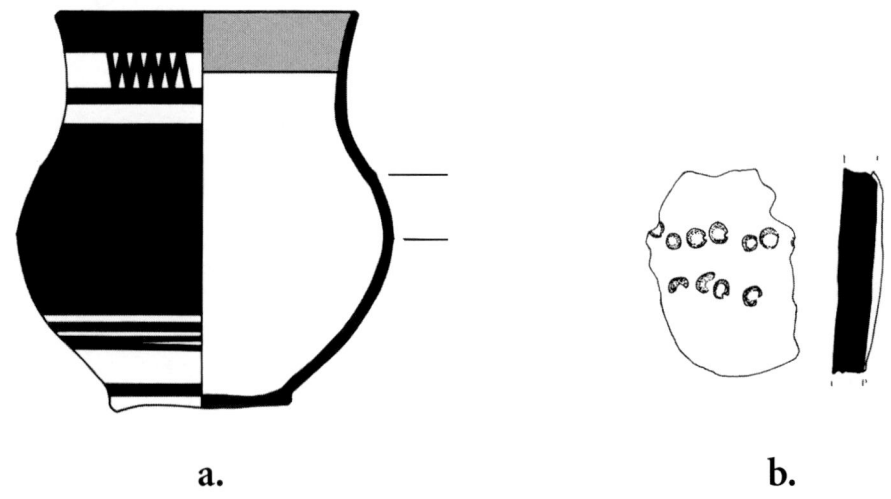

FIGURE 83. Tomb 27. (*a*) **T27-1**. (*b*) **T27-2**.

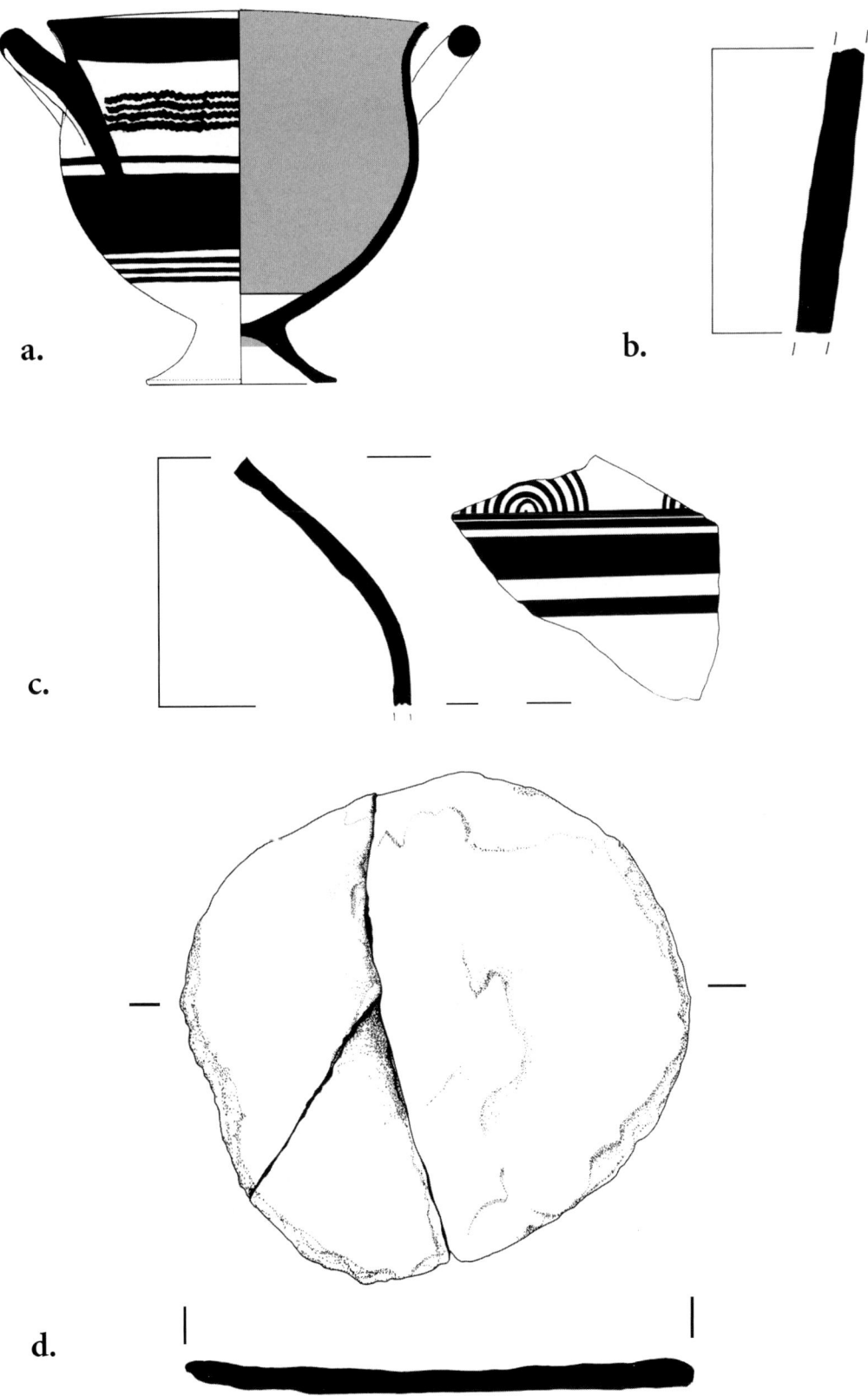

FIGURE 84. Tomb 28. (*a*) **T28-1**. (*b*) **T28-3**. (*c*) **T28-4**. (*d*) **T28-2**.

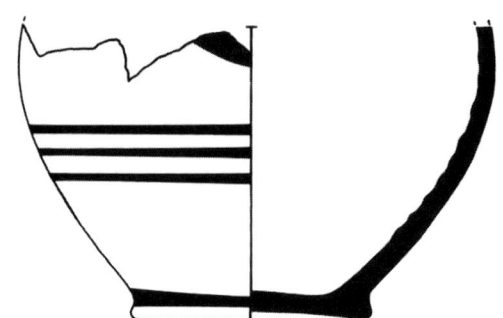

FIGURE 85. Tomb 29. **T29-1.**

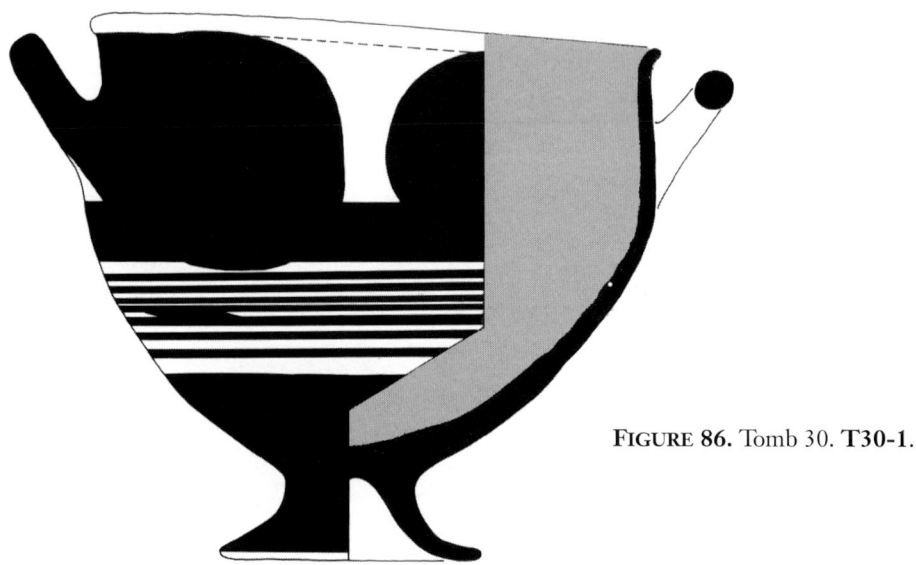

FIGURE 86. Tomb 30. **T30-1.**

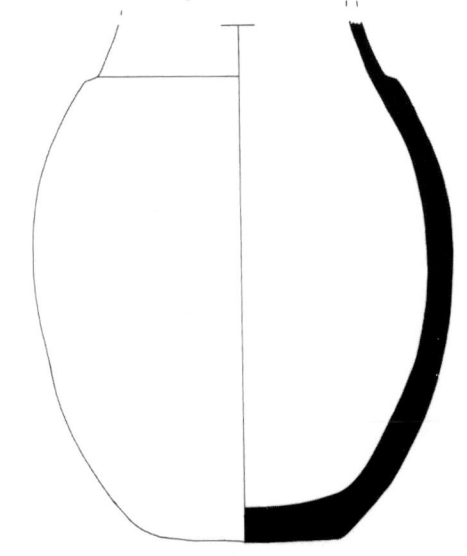

FIGURE 87. Tomb 31. **T31-1.**

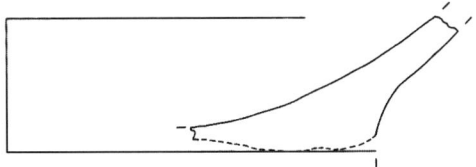

FIGURE 88. Tomb 32. **T32-1.**

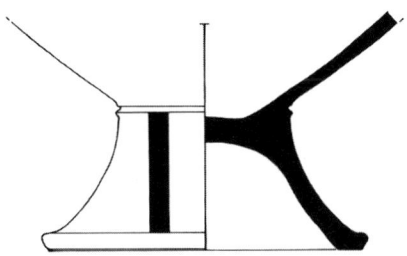

FIGURE 89. Tomb 33. **T33-1**

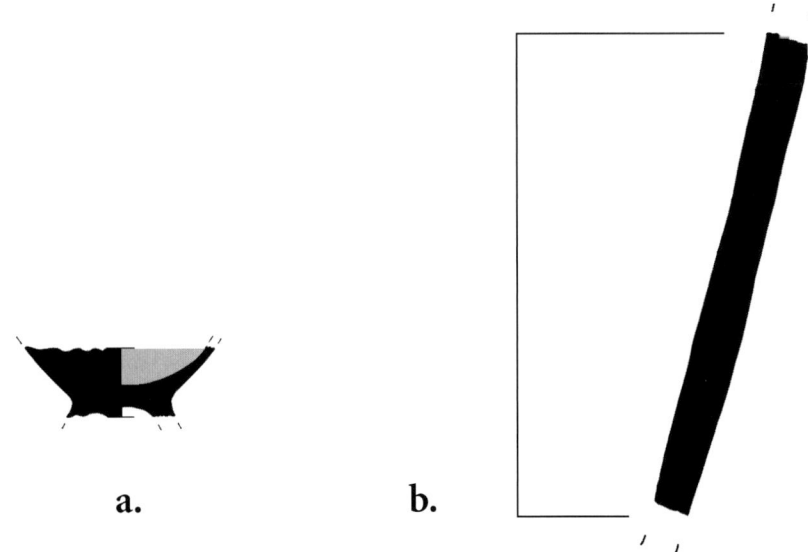

a.   b.

FIGURE 90. Tomb 34. (*a*) **T34-1.** (*b*) **T34-2.**

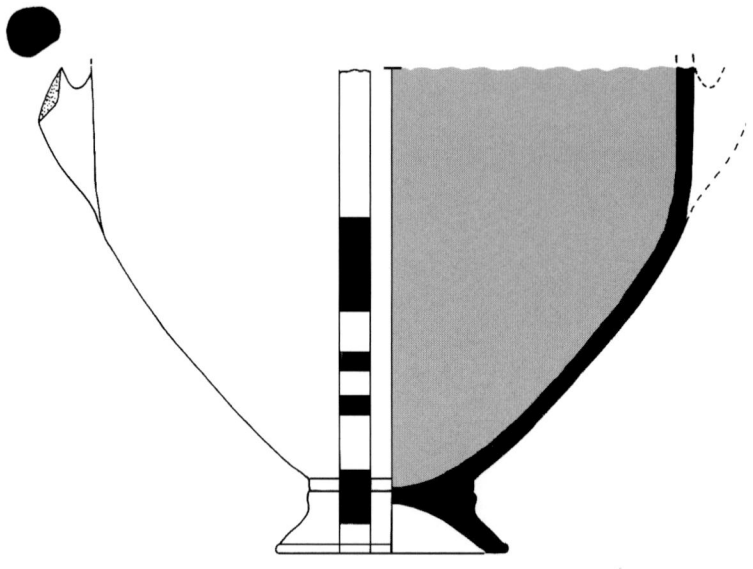

FIGURE 91. Tomb 35. **T35-1**.

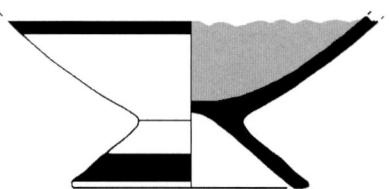

FIGURE 92. Tomb 36. **T36-1**.

FIGURE 93. Tomb 37. **T37-1**.

FIGURE 94. Tomb 38. (*a*) **T38-1**. (*b*) **T38-2**.

FIGURE 95. Tomb 39. **T39-1**.

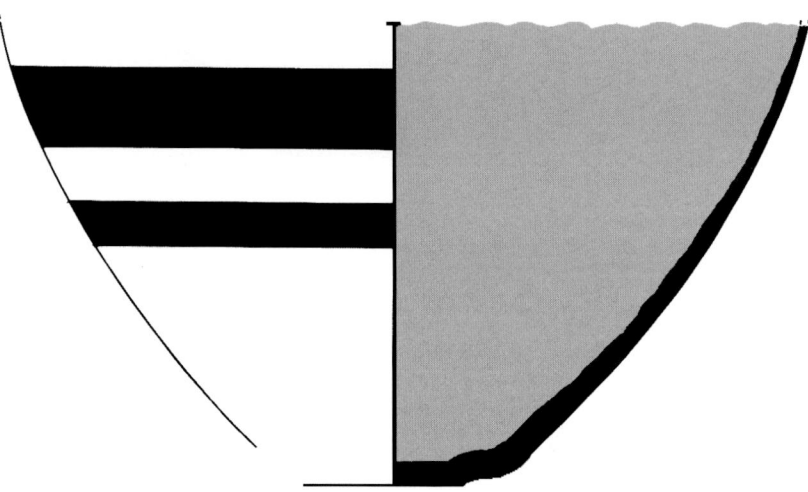

FIGURE 96. Tomb 40. **T40-1**.

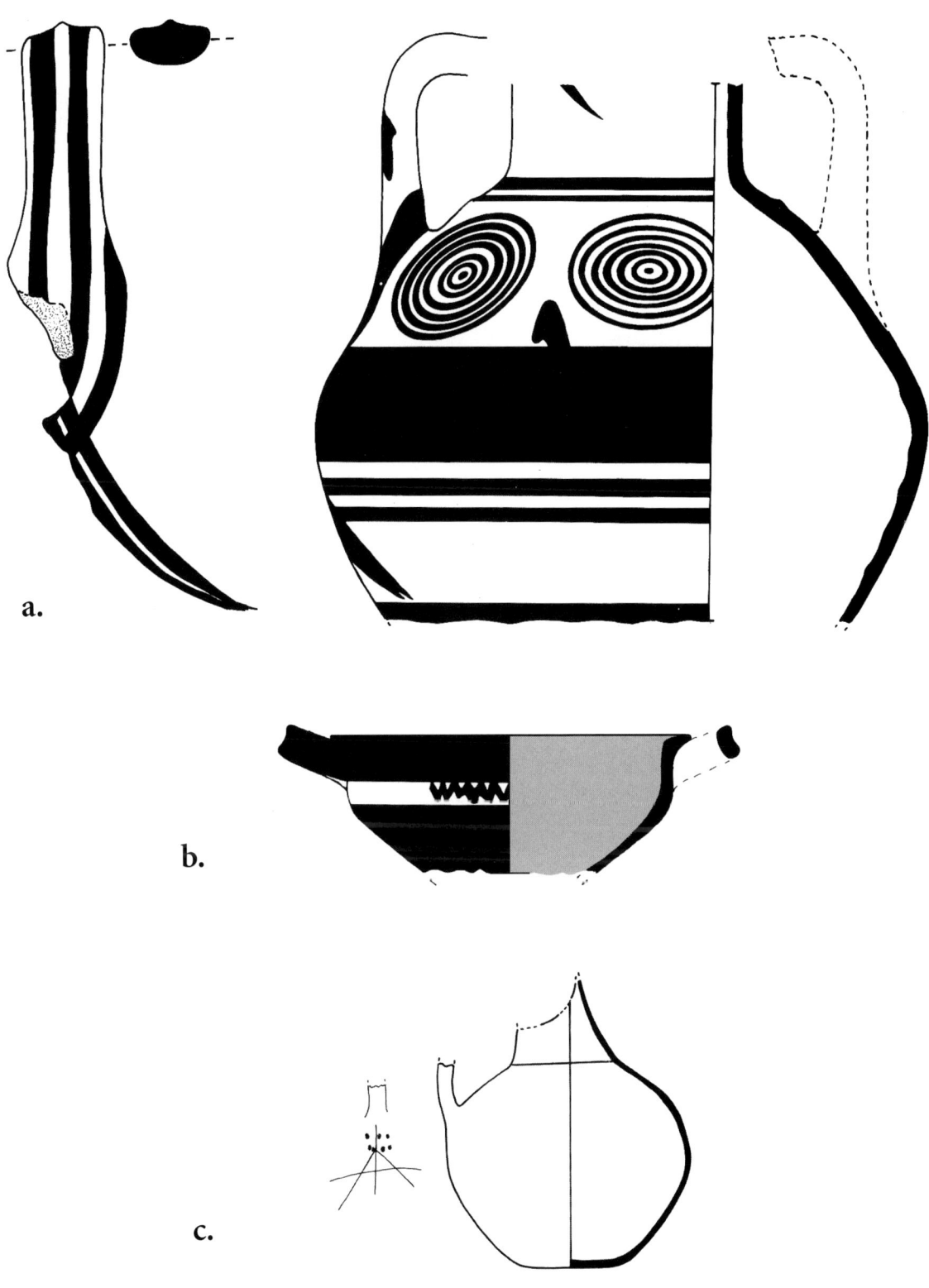

FIGURE 97. Tomb 41. (*a*) **T41-1**. (*b*) **T41-2**. (*c*) **T41-3**.

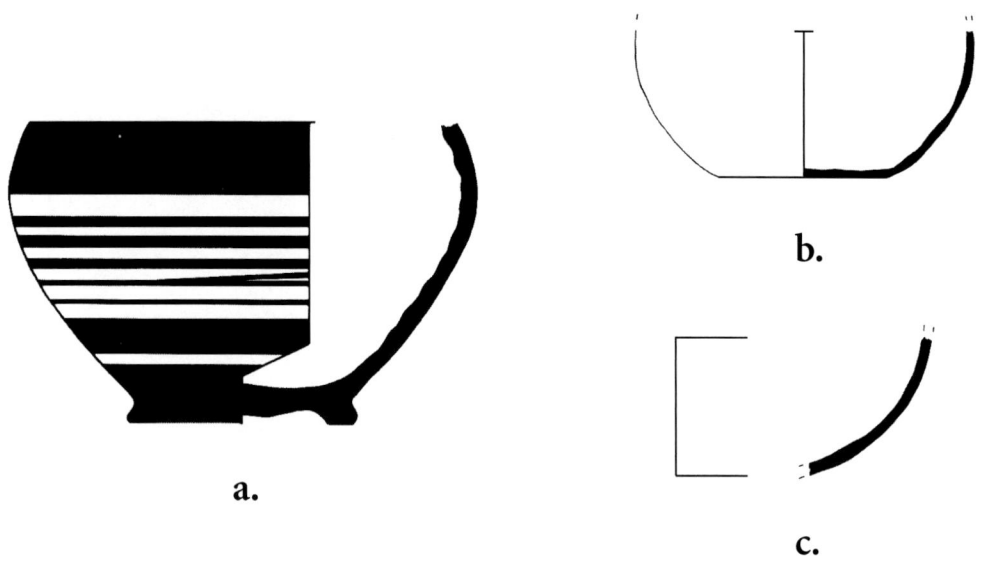

FIGURE 98. Tomb 42. (*a*) **T42-1**. (*b*) **T42-2**. (*c*) **T42-3**.

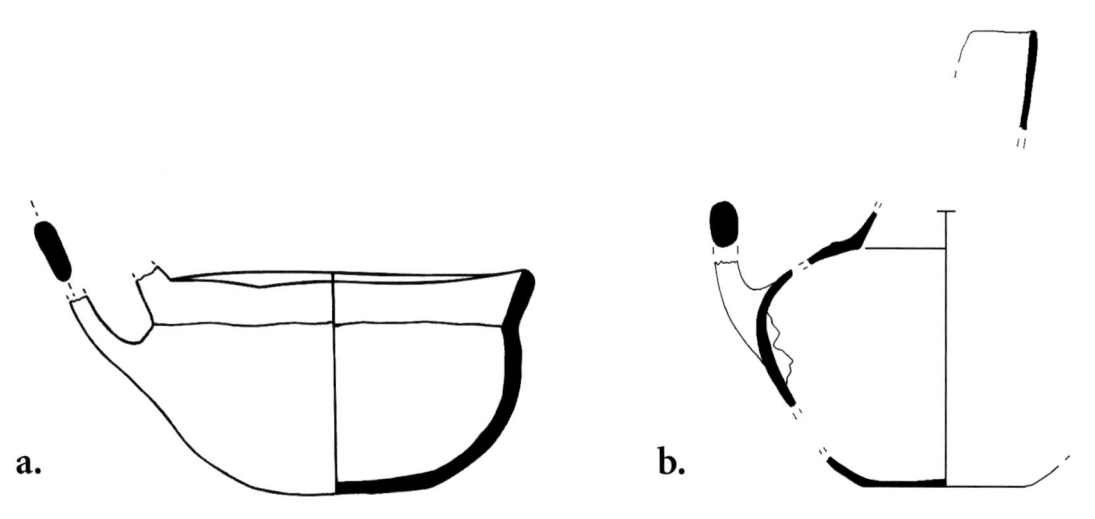

FIGURE 99. Tomb 43. (*a*) **T43-1**. (*b*) **T43-2**.

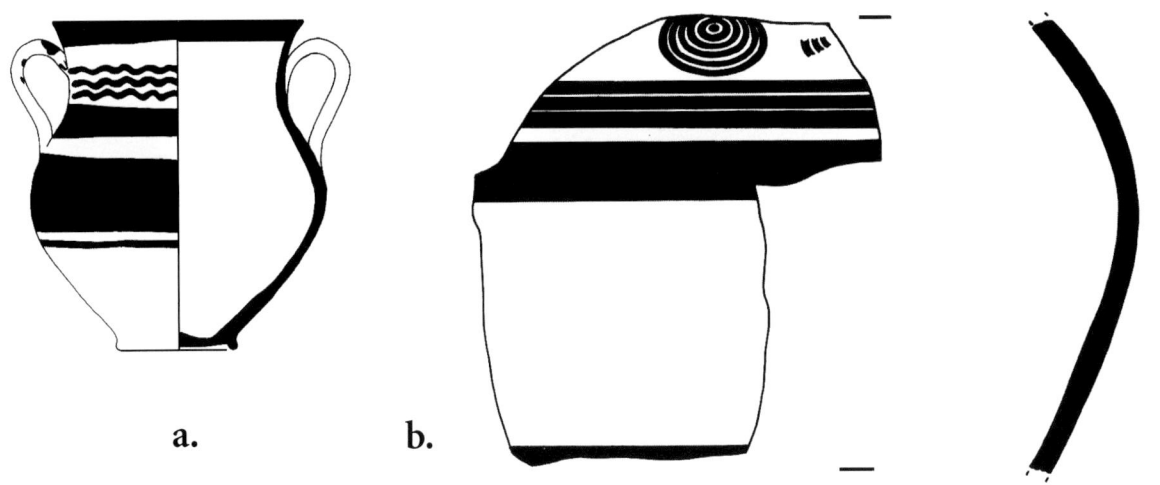

FIGURE 100. Tomb 44. (*a*) **T44-1**. (*b*) **T44-2**.

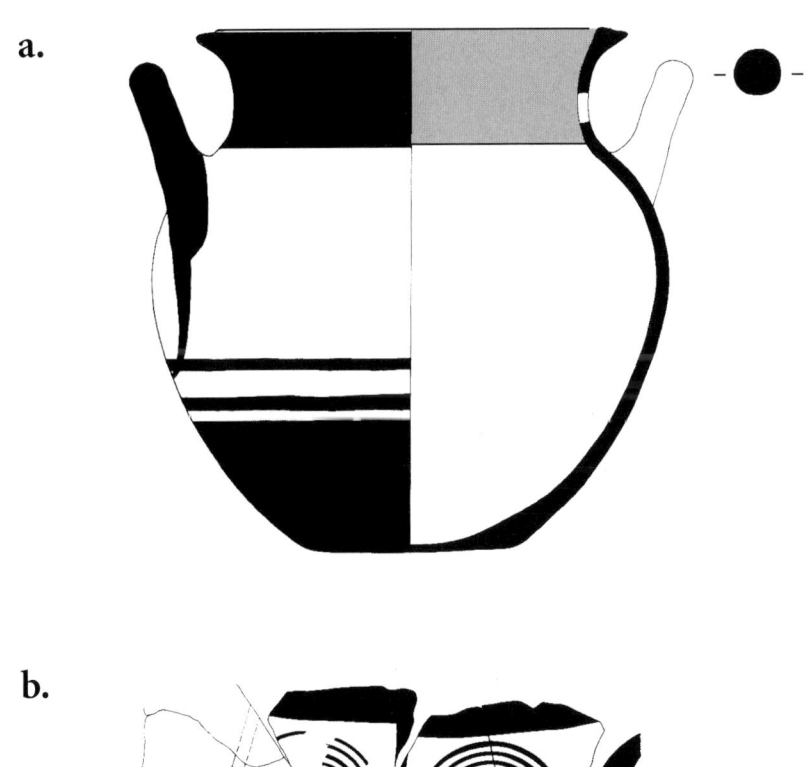

FIGURE 101. Tomb 45. (*a*) **T45-1**. (*b*) Detail of decoration on upper body of **T45-1**.

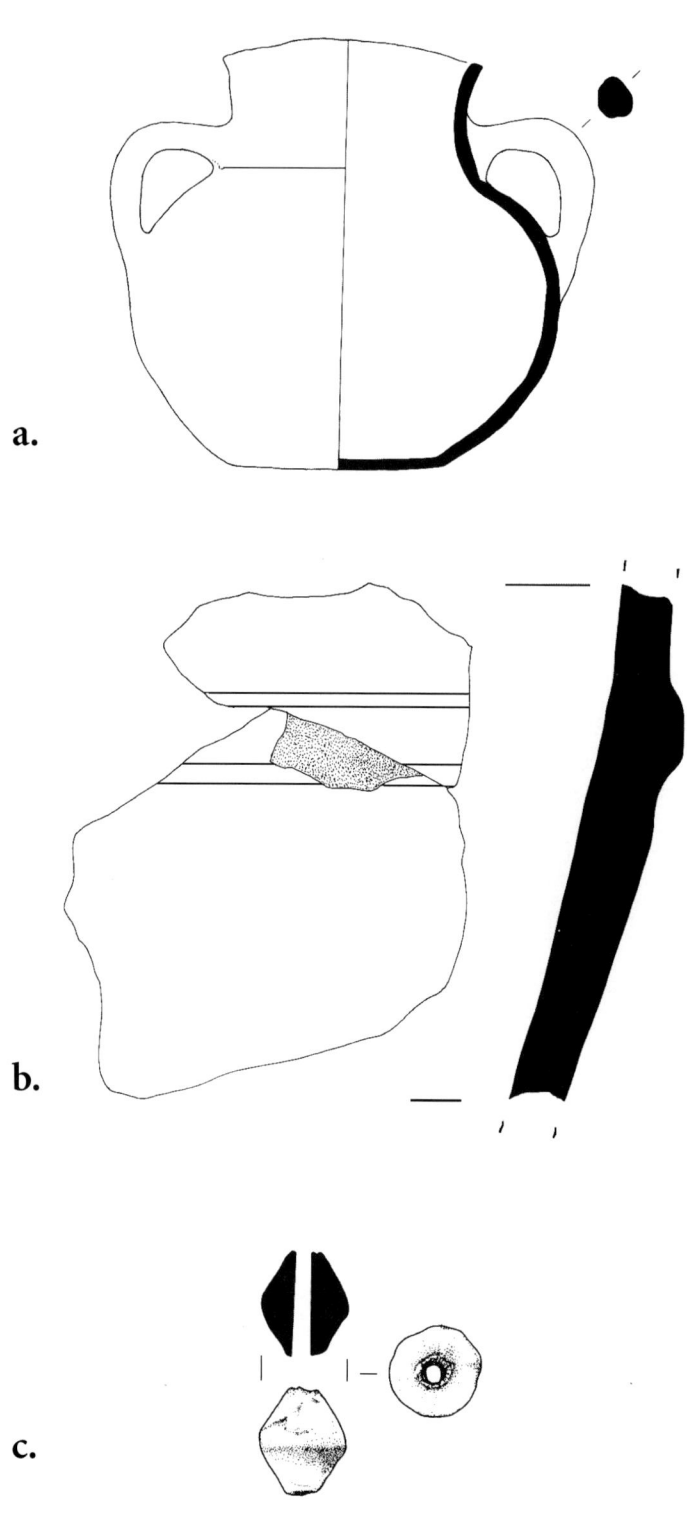

FIGURE 102. Tomb 46. (*a*) **T46-1**. (*b*) **T46-2**. (*c*) **T46-3**.

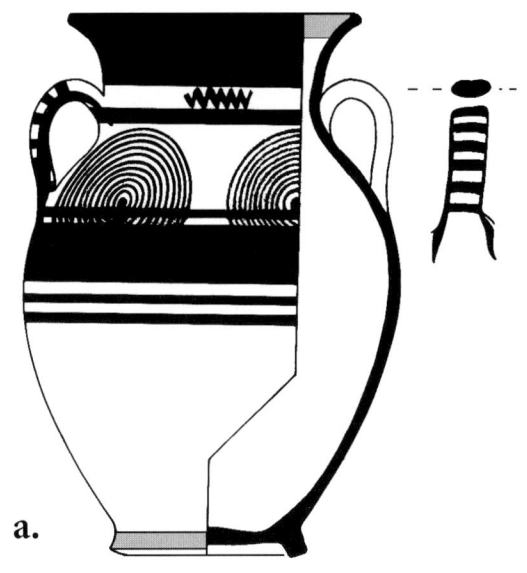

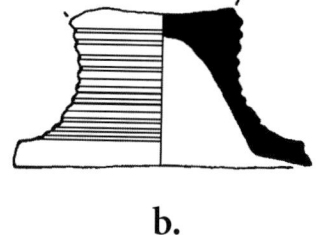

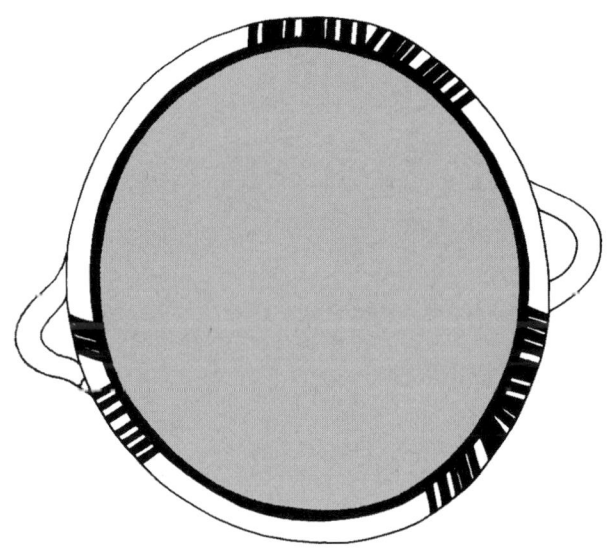

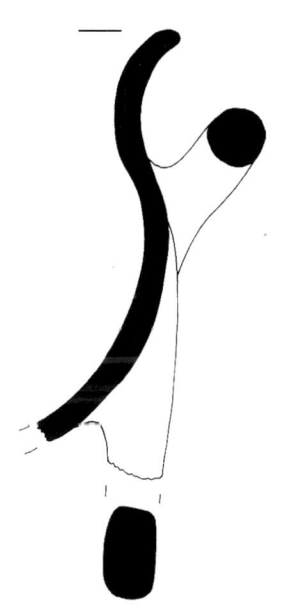

FIGURE 103. Tomb 47. (*a*) **T47-1**.
(*b*) **T47-2**. (*c*) **T47-3**. (*d*) **T47-4**.

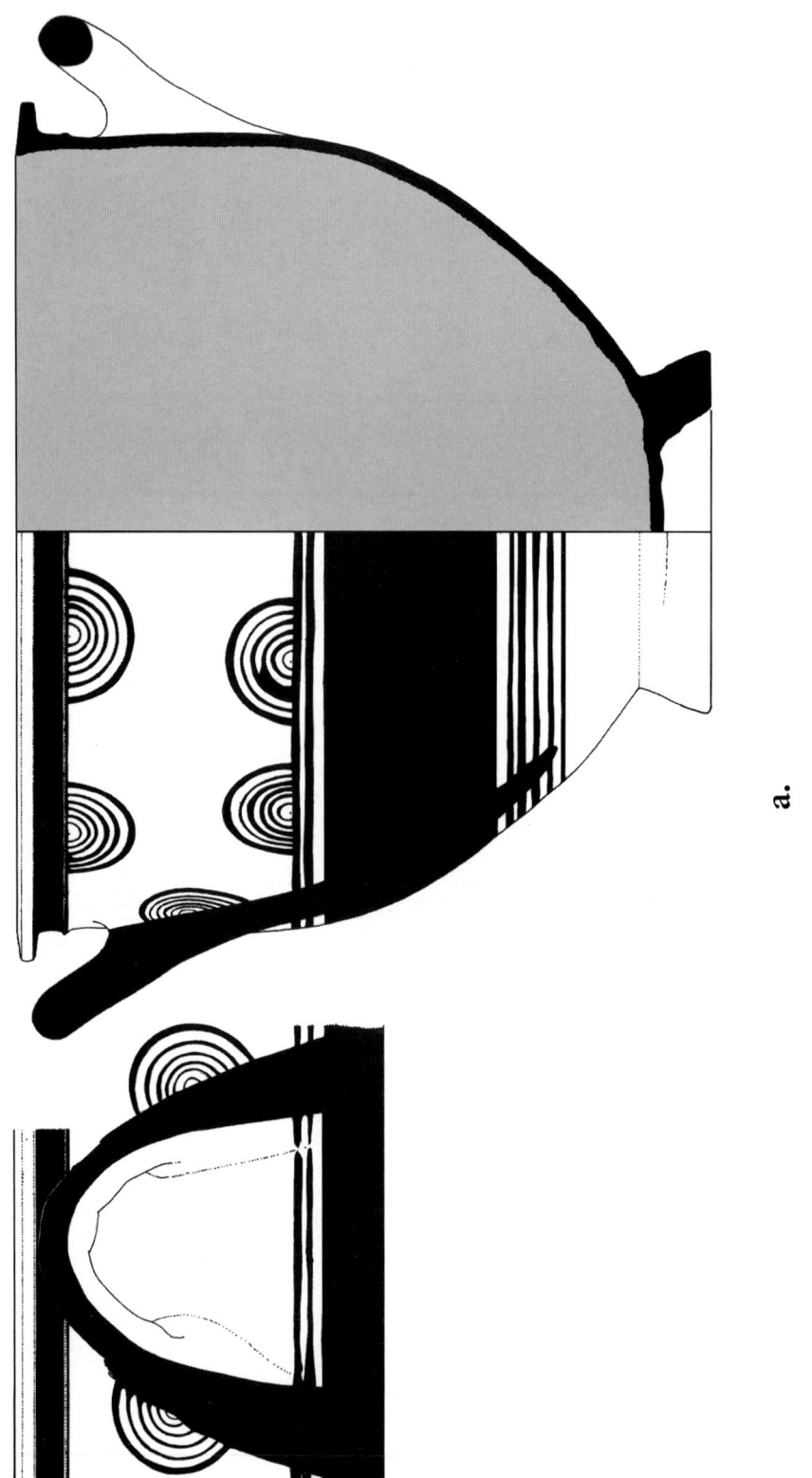

FIGURE 104 (on facing page). Tomb 48. (*a*) **T48-1**. Including handle decoration.

a.

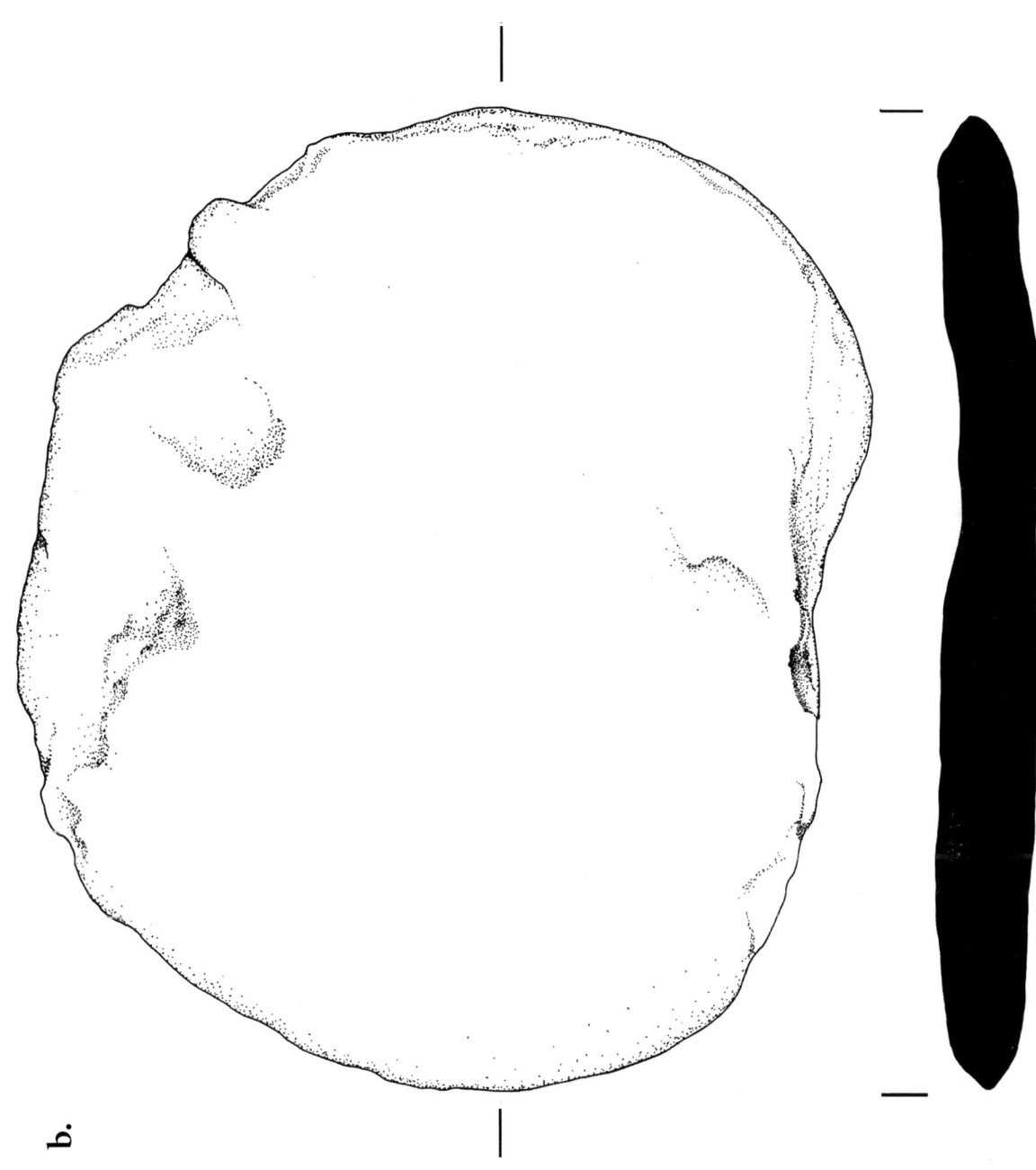

b.

FIGURE 104 (continued).
Tomb 48. (b) T48-2.

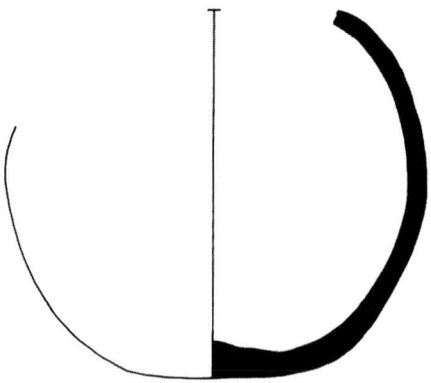

FIGURE 105. Tomb 49. **T49-1**.

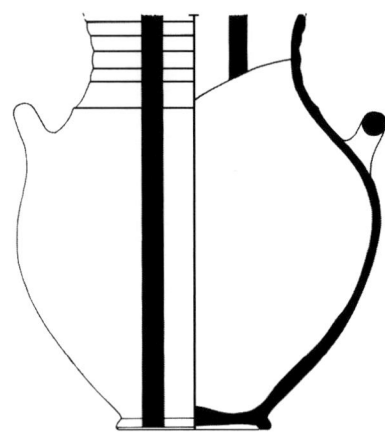

FIGURE 106. Tomb 50. **T50-1**.

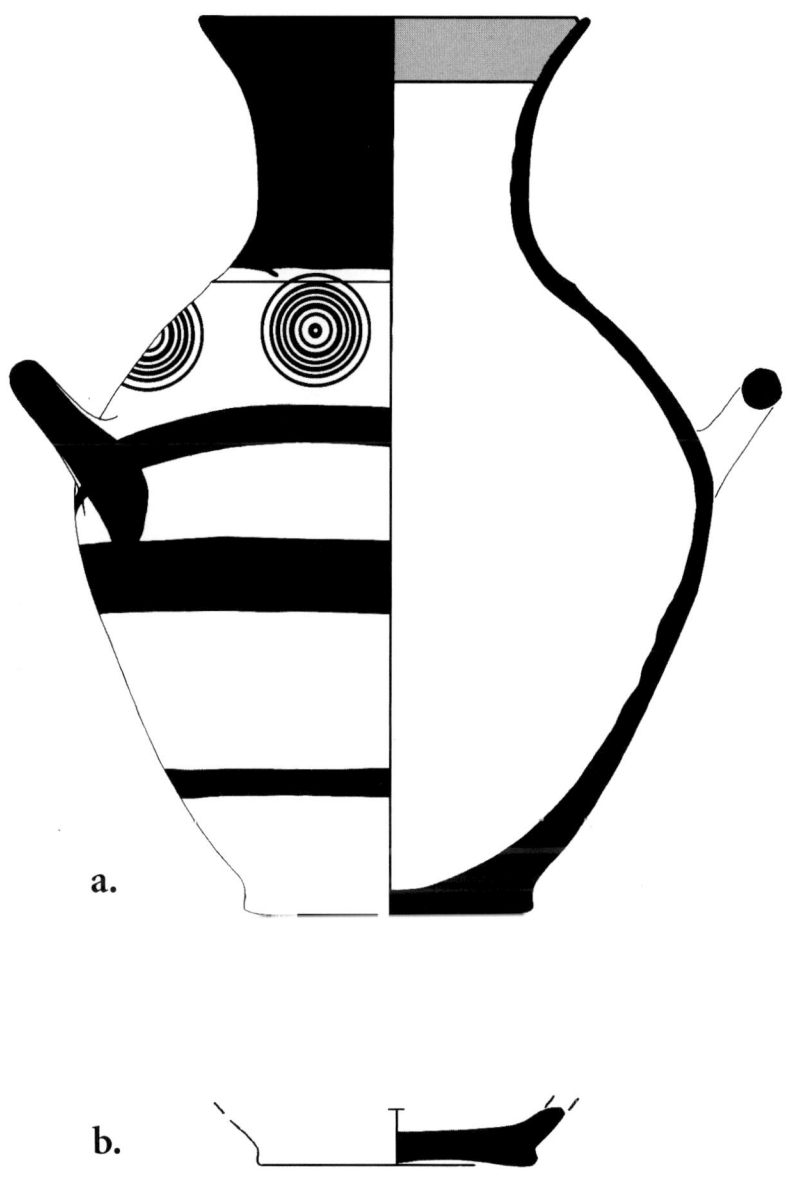

a.

b.

FIGURE 107 (on following page). Tomb 51. (*a*) **T51-1**. (*b*) **T51-2**.

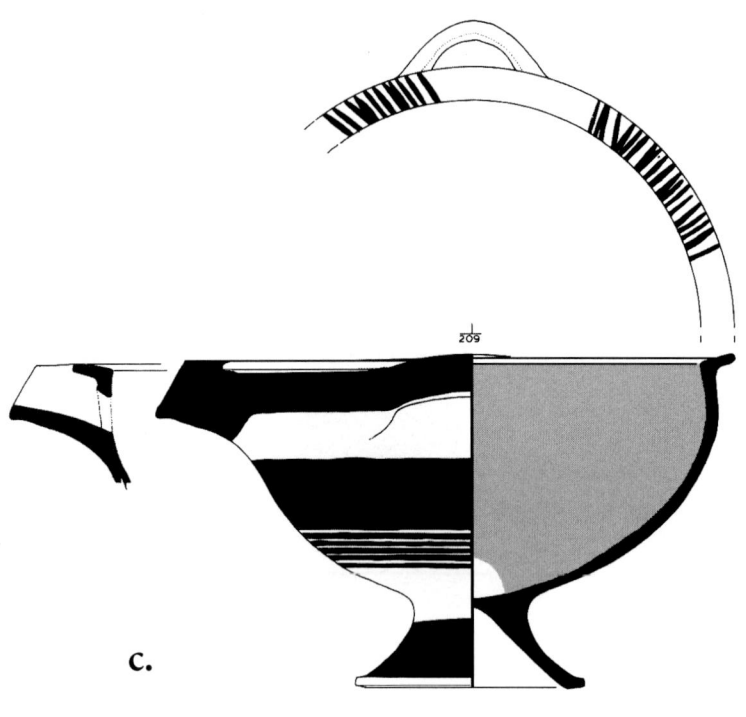

c.

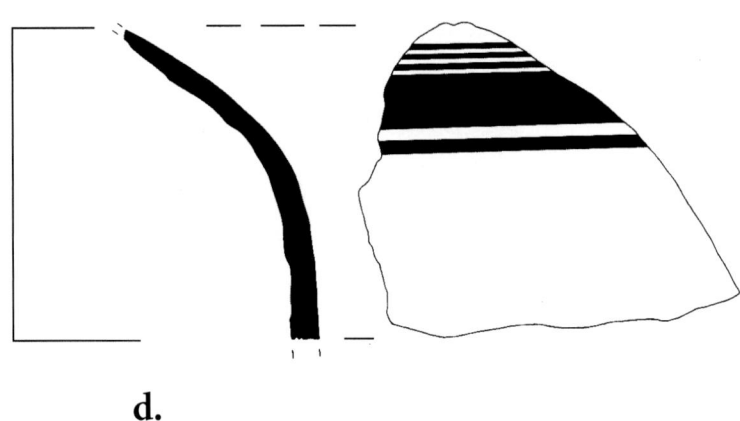

d.

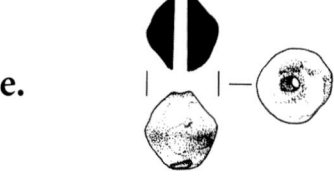

e.

FIGURE 107 (continued). Tomb 51. (*c*) **T51-3**. (*d*) **T51-4**. (*e*) **T51-5**.

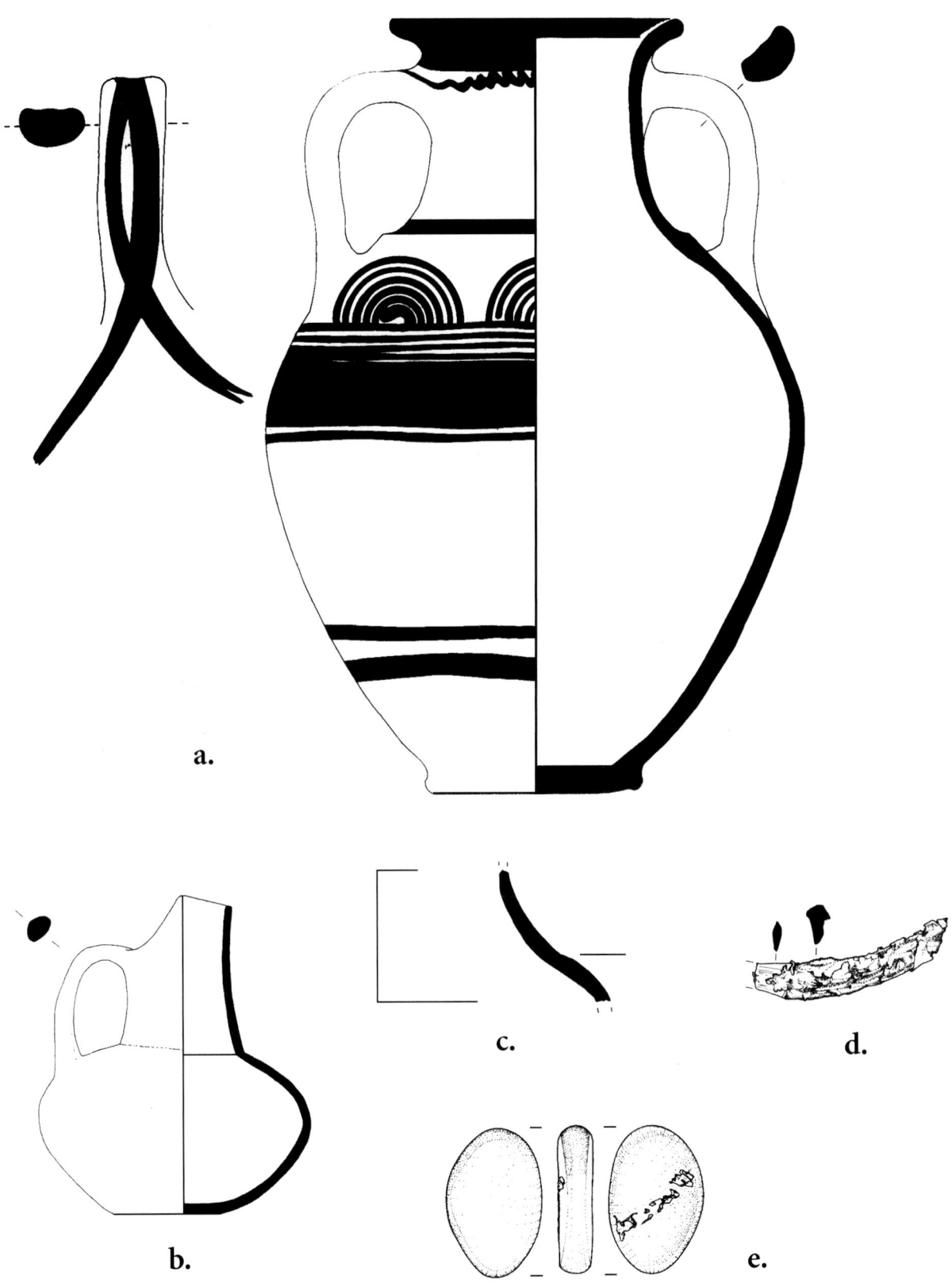

FIGURE 108. Tomb 52. (*a*) **T52-1**. (*b*) **T52-2**. (*c*) **T52-3**. (*d*) **T52-4**. (*e*) **T52-5**.

FIGURE 109. Tomb 53. (*a*) **T53-1**. (*b*) **T53-2**.

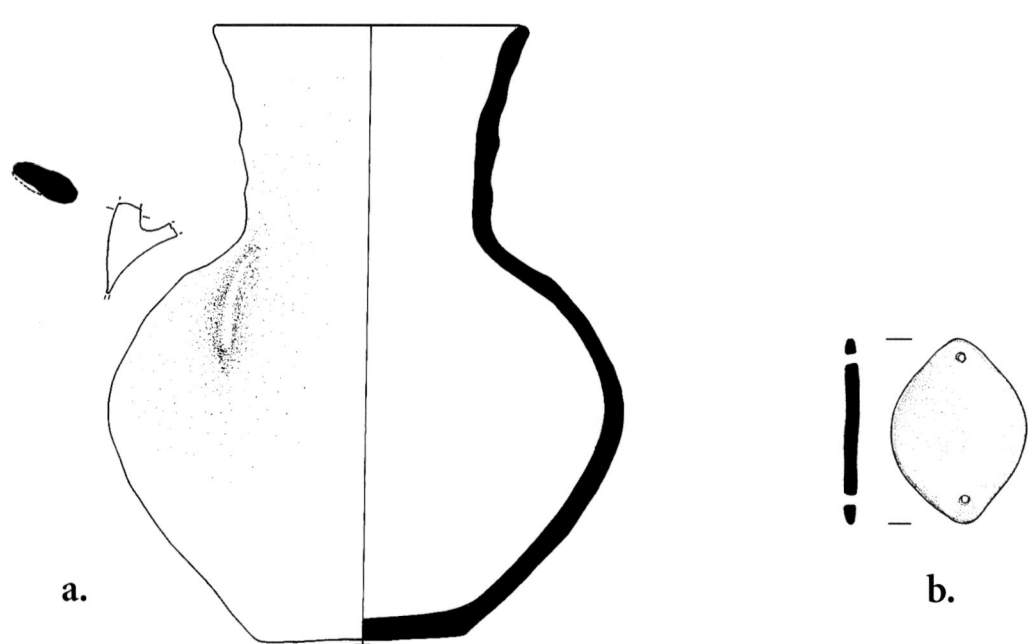

FIGURE 110. Tomb 54. (*a*) **T54-1**. (*b*) **T54-2**.

FIGURE 111. Tomb 55. **T55-1**.

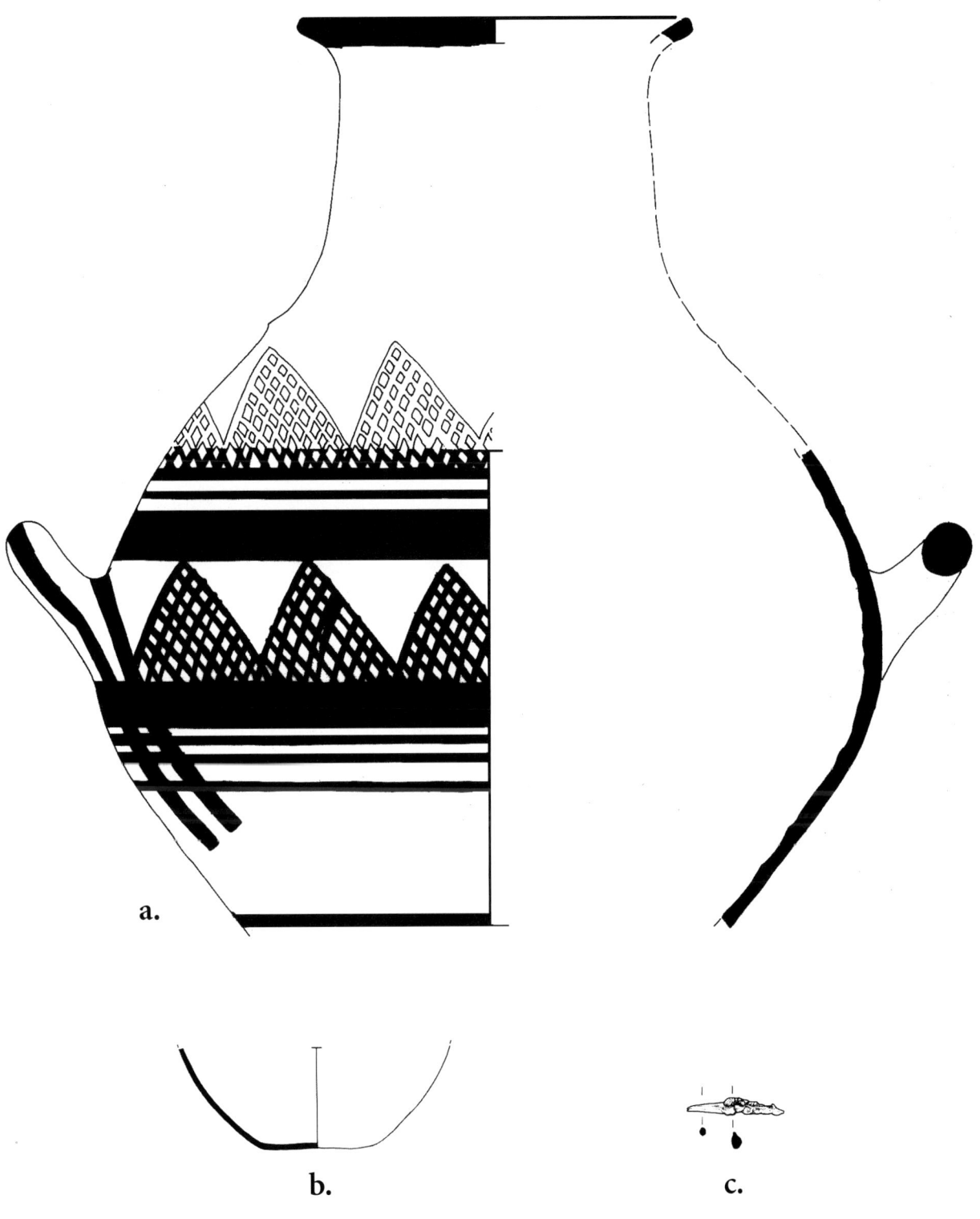

FIGURE 112. Tomb 56. (*a*) **T56-1.** (*b*) **T56-2.** (*c*) **T56-3.**

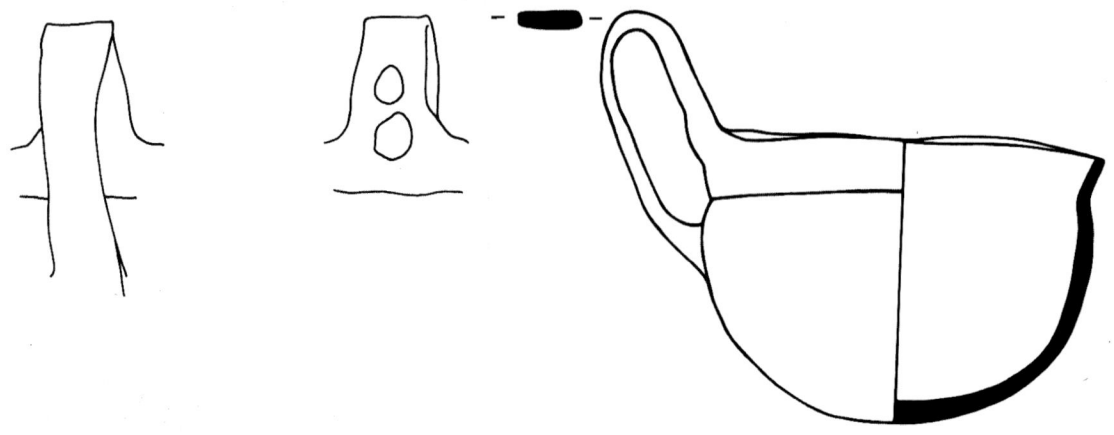

FIGURE 113. Tomb 57. **T57-1**.

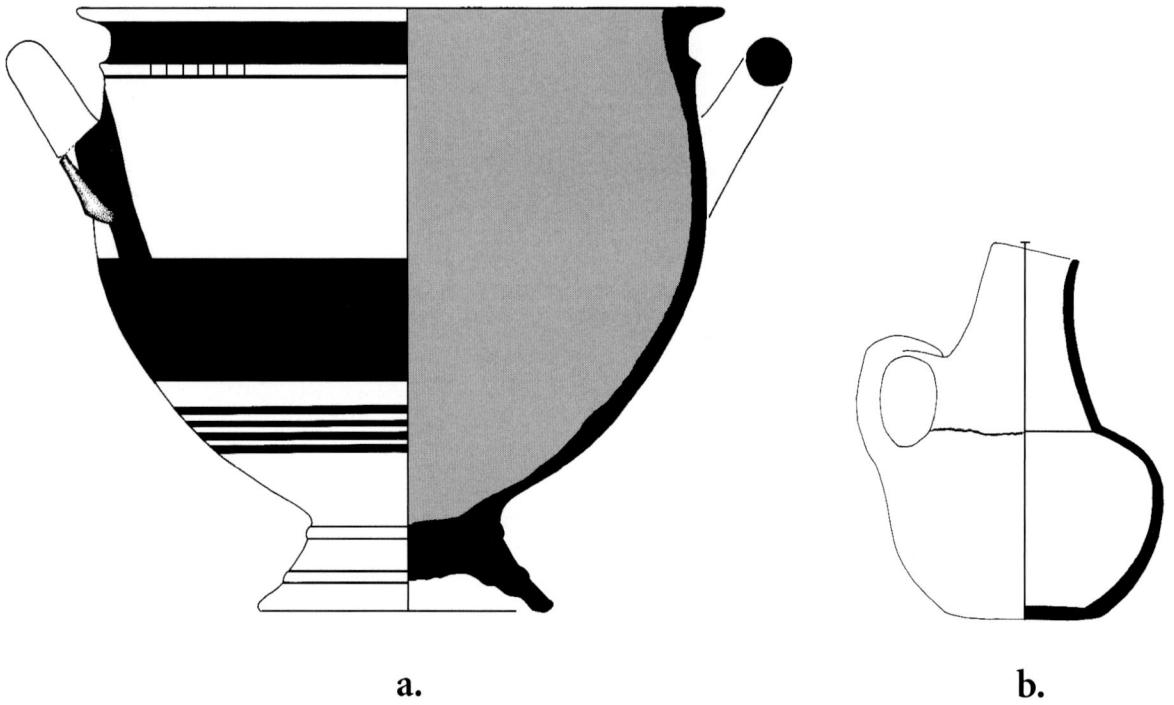

a.   b.

FIGURE 114. Tomb 58. (*a*) **T58-1**. (*b*) **T58-2**.

FIGURE 115. Tomb 59. **T59-1.**

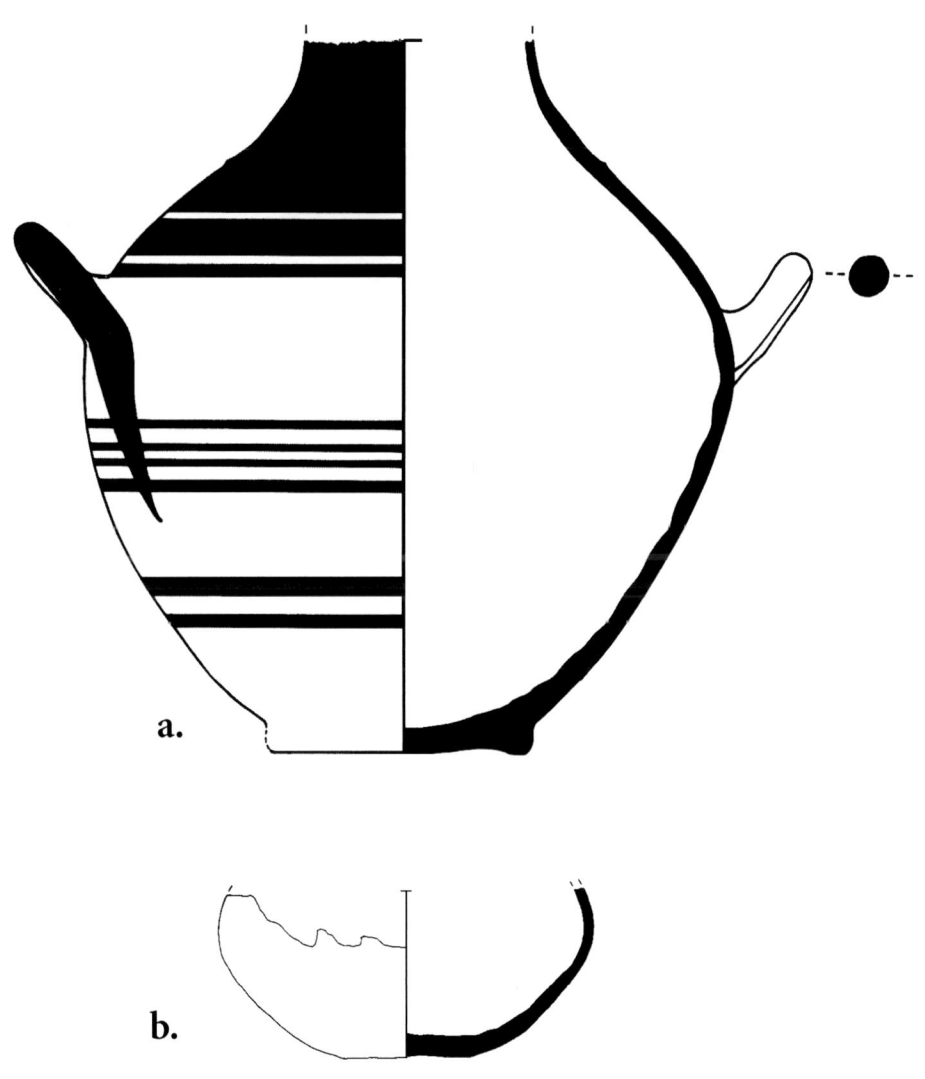

FIGURE 116. Tomb 60. (*a*) **T60-1.** (*b*) **T60-2.**

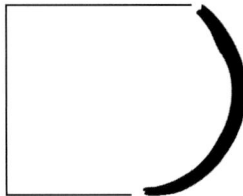

FIGURE 117. Tomb 61. **T61-1**.

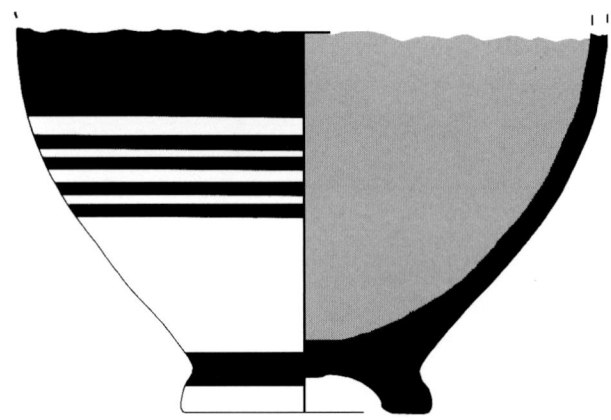

FIGURE 118. Tomb 62. **T62-1**.

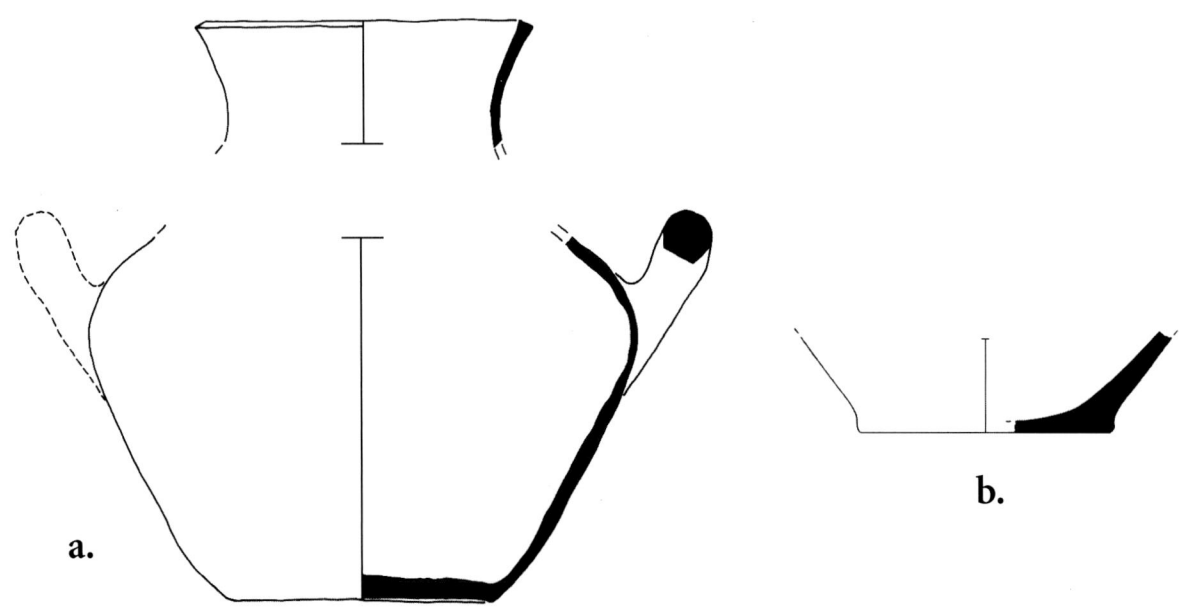

FIGURE 119. Tomb 63. (*a*) **T63-1**. (*b*) **T63-2**.

FIGURE 120. Tomb 64. **T64-1**.

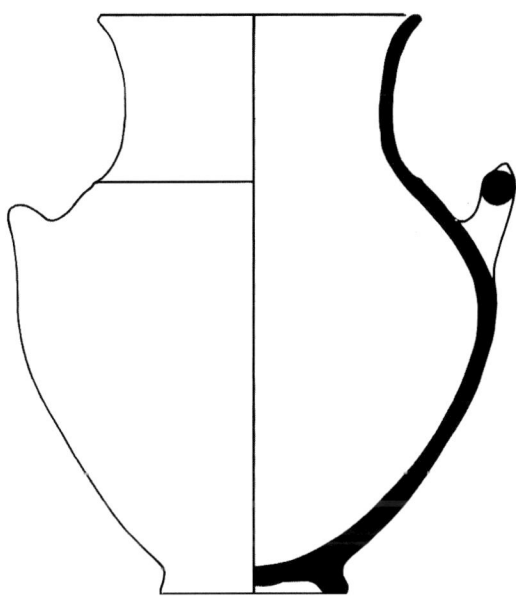

FIGURE 121. Tomb 65. **T65-1**.

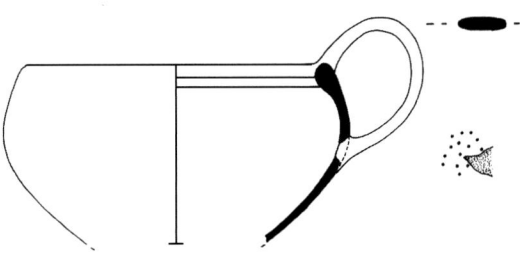

FIGURE 122. Tomb 66. **T66-1**.

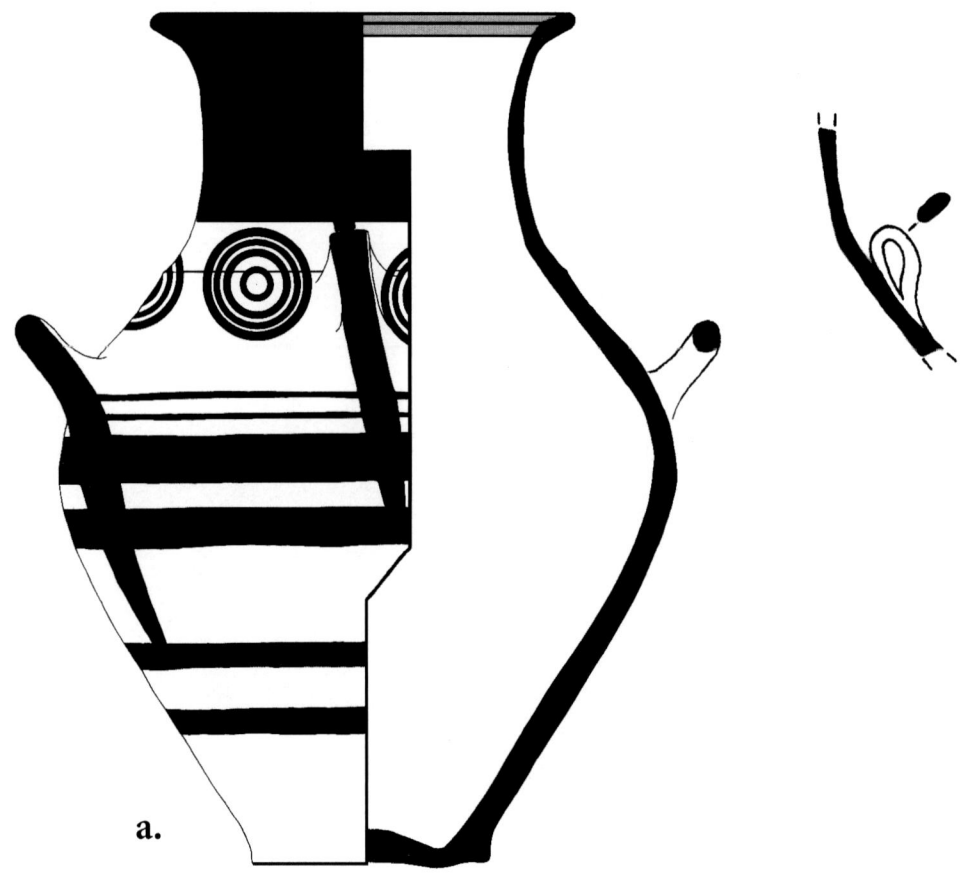

FIGURE 123 (on facing page). Tomb 67. (*a*) **T67-1**.

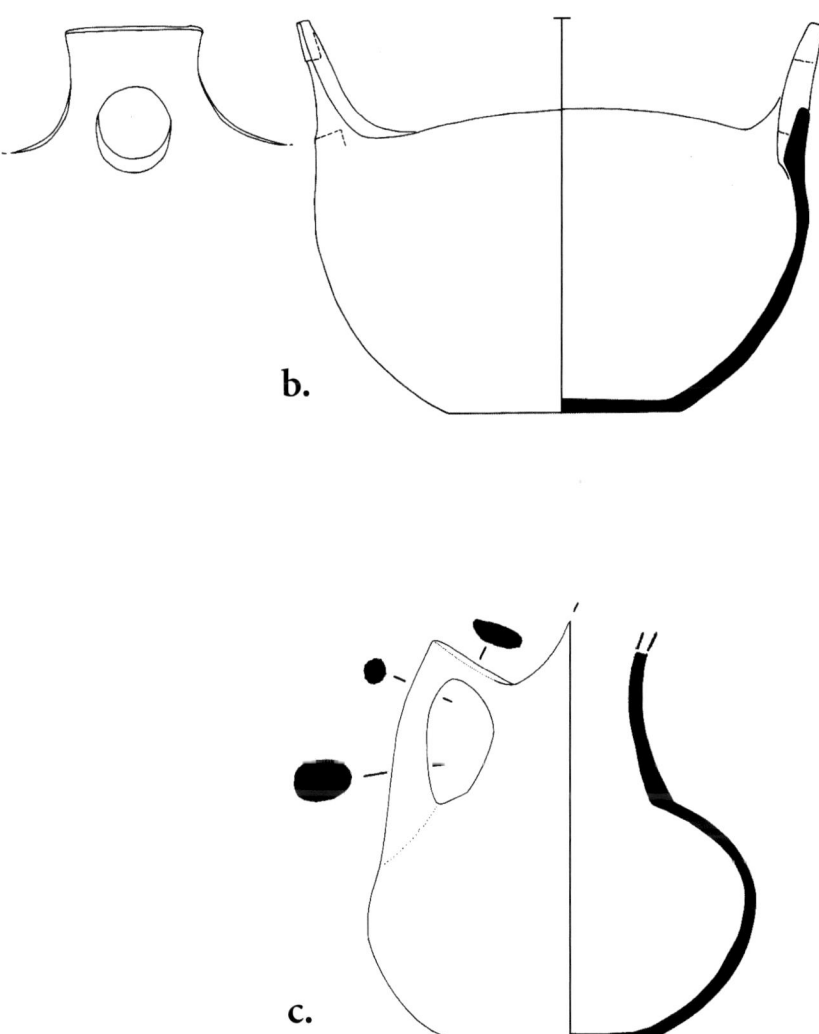

FIGURE 123 (continued). Tomb 67. (*b*) **T67-2.** (*c*) **T67-3.**

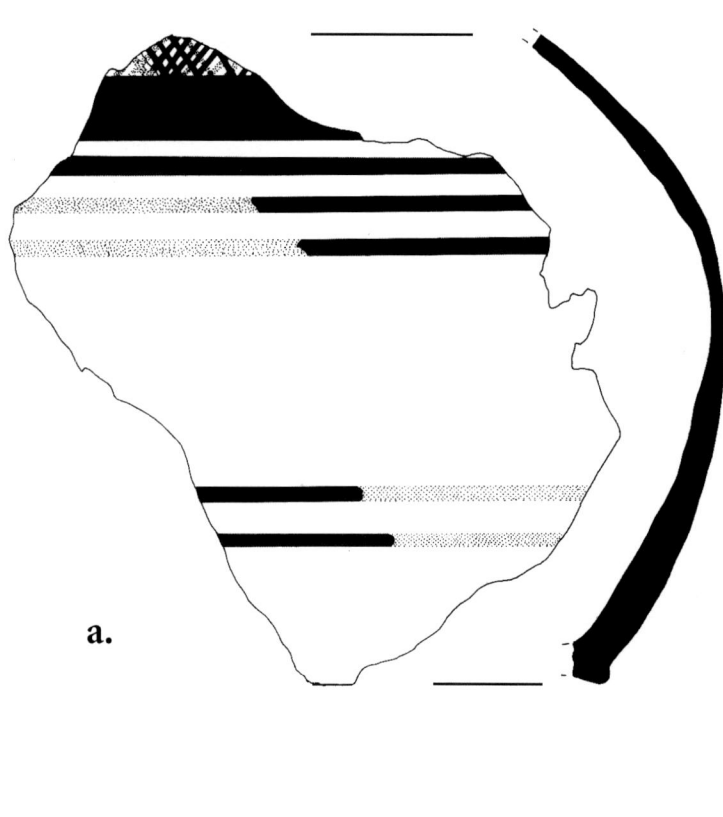

Figure 124. Tomb 68. (*a*) **T68-1**. (*b*) **T68-2**.

a.

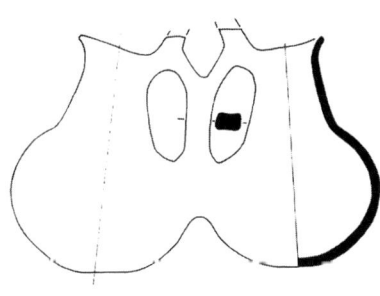

b.

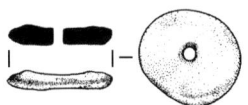

c.

FIGURE 125. Tomb 69. (*a*) **T69-1**. (*b*) **T69-2**. (*c*) **T69-3**.

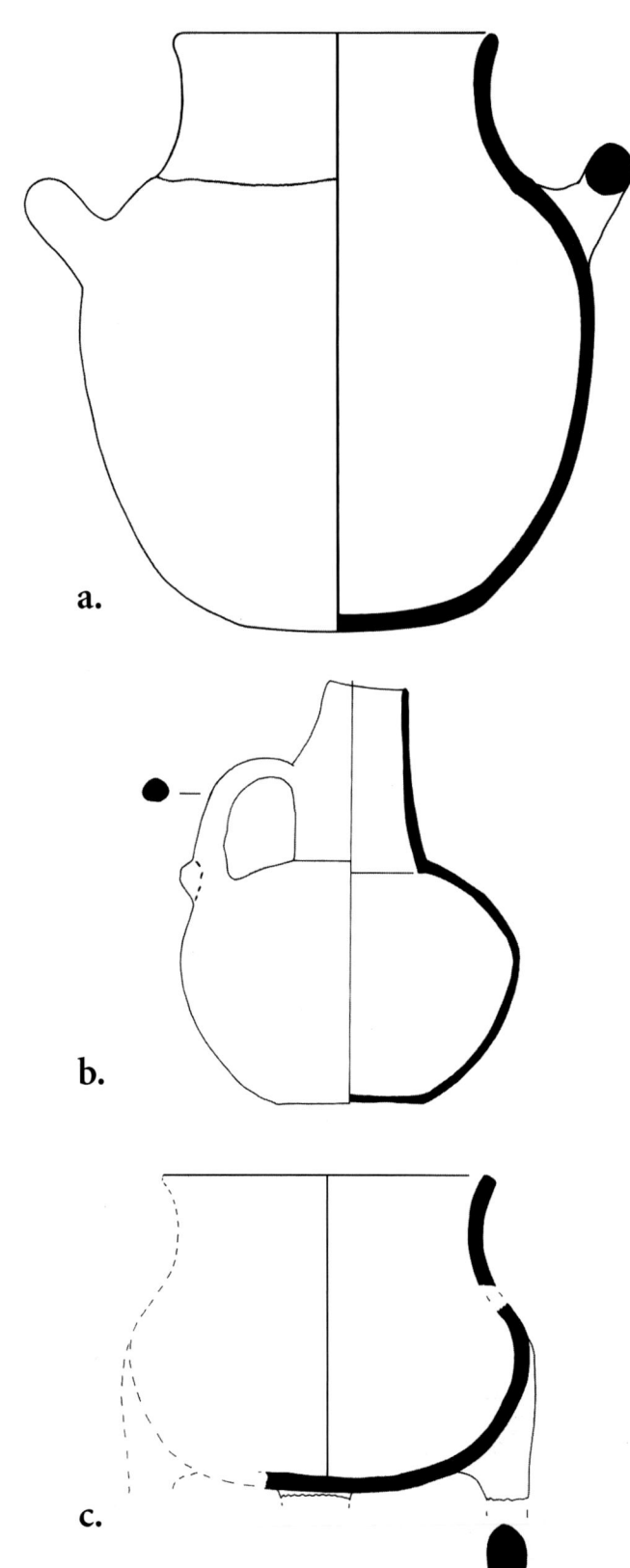

FIGURE 126. Tomb 70.
(*a*) **T70-1.** (*b*) **T70-2.**
(*c*) **T70-3.**

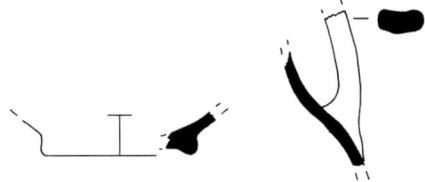

FIGURE 127. Tomb 71. **T71-1.**

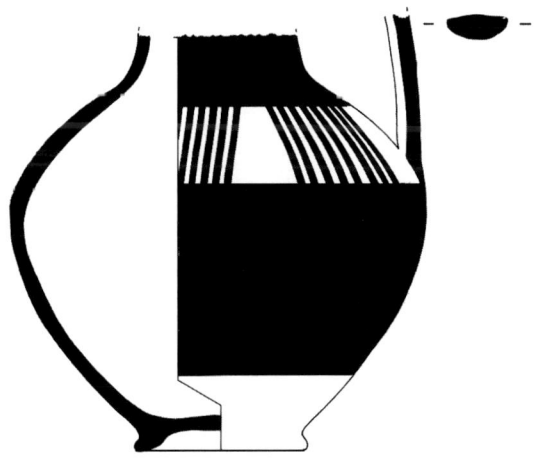

FIGURE 128. Tomb 72. **T72-1.**

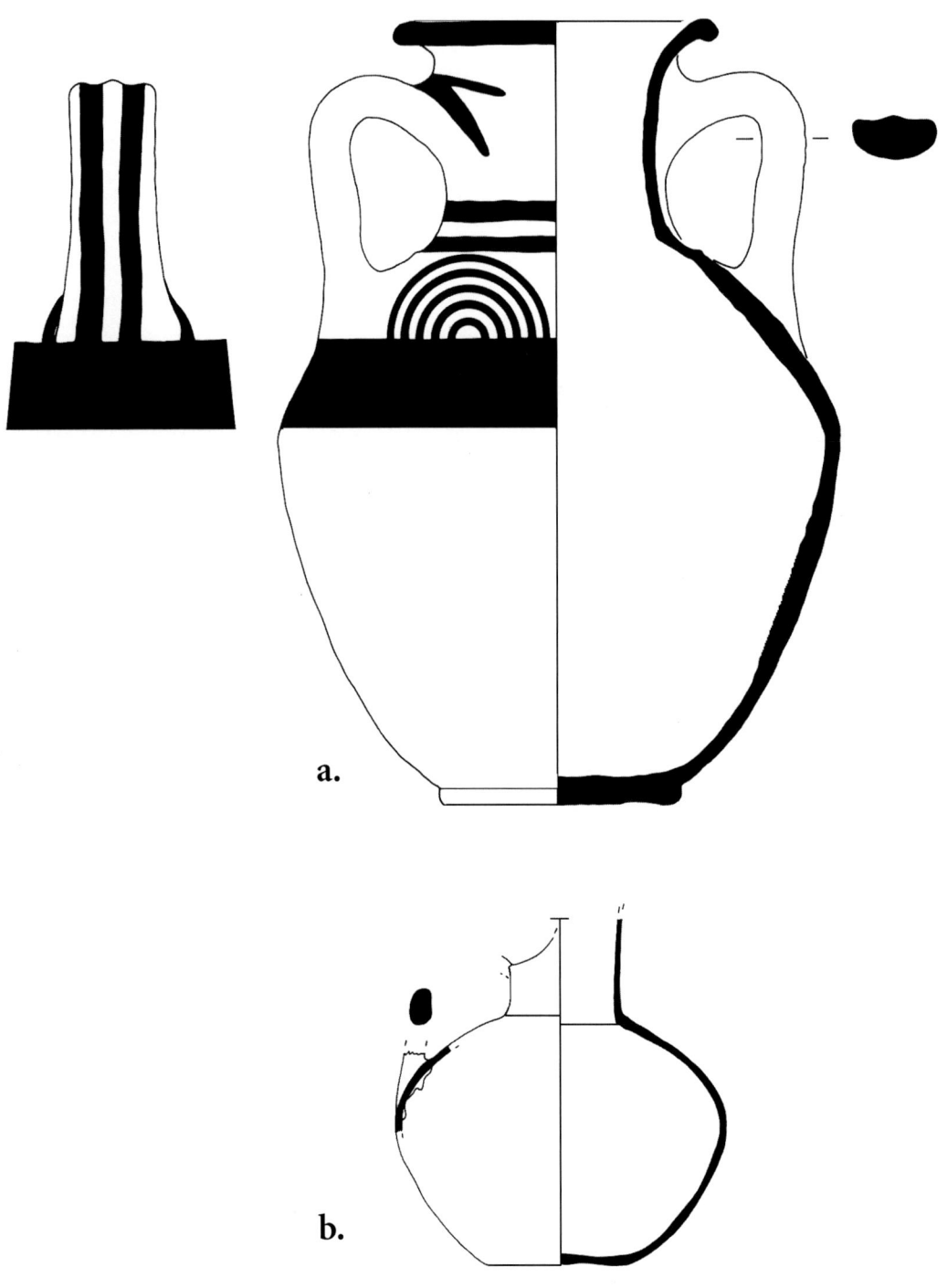

FIGURE 129. Tomb 73. (*a*) **T73-1.** (*b*) **T73-2.**

a.

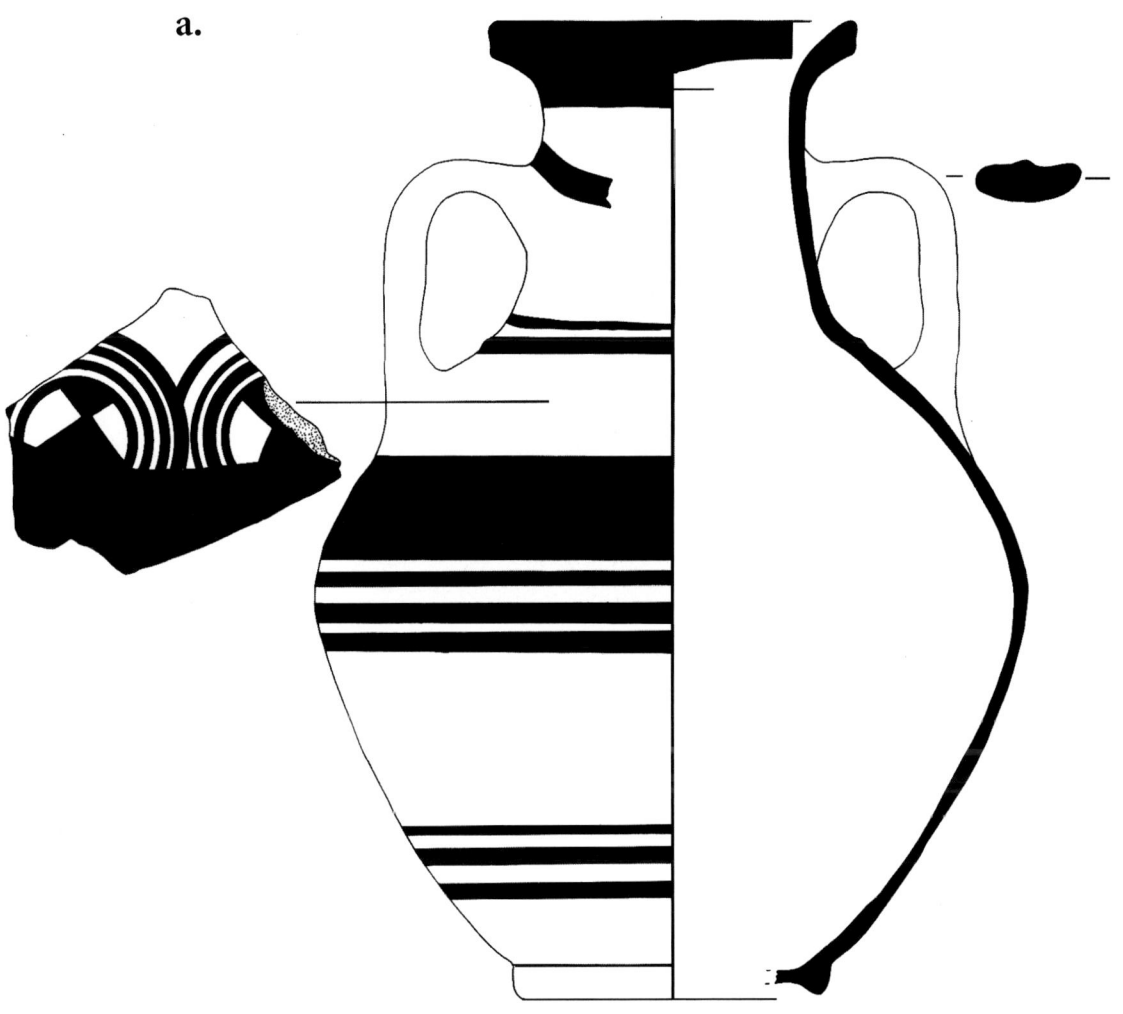

FIGURE 130 (on following page). Tomb 74. (*a*) T74-1.

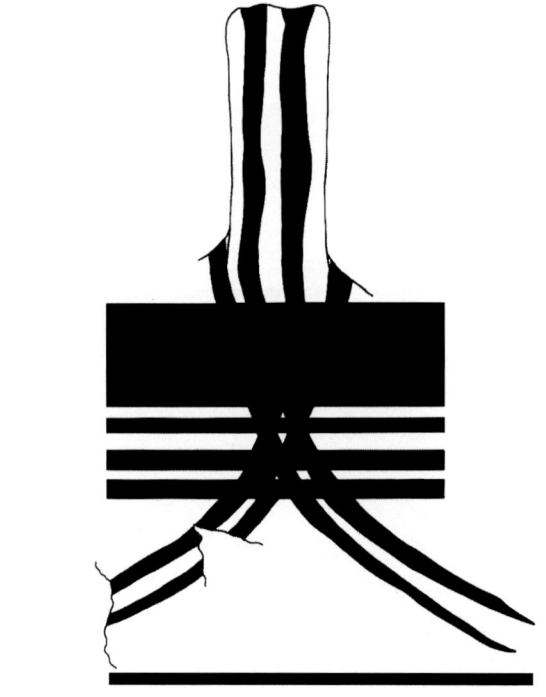

b.

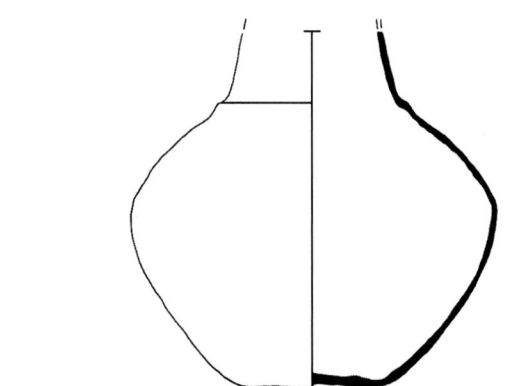

c.

FIGURE 130 (continued). Tomb 74. (*b*) **T74-1**. Handle decoration. (*c*) **T74-2**.

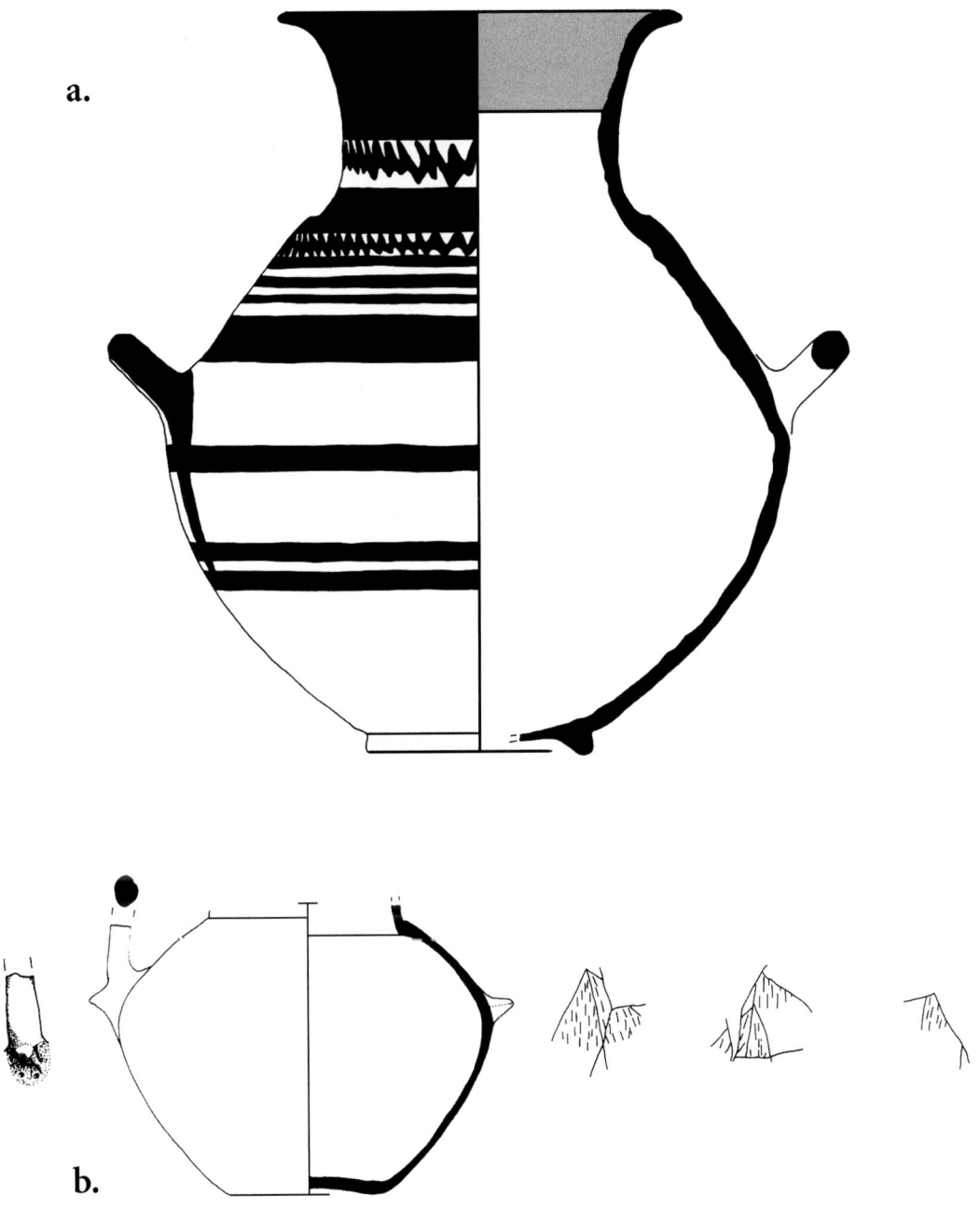

FIGURE 131 (on following page). Tomb 75. (*a*) **T75-1.** (*b*) **T75-2.**

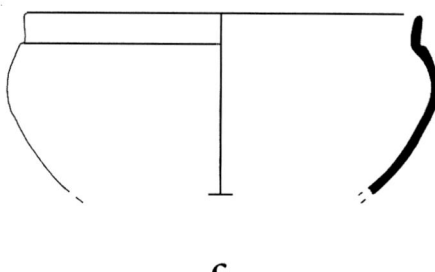

c.

d.

FIGURE 131 (continued). Tomb 75. (*c*) **T75-3**. (*d*) **T75-4**.

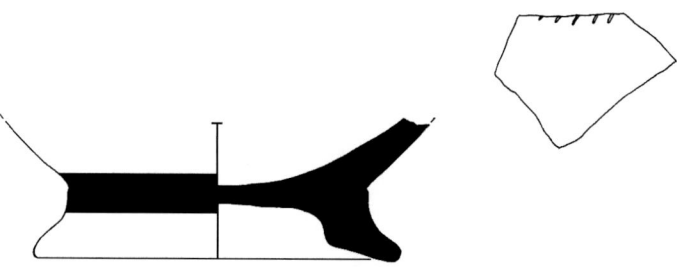

FIGURE 132. Tomb 76. **T76-1**.

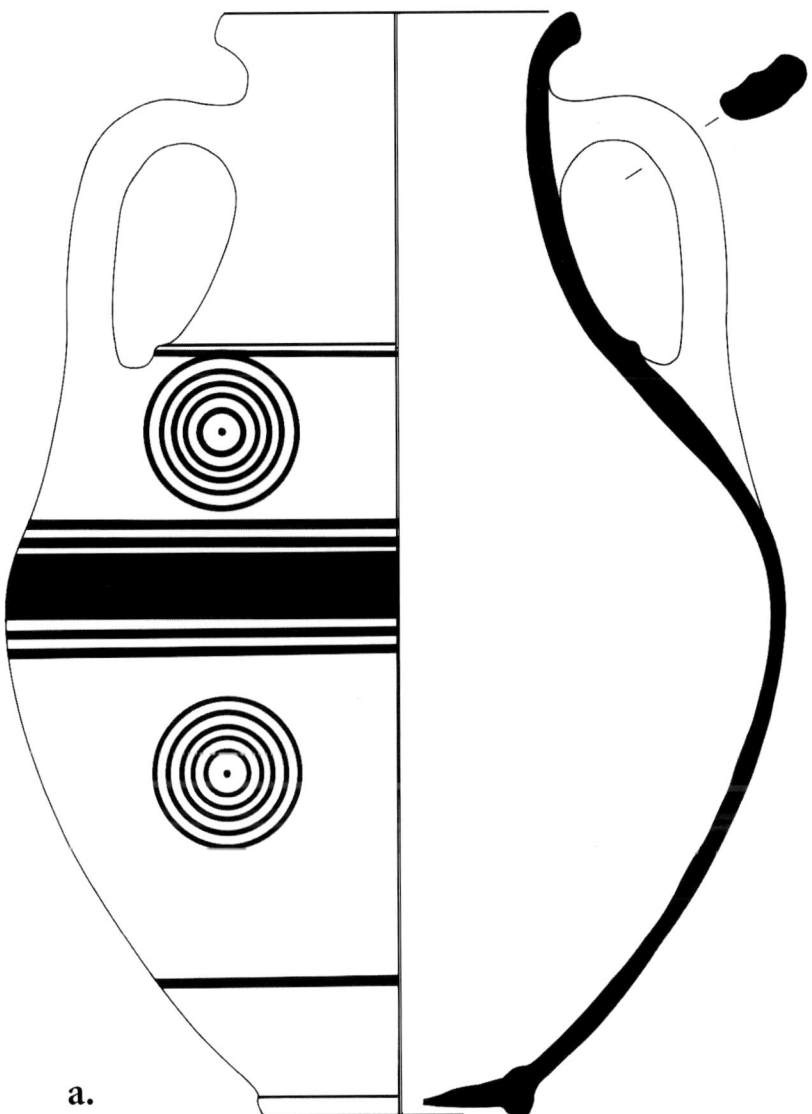

a.

FIGURE 133 (on following page). Tomb 77. (*a*) **T77-1**.

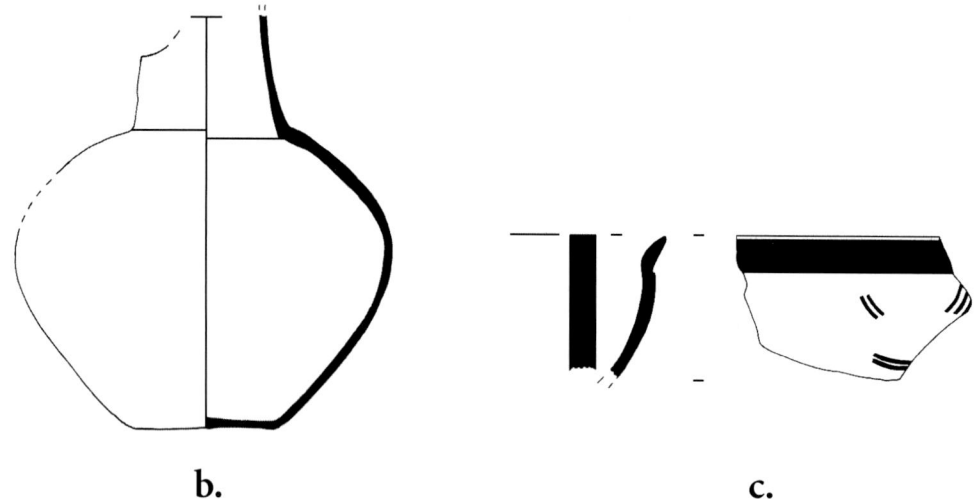

b.

c.

FIGURE 133 (continued). Tomb 77. (*b*) **T77-2**. (*c*) **T77-3**.

FIGURE 134. Tomb 78. **T78-1**.

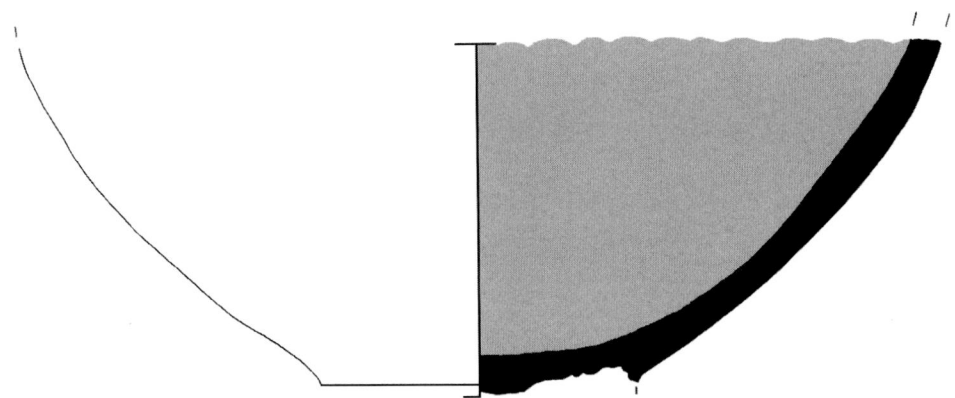

FIGURE 135. Tomb 79. **T79-1.**

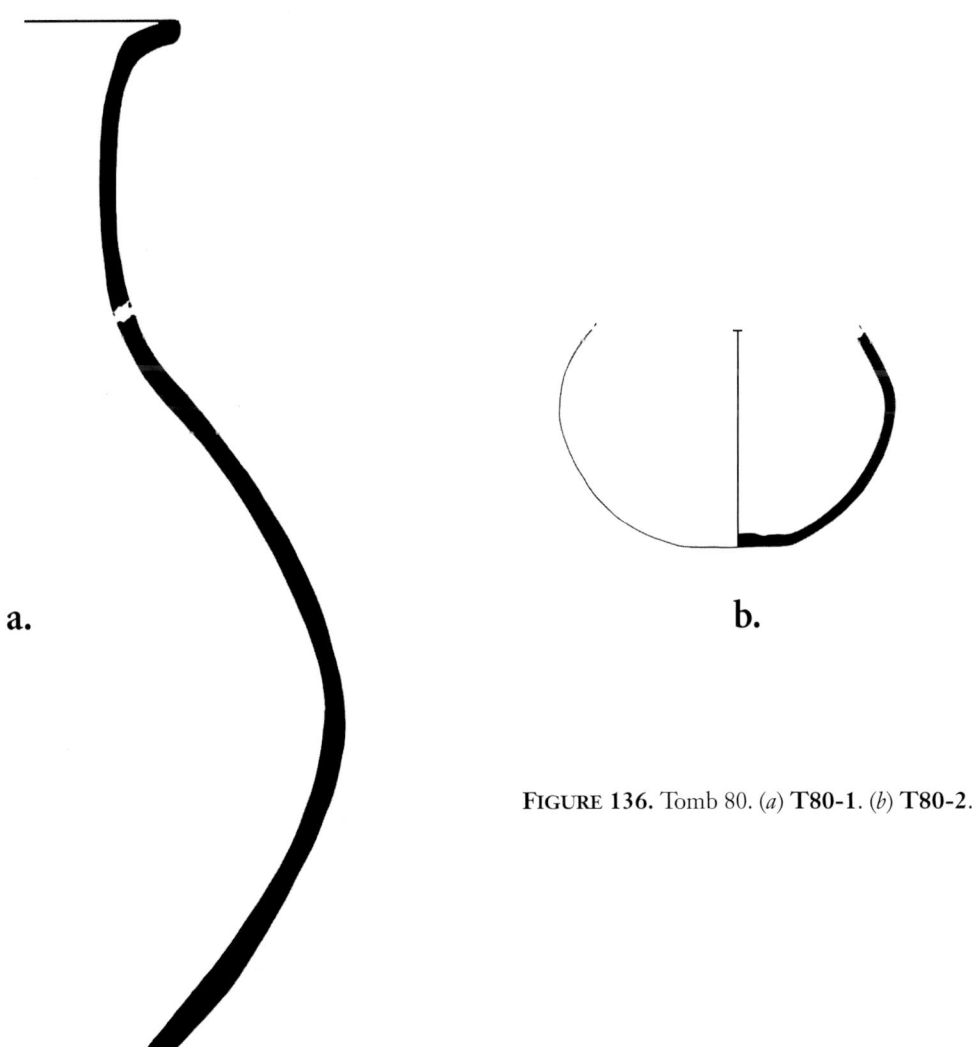

a.

b.

FIGURE 136. Tomb 80. (*a*) **T80-1.** (*b*) **T80-2.**

a.

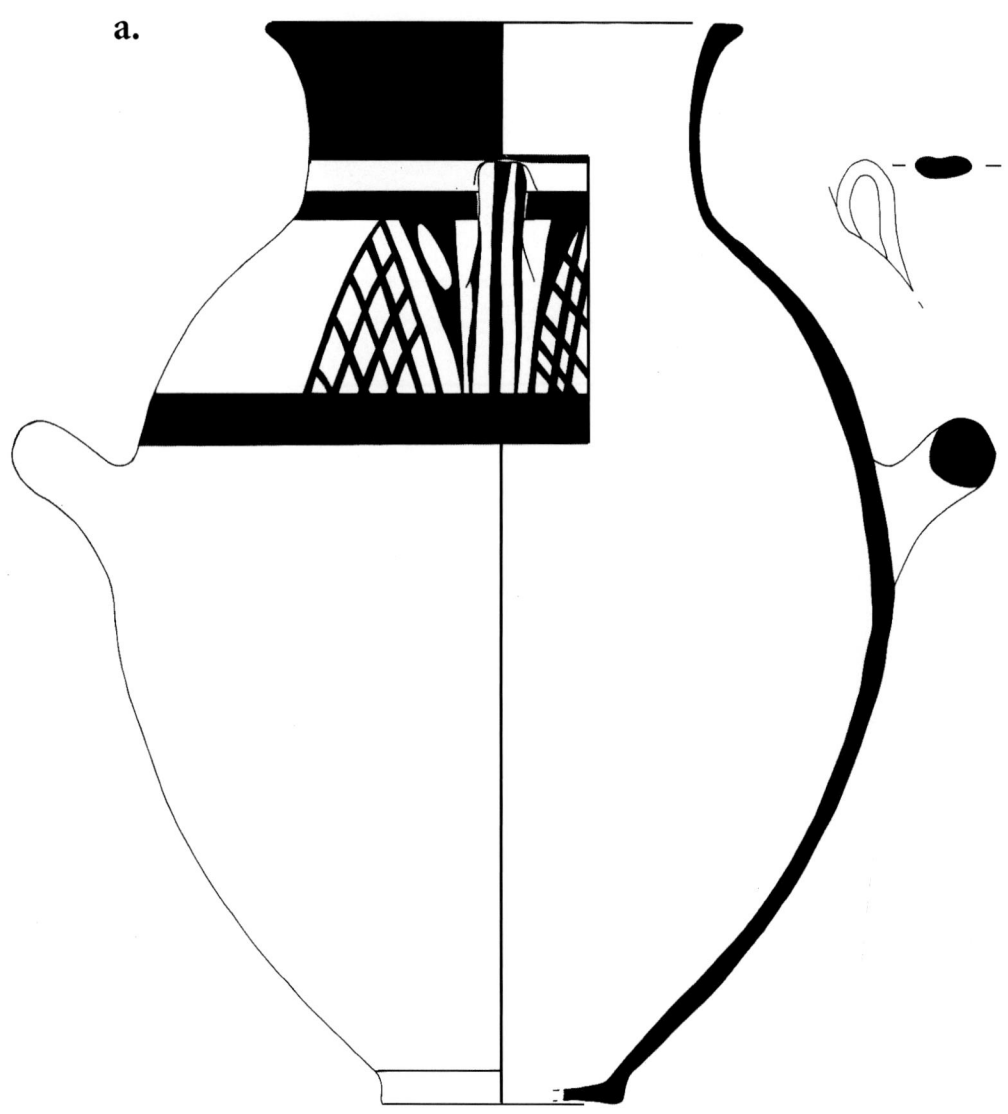

FIGURE 137 (on facing page). Tomb 81. (*a*) **T81-1.**

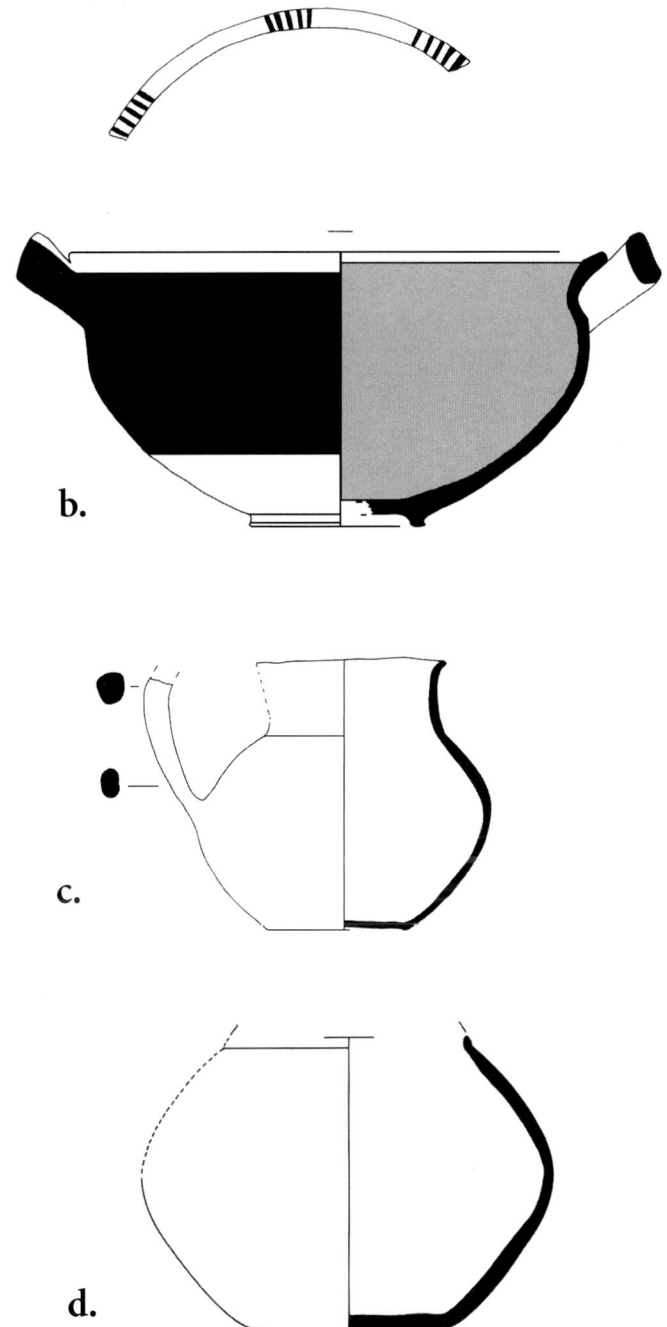

FIGURE 137 (continued). Tomb 81. (*b*) **T81-2**. (*c*) **T81-3**. (*d*) **T81-4**.

a.

b.

FIGURE 138 (on facing page). Tomb 82. (*a*) **T82-1**. (*b*) **T82-2**.

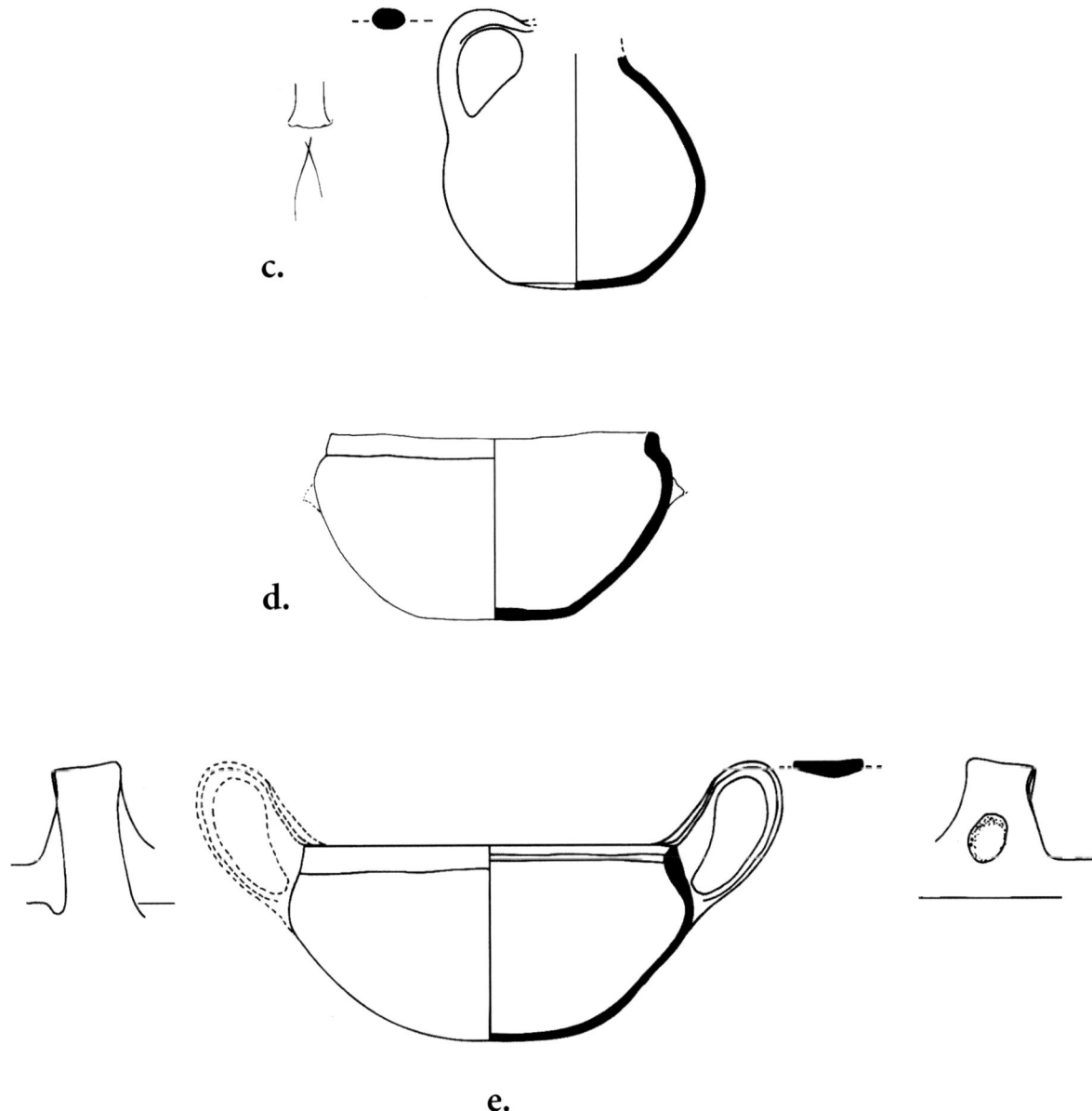

FIGURE 138 (continued). Tomb 82. (*c*) **T82-3**. (*d*) **T82-4**. (*e*) **T82-5**.

FIGURE 139. Tomb 83. (*a*) **T83-1.** (*b*) **T83-2.**

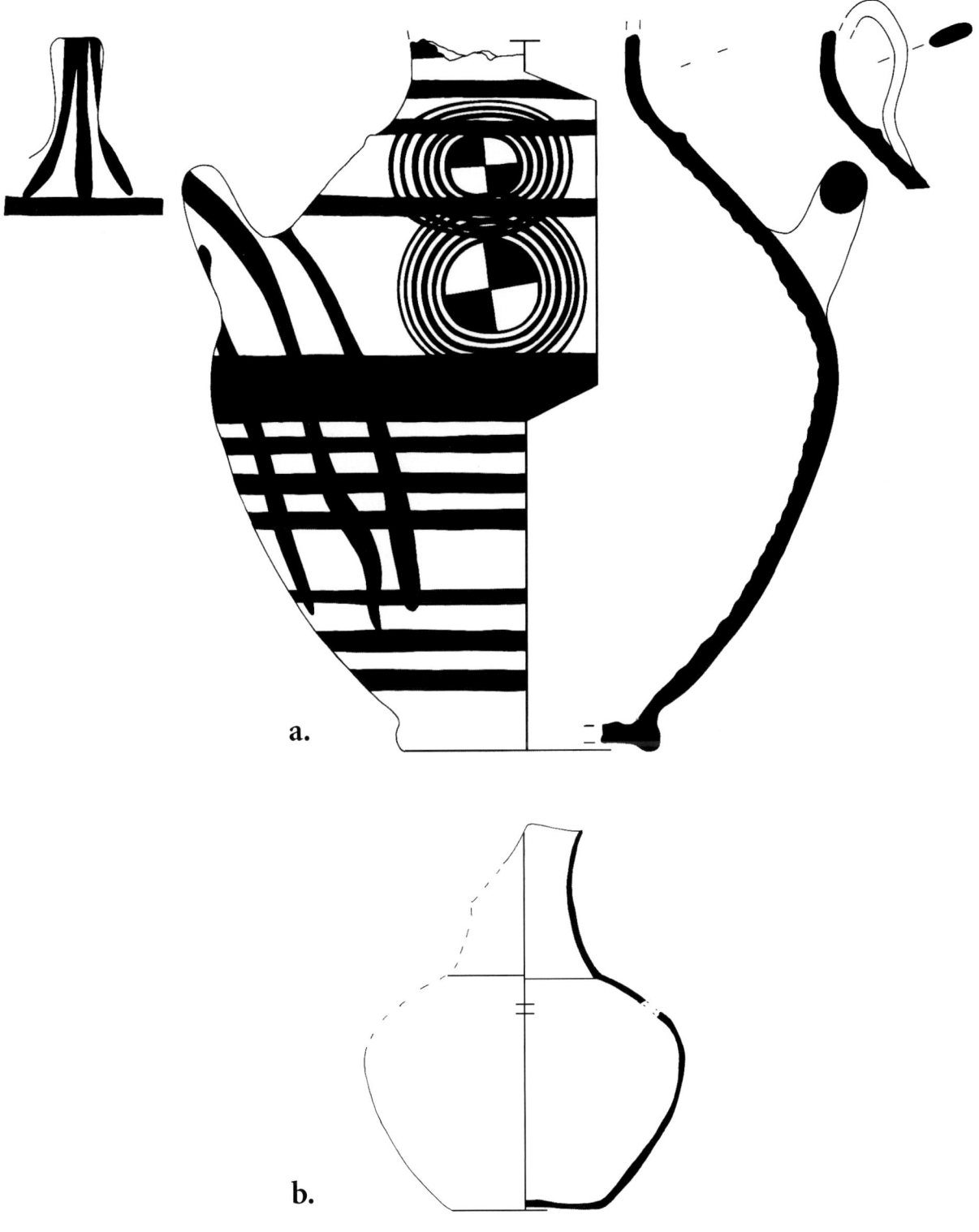

a.

b.

FIGURE 140 (on following page). Tomb 84. (*a*) **T84-1**. (*b*) **T84-2**.

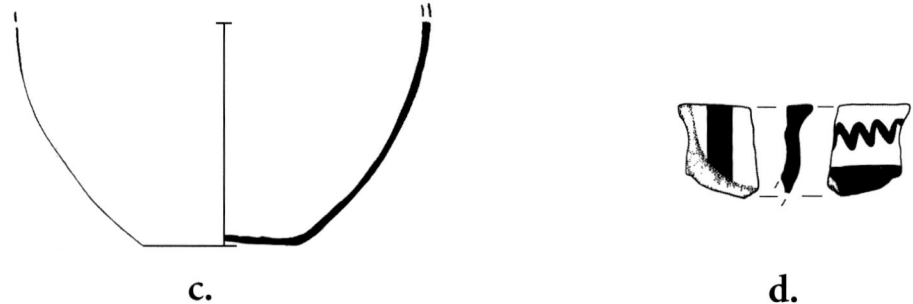

c.   d.

FIGURE 140 (continued). Tomb 84. (*c*) **T84-3**. (*d*) **T84-4**.

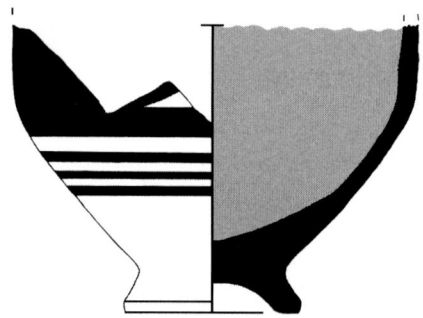

FIGURE 141. Tomb 85. **T85-1**.

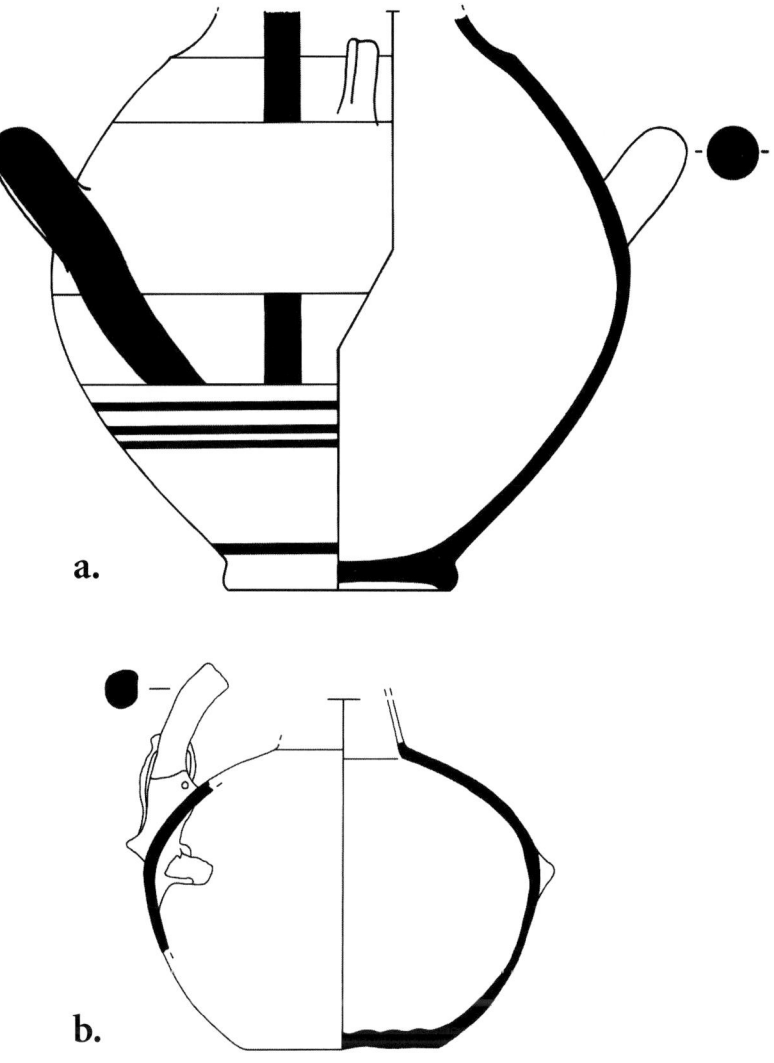

FIGURE 142. Tomb 86. (*a*) **T86-1**. (*b*) **T86-2**.

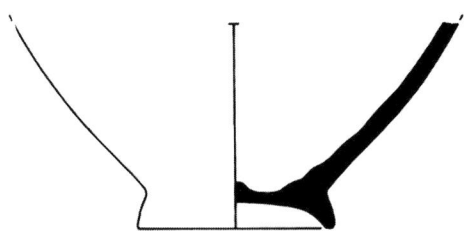

FIGURE 143. Tomb 87. **T87-1**.

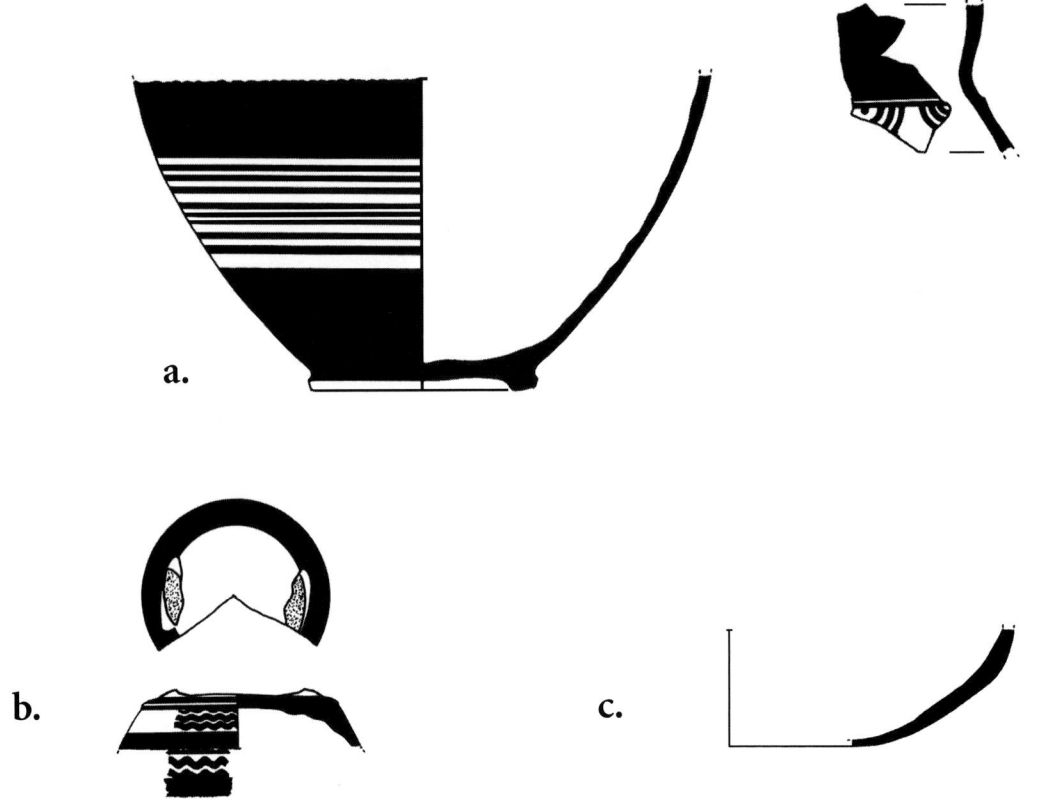

FIGURE 144. Tomb 88. (*a*) **T88-1**. (*b*) **T88-2**. (*c*) **T88-3**.

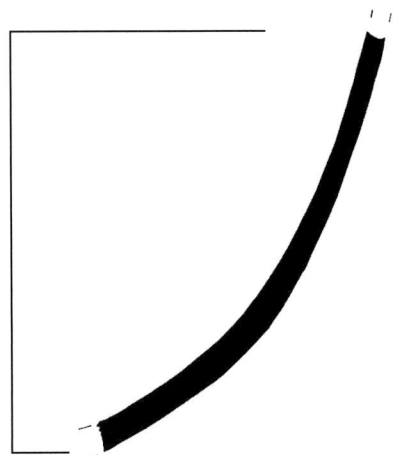

FIGURE 145. Tomb 89. **T89-1**.

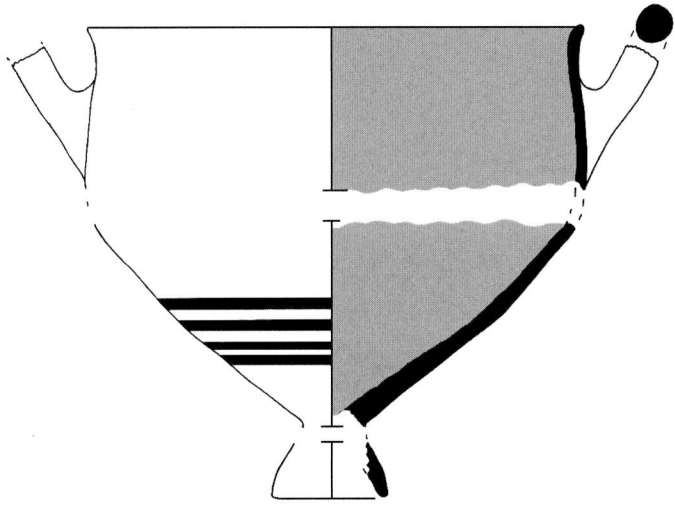

FIGURE 146. Tomb 90. **T90-1**.

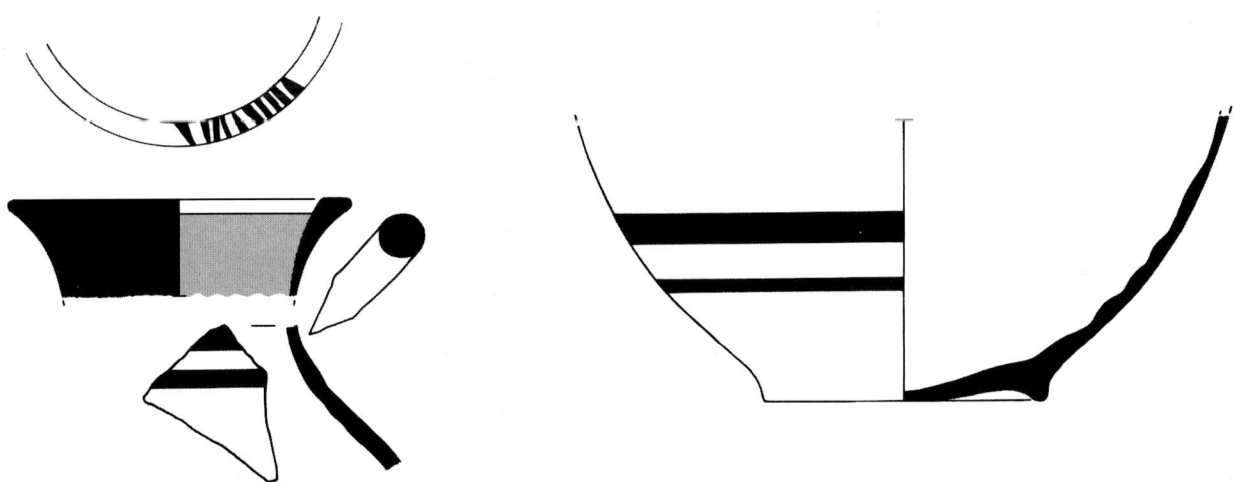

FIGURE 147. Tomb 91. **T91-1**.

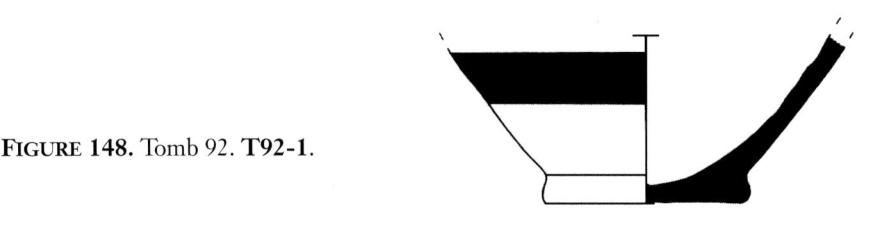

FIGURE 148. Tomb 92. **T92-1.**

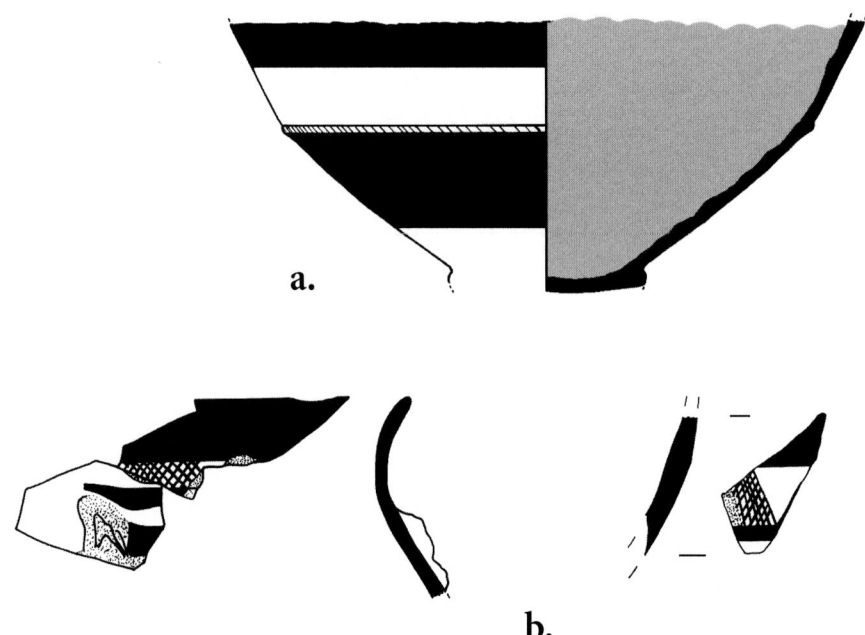

a.

b.

FIGURE 149. Tomb 93. **T93-1** (as preserved). (*a*) Base and lower body. (*b*) Rim and body fragments.

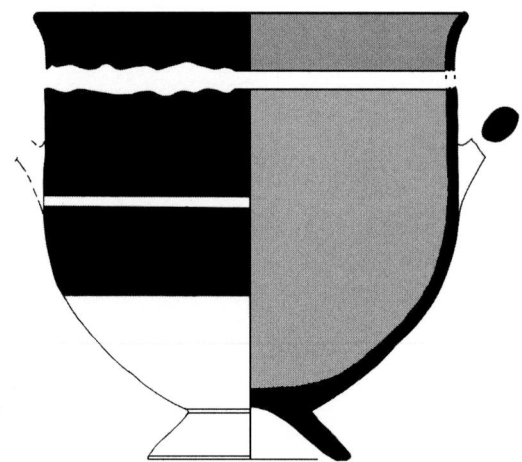

FIGURE 150. Tomb 94. **T94-1.**

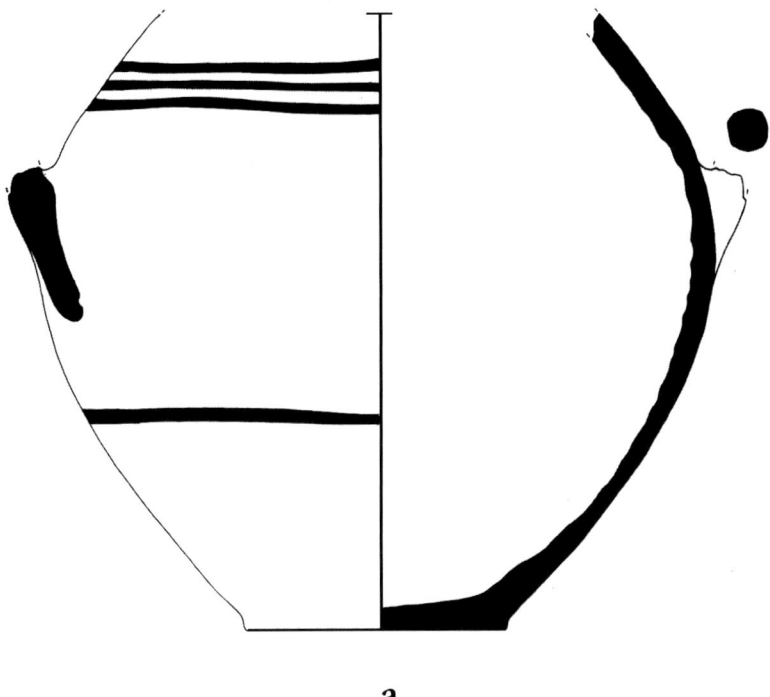

a.

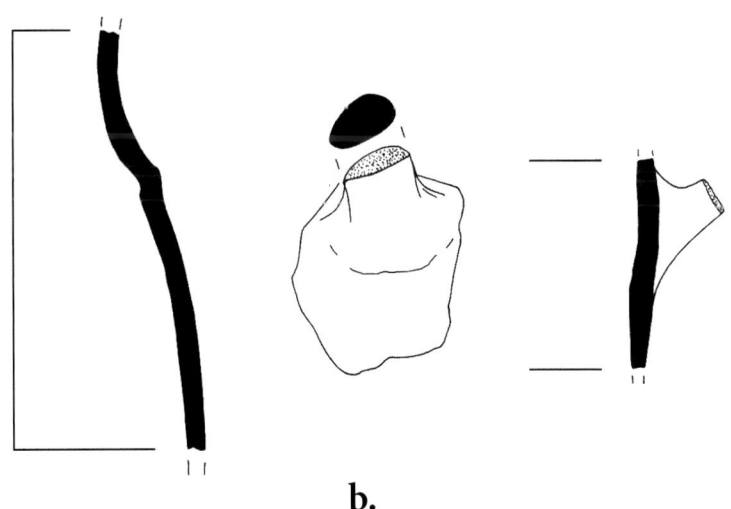

b.

FIGURE 151. Tomb 95. (*a*) **T95-1**. (*b*) **T95-2**.

FIGURE 152. Tomb 96. **T96-1.**

FIGURE 153. Tomb 97. **T97-1**.

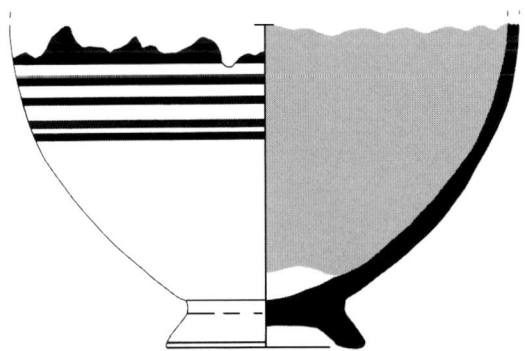

FIGURE 154. Tomb 98. **T98-1**.

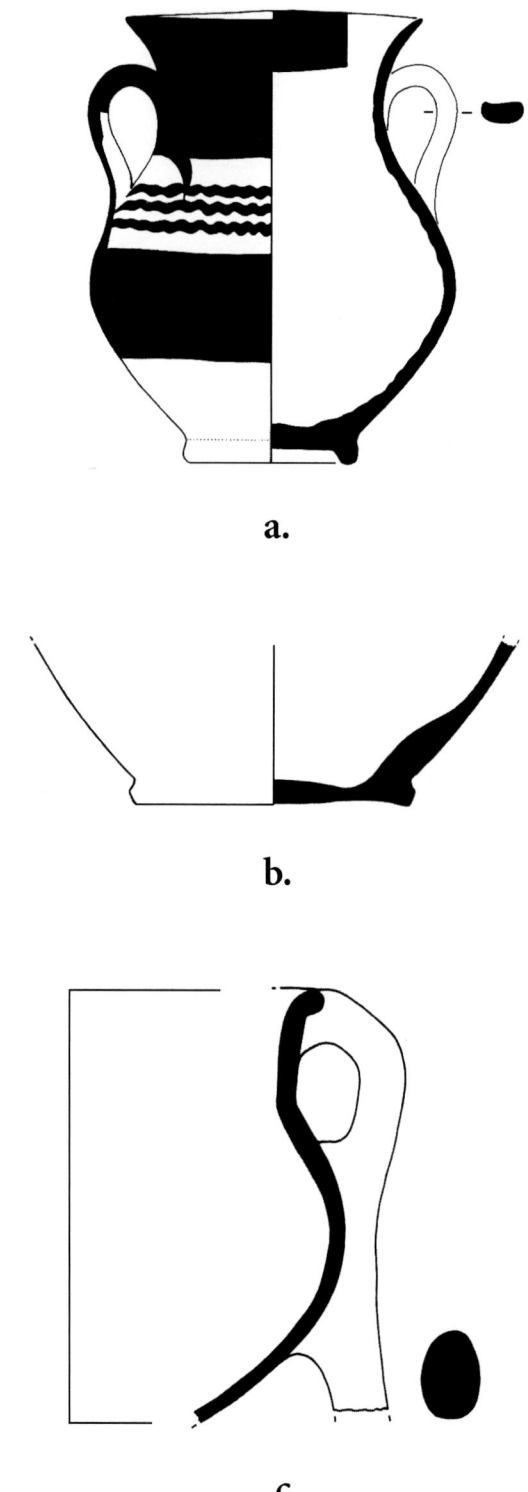

a.

b.

c.

FIGURE 155. Tomb 99. (*a*) **T99-1**. (*b*) **T99-2**. (*c*) **T99-3**.

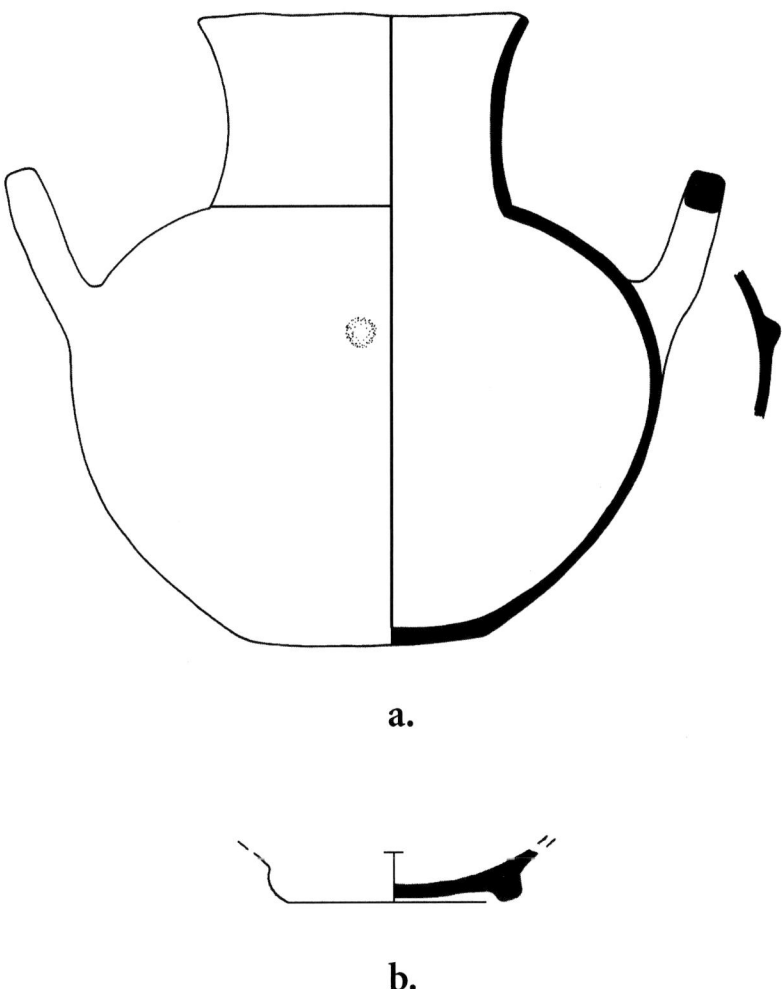

a.

b.

FIGURE 156. Tomb 100. (*a*) **T100-1.** (*b*) **T100-2.**

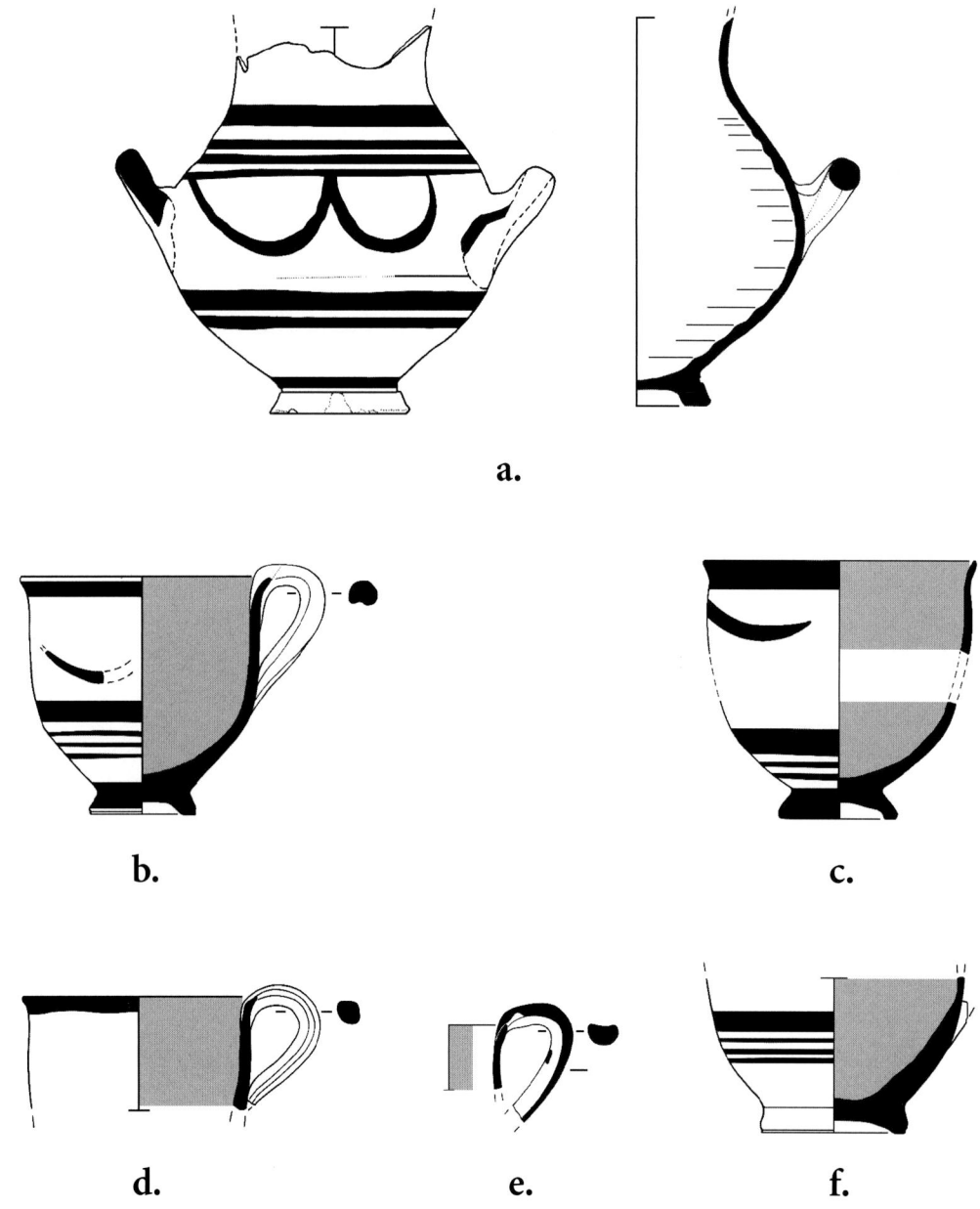

FIGURE 157 (on facing page). Tomb 101. (*a*) **T101-1**. (*b*) **T101-2**. (*c*) **T101-3**. (*d*) **T101-4**. (*e*) **T101-5**. (*f*) **T101-6**.

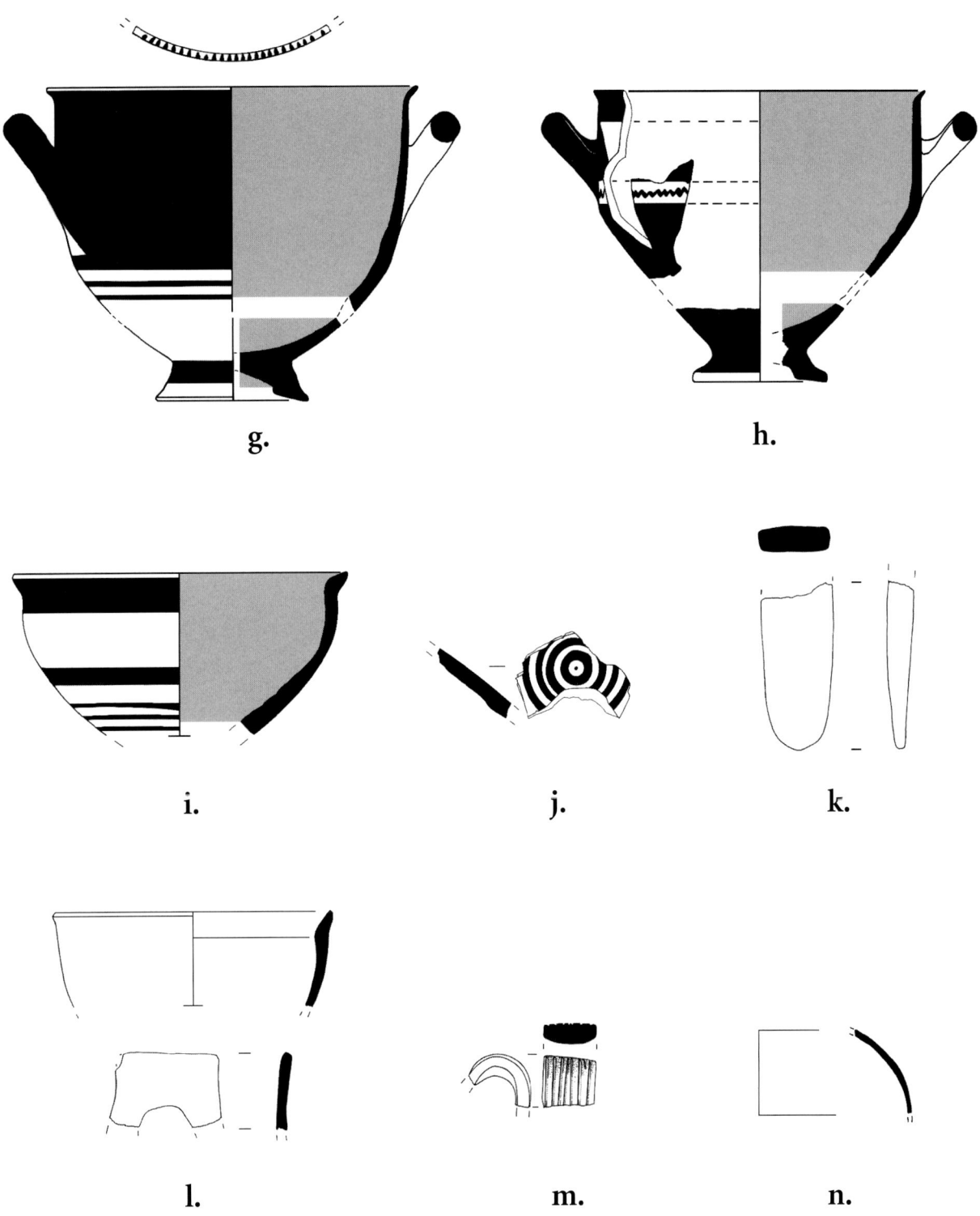

FIGURE 157 (continued). Tomb 101. (g) **T101-7**. (h) **T101-8**. (i) **T101-9**. (j) **T101-10**. (k) **T101-11**. (l) **T101-12**. (m) **T101-13**. (n) **T101-14**.

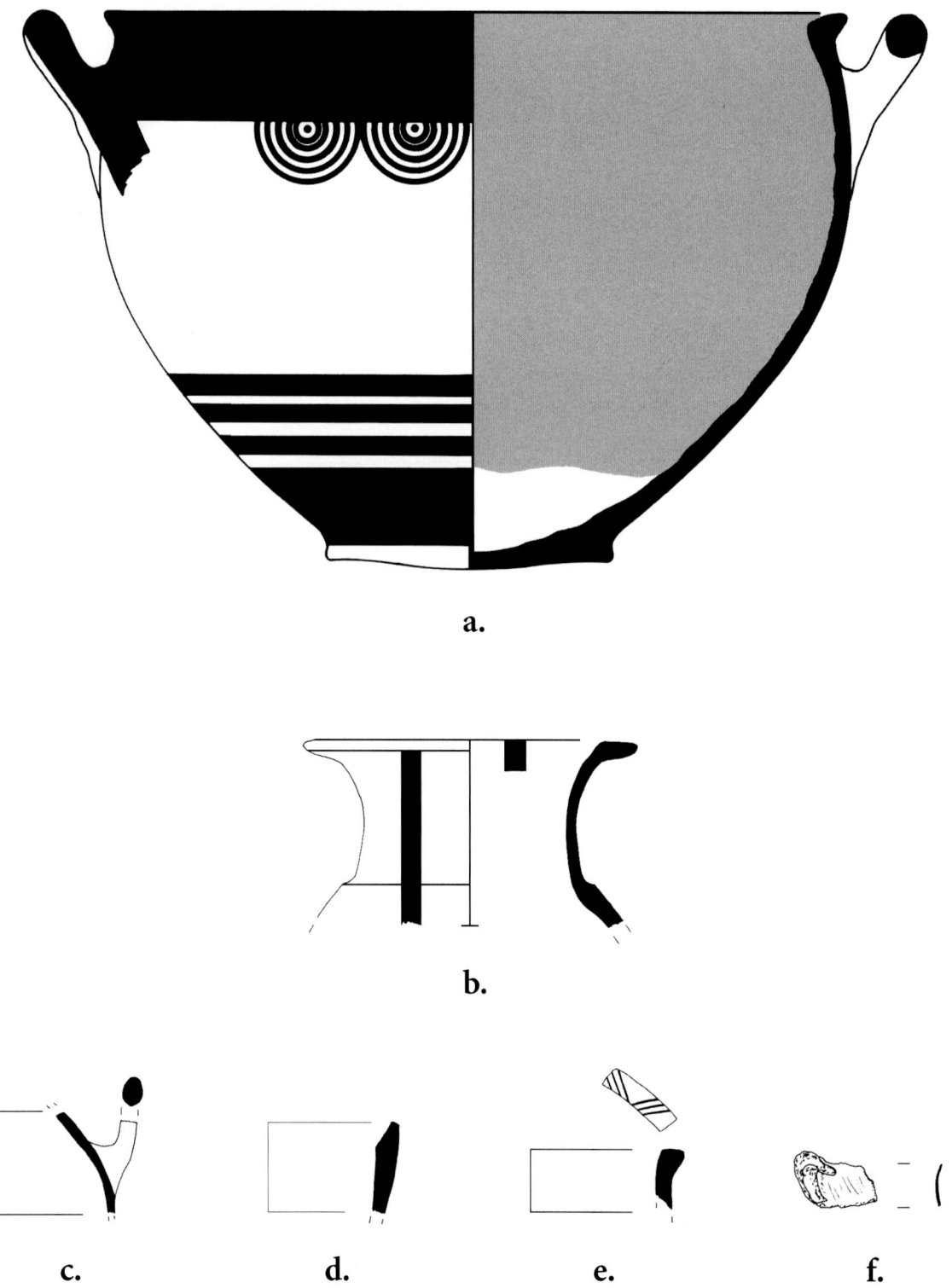

a.

b.

c.   d.   e.   f.

FIGURE 158. Tomb 102. (*a*) **T102-1**. (*b*) **T102-2**. (*c*) **T102-3**. (*d*) **T102-4**. (*e*) **T102-5**. (*f*) **T102-7**.

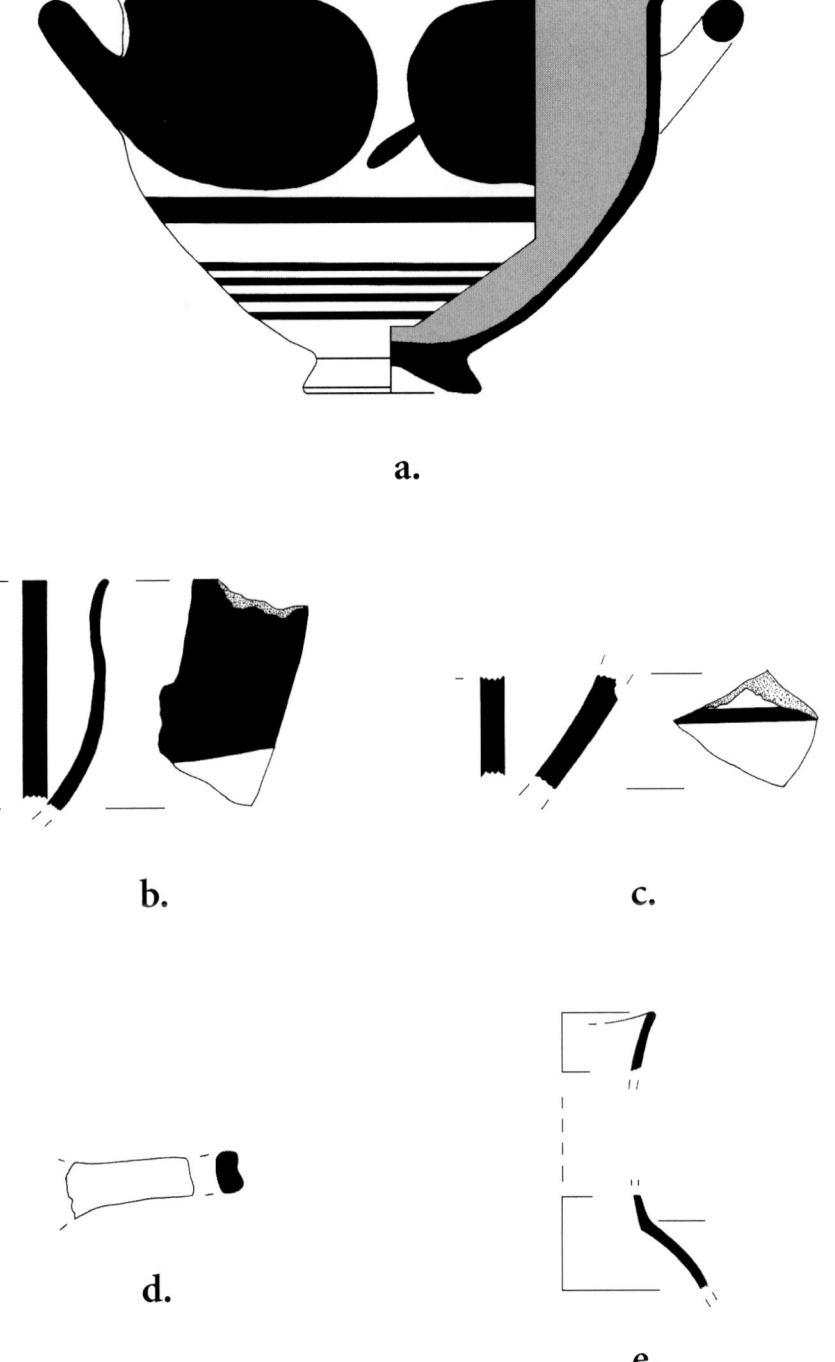

FIGURE 159. Tomb 103. (*a*) **T103-1**. (*b*) **T103-2**. (*c*) **T103-3**. (*d*) **T103-4**. (*e*) **T103-5**.

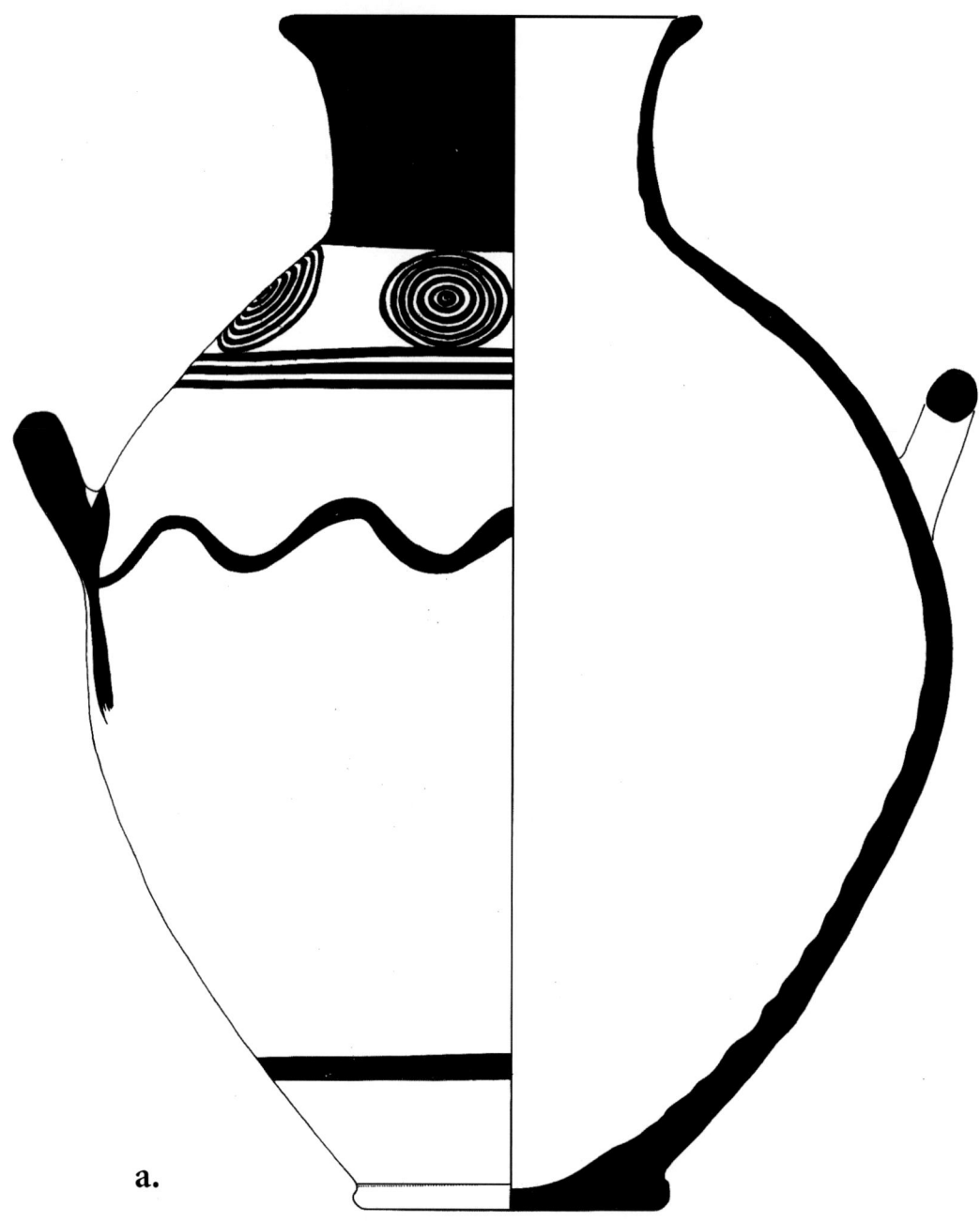

FIGURE 160 (on pages 858–862). Tomb 104. (*a*) **T104-1**.

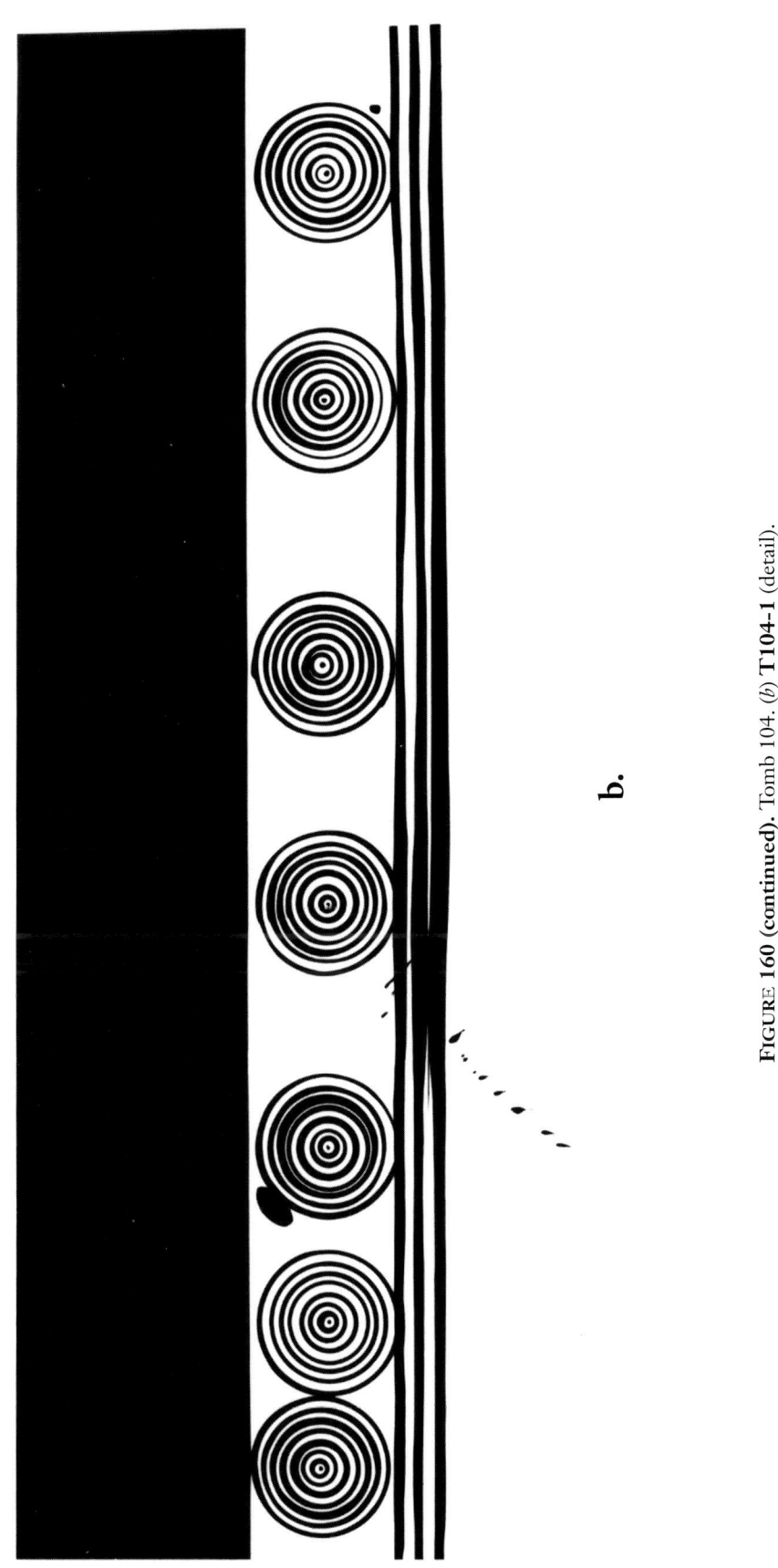

FIGURE 160 (continued). Tomb 104. (b) T104-1 (detail).

b.

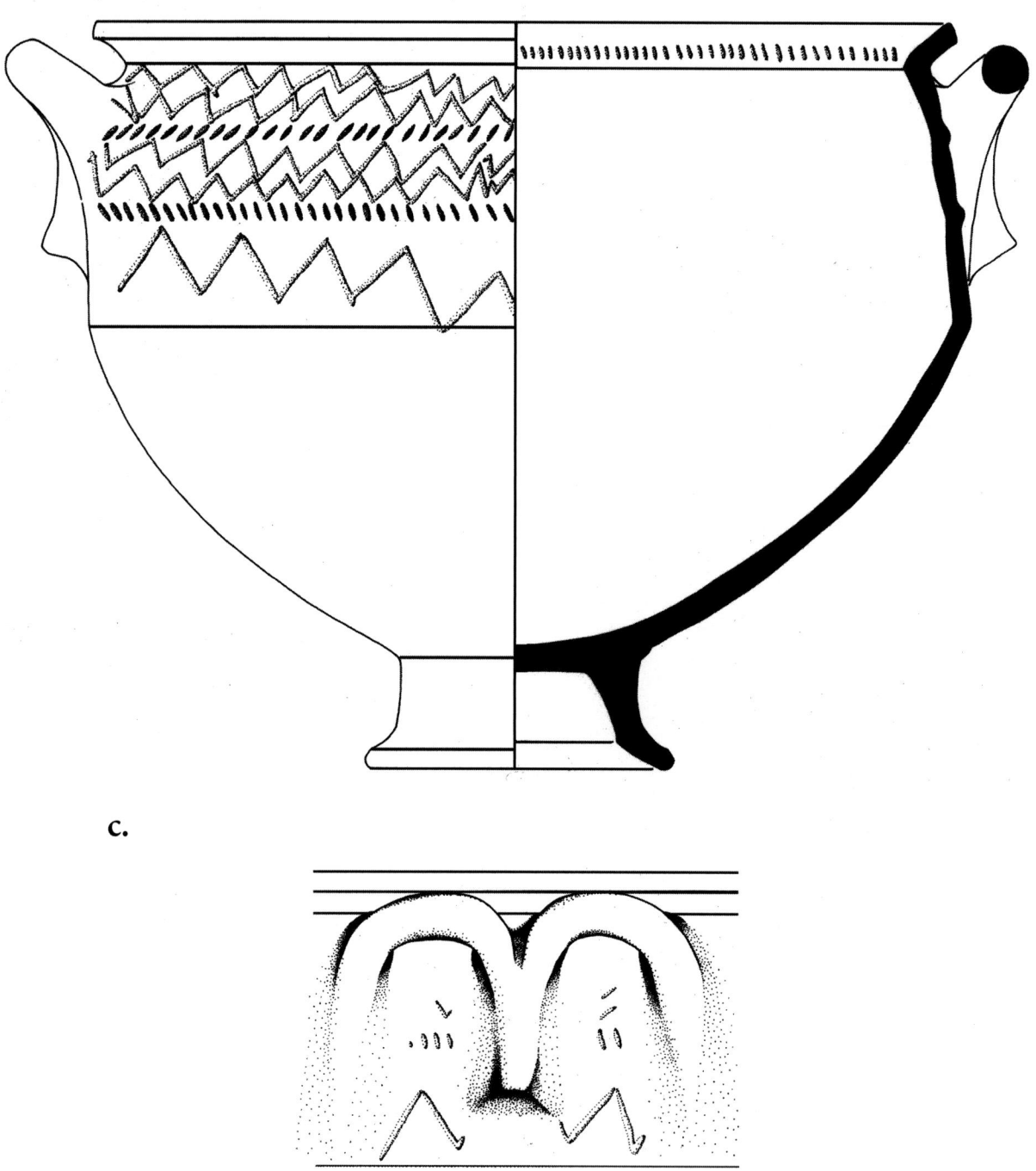

c.

FIGURE 160 (continued). Tomb 104. (*c*) **T104-2**.

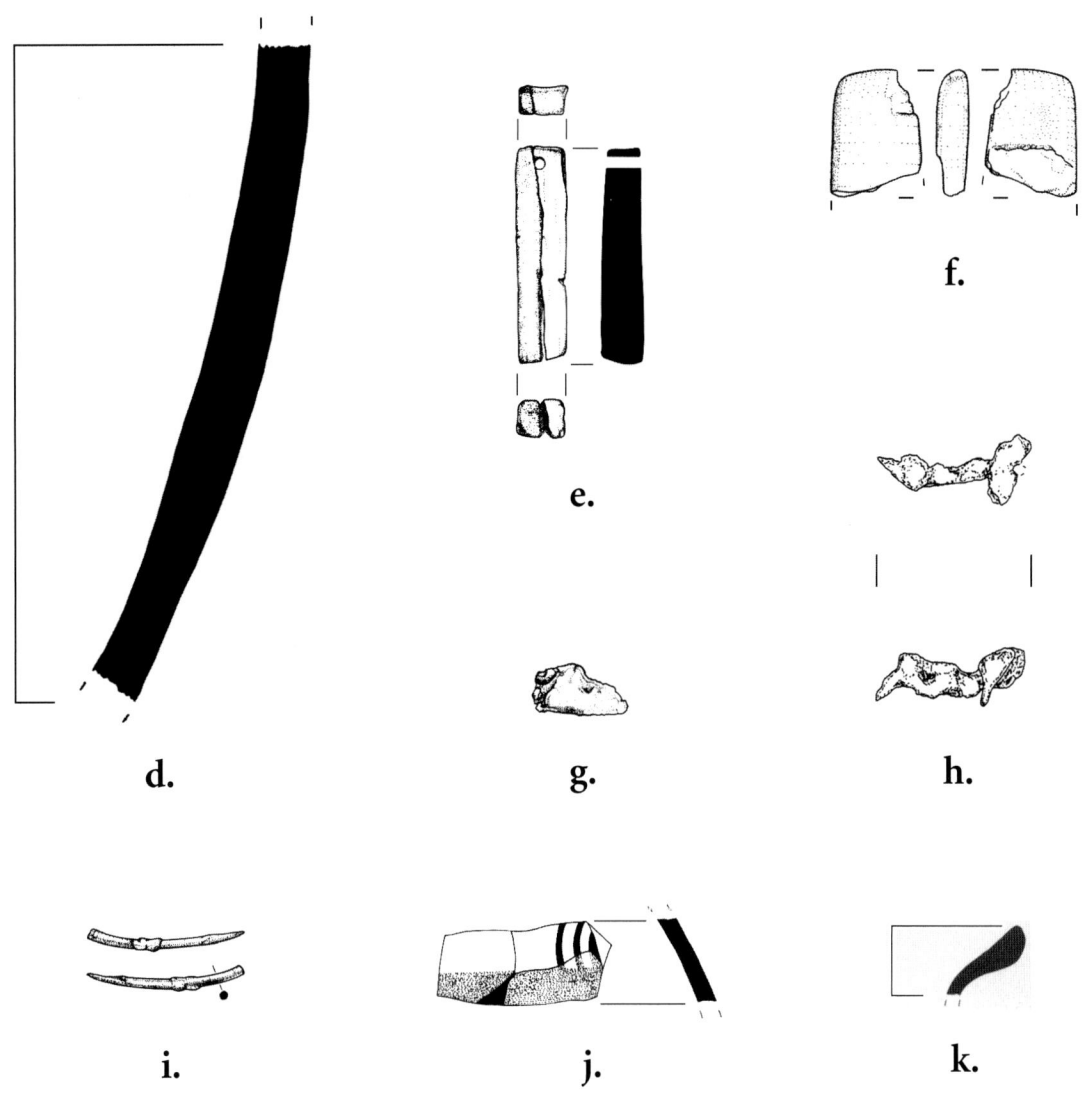

FIGURE 160 (continued). Tomb 104. (*d*) **T104-3**. (*e*) **T104-4**. (*f*) **T104-5**. (*g*) **T104-6**. (*h*) **T104-7**. (*i*) **T104-8**. (*j*) **T104-9**. (*k*) **T104-10**.

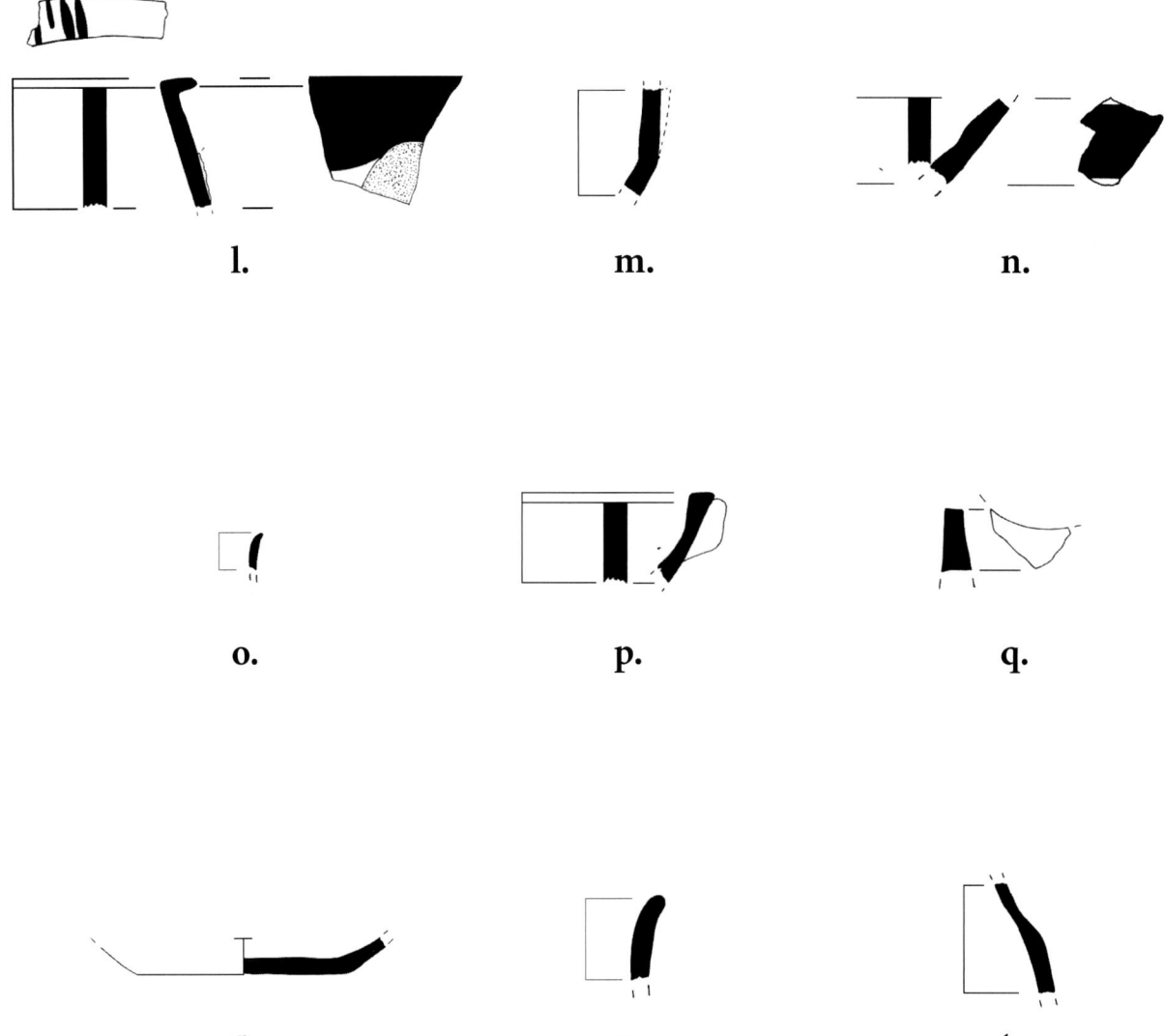

FIGURE 160 (continued). Tomb 104. (*l*) **T104-11**. (*m*) **T104-12**. (*n*) **T104-13**. (*o*) **T104-14**. (*p*) **T104-15**. (*q*) **T104-16**. (*r*) **T104-17**. (*s*) **T104-18**. (*t*) **T104-19**.

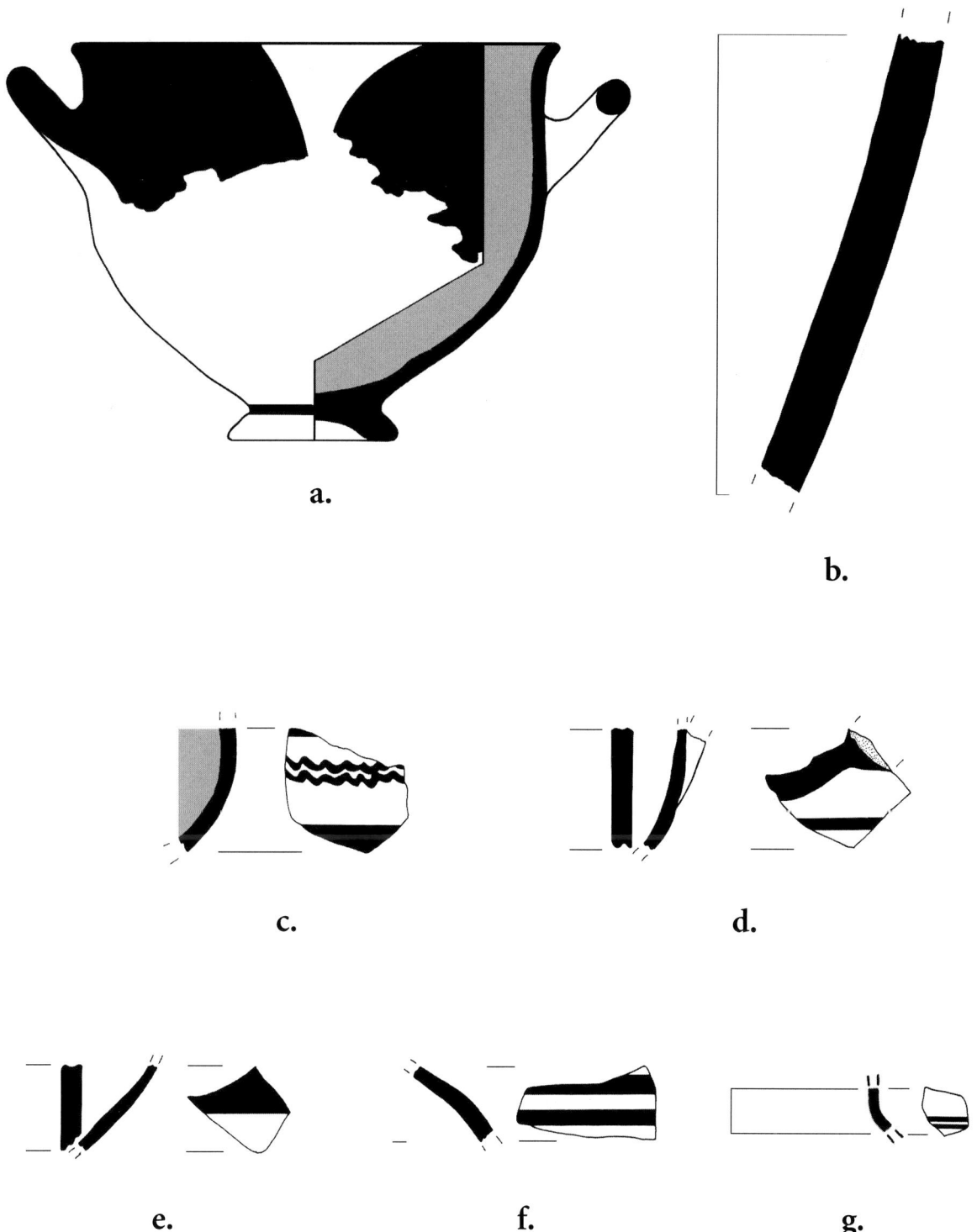

FIGURE 161. Tomb 105. (*a*) **T105-1**. (*b*) **T105-2**. (*c*) **T105-3**. (*d*) **T105-4**. (*e*) **T105-5**. (*f*) **T105-6**. (*g*) **T105-7**.

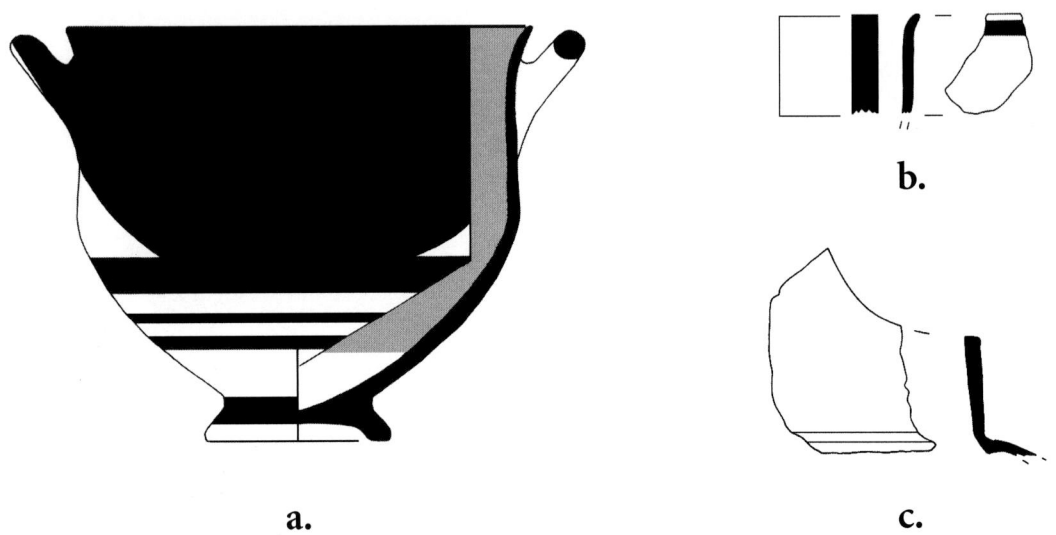

FIGURE 162. Tomb 106. (*a*) **T106-1**. (*b*) **T106-2**. (*c*) **T106-3**.

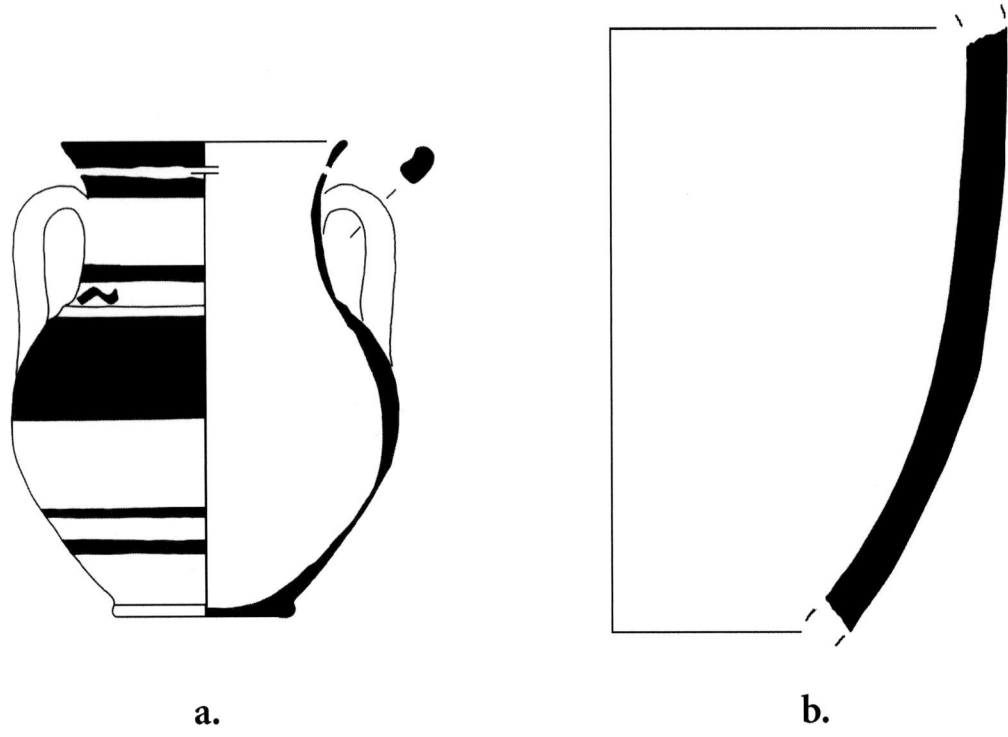

FIGURE 163. Tomb 107. (*a*) **T107-1**. (*b*) **T107-2**.

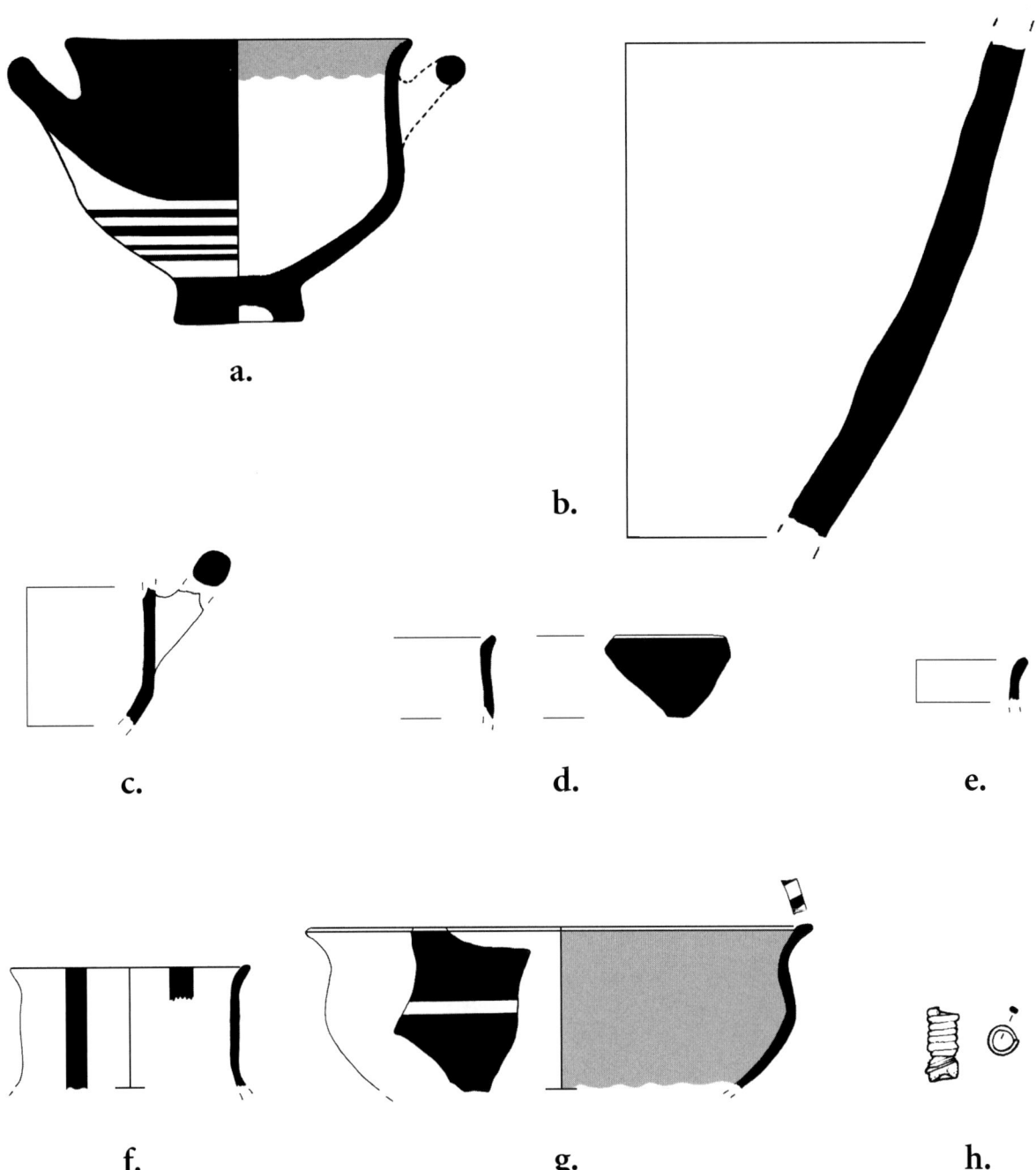

FIGURE 164. Tomb 108. (*a*) **T108-1**. (*b*) **T108-2**. (*c*) **T108-3**. (*d*) **T108-4**. (*e*) **T108-5**. (*f*) **T108-6**. (*g*) **T108-7**. (*h*) **T108-8**.

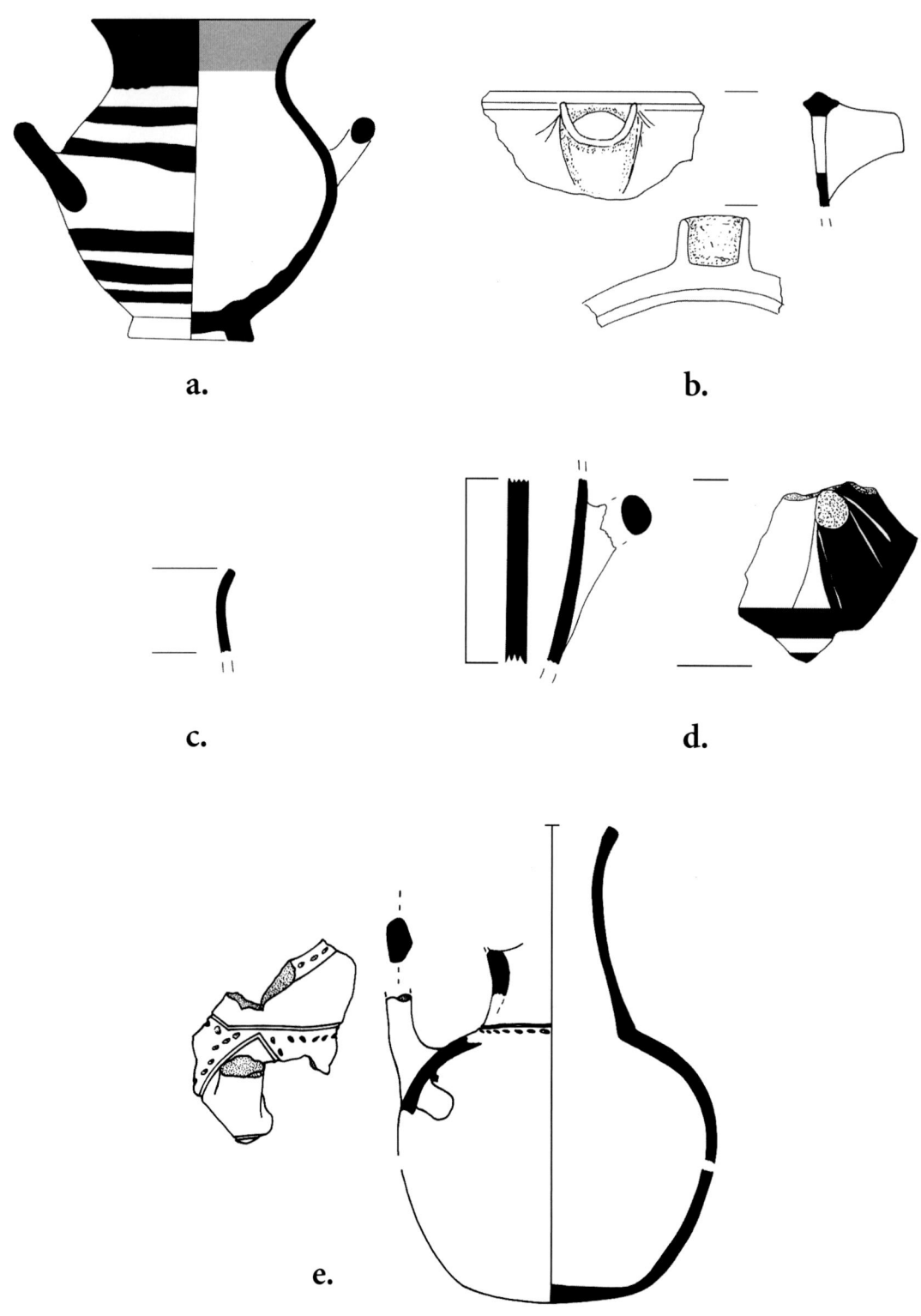

FIGURE 165. Tomb 109. (*a*) **T109-1**. (*b*) **T109-2**. (*c*) **T109-3**. (*d*) **T109-4**. (*e*) **T109-5**.

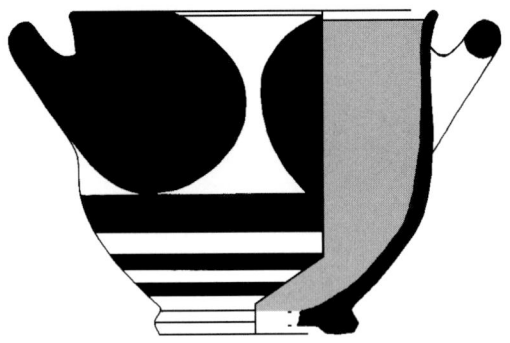

FIGURE 166. Tomb 110. **T110-1.**

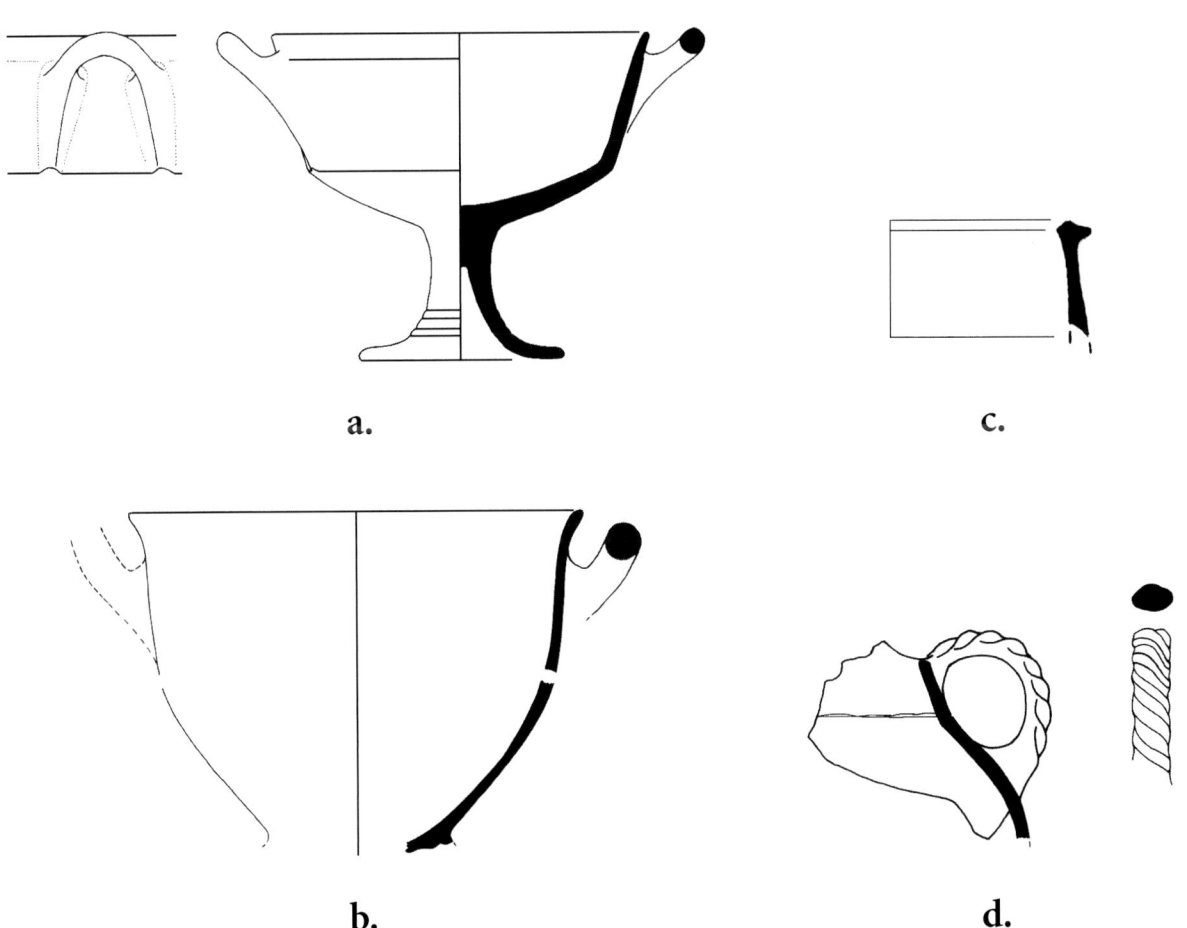

a.

b.

c.

d.

FIGURE 167. Tomb 111. (*a*) **T111-1.** (*b*) **T111-2.** (*c*) **T111-3.** (*d*) **T111-4.**

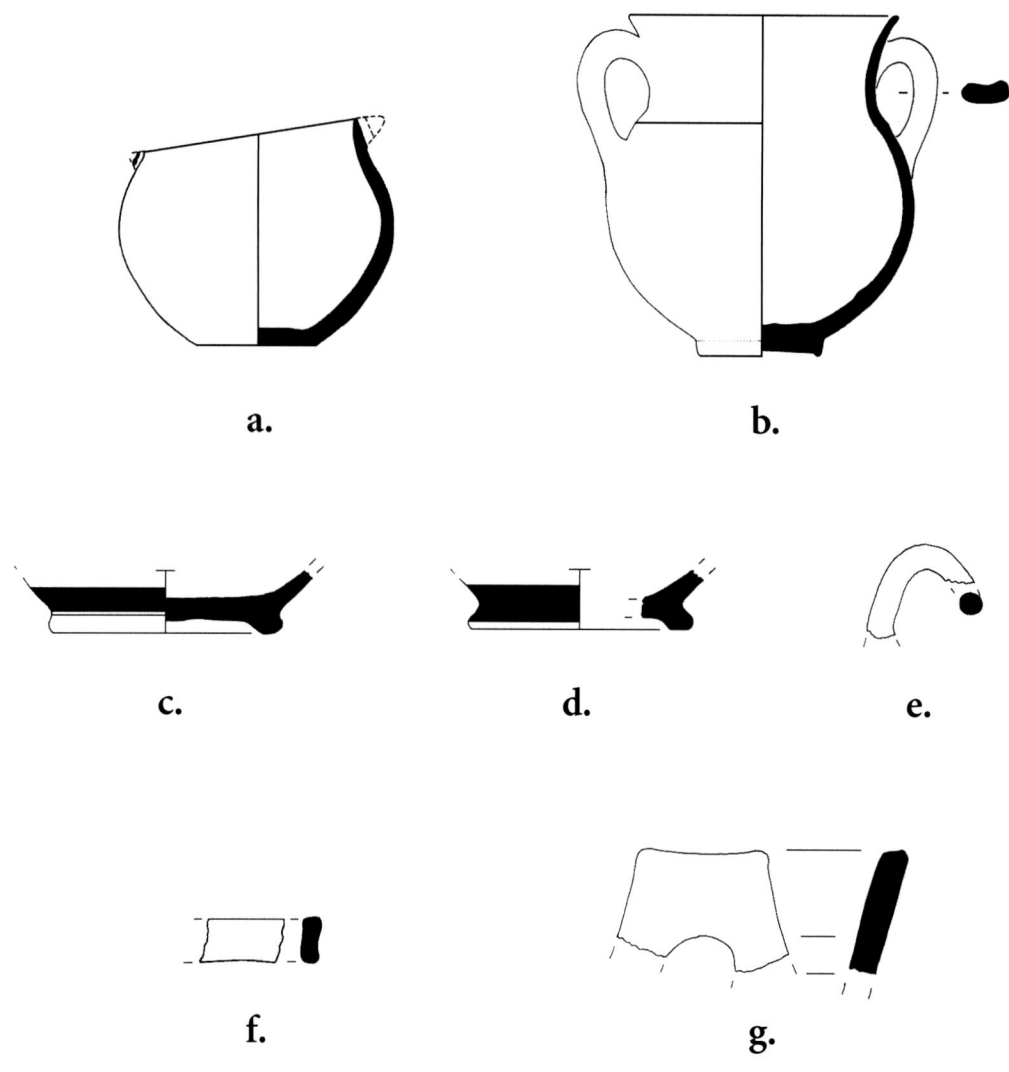

FIGURE 168. Tomb 112. (*a*) **T112-1**. (*b*) **T112-2**. (*c*) **T112-3**. (*d*) **T112-4**. (*e*) **T112-5**. (*f*) **T112-6**. (*g*) **T112-7**.

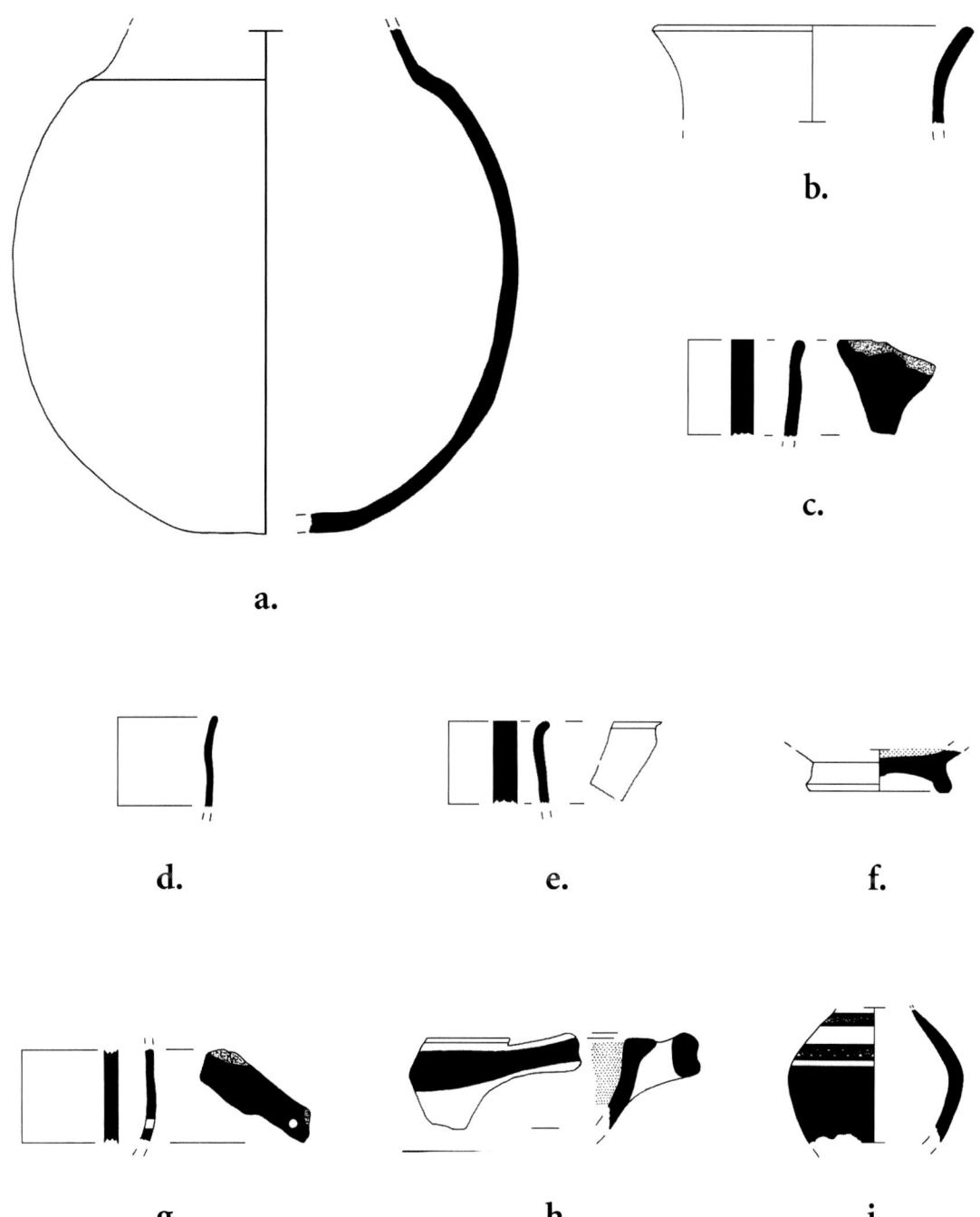

FIGURE 169 (on following page). Tomb 113. (*a*) **T113-1.** (*b*) **T113-2.** (*c*) **T113-3.** (*d*) **T113-4.** (*e*) **T113-5.** (*f*) **T113-6.** (*g*) **T113-7.** (*h*) **T113-8.** (*i*) **T113-9.**

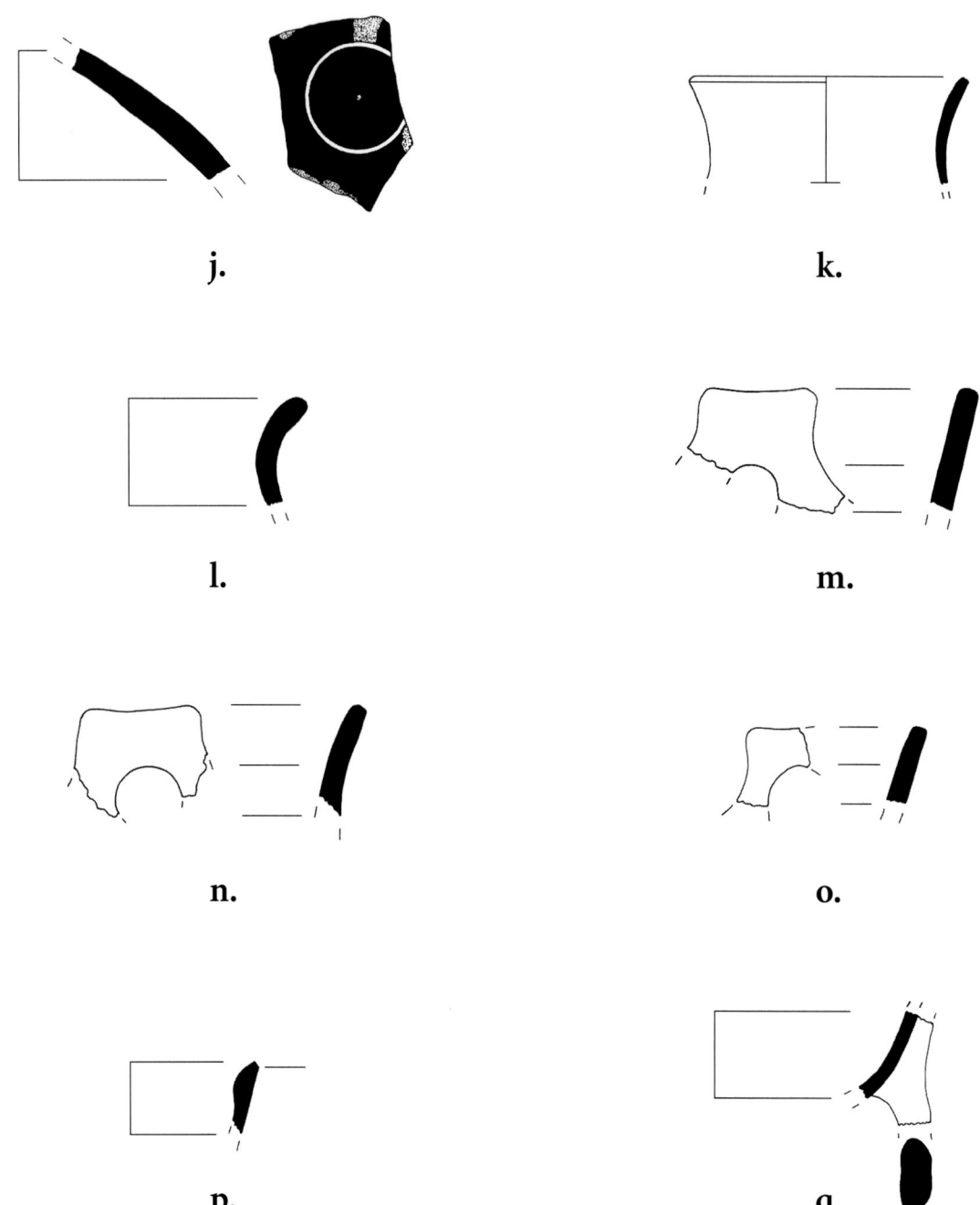

FIGURE 169 (continued). Tomb 113. (*j*) **T113-10.** (*k*) **T113-11.** (*l*) **T113-12.** (*m*) **T113-13.** (*n*) **T113-14.** (*o*) **T113-15.** (*p*) **T113-16.** (*q*) **T113-17.**

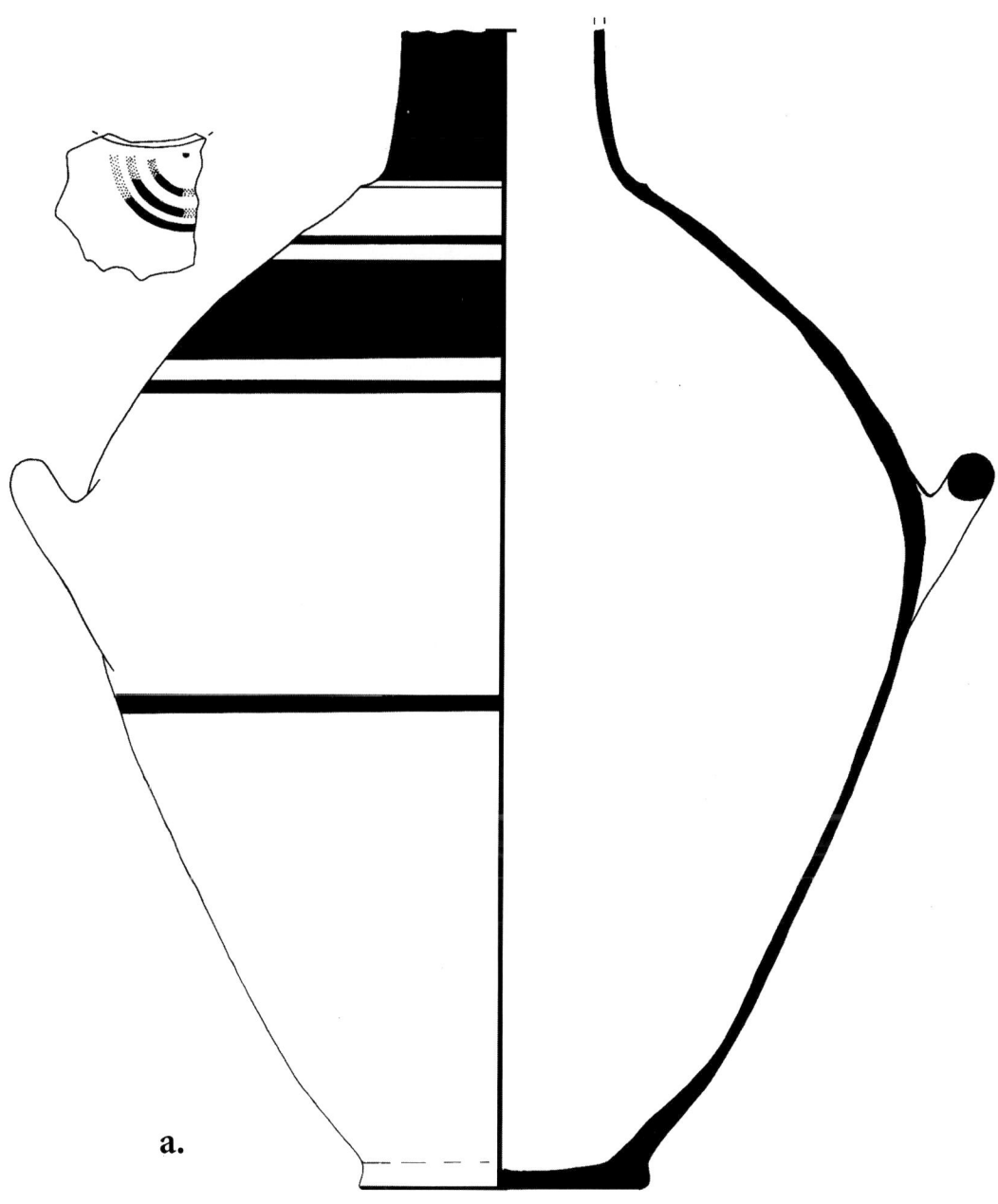

FIGURE 170 (on following page). Tomb 114. (*a*) **T114-1**.

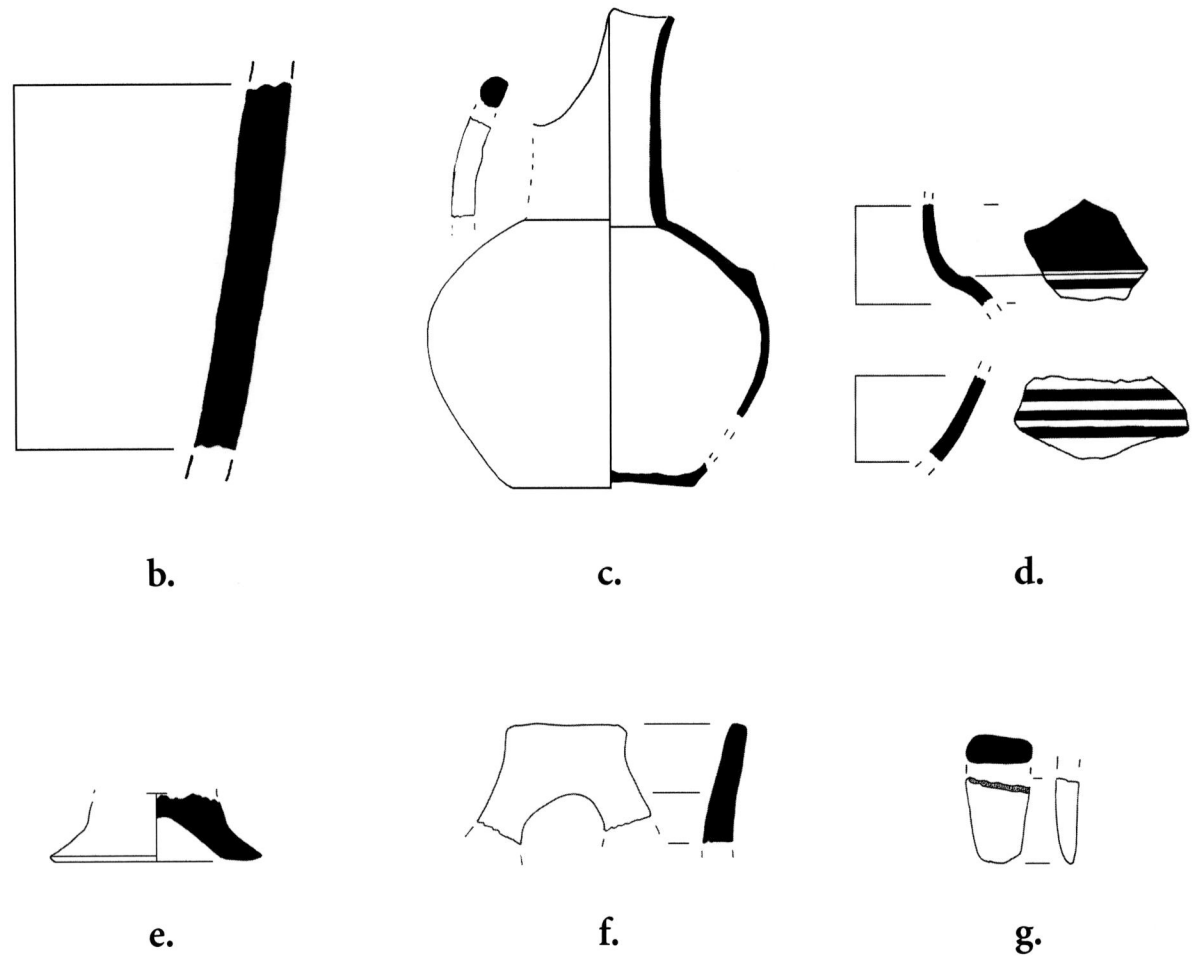

b. c. d.

e. f. g.

FIGURE 170 (continued). Tomb 114. (*b*) **T114-2**. (*c*) **T114-3**. (*d*) **T114-4**. (*e*) **T114-5**. (*f*) **T114-6**. (*g*) **T114-7**.

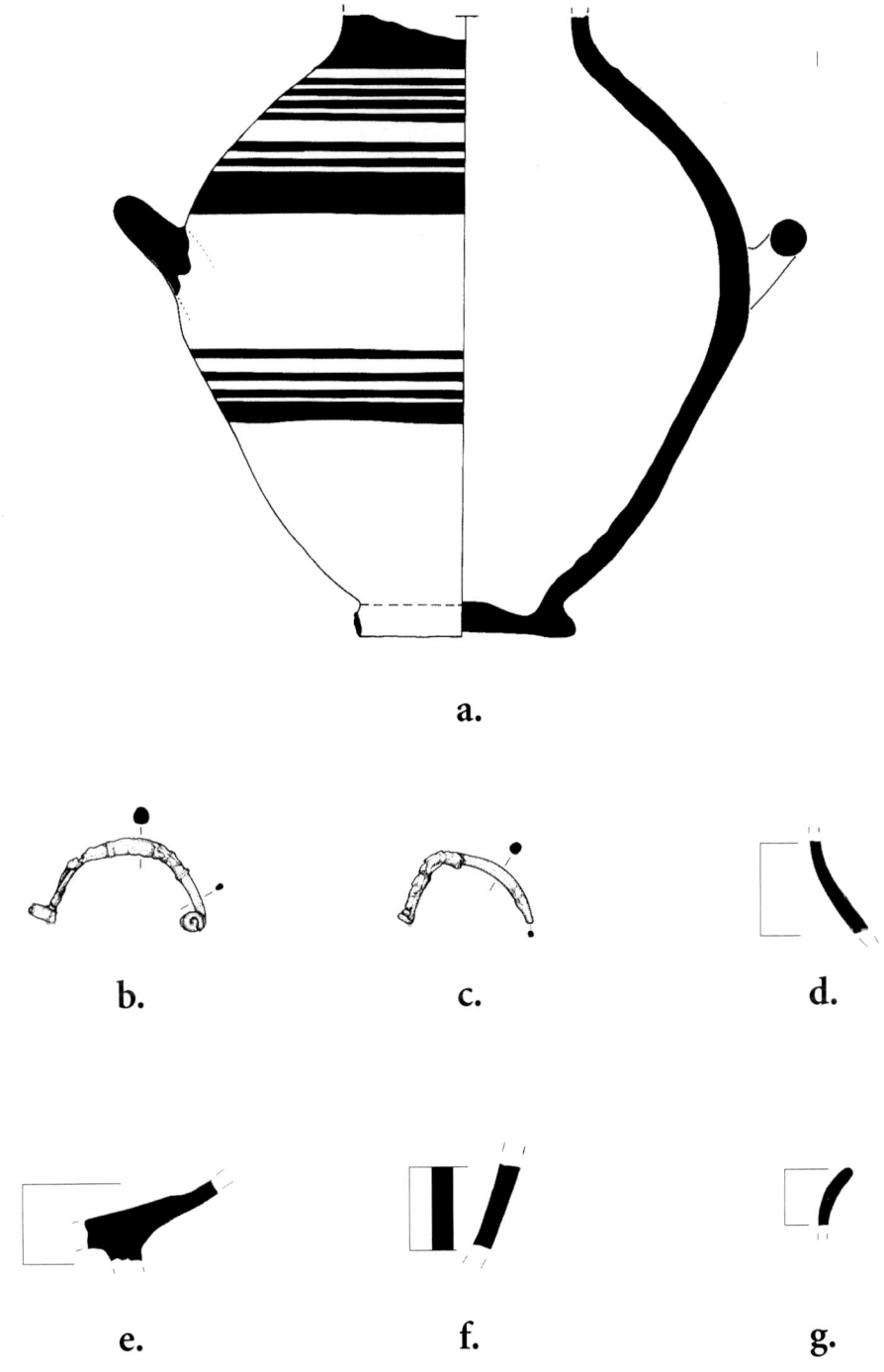

a.

b.   **c.**   **d.**

e.   **f.**   **g.**

FIGURE 171 (on following page). Tomb 115. (*a*) **T115-1**. (*b*) **T115-2**. (*c*) **T115-3**. (*d*) **T115-5**. (*e*) **T115-6**. (*f*) **T115-7**. (*g*) **T115-8**.

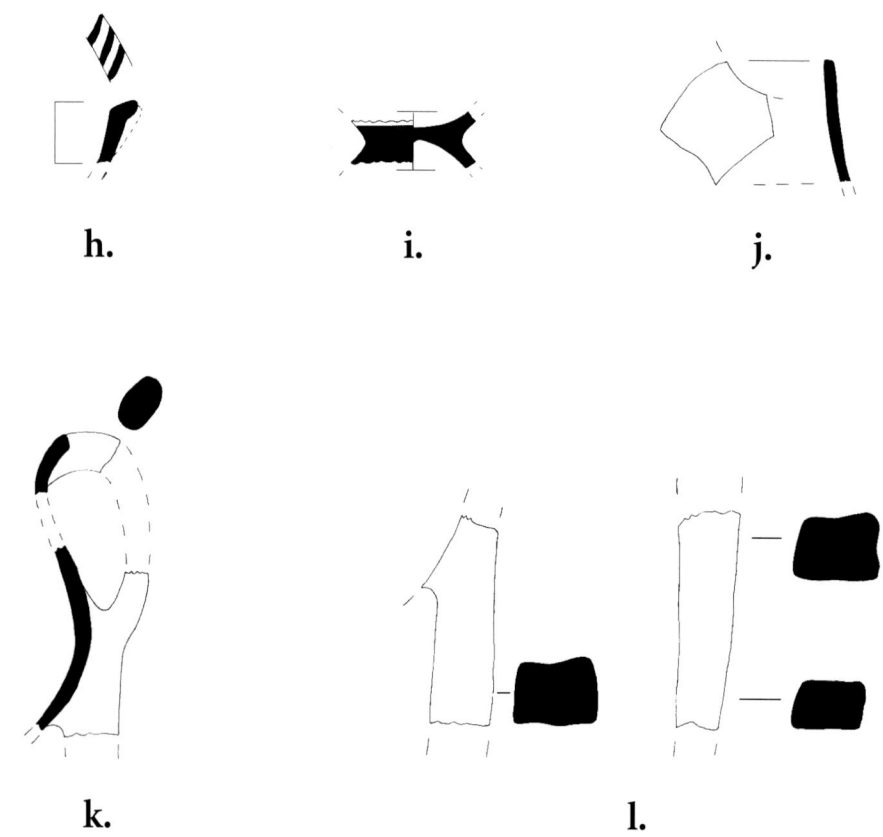

FIGURE 171 (continued). Tomb 115. (*h*) **T115-9.** (*i*) **T115-10.** (*j*) **T115-11.** (*k*) **T115-12.** (*l*) **T115-13.**

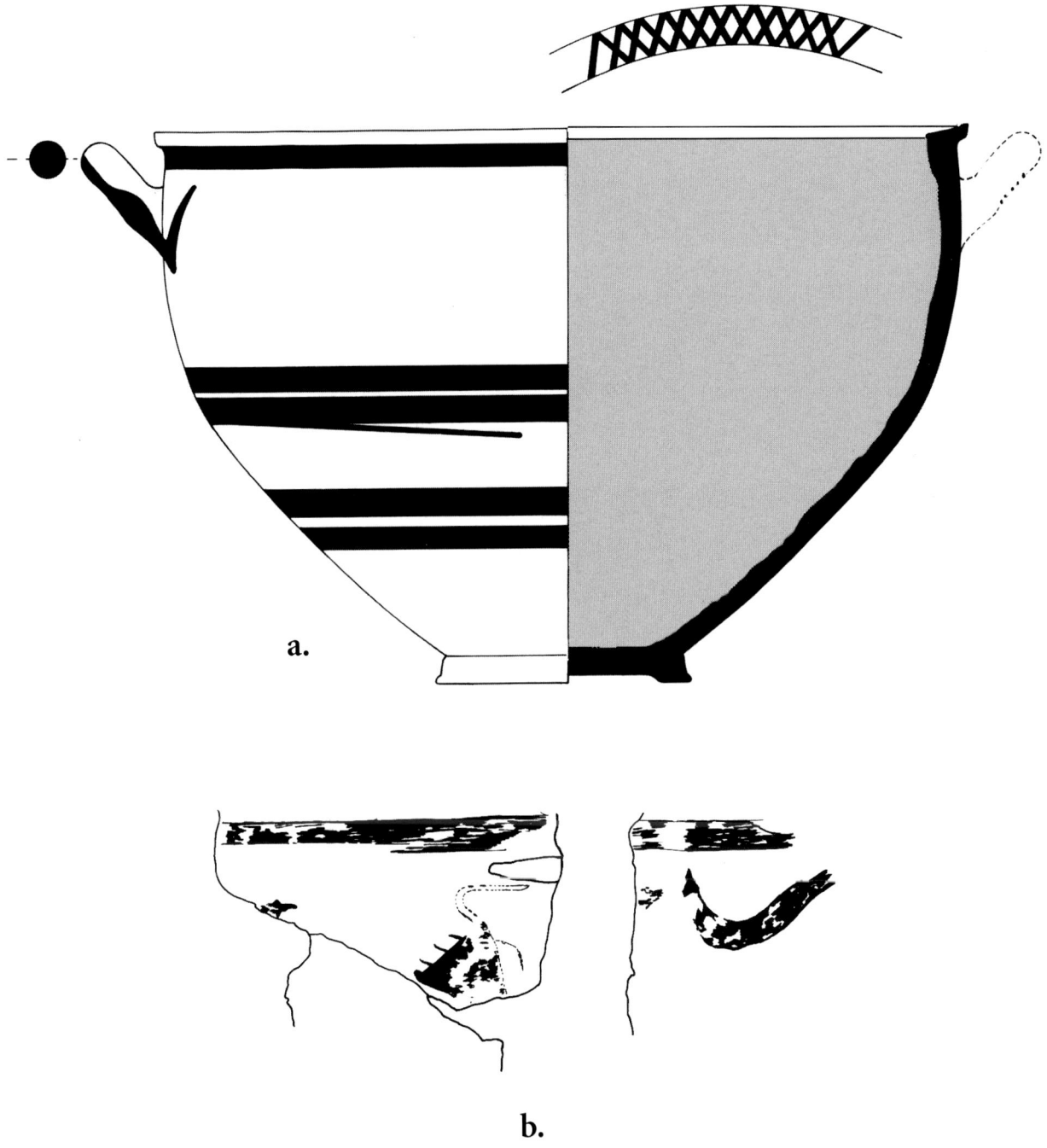

FIGURE 172 (on following page). Tomb 116. (*a*) **T116-1**. (*b*) **T116-1**. Painted decoration on upper body as preserved.

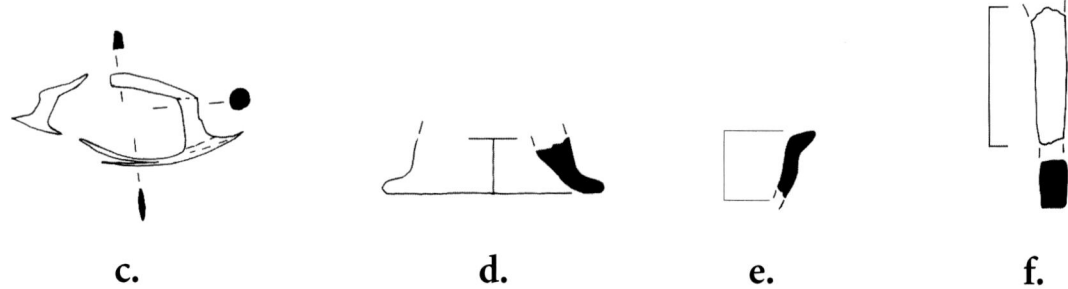

c.   **d.**   **e.**   **f.**

FIGURE 172 (continued). Tomb 116. (c) **T116-1**. Lead mending clamp. (d) **T116-2**. (e) **T116-3**. (f) **T116-4**.

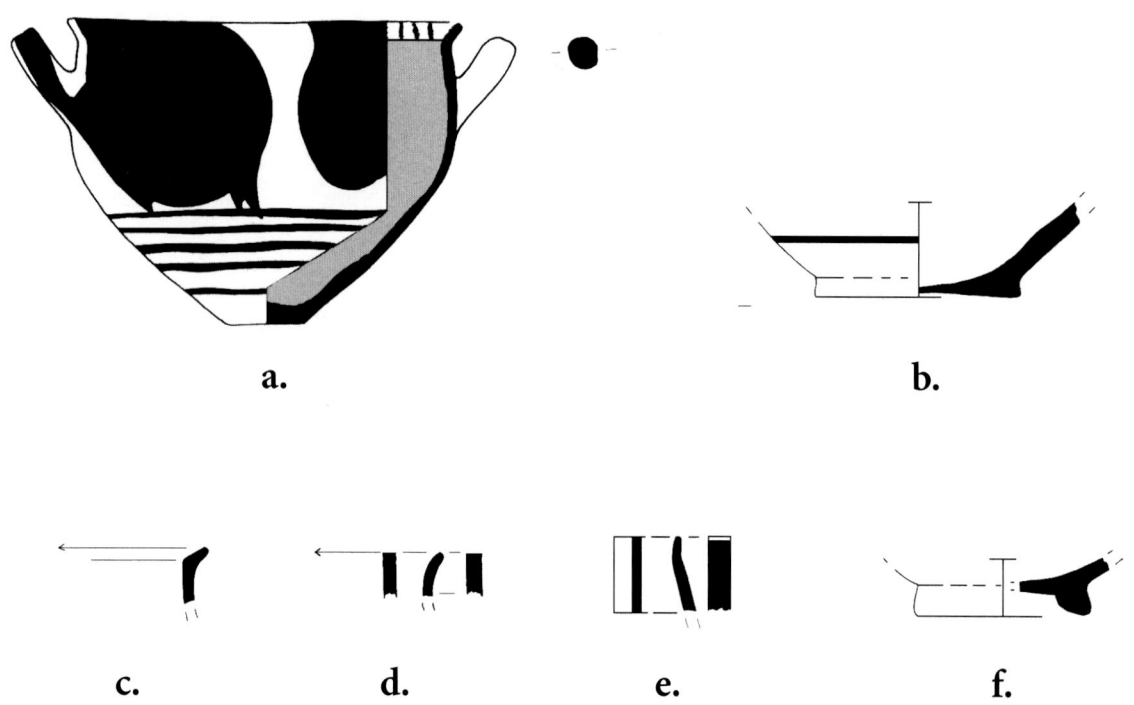

a.   **b.**

c.   **d.**   **e.**   **f.**

FIGURE 173 (on facing page). Tomb 117. (a) **T117-1**. (b) **T117-2**. (c) **T117-3**. (d) **T117-4**. (e) **T117-5**. (f) **T117-6**.

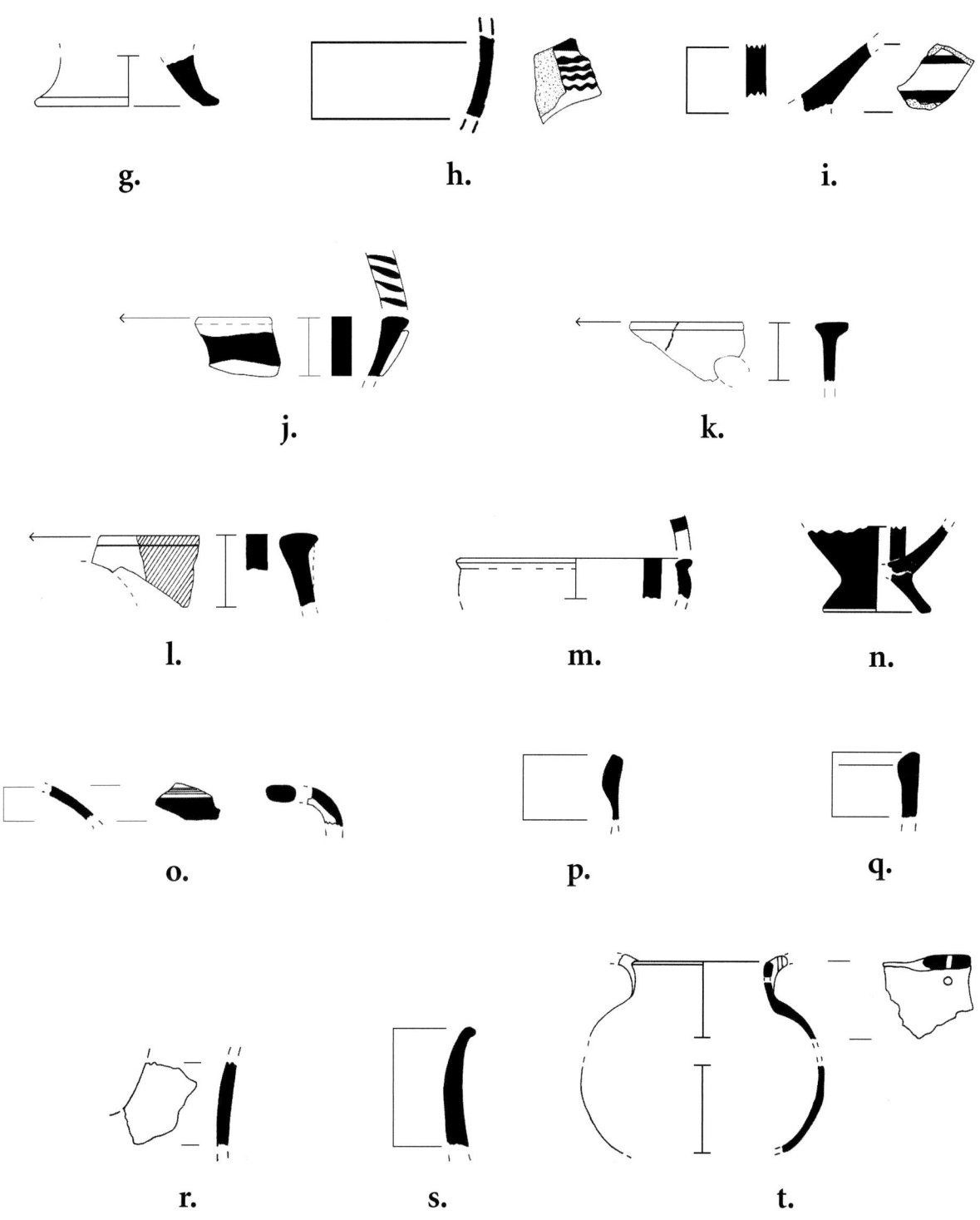

FIGURE 173 (continued). Tomb 117. (*g*) **T117-7**. (*h*) **T117-8**. (*i*) **T117-9**. (*j*) **T117-10**. (*k*) **T117-11**. (*l*) **T117-12**. (*m*) **T117-13**. (*n*) **T117-14**. (*o*) **T117-15**. (*p*) **T117-16**. (*q*) **T117-17**. (*r*) **T117-18**. (*s*) **T117-19**. (*t*) **T117-20**.

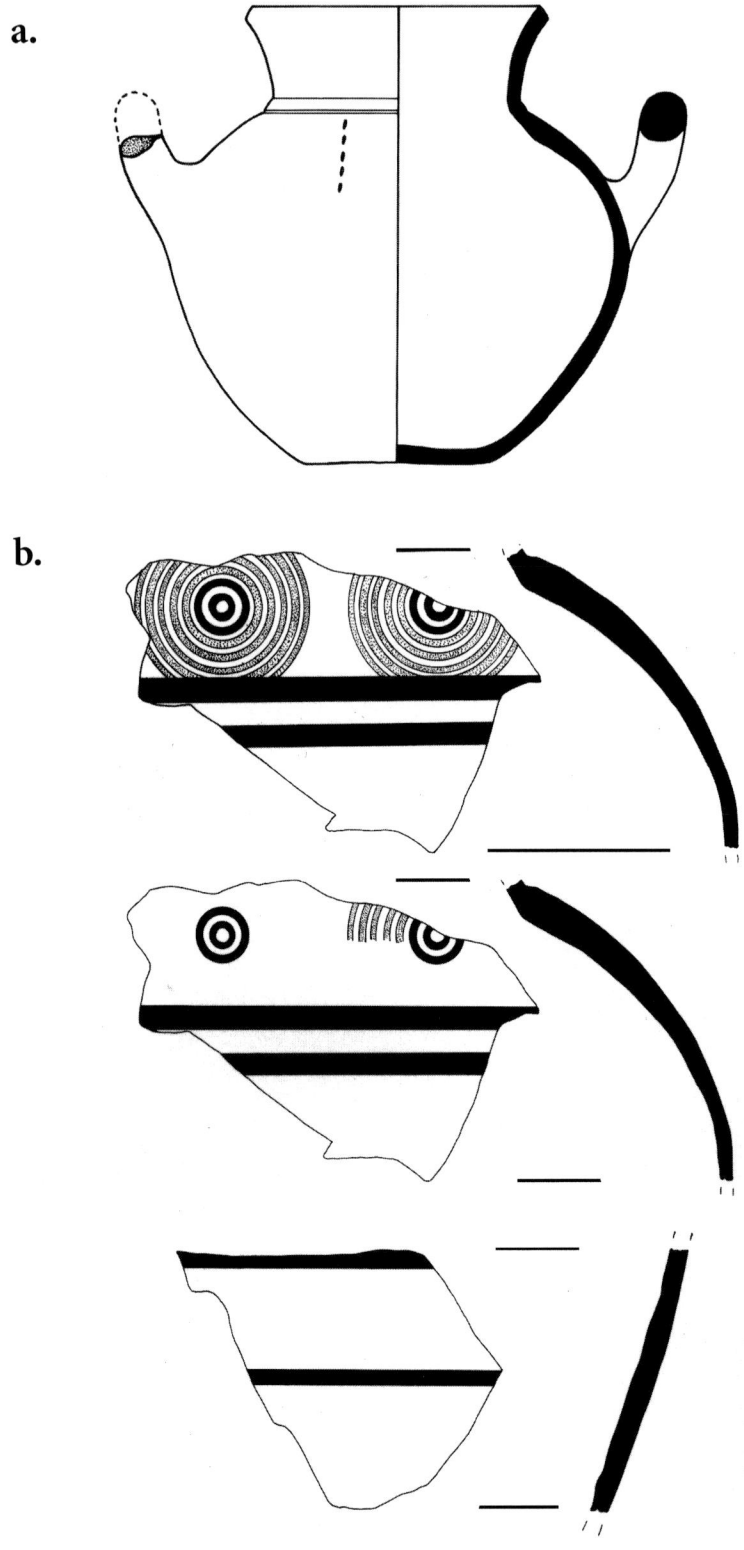

FIGURE 174 (on facing page). Tomb 118. (*a*) **T118-1**. (*b*) **T118-2**.

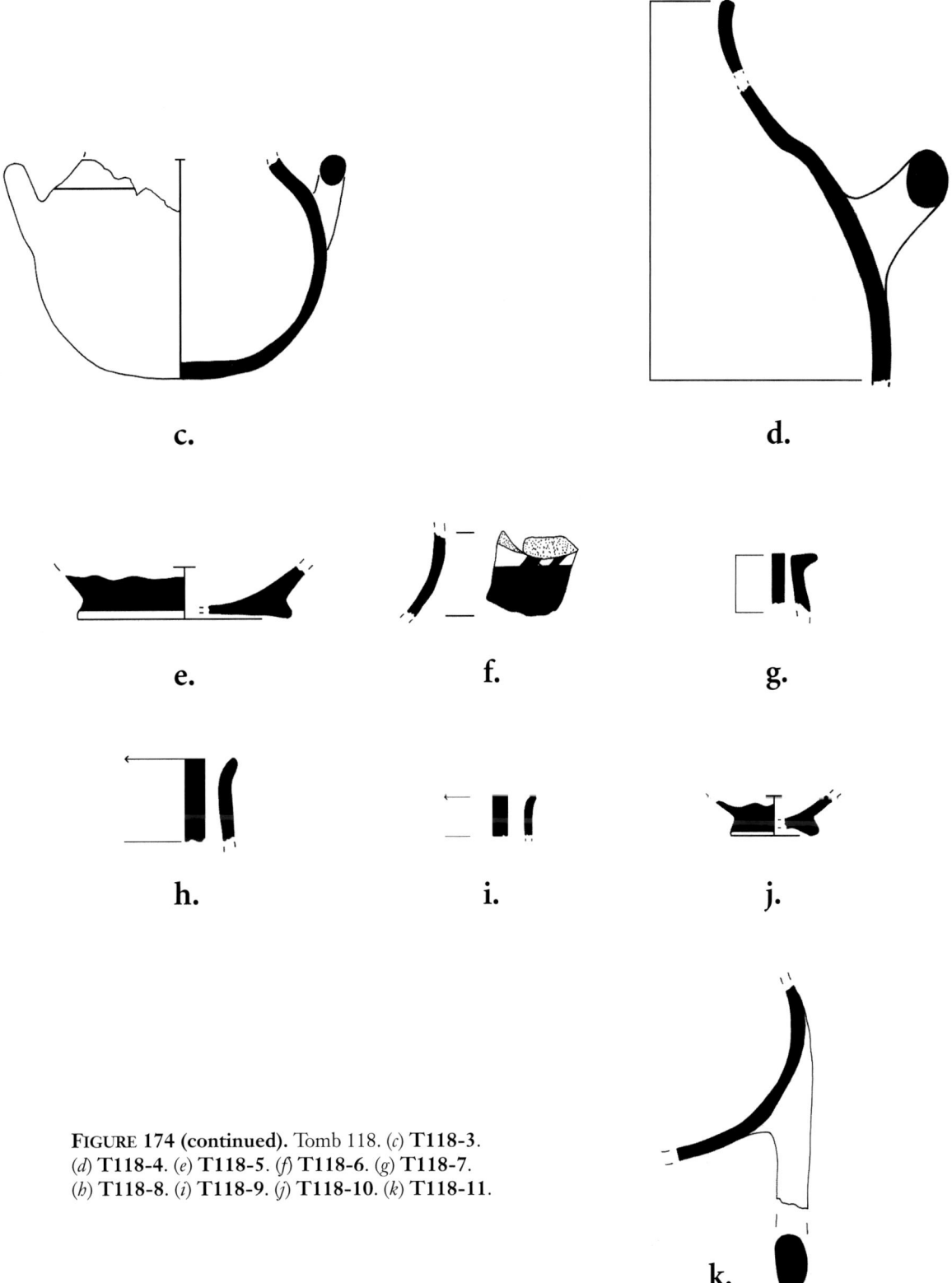

FIGURE 174 (continued). Tomb 118. (c) **T118-3.**
(d) **T118-4.** (e) **T118-5.** (f) **T118-6.** (g) **T118-7.**
(h) **T118-8.** (i) **T118-9.** (j) **T118-10.** (k) **T118-11.**

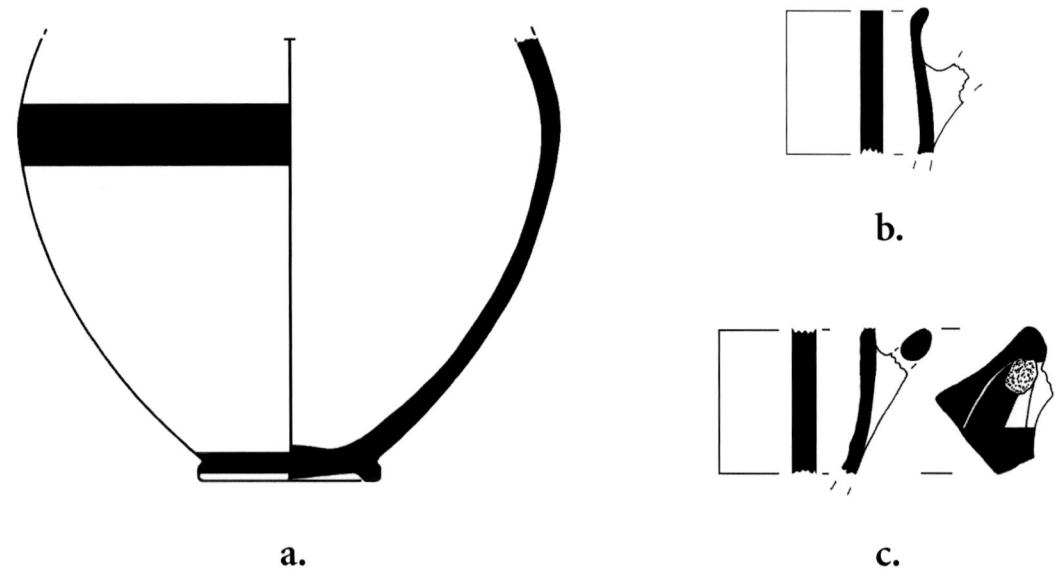

a. b. c.

FIGURE 175. Tomb 119. (*a*) **T119-1**. (*b*) **T119-2**. (*c*) **T119-3**.

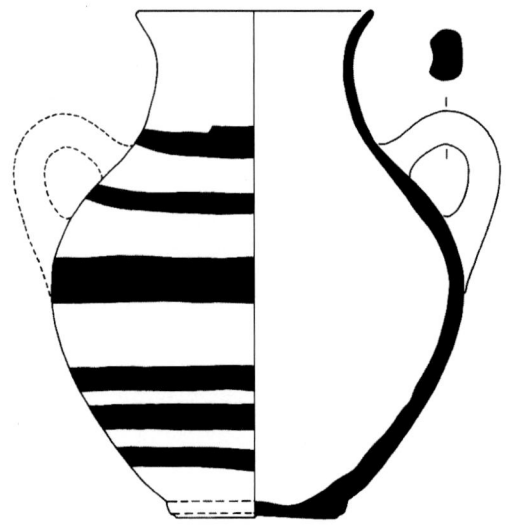

FIGURE 176. Tomb 120. **T120-1**.

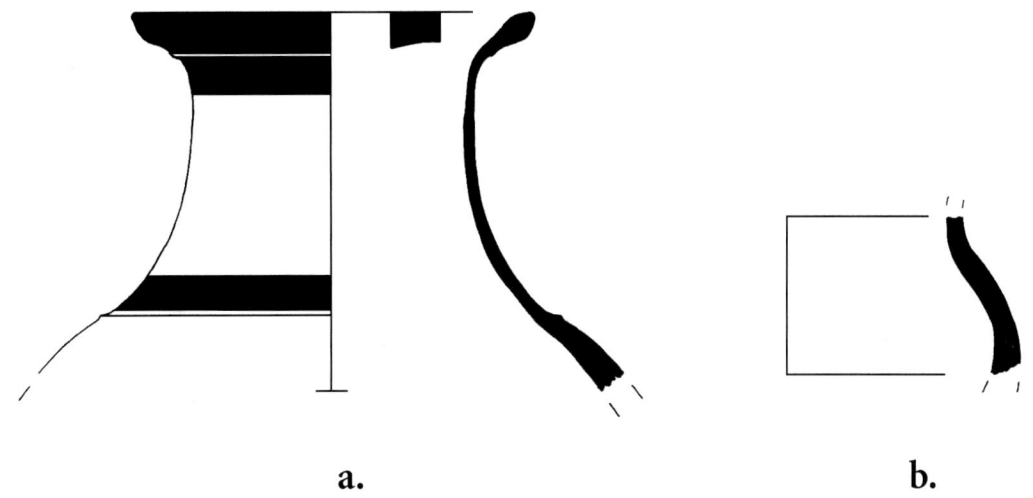

a.

b.

FIGURE 177. Tomb 121. (*a*) **T121-1**. (*b*) **T121-2**.

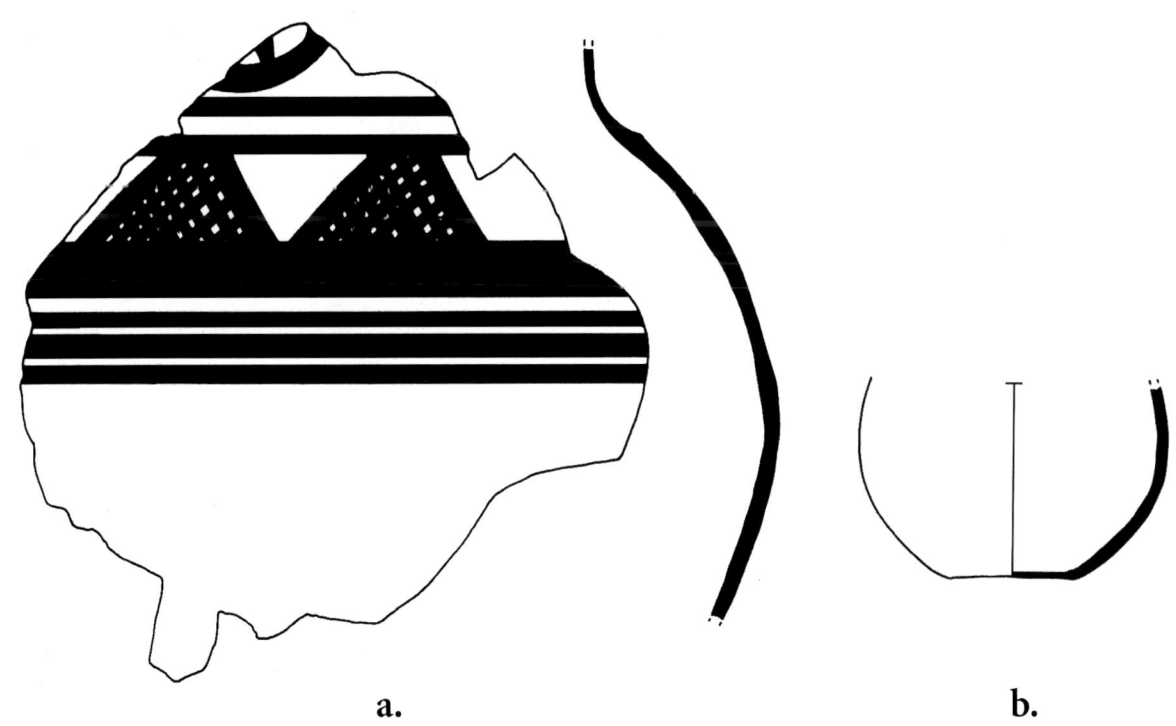

a.

b.

FIGURE 178. Tomb 122. (*a*) **T122-1**. (*b*) **T122-2**.

a.

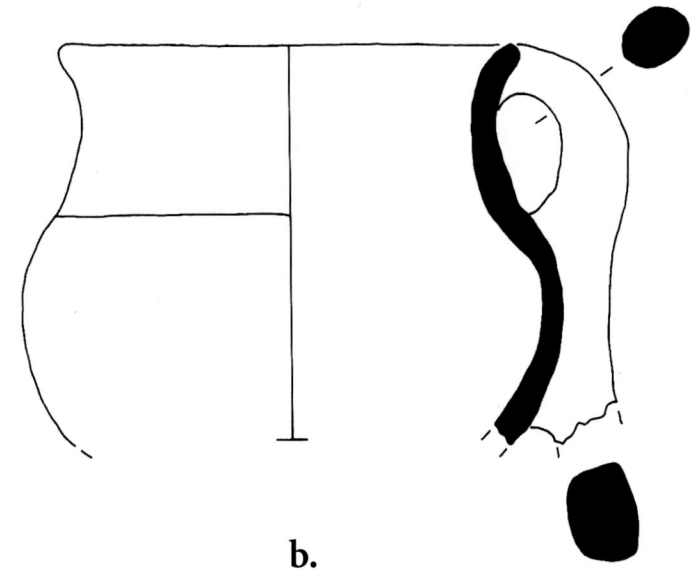

b.

FIGURE 179 (on facing page). Tomb 123. (*a*) **T123-1**. (*b*) **T123-2**.

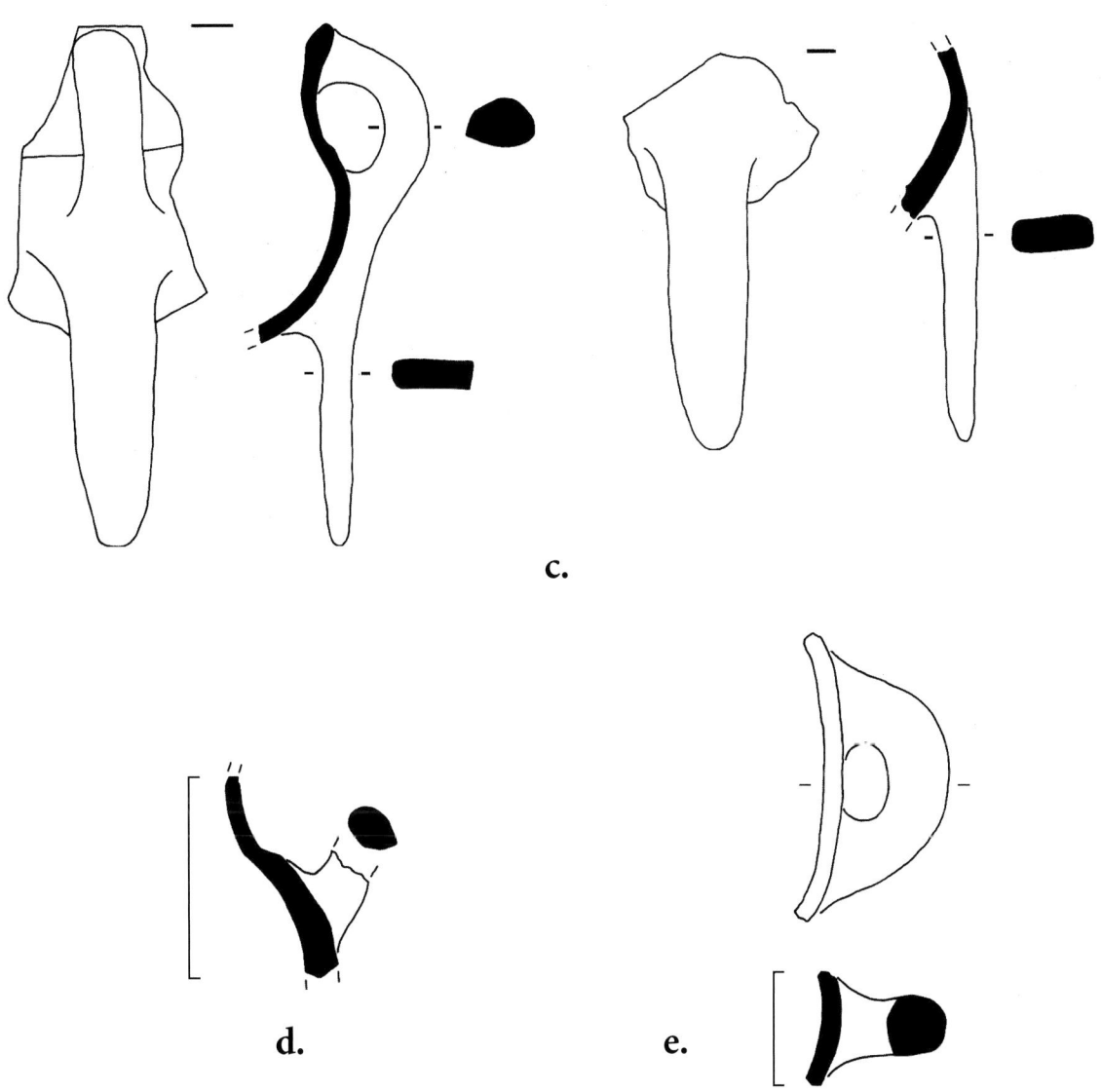

FIGURE 179 (continued). Tomb 123. (*c*) **T123-3**. (*d*) **T123-4**. (*e*) **T123-5**.

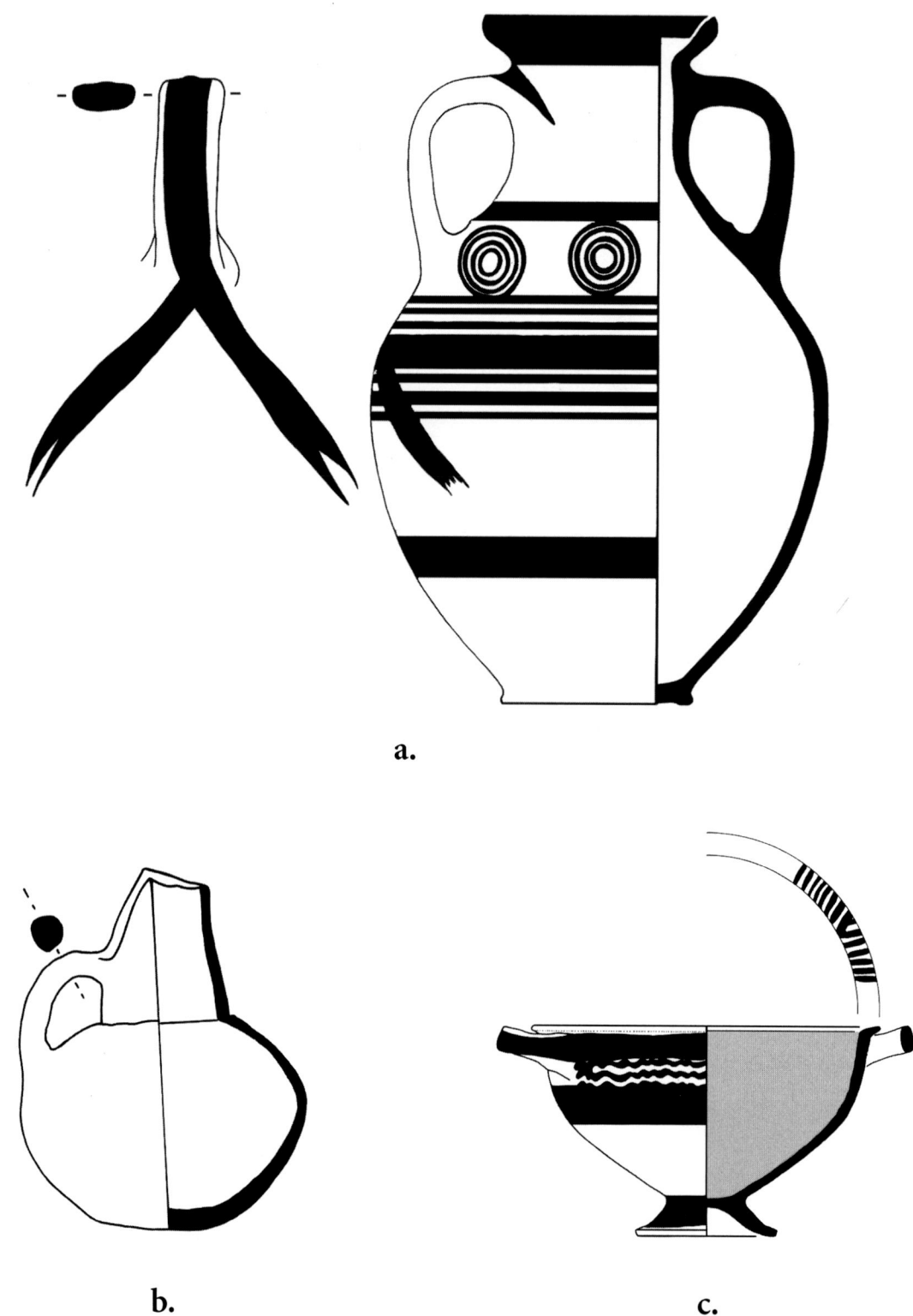

a.

b.   c.

FIGURE 180. Tomb 124. (*a*) **T124-1**. (*b*) **T124-2**. (*c*) **T124-3**.

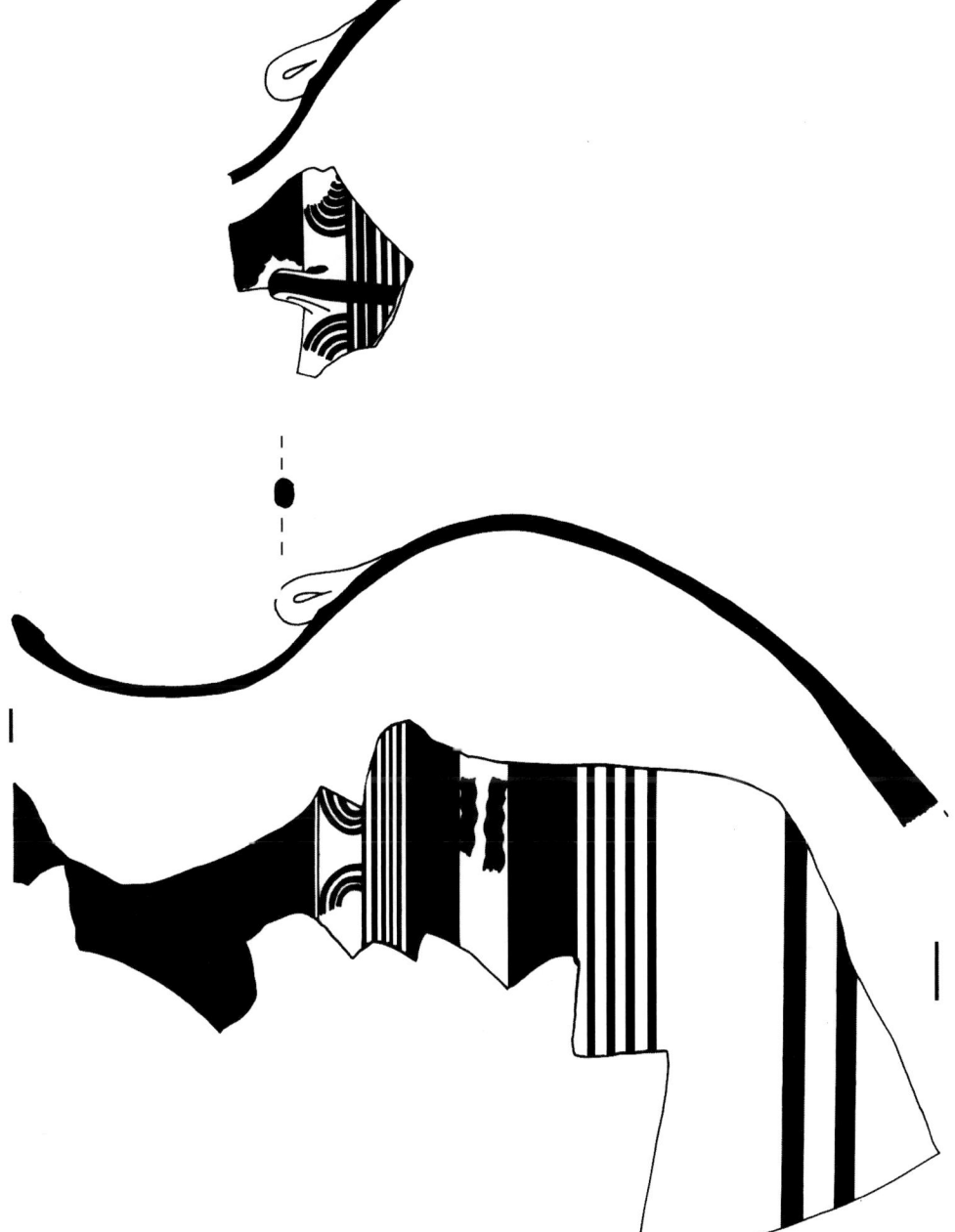

FIGURE 181 (on following page). Tomb 125. (*a*) T125-1.

a.

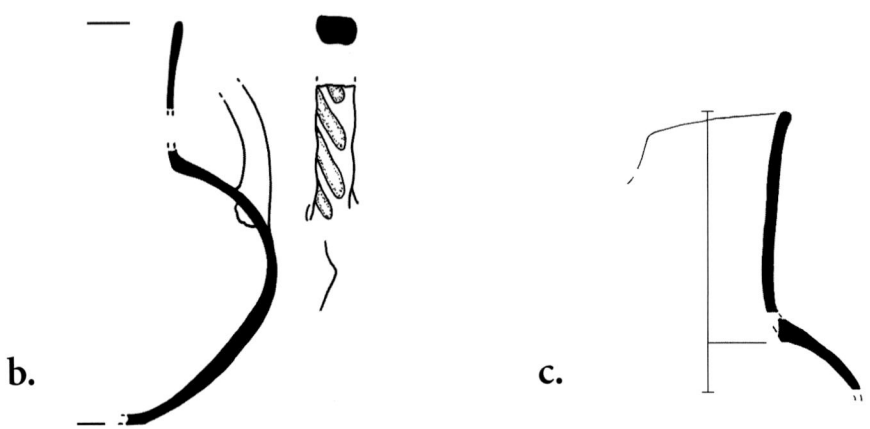

b.   **c.**

FIGURE 181 (continued). Tomb 125. (*b*) **T125-2**. (*c*) **T125-3**.

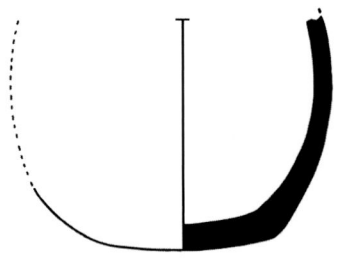

FIGURE 182. Tomb 126. **T126-1**.

FIGURE 183. Tomb 127. **T127-1**.

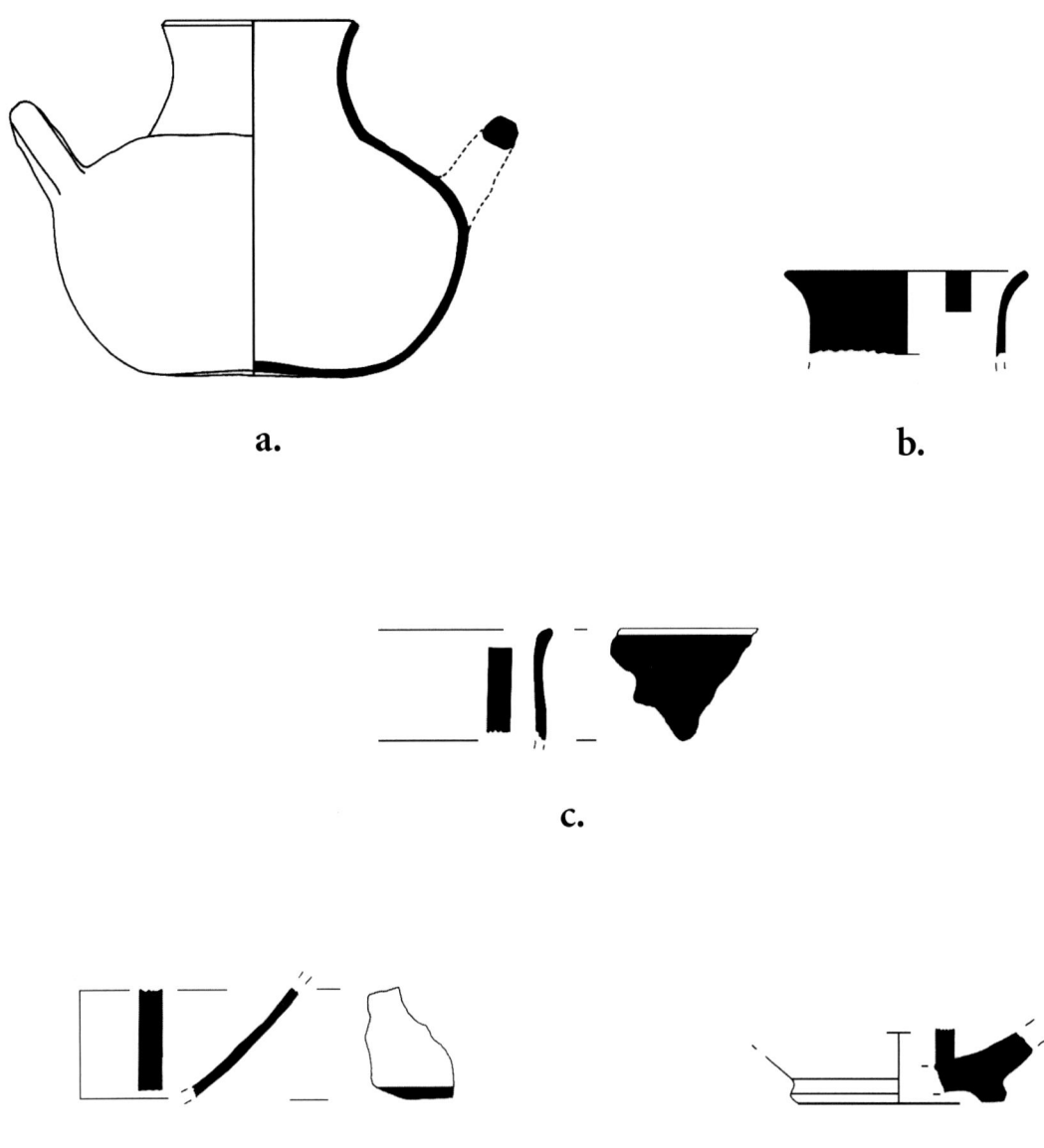

a.

b.

c.

d.

e.

FIGURE 184. Tomb 128. (*a*) **T128-1**. (*b*) **T128-2**. (*c*) **T128-3**. (*d*) **T128-4**. (*e*) **T128-5**.

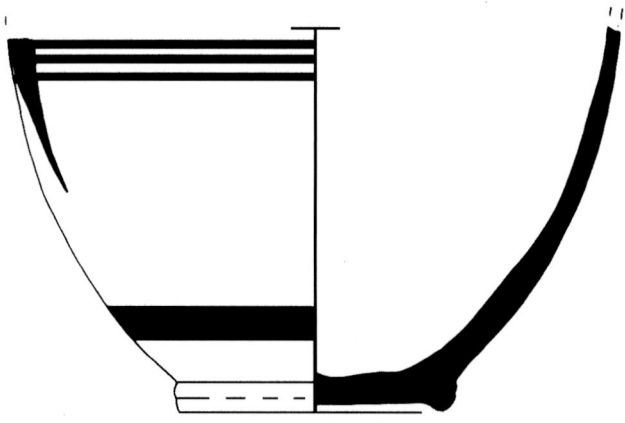

FIGURE 185. Tomb 129. **T129-1**.

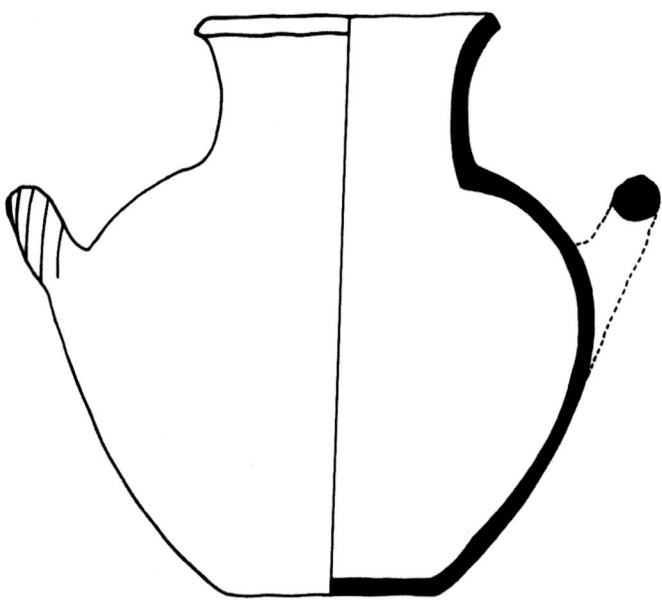

FIGURE 186. Tomb 130. **T130-1**.

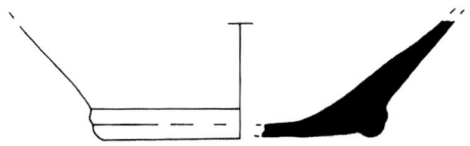

FIGURE 187. Tomb 131. **T131-1.**

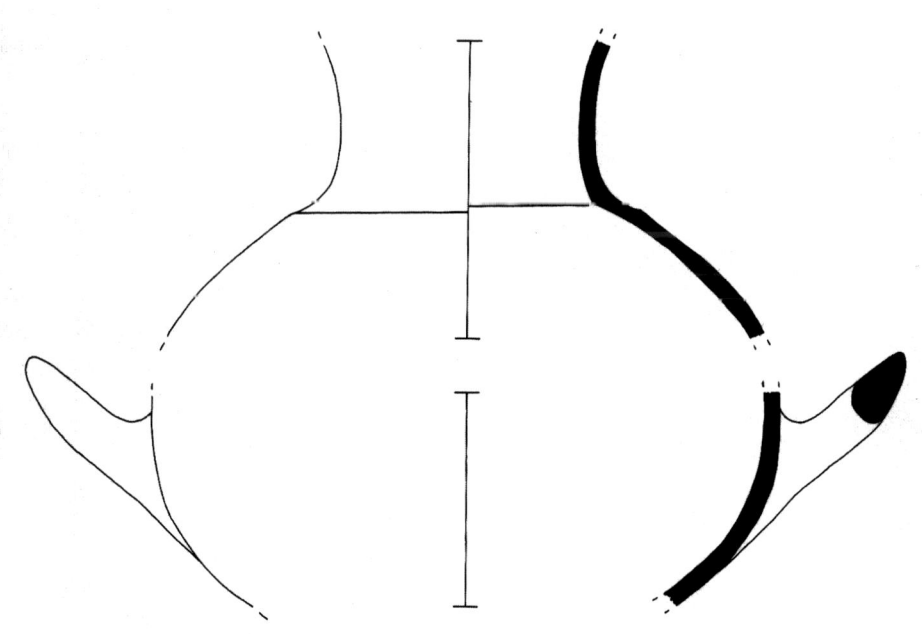

FIGURE 188. Tomb 132. **T132-1.**

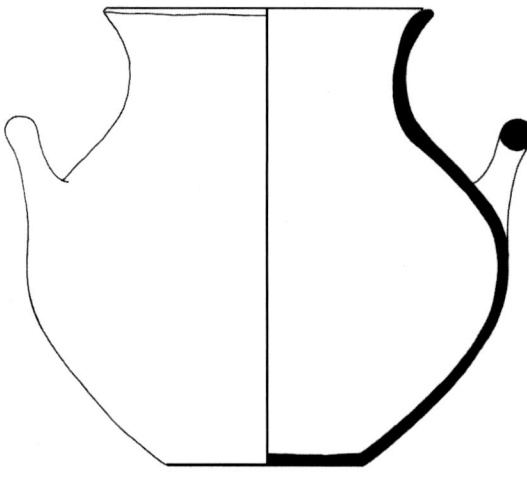

FIGURE 189. Tomb 133. **T133-1**.

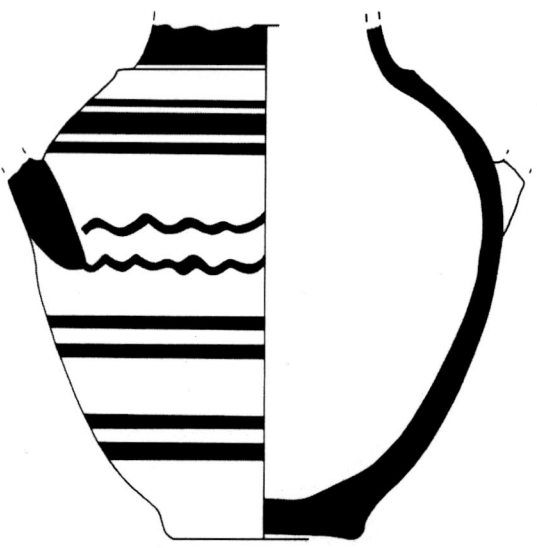

FIGURE 190. Tomb 134. **T134-1**.

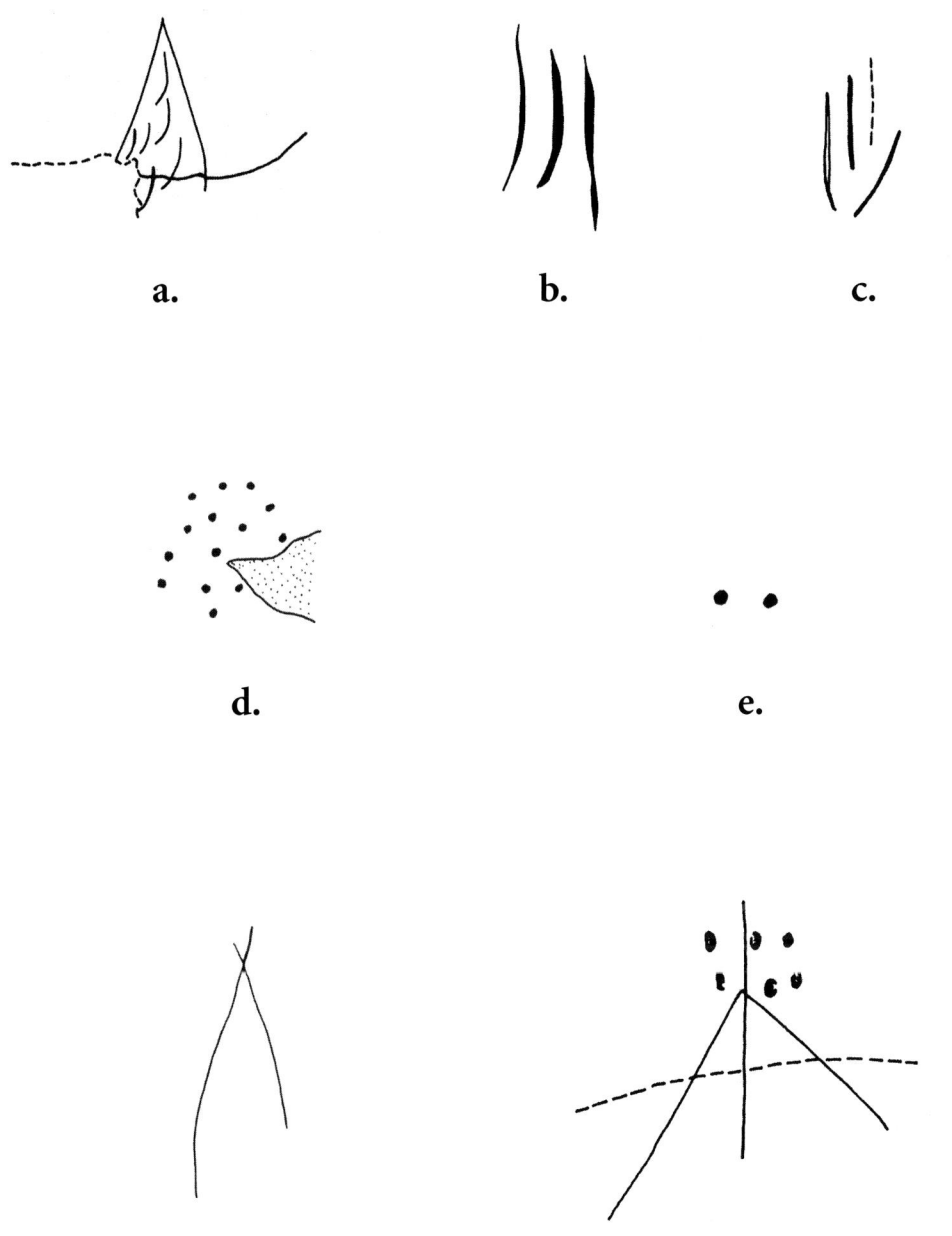

FIGURE 191. Early Iron Age potters' marks. (*a*) **T10-1**. (*b*) **T10-3**. (*c*) **T38-2**. (*d*) **T66-1**. (*e*) **T75-2**. (*f*) **T82-3**. (*g*) **T41-3**. (scale 1:1)

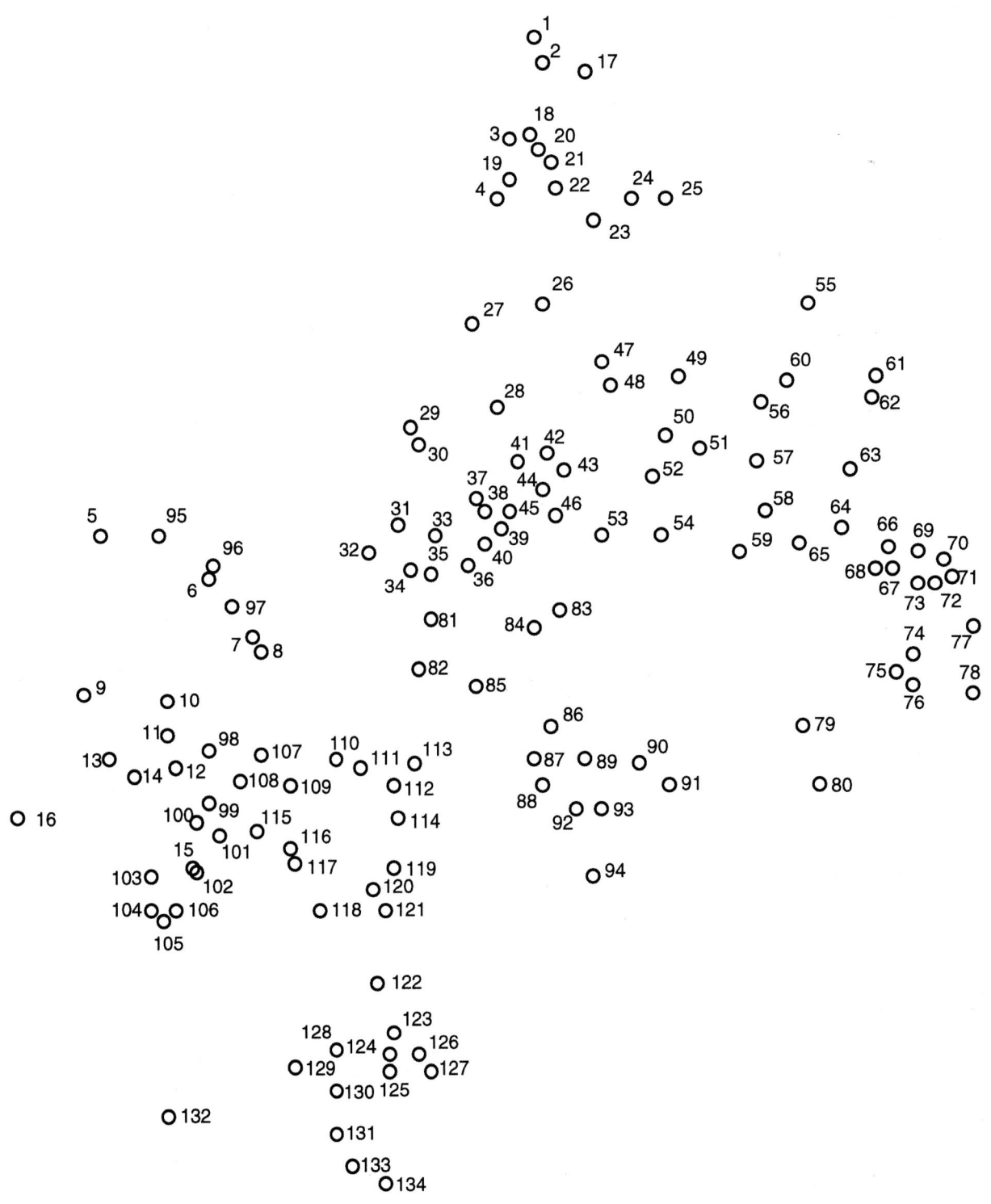

FIGURE 192. Schematic plan of all Early Iron Age tombs.

Tomb Group Plan:

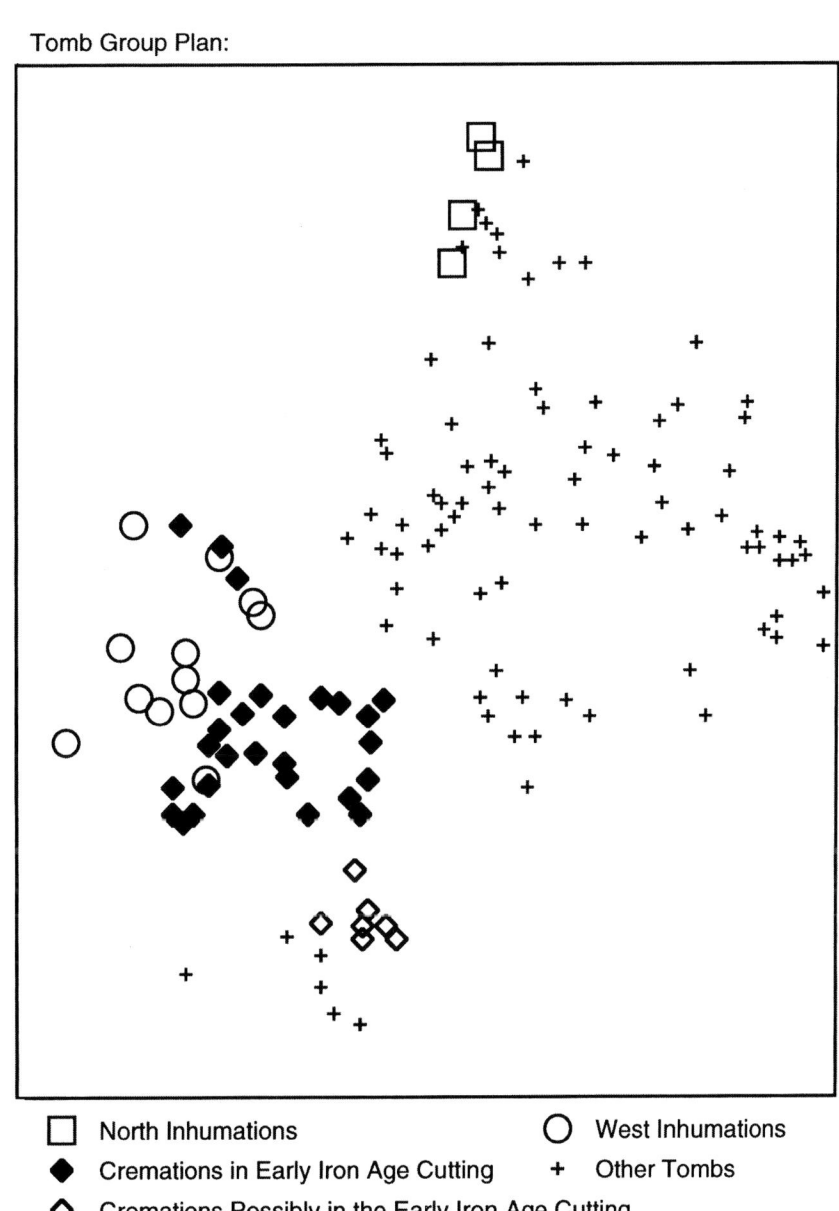

☐ North Inhumations   ◯ West Inhumations

◆ Cremations in Early Iron Age Cutting   + Other Tombs

◇ Cremations Possibly in the Early Iron Age Cutting

FIGURE 193. Schematic plan of the cemetery showing the location of the north and west groups of inhumations and cremations in the area of the Early Iron Age cutting.

Pyre Remains Plan:

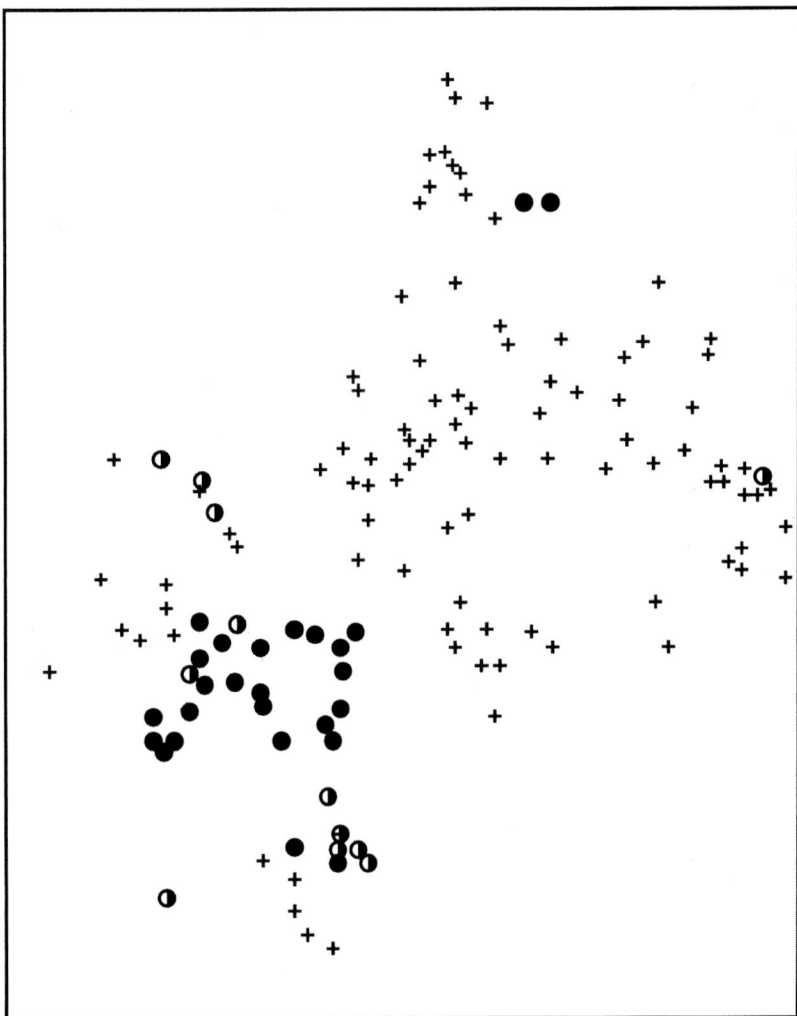

●   Remains of Pyre and Burnt Sherds

◑   Pyre Remains

+   No Pyre Remains

FIGURE 194. Schematic plan of the cemetery showing tombs with remains of the pyre and burned sherds.

Tomb Phase Plan:

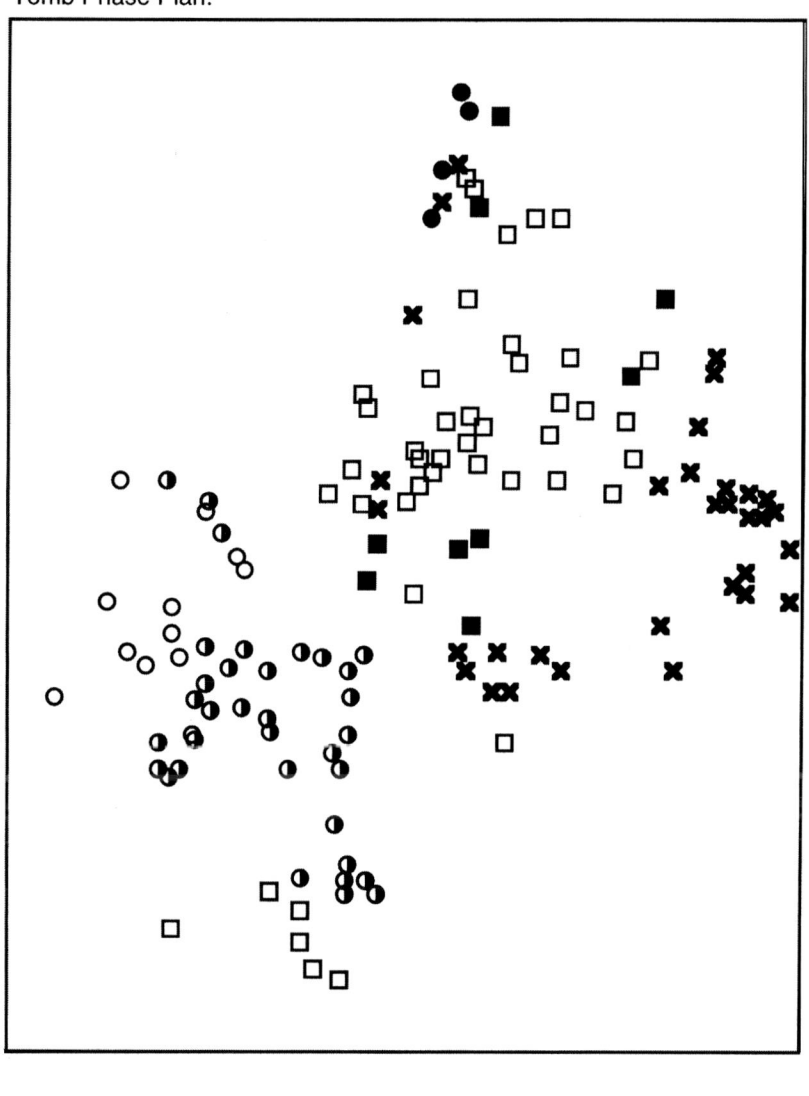

$\mathbf{0}$ I/II $\bigcirc$ IA $\bullet$ IB $\square$ III $\pmb{\times}$ III/IV $\blacksquare$ IV

FIGURE 195. Schematic plan of the cemetery showing tombs according to chronological phases.
KEY: 1A = inhumations within the area of the Early Iron Age cutting (among the earliest tombs of the cemetery).
1B = the four northern inhumation tombs, which may or may not be contemporary with those in the area of the cutting.
I/II = Phases I and II—all the cremation tombs within the area of the cutting.

Tomb Type Plan:

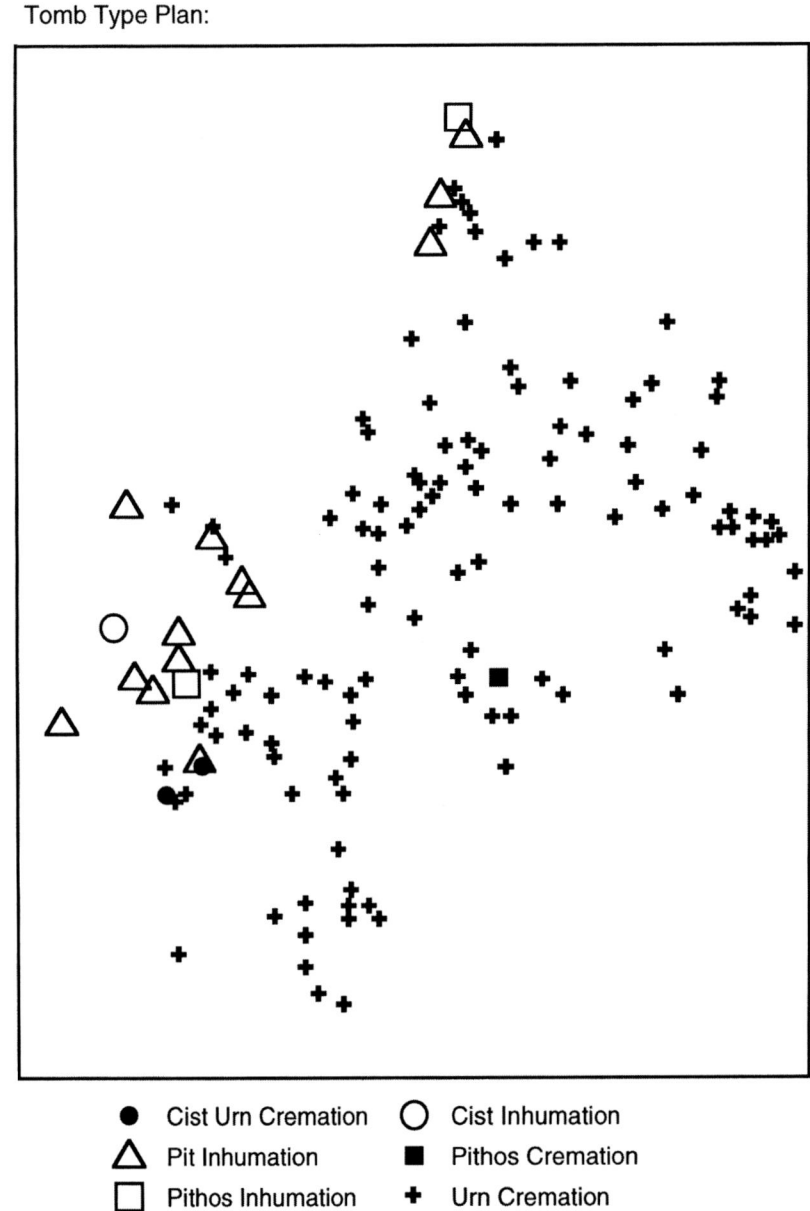

FIGURE 196. Schematic plan of the cemetery showing distribution of different tomb types.

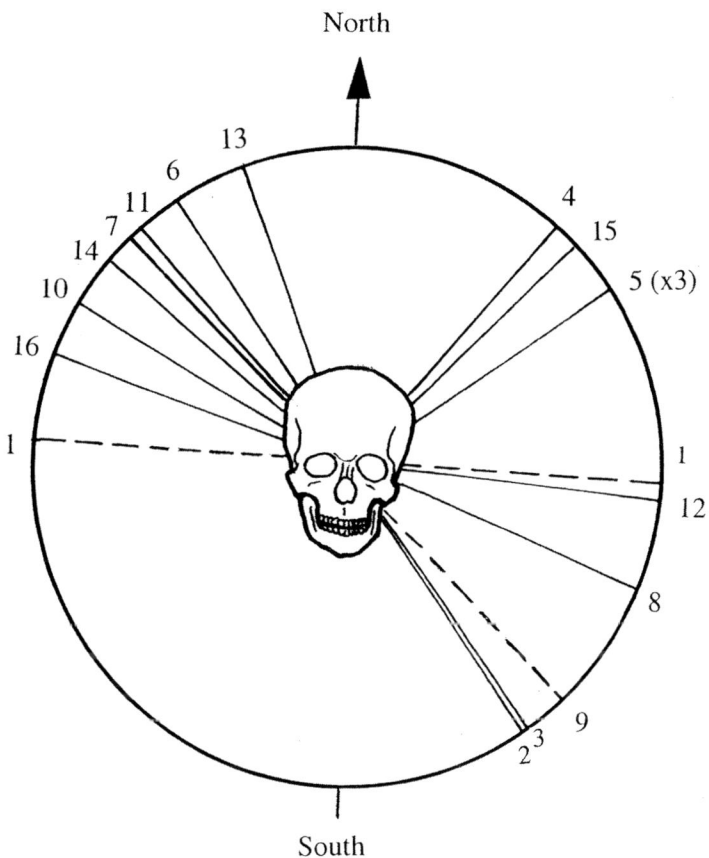

FIGURE 197. Diagram showing the orientation of inhumation tombs.

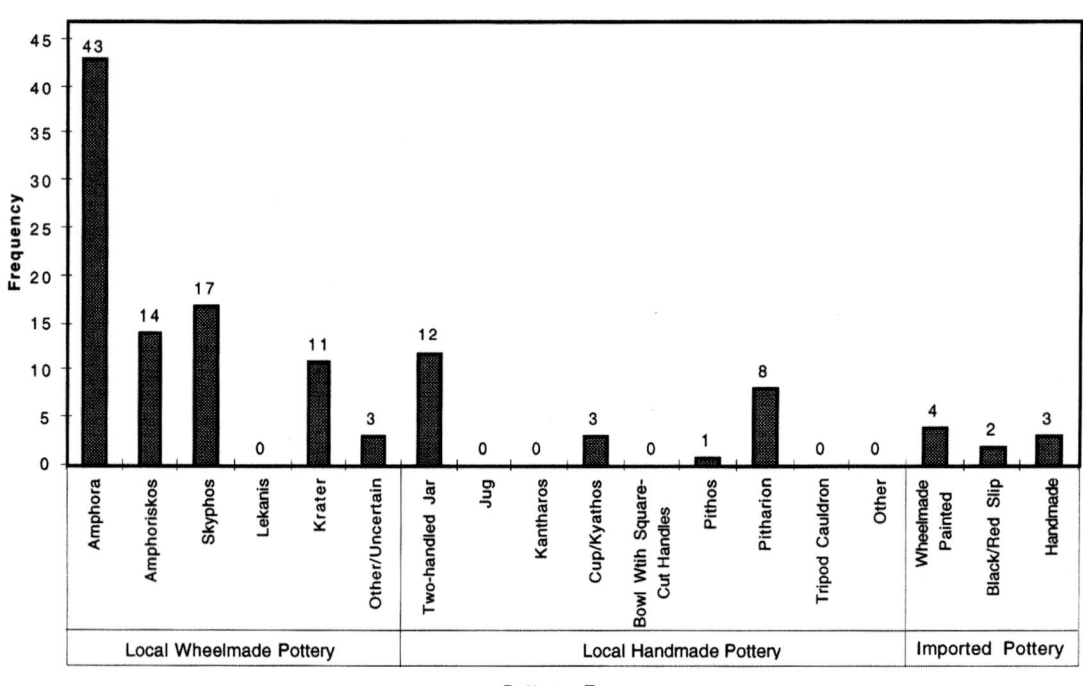

FIGURE 198. Histogram showing the frequency of different pot shapes used as ash-urns in the cemetery.

Pottery Plan:

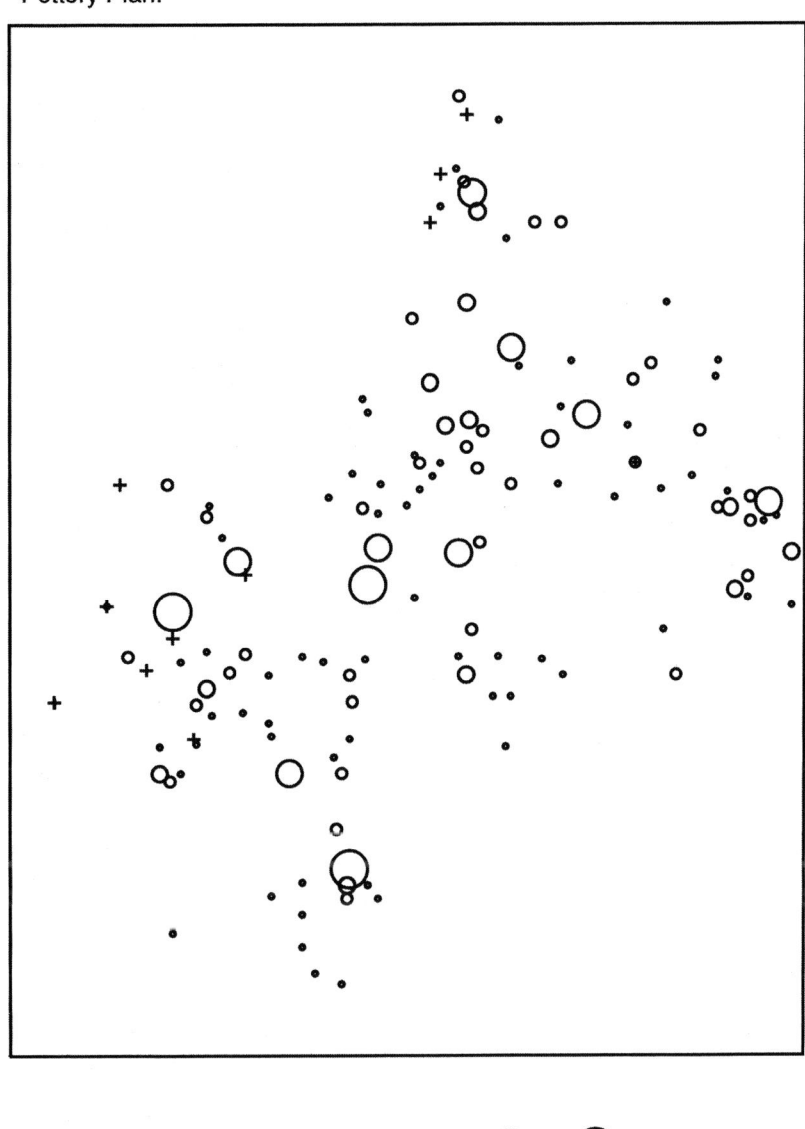

+ 0 • 1 ○ 2 ⊙ 3 ◯ 4 ◯ 5

FIGURE 199. Schematic plan of the cemetery showing the number of pots in individual tombs (inhumations and cremations).

Terracottas Plan:

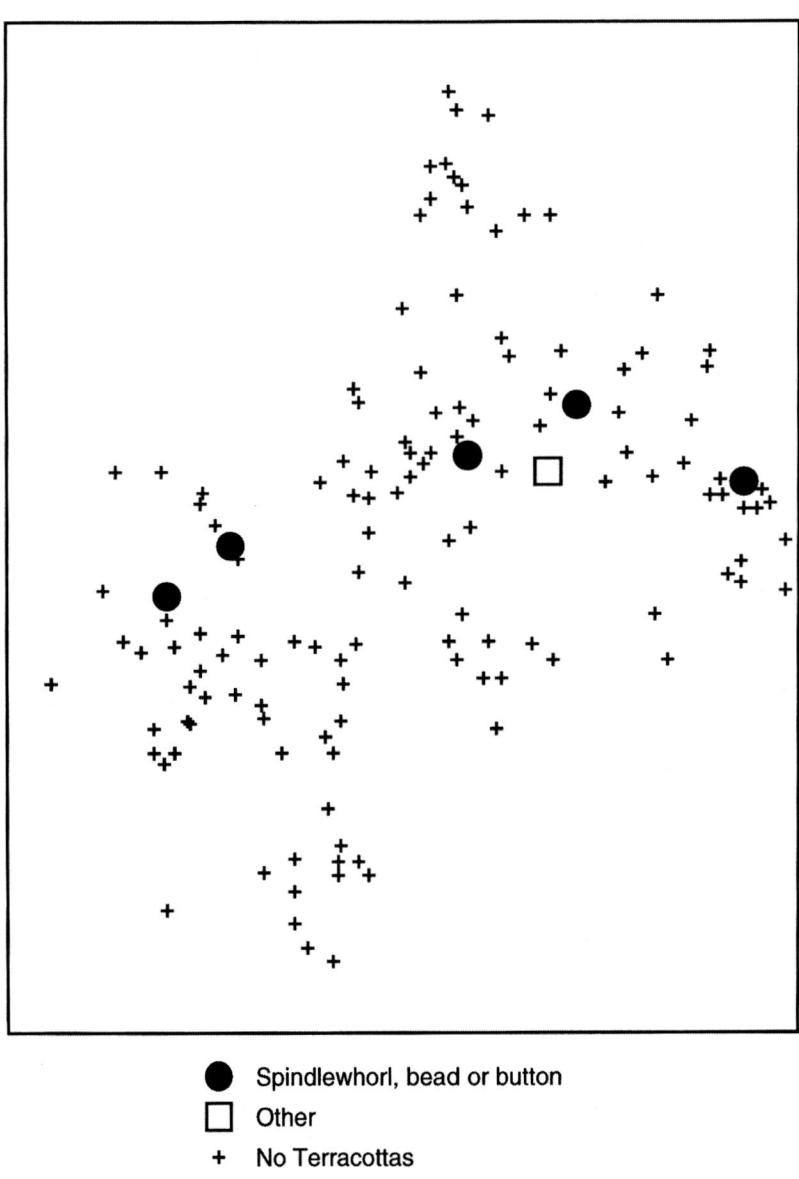

FIGURE 200. Schematic plan of the cemetery showing distribution of terracotta objects other than pottery in tombs.

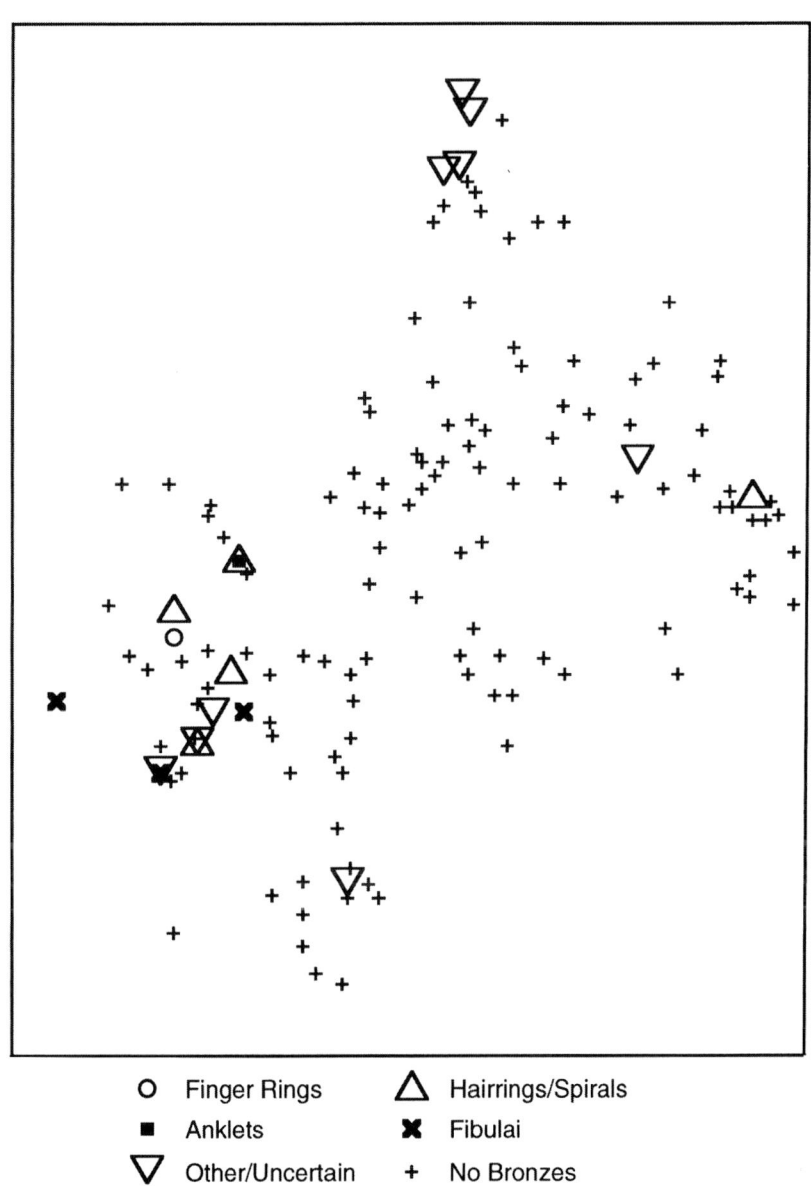

FIGURE 201. Schematic plan of the cemetery showing distribution of bronze objects in tombs.

Other Grave Goods Plan:

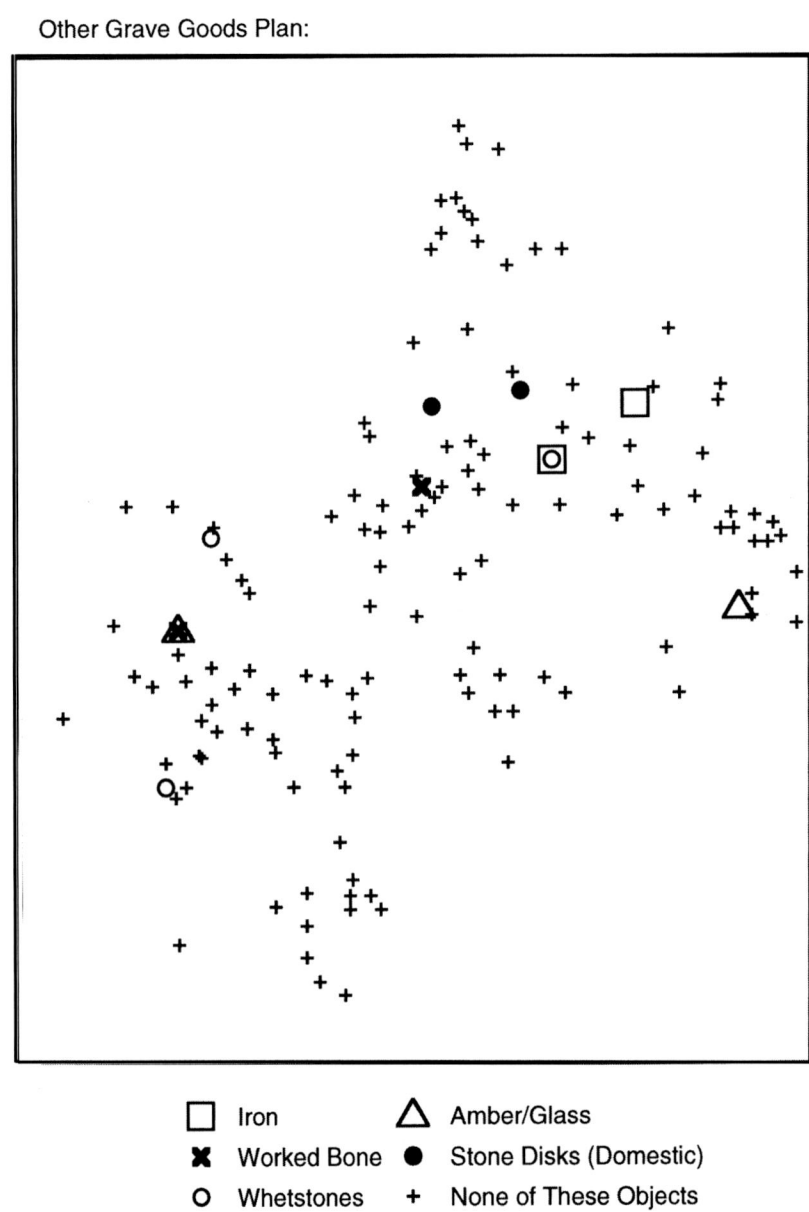

FIGURE 202. Schematic plan of the cemetery showing distribution of iron, amber/glass, worked bone, stone disks, and whetstones in tombs.

Age Plan:

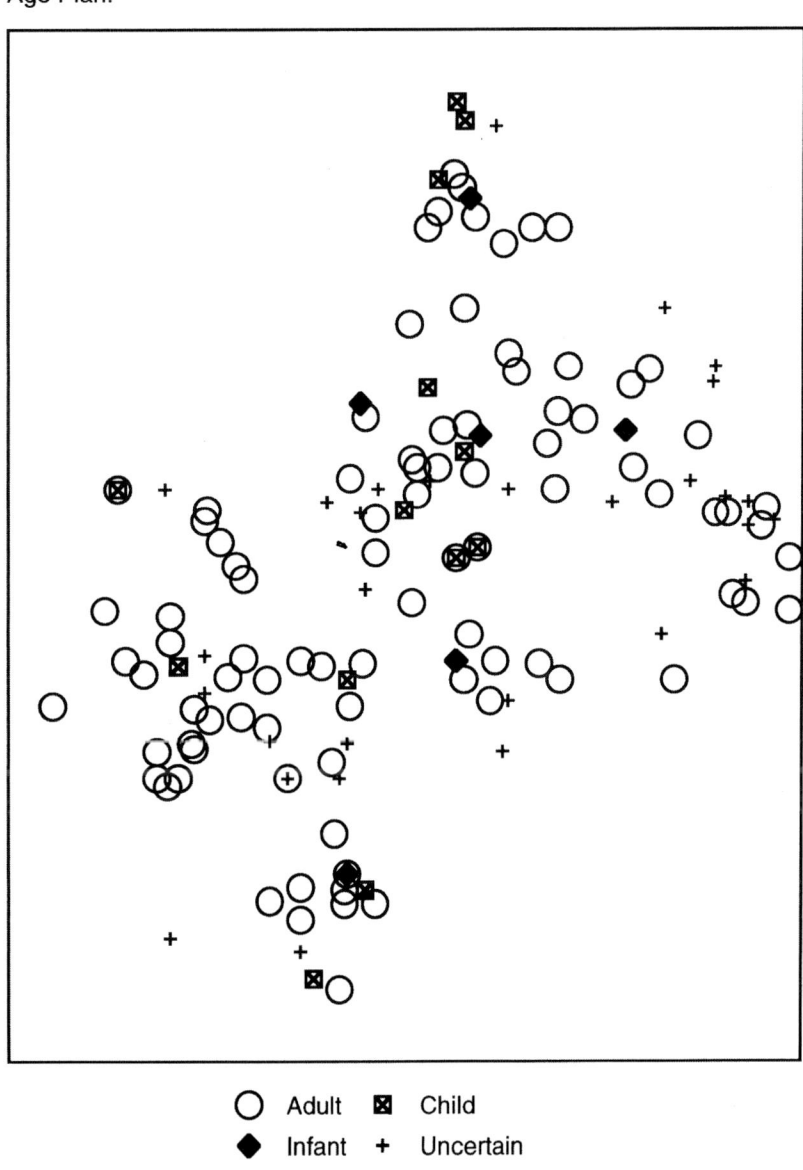

FIGURE 203. Schematic plan of the cemetery showing distribution of adult, child, and infant tombs.

Sex Plan:

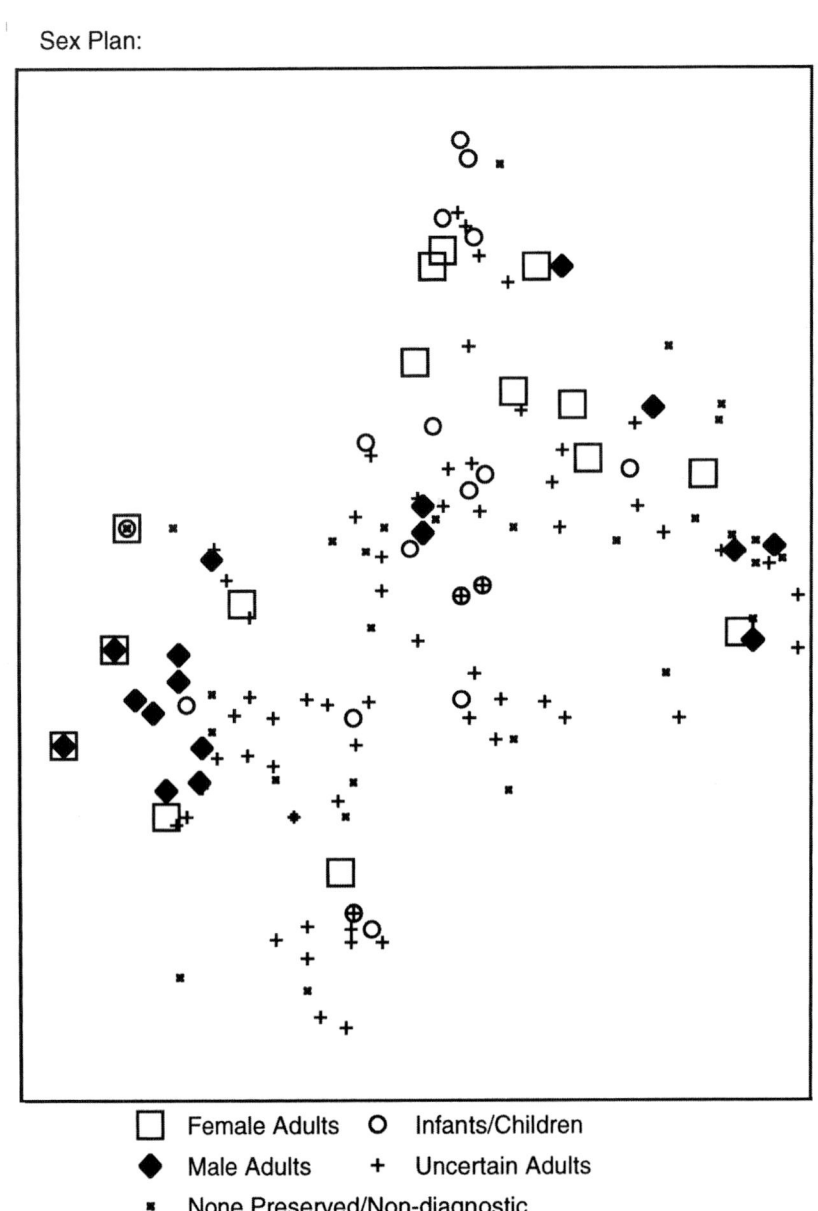

Female Adults □   Infants/Children ○

Male Adults ◆   Uncertain Adults +

None Preserved/Non-diagnostic ▪

FIGURE 204. Schematic plan of the cemetery showing distribution of tombs according to age and sex of the deceased.

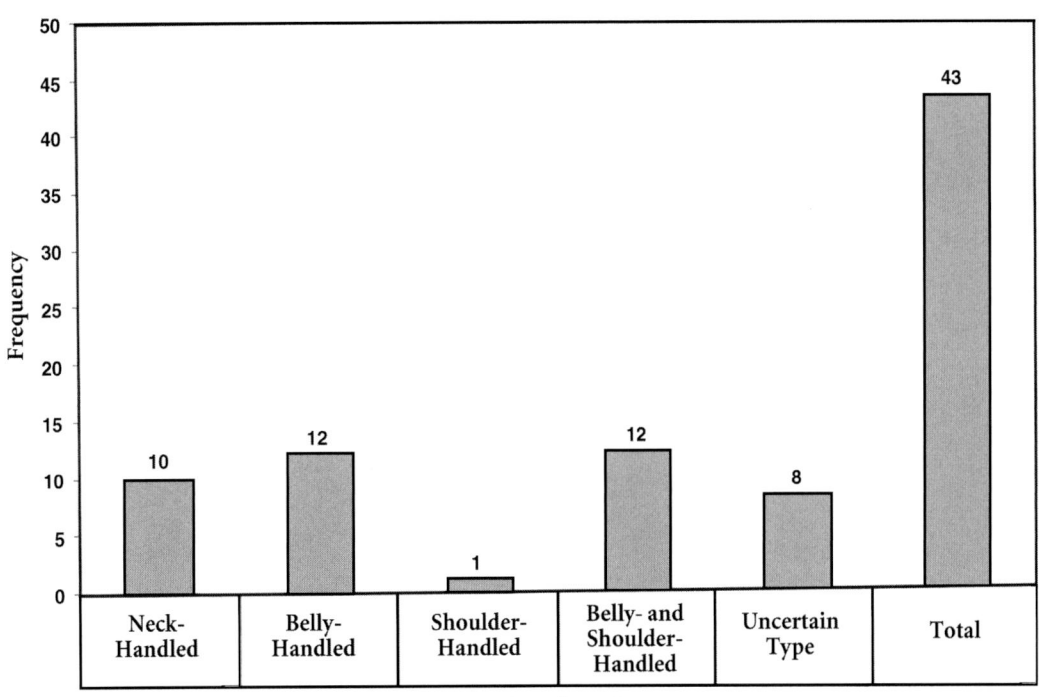

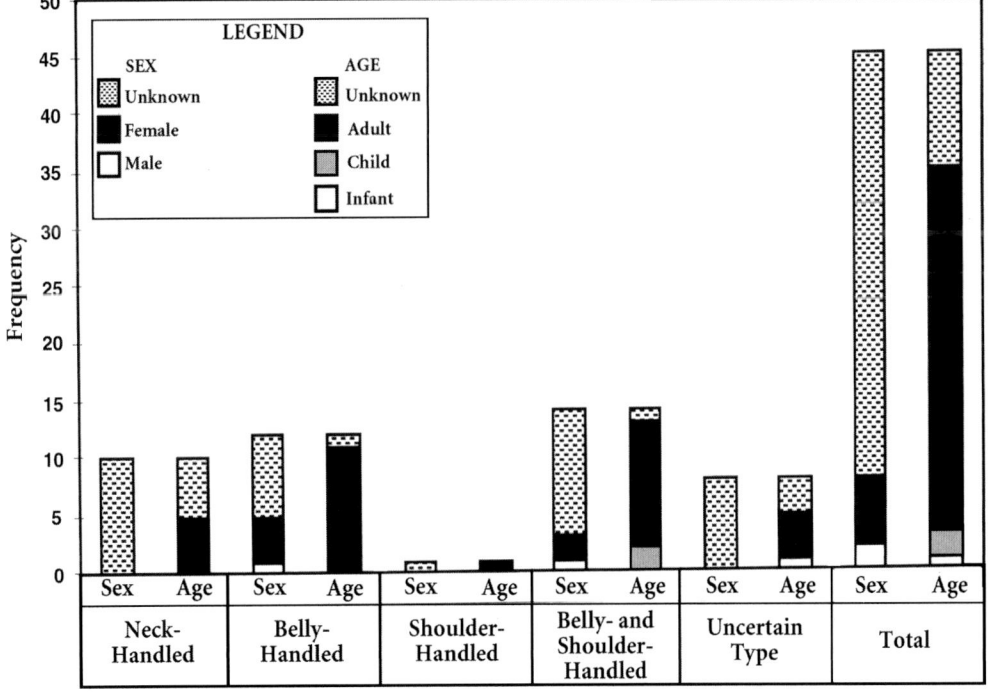

Tombs 83 and 84 each containing adult and child

FIGURE 205. Histograms showing frequency of amphorai used as ash-urns together with age and sex determinations of the deceased.

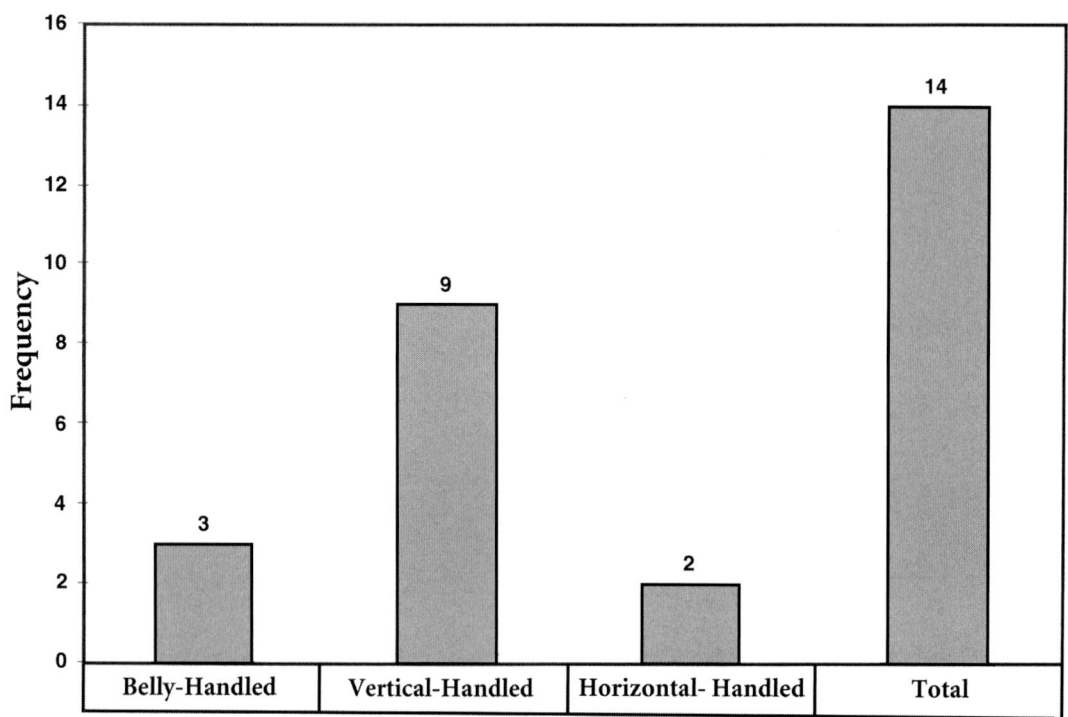

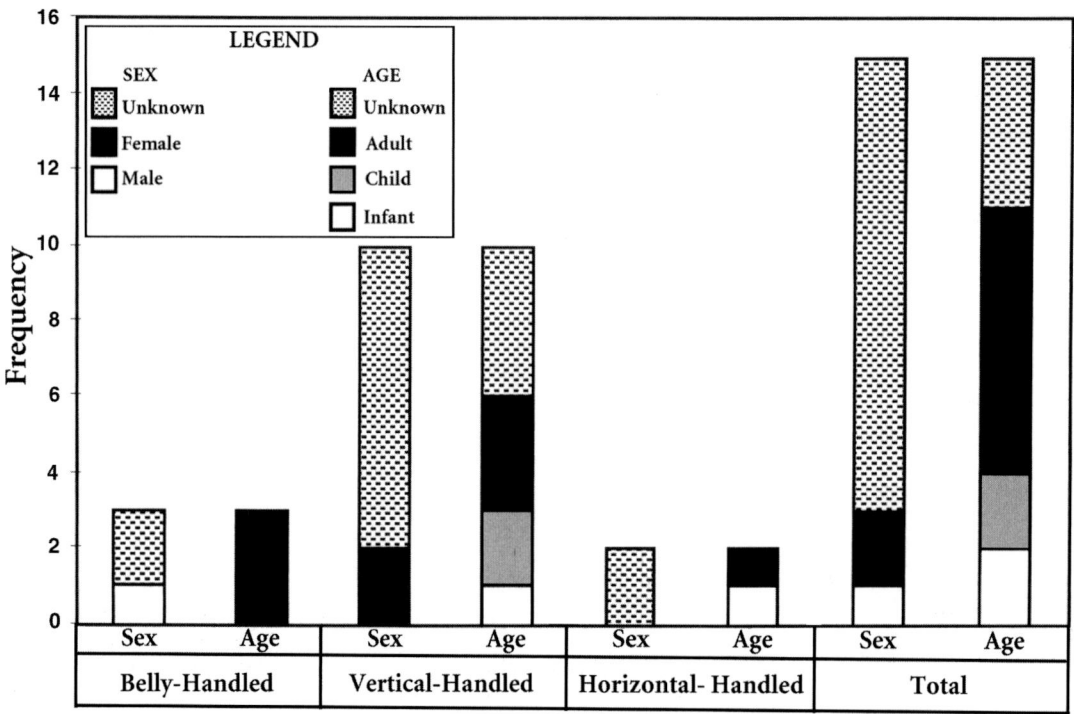

FIGURE 206. Histograms showing frequency of amphoriskoi used as ash-urns, together with age and sex determinations of the deceased.

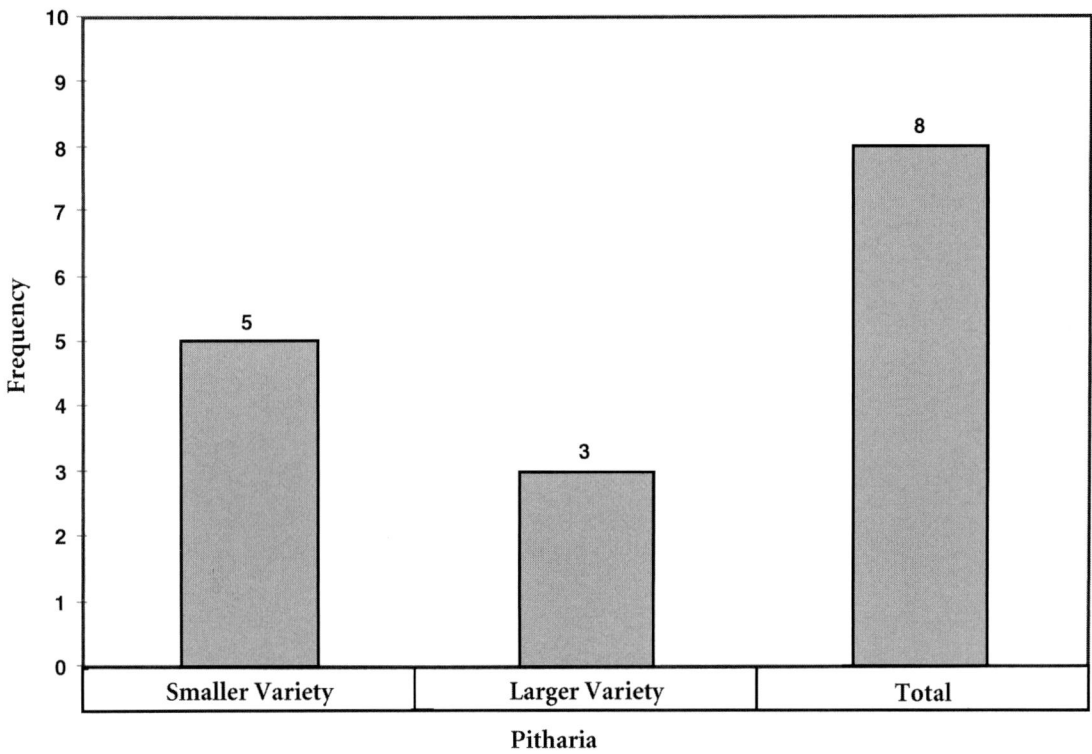

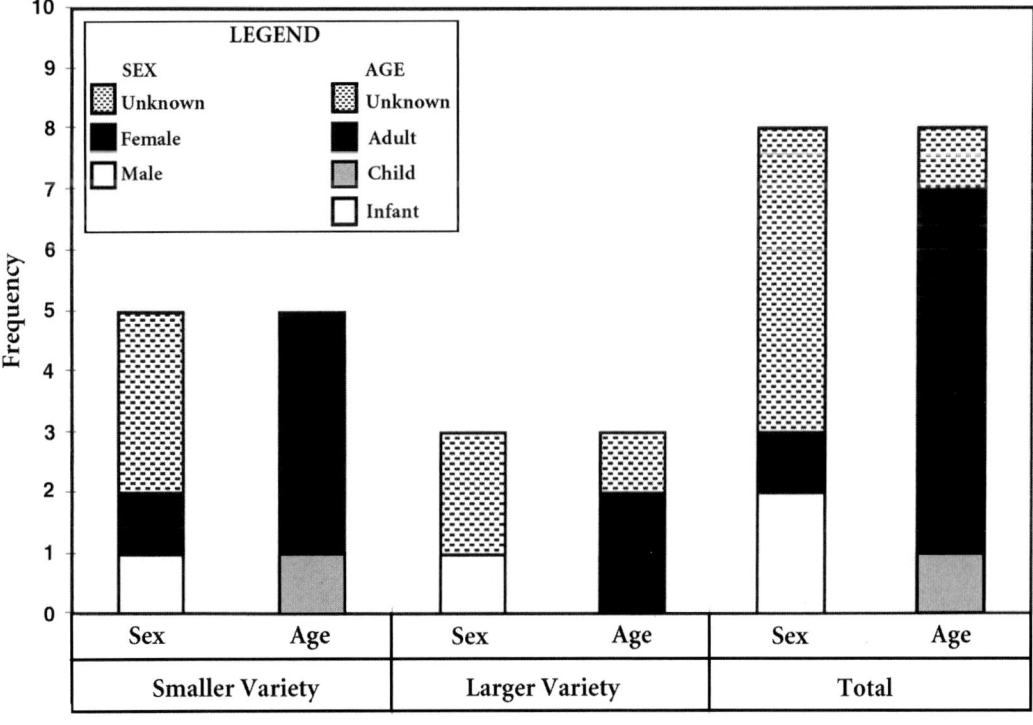

FIGURE 207. Histograms showing frequency of handmade pitharia used as ash-urns, together with age and sex determinations of the deceased.

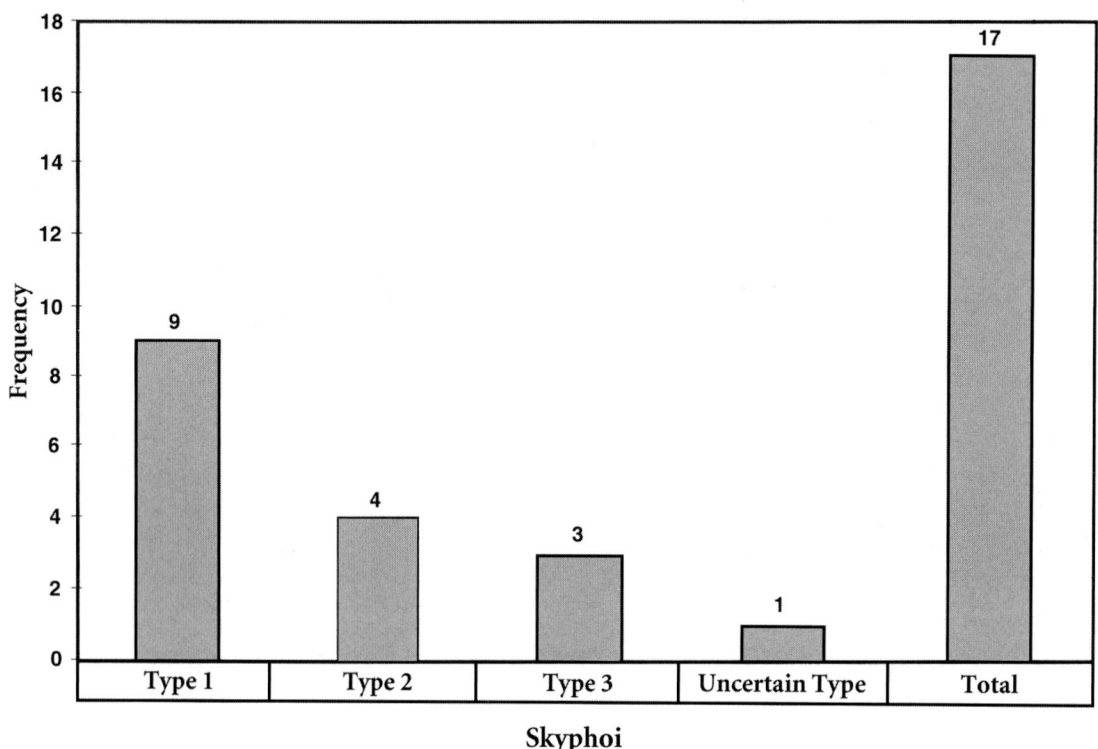

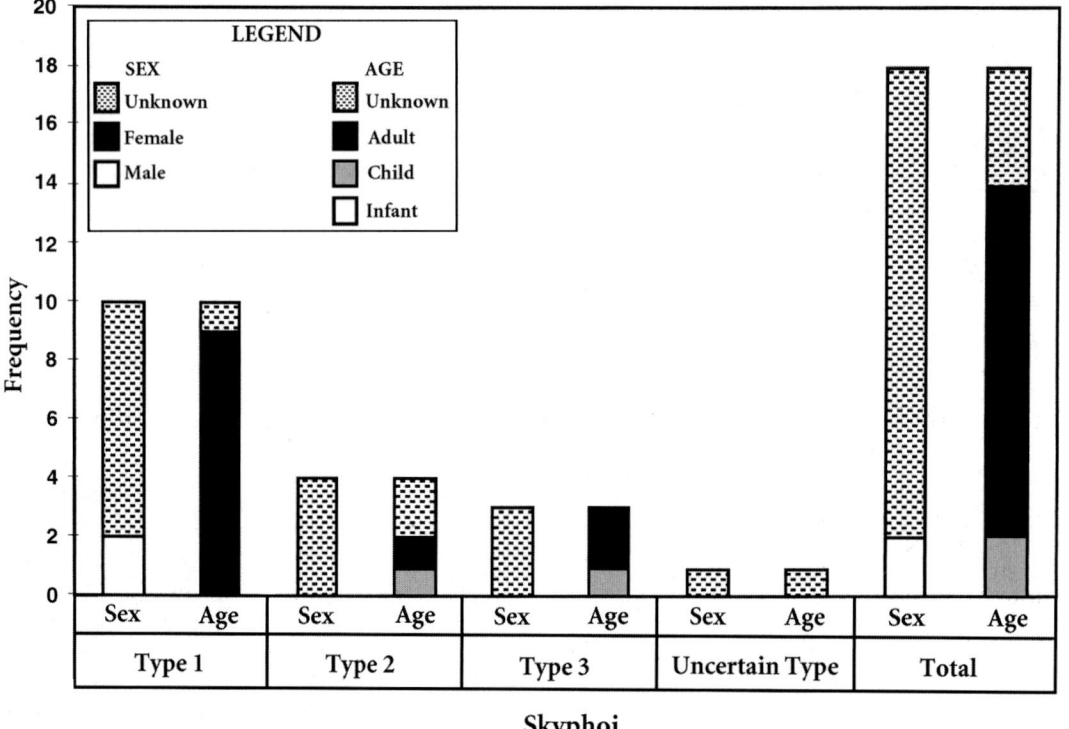

FIGURE 208. Histograms showing frequency of skyphoi used as ash-urns, together with age and sex determinations of the deceased.

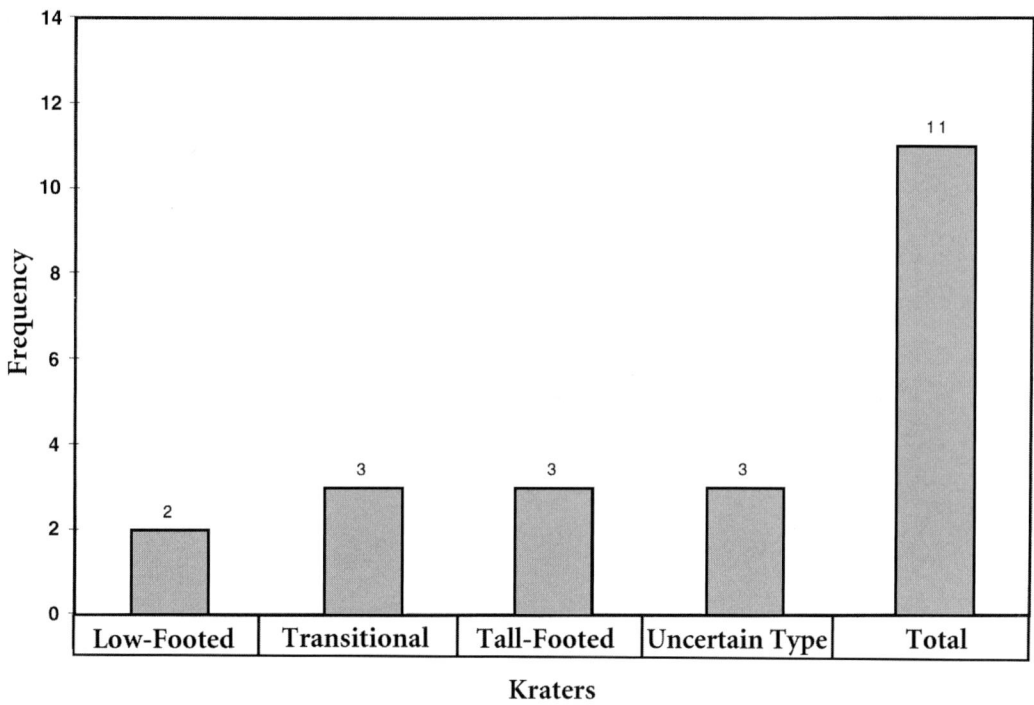

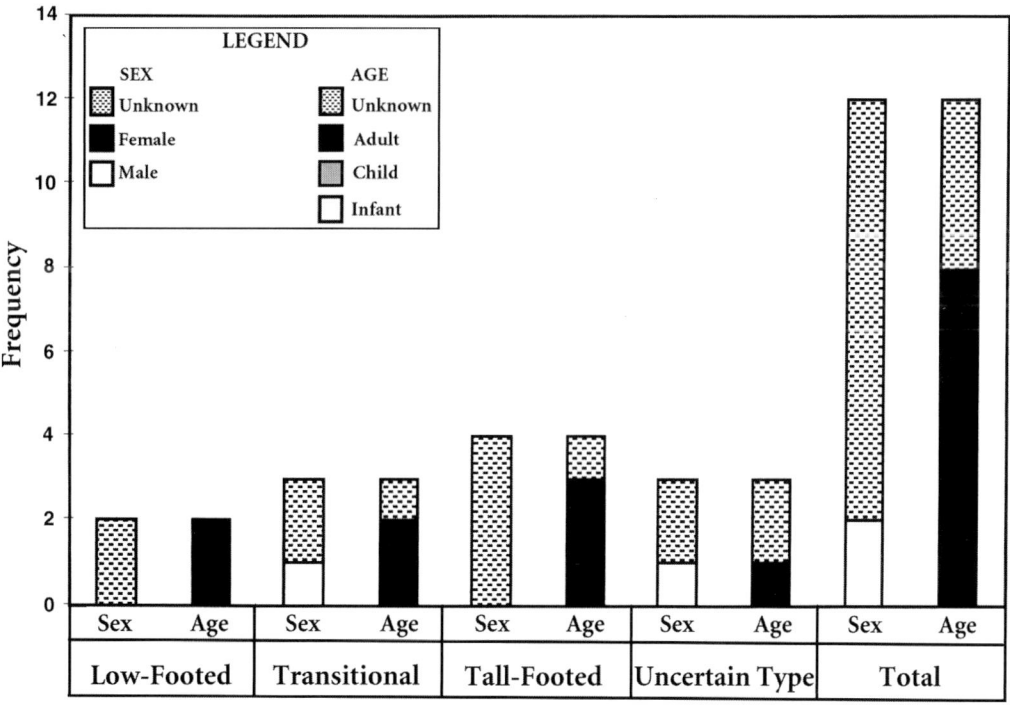

T58-1 has 2 adults, unknown sex

FIGURE 209. Histograms showing frequency of kraters used as ash-urns together with age and sex determinations of the deceased.

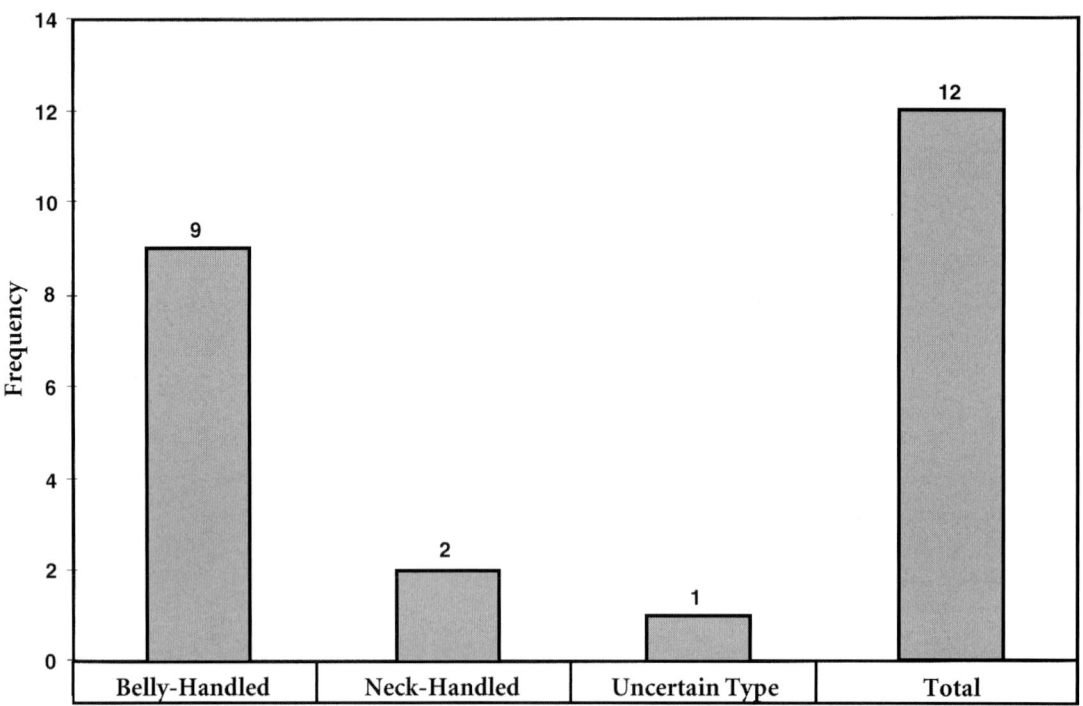

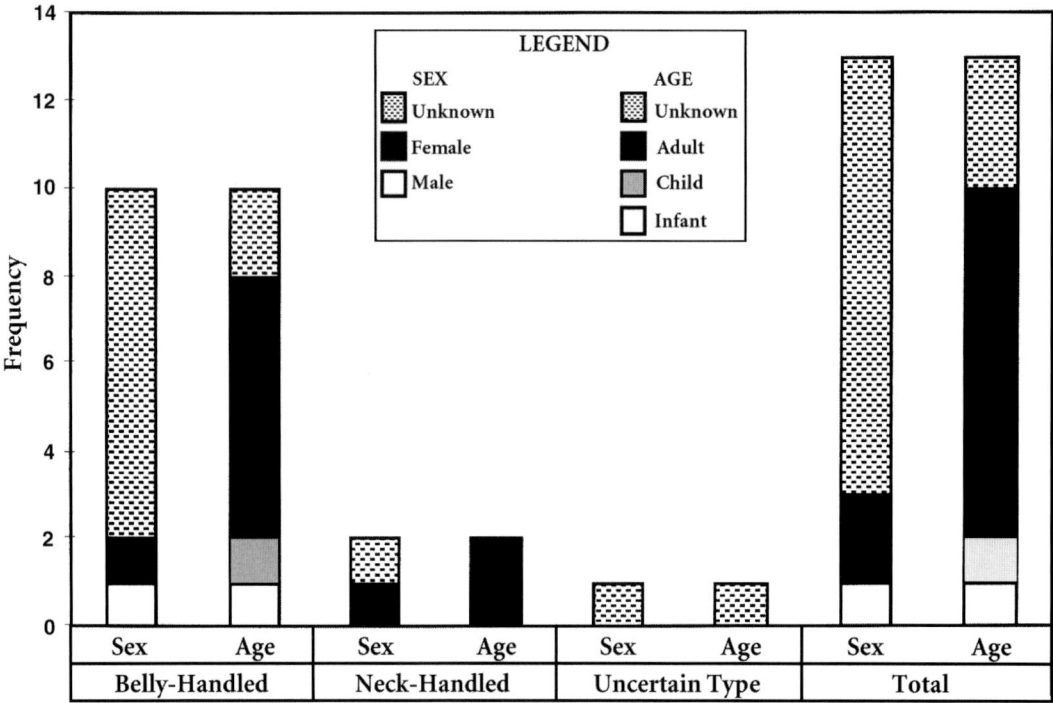

FIGURE 210. Histograms showing frequency of handmade two-handled jars used as ash-urns, together with age and sex determinations of the deceased.

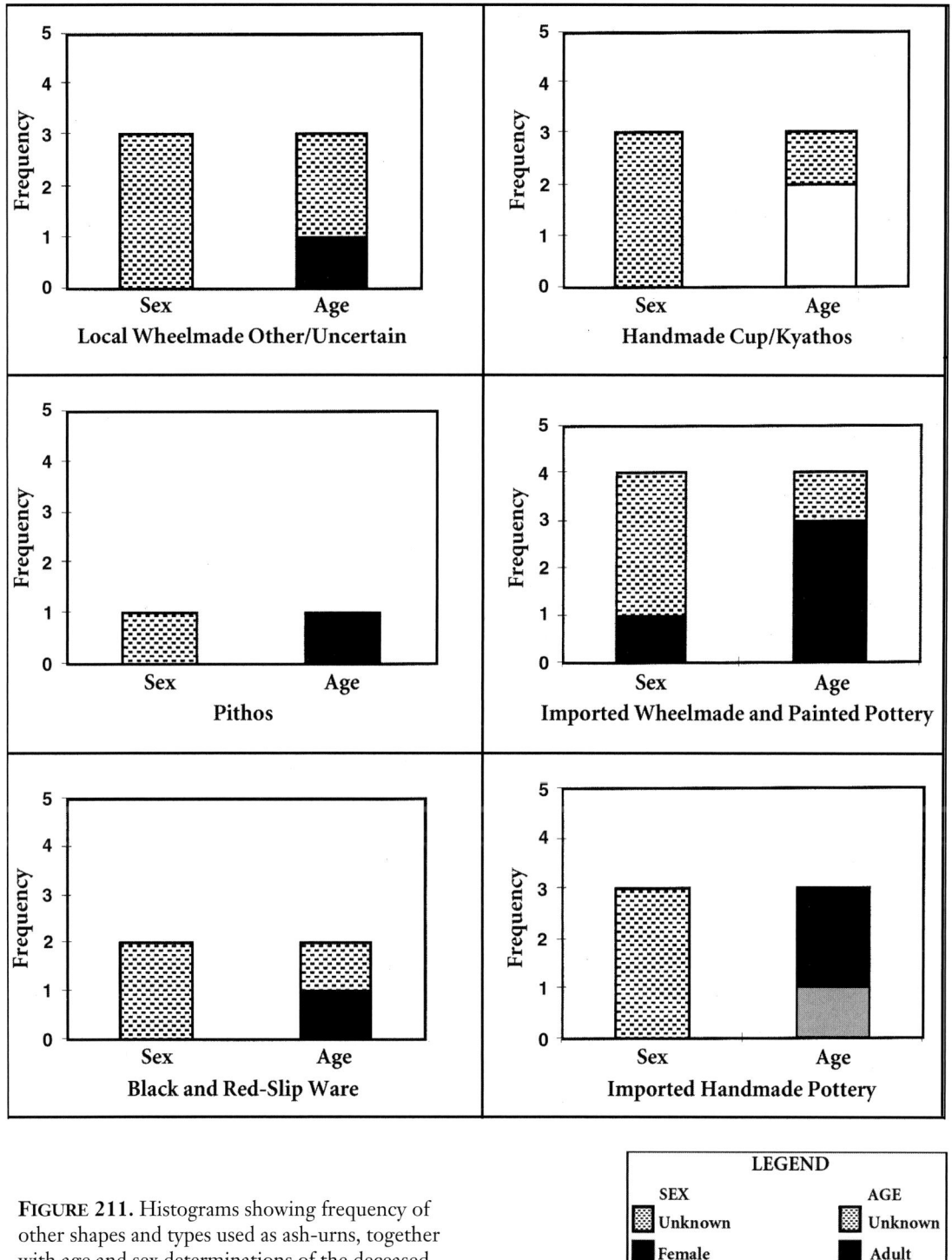

FIGURE 211. Histograms showing frequency of other shapes and types used as ash-urns, together with age and sex determinations of the deceased.

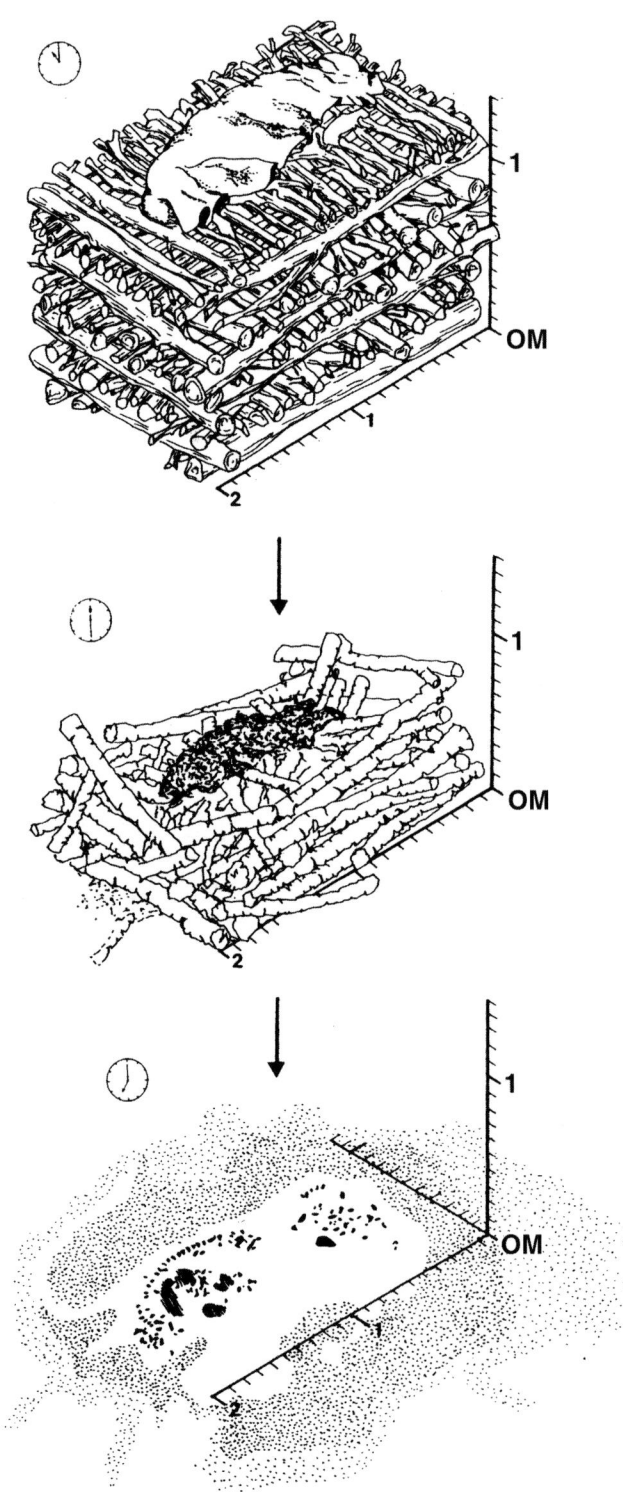

FIGURE 212. Schematic diagram of a cremation pyre and its collapse (after Parker Pearson 1999:8, fig. 1.1). The experiment involved a pig, not a person, and illustrates how long cremation takes and what is left behind.

Faunal Plan:

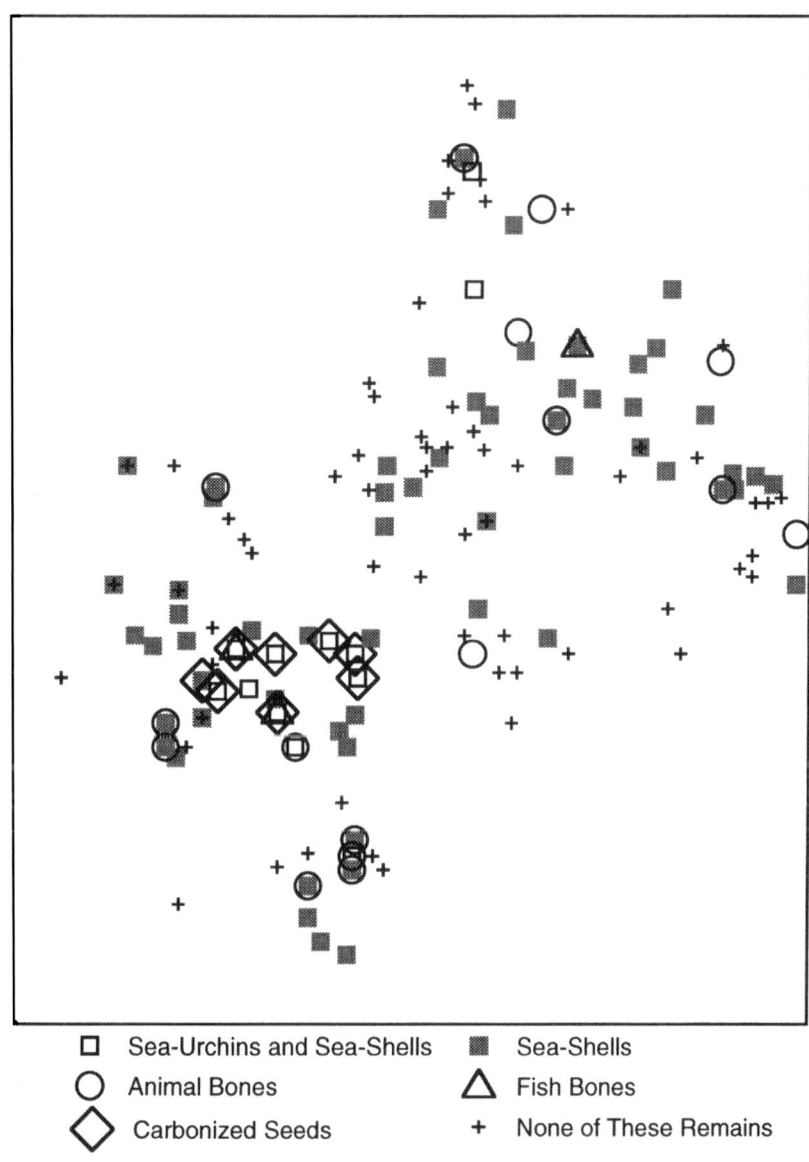

FIGURE 213. Schematic plan of the cemetery showing distribution of faunal, floral, and marine remains in tombs.

a.

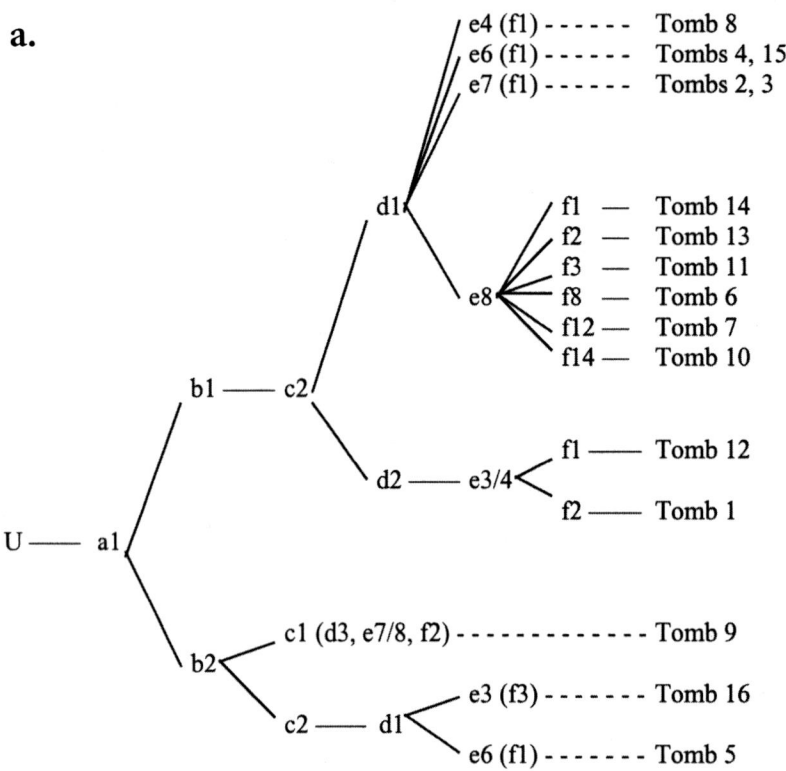

Key Diagram (Inhumation Tombs)

Variables

U = Universe

a1 = Inhumation
a2 = Cremation

b1 = Single
b2 = Multiple

c1 = Burnt debris in tomb pit
c2 = No burnt debris in tomb pit

d1 = Pit grave
d2 = "Pithos" grave
d3 = Cist grave
d4 = Urn cremation
d5 = "Pithos" cremation
d6 = Cist cremation

e1 = N-S
e2 = S-N
e3 = E-W
e4 = W-E
e5 = NE-SW
e6 = SW-NE
e7 = NW-SE

e8 = SE-NW
e9 = Upright
e10 = Upside-down

f1 = No kterismata
f2 = Vase(s)
f3 = Bronze
f4 = Iron
f5 = Terracotta
f6 = Vase(s), bronze
f7 = Vase(s), iron
f8 = Vase(s), stone
f9 = Vase(s), terracotta
f10 = Vase(s), amber
f11 = Vase(s), bronze, stone
f12 = Vase(s), bronze, terracotta
f13 = Vase(s), iron, stone
f14 = Vase(s), bronze, terracotta, glass compound/bone

FIGURE 214 (on facing page). Key diagram of the Early Iron Age cemetery at Torone. (*a*) Inhumation tombs.

b.

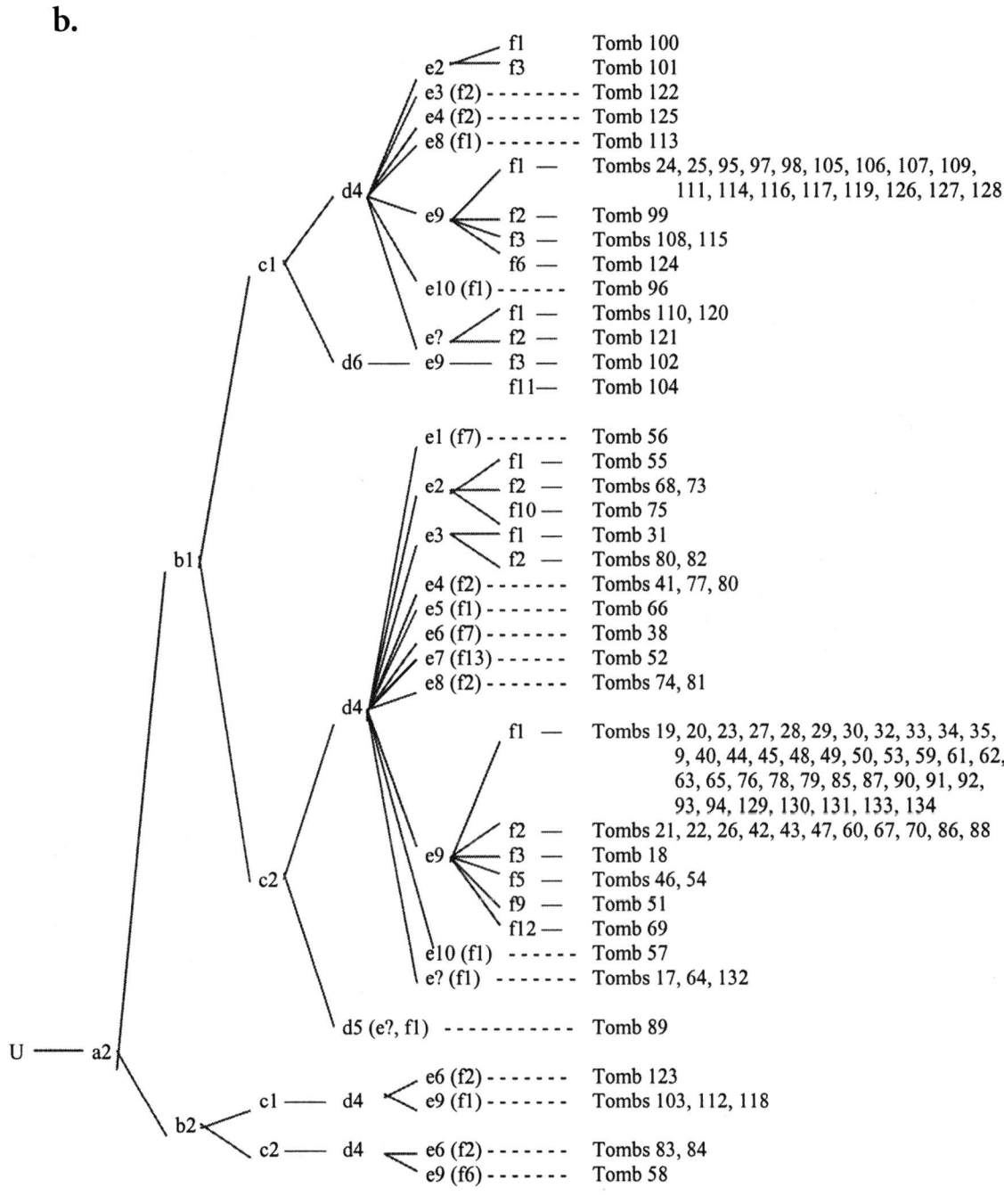

Key Diagram (Cremation Tombs)

FIGURE 214 (continued). Key diagram of the Early Iron Age cemetery at Torone.
(*b*) Cremation tombs.

a) Dimensions of differentiation

| | Number of dimensions different from the modal definition | | | | | | |
	0	1	2	3	4	5	6
No. of graves:	43	40	26	14	8	1	1

b) Calculation of variability

| | Score on the V-axis[1] | | | | | | |
	0	.166	.332	.498	.664	.83	1
Score on the N-axis:[2]	.3225	.6225	.8175	.9225	.9825	.99	1

Variability score for the cemetery as a whole: .1673.

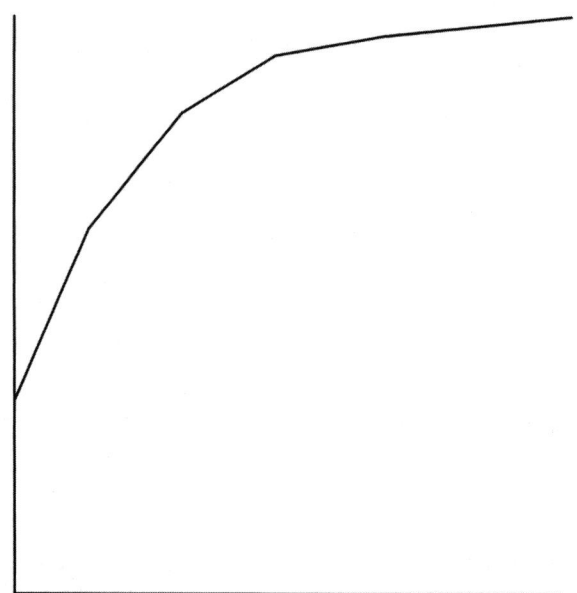

----

[1] Since there are six dimensions of differentiation, each dimension in which a grave differs from the mode (a2/b1/c2/d4/e9/f1) scores 0.166 on a scale of 0-1.

[2] Since there are 133 graves, each burial scores .0075 on a 0-1 scale.

FIGURE 215. The measurement of variability.

Tomb Cluster Plan:

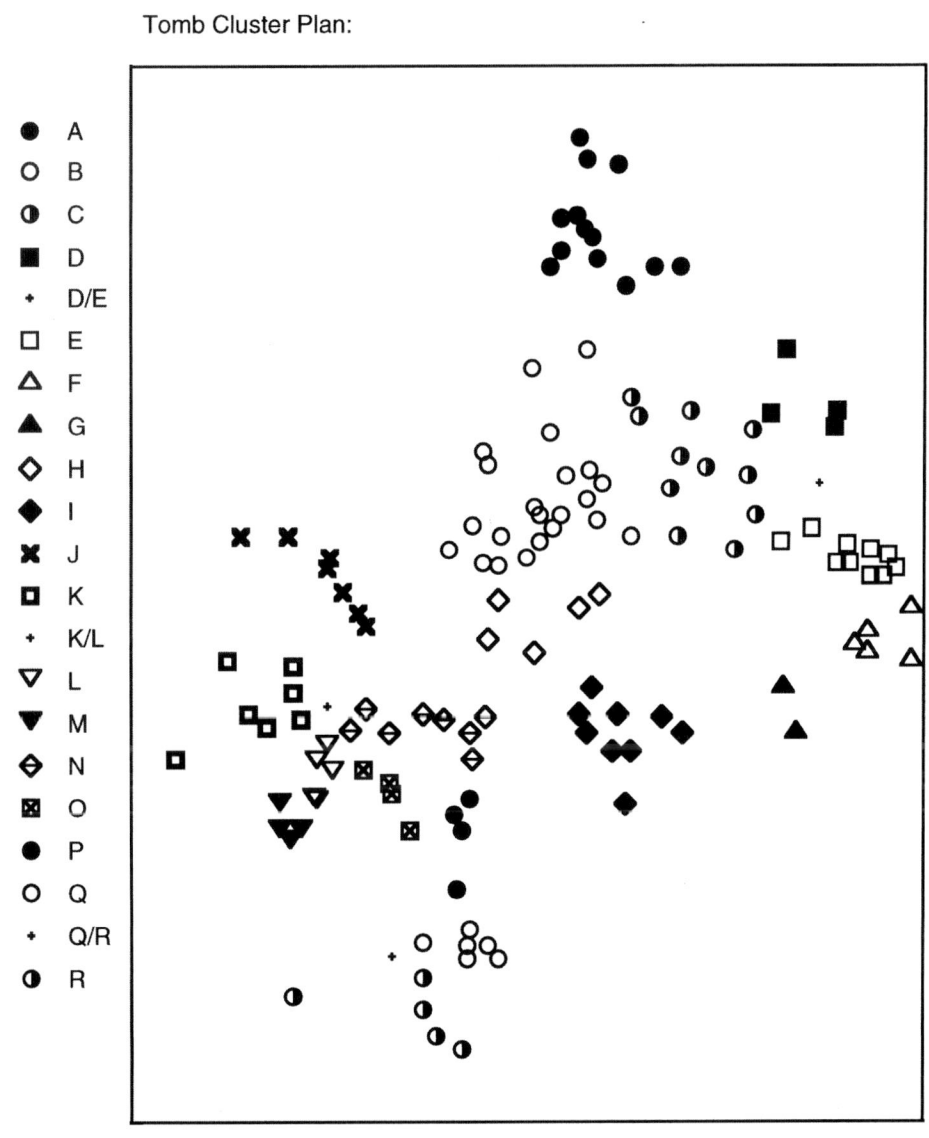

FIGURE 216. Schematic plan of the cemetery showing distribution of tombs according to discrete clusters.

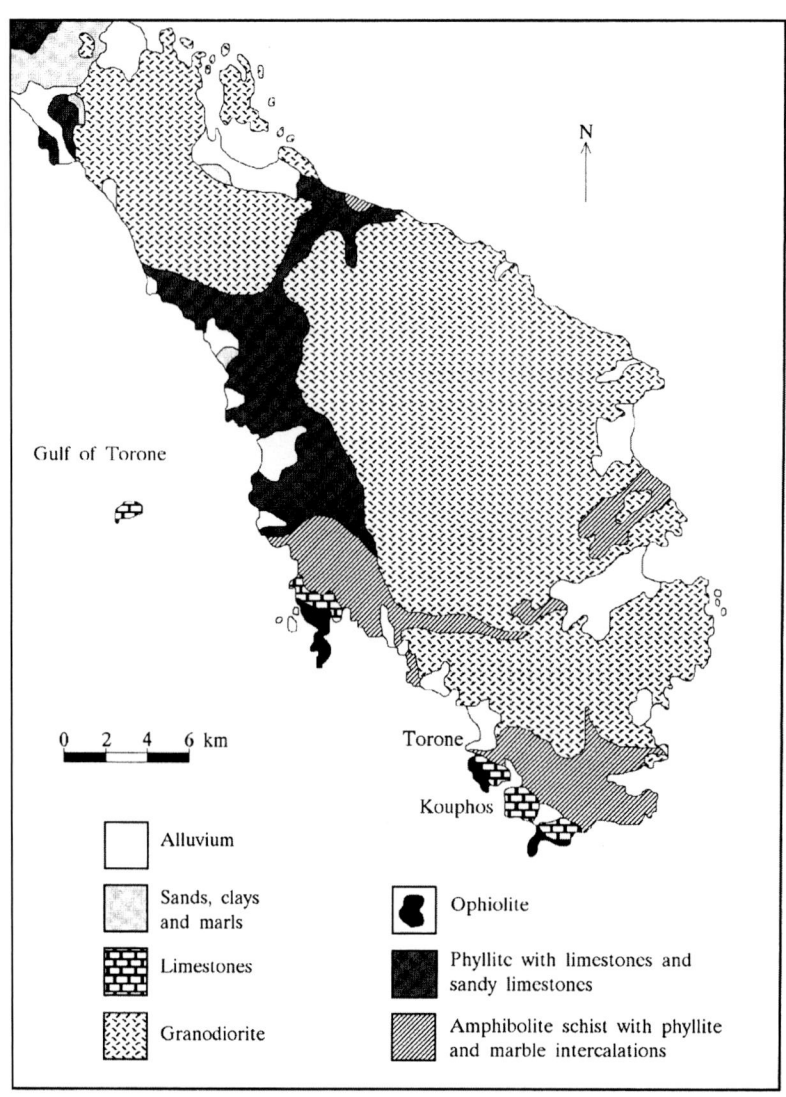

FIGURE 217. Geology of the Sithonia peninsula (after Sapountzis et al. 1976).

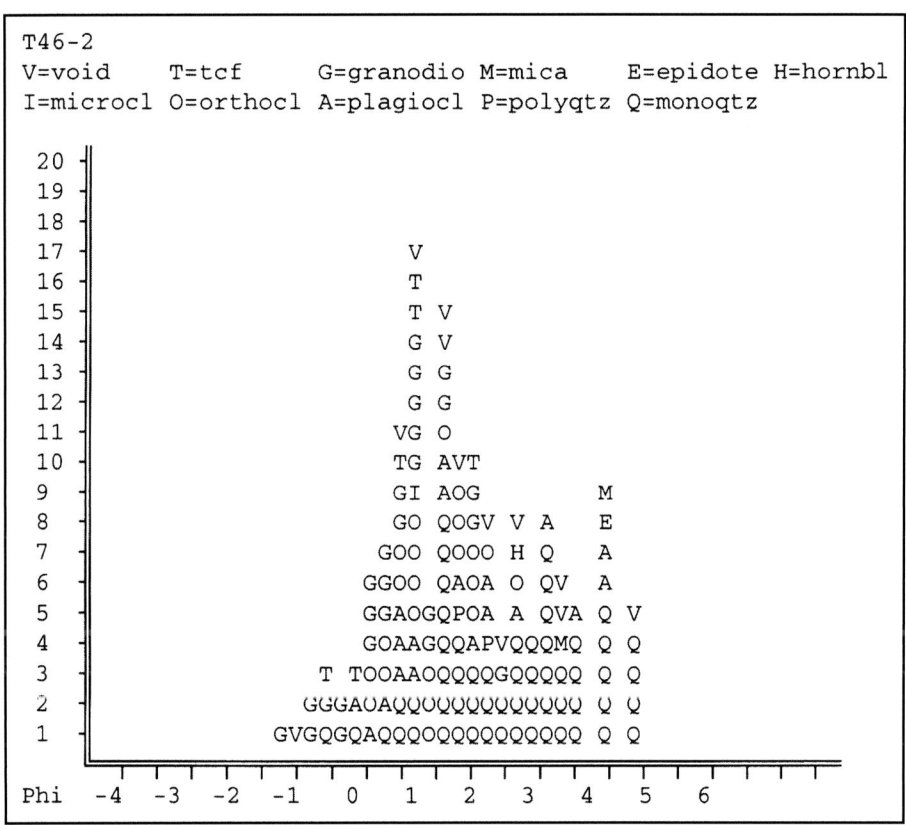

FIGURE 218. Grain-size composition graph of a granodiorite fabric with coarse-grained inclusions (**T46-2**).

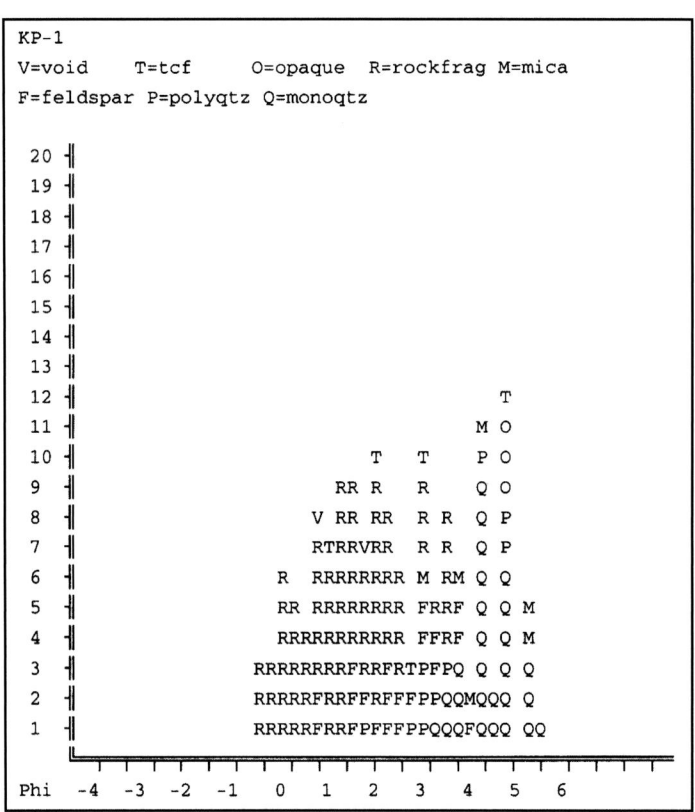

FIGURE 219. Grain-size composition graph of a metamorphic fabric (**KP-1**).

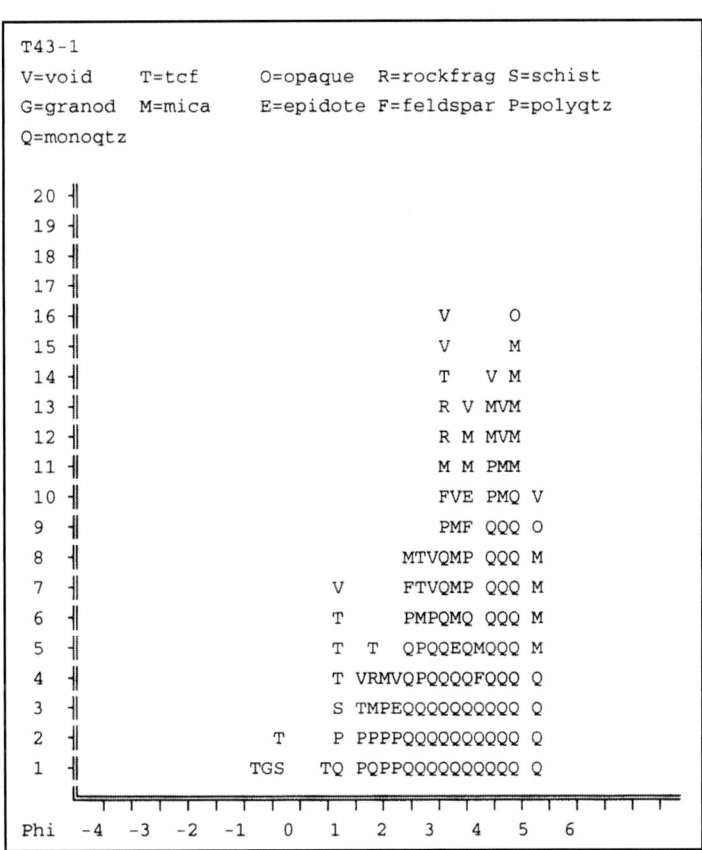

FIGURE 220. Grain-size composition graph of a fine sand fabric (**T43-1**).

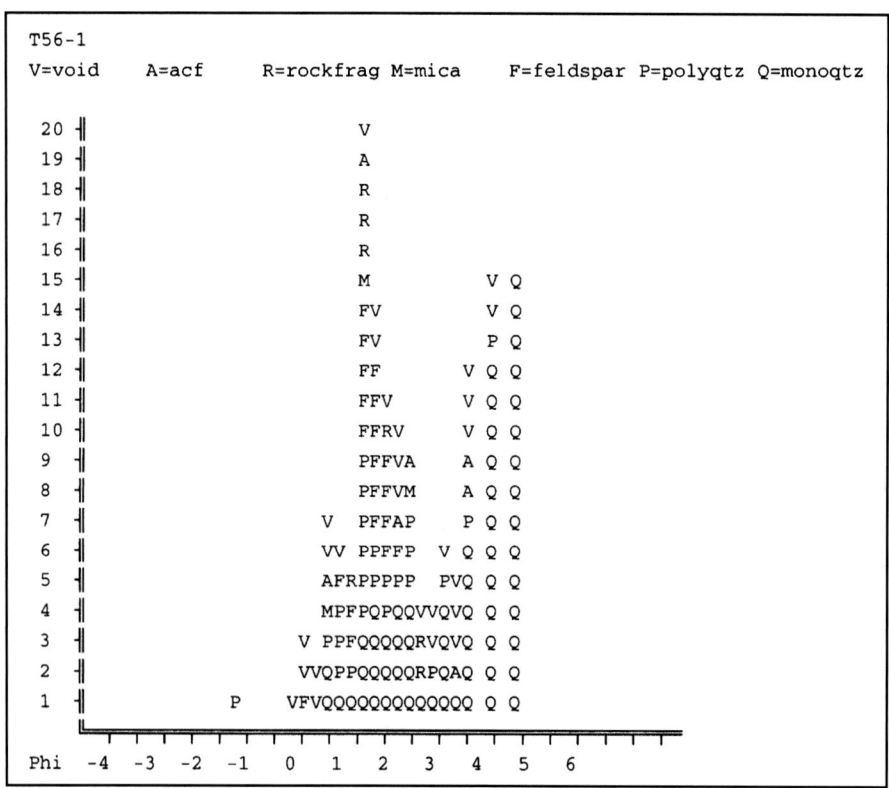

FIGURE 221. Grain-size composition graph of a well-sorted, medium sand-grained fabric (**T56-1**).

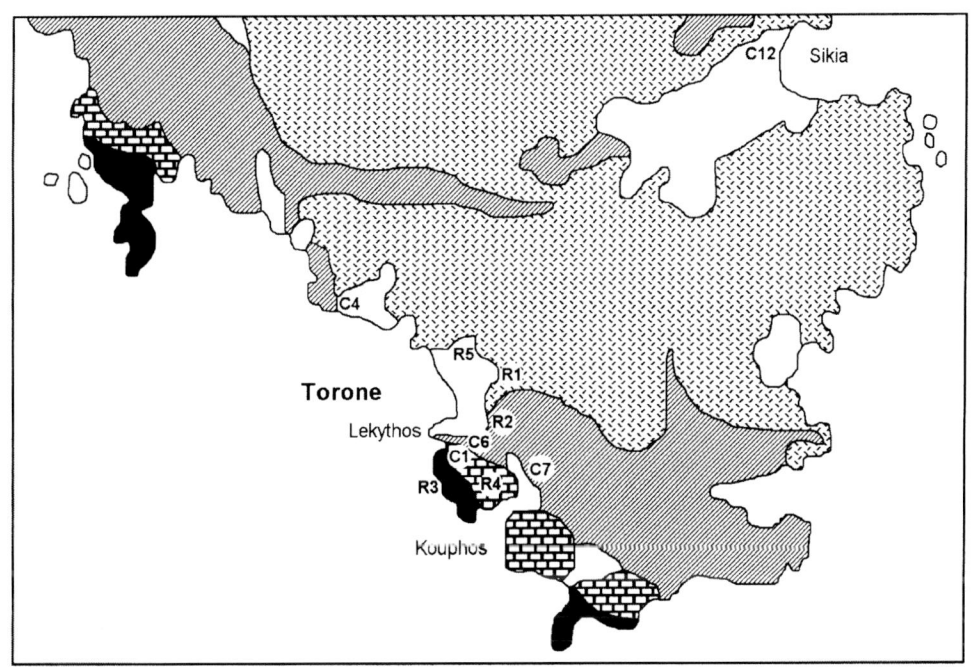

FIGURE 222. Sample locations for rocks and clays relative to the local regional geology (after Sapountzis et al. 1976; Kockel et al. 1978).

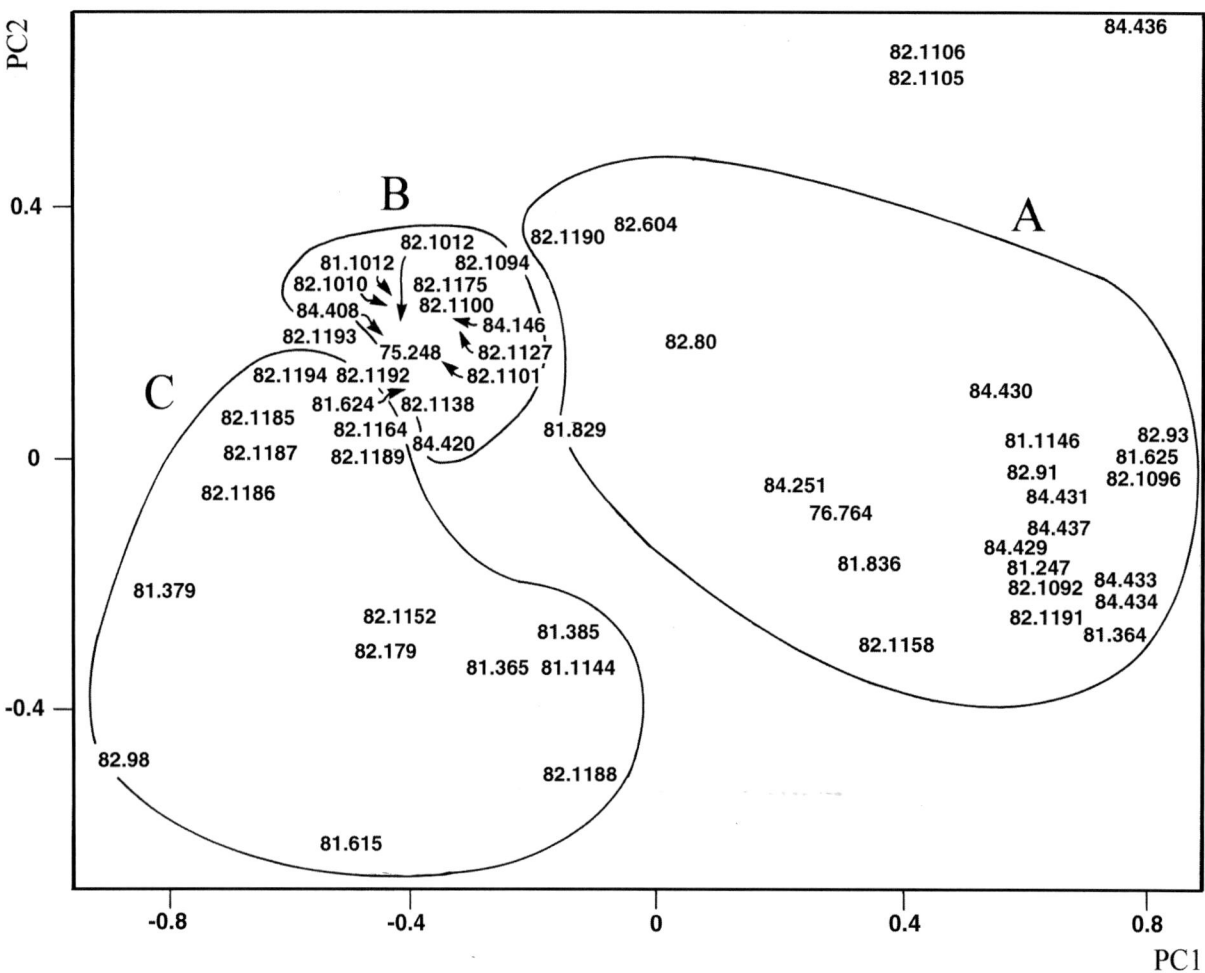

FIGURE 223. Principal components plot (PC1 vs. PC2) of the chemical data (all elements except Si and Ti) for all samples excluding **T99-1**. The three clusters (A, B, and C) observed in fig. 224 have been superimposed. In the dendrogram **KP-13** belongs to cluster C. The boundary of cluster A is drawn to indicate that the cluster includes three outliers (**53, 54** and **T101-8**).

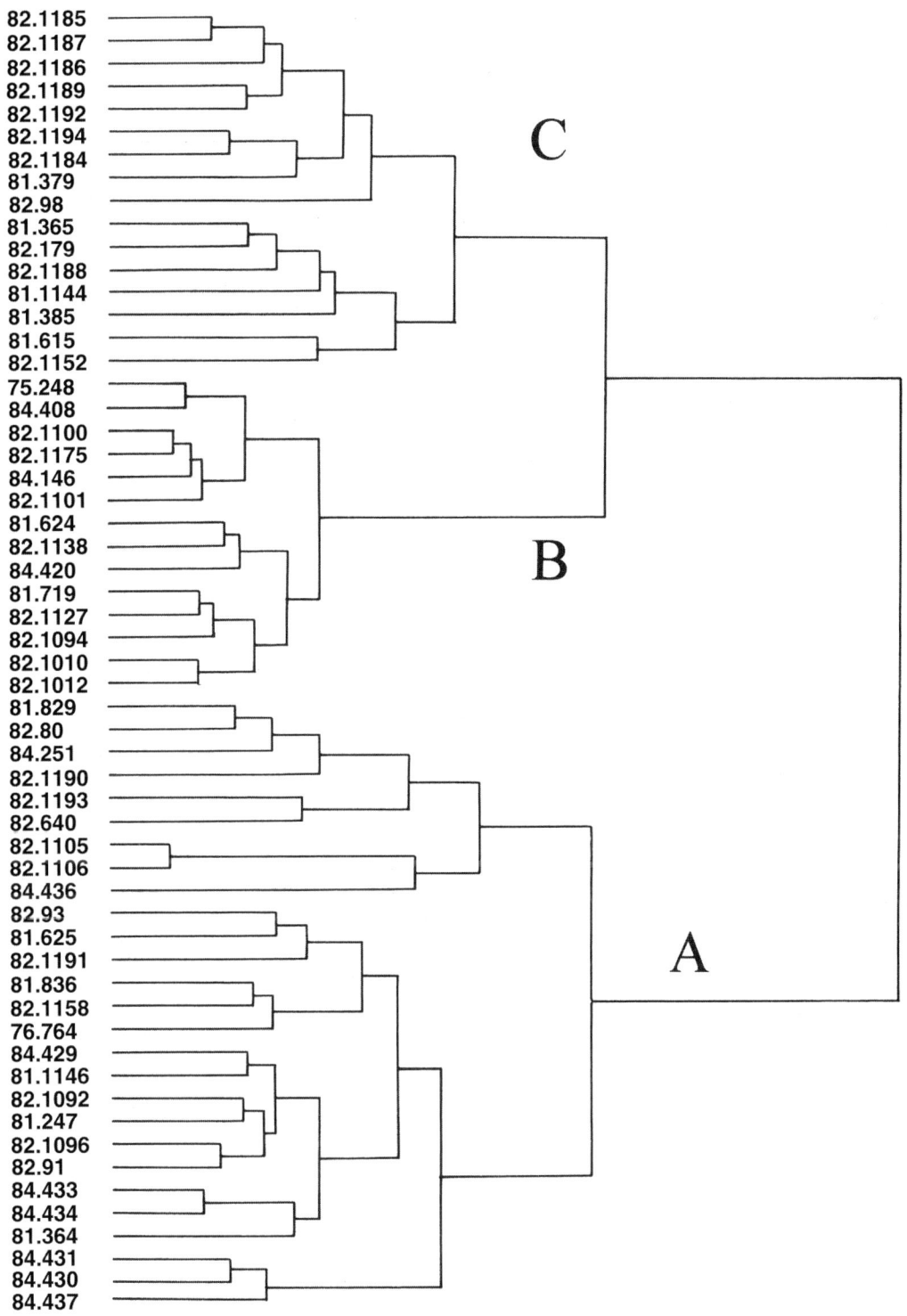

FIGURE 224. Dendrogram resulting from Ward's method cluster analysis of the same data set as in fig. 223.

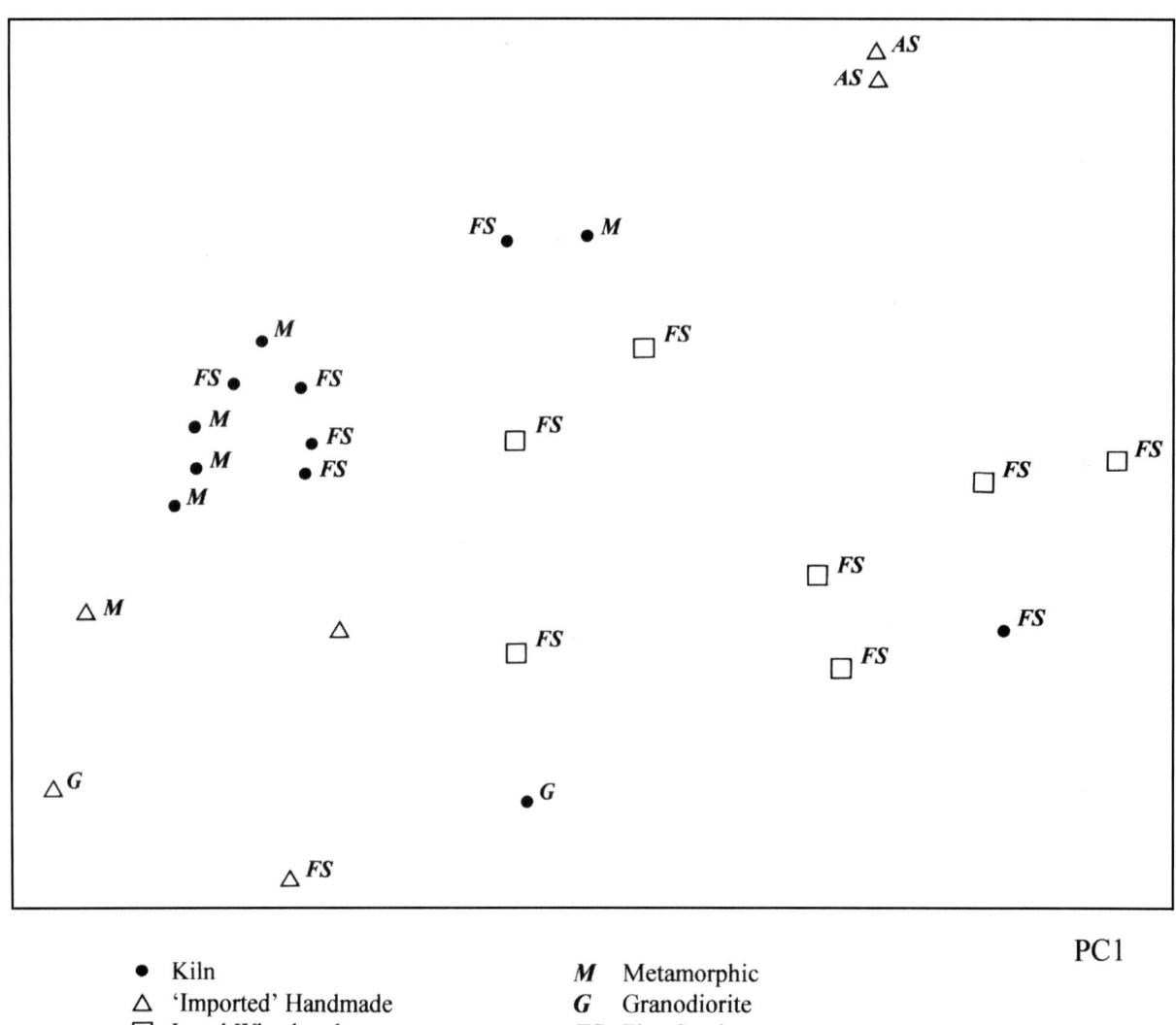

PC1

- ● Kiln
- △ 'Imported' Handmade
- □ Local Wheelmade

- *M* Metamorphic
- *G* Granodiorite
- *FS* Fine Sand
- *AS* Amphibole Schist

FIGURE 225. Correlation of the classification of the chemical data (by PCA) and petrographic data for the kiln pottery, local wheelmade, and "imported handmade." Petrographic fabrics: M = metamorphic; G = granodiorite; FS = (very) fine sand; AS = amphibolite schist.

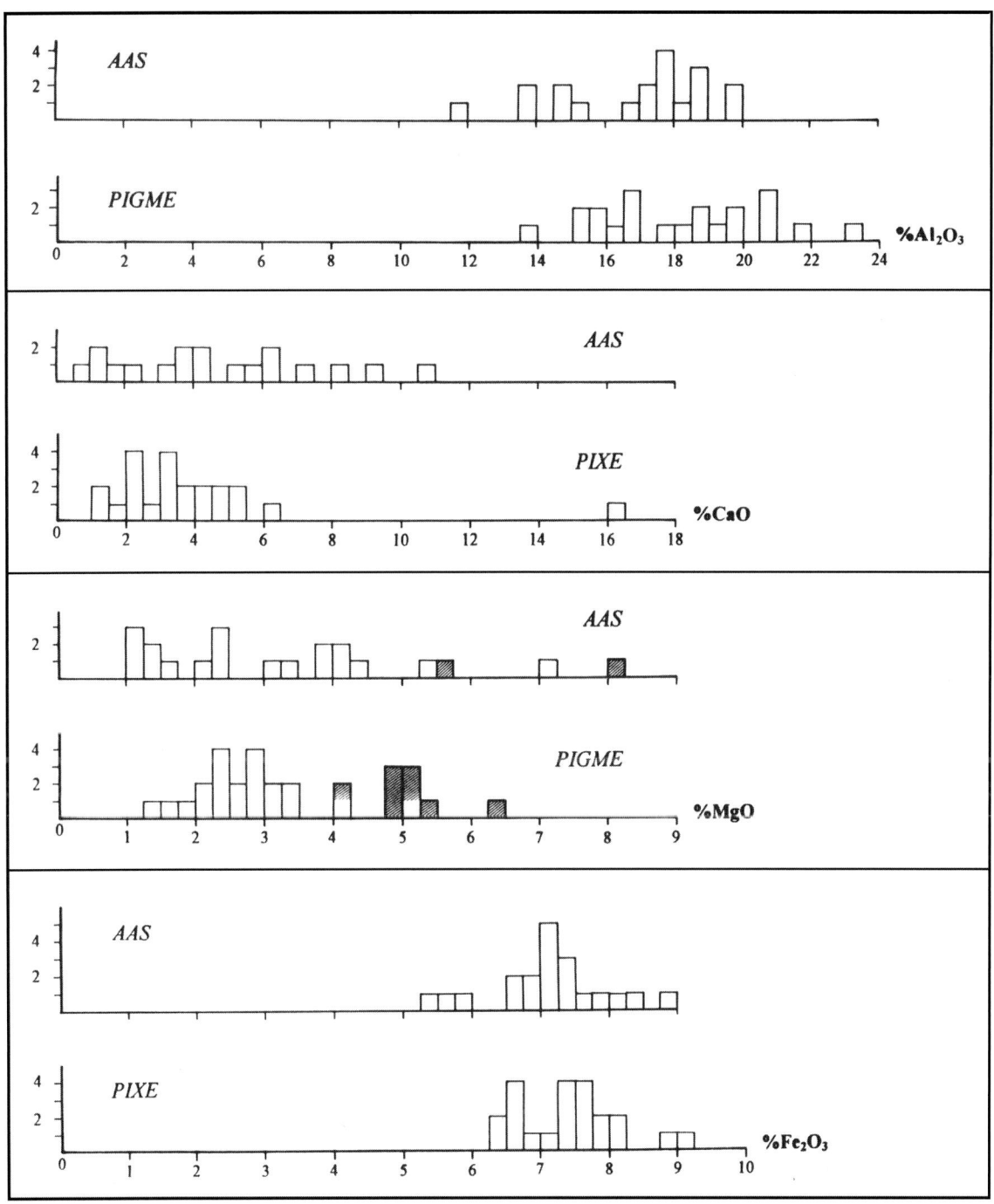

FIGURE 226 (on following page). Distribution of Al, Ca, Mg, and Fe contents in the kiln and local wheelmade pottery (AAS) (top) and Classical local, mainly decorated pottery (PIXE-PIGME) (bottom) (from Tudor Jones 1995). In the Mg distribution are included the two likely Early Iron Age Attic imports (AAS) and examples of Attic BG and RF (PIXE-PIGME).

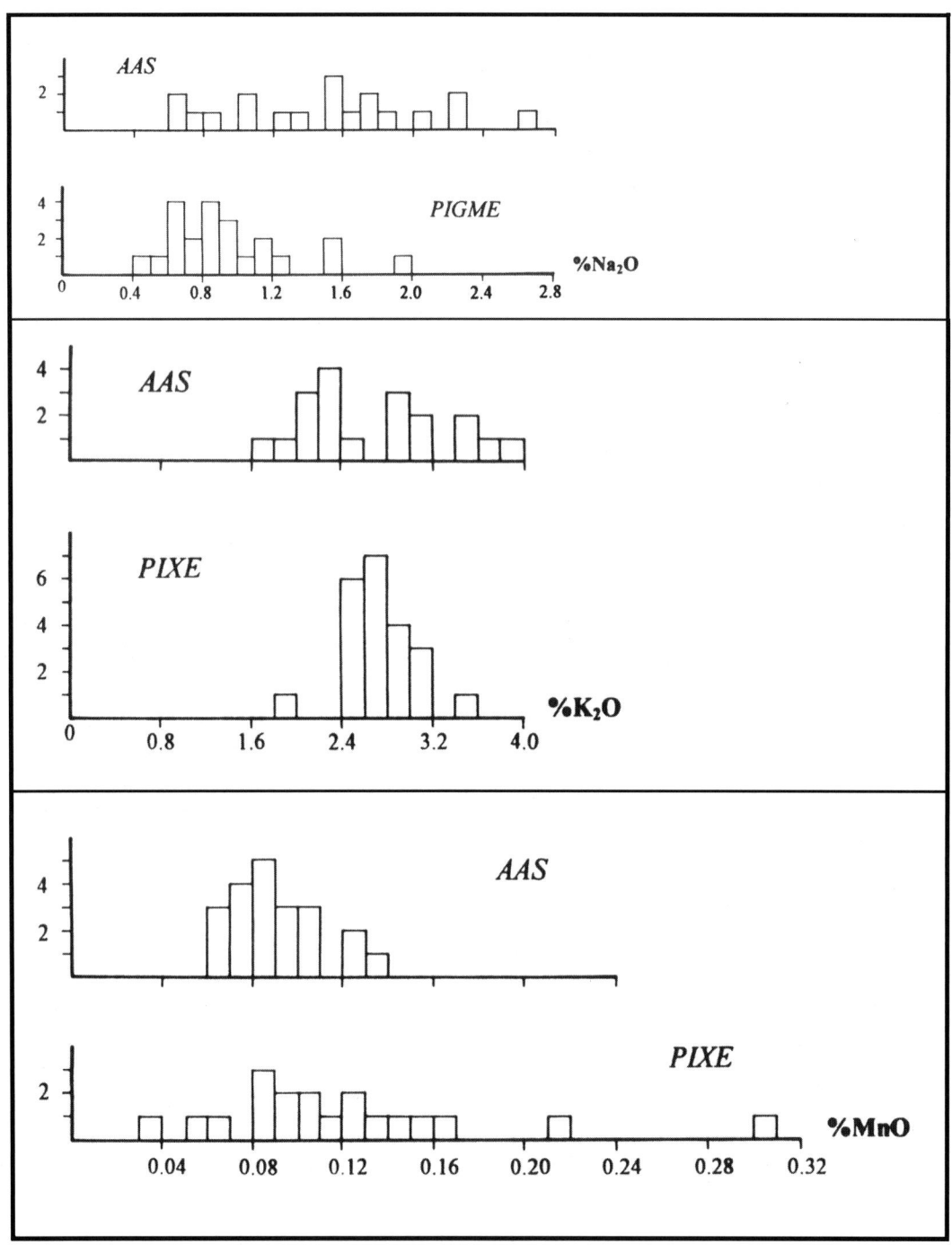

FIGURE 226 (continued). Distribution of Na, K, and Mn contents in the kiln and local wheelmade pottery (AAS) (top) and Classical local, mainly decorated pottery (PIXE-PIGME) (bottom) (from Tudor Jones 1995).

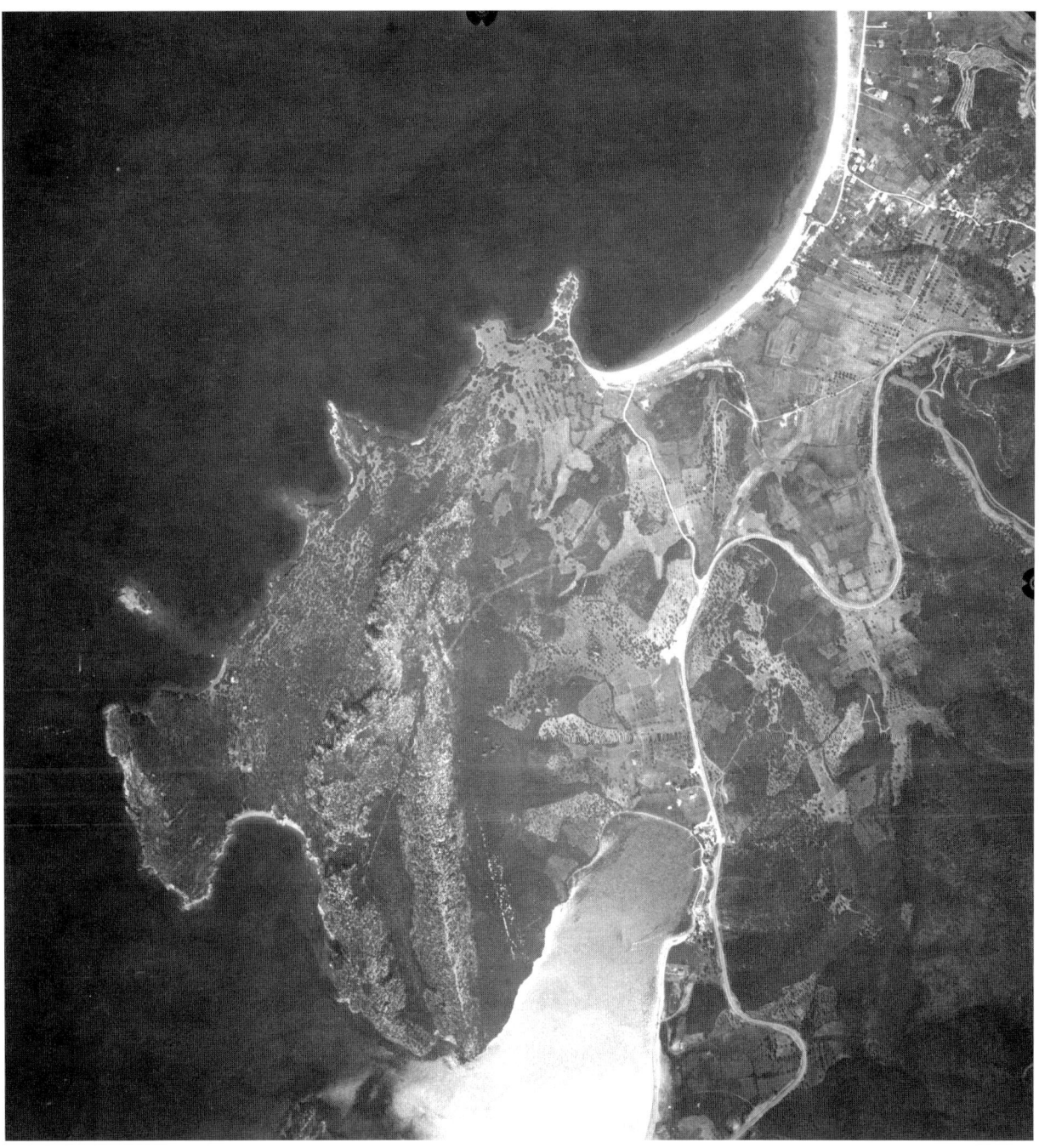

PLATE 1. Aerial photograph of the Torone peninsula, with the harbor of Kophos, taken by the Greek Airforce, 3 August 1979. Approximate scale 1:14000.

PLATE 2. Aerial view of Torone (1986) from the north.

PLATE 3. General view of the site and bay of Torone from NE.

PLATE 4. General view of the site looking across the bay of Torone, from the north.

PLATE 5. General view across SE Sithonia, looking east toward Akte, with Mount Athos in the distance.

PLATE 6. The entrance to Kophos from Hill 1 looking south. The small promontory in the distant background is Cape Derris, the SW tip of Sithonia.

a.

b.

PLATE 7. Hill 1 (Vigla) from Porto Kophos. (*a*) View from ESE. (*b*) View from the south.

a.

b.

PLATE 8. The entrance to the harbor of Kophos, Hill 1 to the right, Pallene in the distant background. (*a*) From the east. (*b*) Detail.

PLATE 9. View of the site across the plain of Torone, looking WSW. Pallene in distant background to right.

PLATE 10. View of the site from the north: Promonotory 1 in foreground, Hill 1 in background, Promontory 2 to the right.

PLATE 11. General view of the site and bay of Torone from Hill 1, looking north.

PLATE 12. General view of the site from the upper terraces of Hill 2 looking NNW,
showing Promontory 1 and Terrace V in center.

PLATE 13. Terrace V from the south at the end of the 1984 season.

PLATE 14. View of the northern part of the plain of Torone, looking NW.

PLATE 15. Promontory 1 (excavations of 1986–1990) Trench 61/62 showing
Early Iron Age pithoi in situ. View from SE.

a.

b.

PLATE 16. Terrace V from NW showing trenches as excavated.
(*a*) At the end of the 1981 season. (*b*) At the end of the 1984 season.

PLATE 17. Terrace V. View from SE at the end of the 1982 season. Trenches 27, 26, and 26 East Baulk in foreground; Trenches 22 and 40 partly visible at left; Trenches 46 and 43 to the right.

PLATE 18. Terrace V. South–north view of the east part of the excavated area (1982). View from the south showing Trenches 29, 27, 46, and 43.

PLATE 19. Terrace V. View at the end of the 1984 season of the trenches in the north sector of the terrace showing Trenches 56, 56 East Baulk, 57, and 57 East Baulk; Trench 55 in background. View from SE, "Pyrgos" visible in background.

PLATE 20. Trench 1 during excavation showing Tombs 20, 21, 22, and 23 from NW.

PLATE 21. Terrace IV at the end of the 1982 season from the west showing Classical domestic architecture and Late Roman tombs.

a.

PLATE 22 (on facing page). Terrace IV. (*a*) At the end of the 1984 season. View from NE showing embankment between Terraces IV and V.

b.

c.

PLATE 22 (continued). Terrace IV. (*b*) Classical domestic architecture, including house wall used for terrace retention. View from NW (1982). (*c*) View of Classical wall cut vertically in bedrock and lined with plaster, separating Terraces IV and V; Late Roman tombs in left foreground. View from NE.

PLATE 23. Trench 6 during excavation showing Tomb 42 in foreground (right), Tomb 43 at center left, and Tomb 46 behind, near wall *a*. View from the north.

PLATE 24. Trench 6 during excavation showing Tombs 44, 45, and 40 from NNW.

PLATE 25. Trench 6. Cremation tomb pits at end of the 1981 season, view from the west.

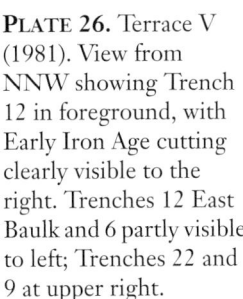

PLATE 26. Terrace V (1981). View from NNW showing Trench 12 in foreground, with Early Iron Age cutting clearly visible to the right. Trenches 12 East Baulk and 6 partly visible to left; Trenches 22 and 9 at upper right.

a.

b.

PLATE 27. Trench 12. (*a*) Deposit Type 2 partly cleared; Early Iron Age cutting in foreground, unworked bedrock with cuttings for cremation tombs (pits of Tombs 31 and 32) in the center. (*b*) View from the west.

PLATE 28. Trench 12. View from NE showing wall *a*, portion of Early Iron Age cutting, and unworked bedrock in foreground.

PLATE 29. Trench 13 during excavation. View from the north showing Tombs 56 (foreground) and 57 (center).

PLATE 30. Trench 15 from the west at the end of the 1981 season.

PLATE 31. East portion of Trench 15 during excavation showing horizontal extent of deposit type 2 (foreground) and Pit 1 at center. View from the south.

a.

b.

PLATE 32. Trench 22. (*a*) View from the west during early stages of excavation (1981: Stage 1). Pit for Tomb 111 prominent at upper left. (*b*) After continued excavation (1982). View from NW.

PLATE 33. Trench 22 during excavation (Stages 2 and 3) showing relationship between Classical walling and Early Iron Age tombs (Tomb 115 in foreground; wall *a* in background). View from NW.

a.

b.

PLATE 34. Trench 22 North Baulk. (*a*) Detail of wall *e* from above, south. (*b*) Detail of deposit type 2 from the south.

PLATE 35. Trenches 22 North Baulk, 25 North Baulk, and 25 East Baulk. General view from the east showing Trench 22 North Baulk wall *e* in foreground; Promontory 2 in background.

a.

b.

PLATE 36. Trenches 22 North Baulk, 25 North Baulk, and 25 East Baulk. (*a*) View from the west showing cuttings for Tombs 9 and 10 (Trench 60 in background). (*b*) View from SW showing Trench 25 East Baulk wall *b/d* in foreground, Trenches 55–57 in background.

a.

PLATE 37. Trenches 25 North Baulk, 25 East Baulk, and 22 North Baulk. (*a*) Detail from NNE showing Trench 25 East Baulk wall *a* in foreground, cuttings for tombs; wall *b/d* in background. (*b*) View from SW.

b.

PLATE 38. Trench 25 during excavation. Tombs 13 and 14 in foreground (left); cuttings for Tombs 103, 104, and 105 at upper left; wall *a* and cutting for Tomb 16 at center right. View from the north.

a.

b.

PLATE 39. Trenches 25 North Baulk and 25 East Baulk during excavation. (*a*) View from NE showing Tomb 10 in foreground, pithos fragments of Tomb 12 at center (protruding from scarp), Tomb 9 to right, and Tomb 15 at upper left. (*b*) View from NW showing Tombs 9 (right) and 10 (left) in foreground, Tomb 15 at top, and Tomb 12, just visible protruding from scarp at center.

PLATE 40. Trench 25 East Baulk. Detail of deposit type 2, view from the south.

PLATE 41. Trench 25 East Baulk. Detail of wall *b/d* in the south part of the baulk; Tomb 15 below. View from WNW.

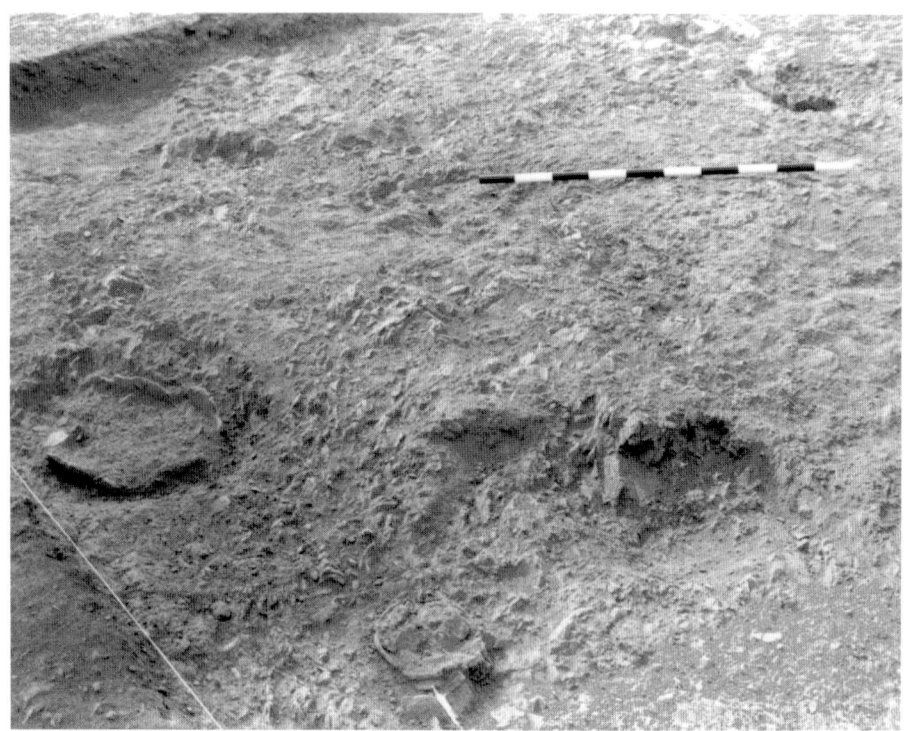

PLATE 42. Trench 26. View from NW showing Tombs 87 (foreground) and 89 (left), pit for Tomb 88 (right), and Tomb 94 in background (right).

PLATE 43. Trench 26. View from SW at the end of the 1982 season showing cremation tomb pits. SE corner of Trench 22 visible at left, NW corner of Trench 28 at right.

PLATE 44. Trenches 26 (foreground) and 28 (background). View from the north showing cremation tomb pits.

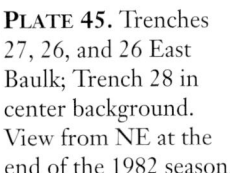

PLATE 45. Trenches 27, 26, and 26 East Baulk; Trench 28 in center background. View from NE at the end of the 1982 season.

PLATE 46. Trench 28 at the end of the 1982 season. View from the south.

PLATE 47. Trench 29 at the end of the 1982 season. View from SE.

PLATE 48. Trench 40. View from the north at the end of the 1982 season showing Early Iron Age cutting.

a.

b.

PLATE 49. Trench 43 during excavation. (*a*) Central and east part, view from the north. (*b*) View from the west (small cutting for Tomb 55 visible at right of center).

PLATE 50. Trench 43 at the end of the 1982 season. View from NW.

PLATE 51. Trench 43. Detail of Early Iron Age kiln during excavation. View from above, NE.

PLATE 52. Trench 43. Detail of kiln after partial excavation showing pithos **KP-1** in situ.
View from above, SW.

PLATE 53. Trench 43. Detail of kiln at the conclusion of excavation. View from SE.

PLATE 54. Trench 44 at the end of the 1982 season.

PLATE 55. Trench 46. View from the north showing wall *a* at center, pit of Tomb 79 behind (at scarp), and pits of Tombs 75 and 76 to left.

a.

b.

PLATE 56. Trenches 47 and 48 at the end of the 1984 season. (*a*) View from NW. (*b*) Detail of Trench 47 from the north.

PLATE 57. Trenches 47 and 48. View from SW.

a.

b.

PLATE 58. Trenches 47 and 48 (mostly 47). (*a*) View from SE. (*b*) View from NE.

PLATE 59. Trenches 47 and 48 (mostly 48). View from SW.

PLATE 60. Trenches 47 and 48. Paved structure, detail from the west.

PLATE 61. Trench 47 North Baulk during excavation. Detail showing Classical pottery partly underlying wall *1*. View from NW.

PLATE 62. Trench 47 East Baulk during excavation showing stone tumble and tile and pottery smash. Trench 48 wall *1* in foreground, wall *5* at center. View from the south.

PLATE 63. Trench 48. Detail of remnant of pebble floor surface. View from NE.

PLATE 64. Trench 55. Stones at upper level of Pit 1. View from NW.

PLATE 65. Trench 55 at the end of the 1984 season. View from SE (note the unexcavated circular structure "Pyrgos" in background).

PLATE 66. Trenches 56 and 56 East Baulk at the end of the 1984 season. View from SW showing cuttings in bedrock for tomb pits.

PLATE 67. Trenches 57, 57 East Baulk, 56, and 56 East Baulk. View from NW
at the end of the 1984 season.

PLATE 68. Trench 57 during excavation. Detail from the north showing deposit
type 2 in NE corner of the trench.

a.

b.

PLATE 69. Trench 58 (with Trench 13 East Baulk). (*a*) Stage 1, view from the north. (*b*) Stage 2, view from SW.

PLATE 70. Trench 59. View from the NW toward the end of the 1984 season.

PLATE 71. Tomb 1 from above, east. Pithos fragments (**T1-1**) used as bedding;
handle fragment of **T1-2** as encountered.

PLATE 72. Tomb 2, as preserved, from above, south.

PLATE 73. Tomb 3 from SW.

PLATE 74. Tomb 4, as preserved, from the north.

PLATE 75. Tomb 5 from above, NW.

PLATE 76. Tomb 5 from the SW.

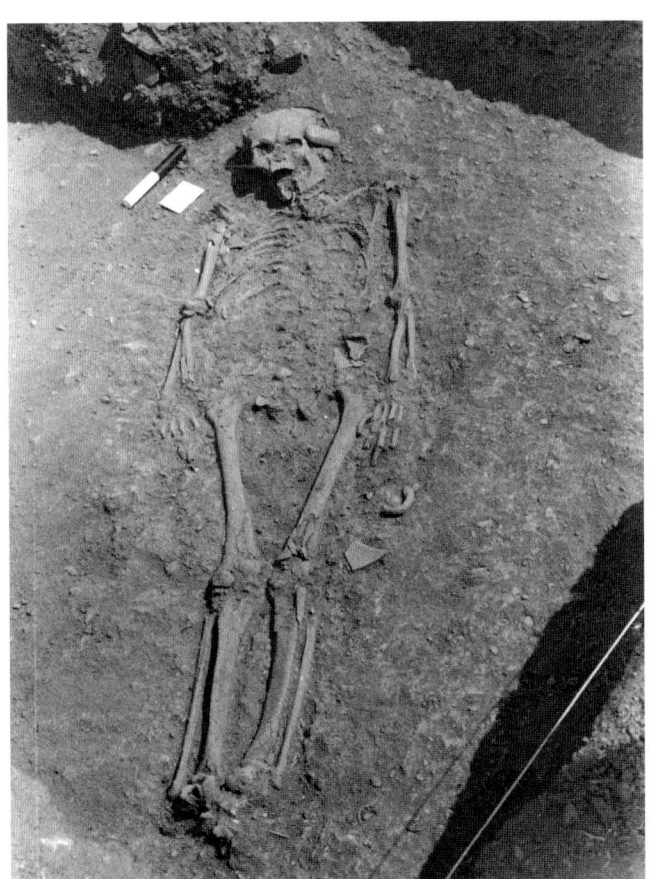

PLATE 77. Tomb 6 from NW (Tomb 97 just visible in background to left of cranium).

PLATE 78. Tomb 6 from NE. Note the level surface of the Early Iron Age cutting.

PLATE 79. Tomb 7 from above, NW.

PLATE 80. Tomb 7 from SE.

PLATE 81. Tomb 7. Detail of mandible and the atlas and axis of the spine as preserved in situ. Detail from the south also showing **T7-6**.

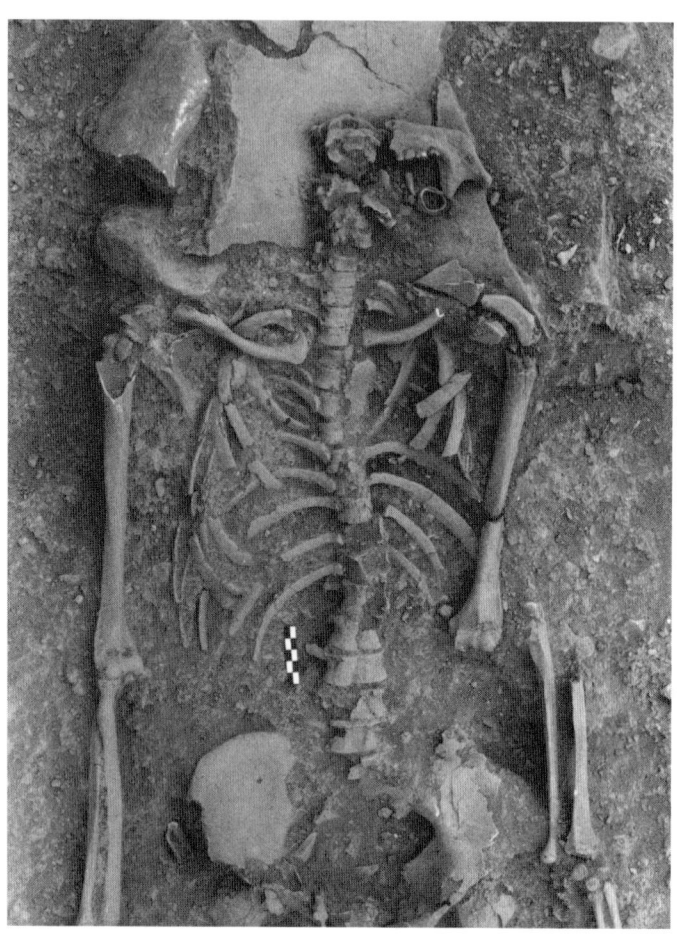

PLATE 82. Tomb 7. Detail of upper torso from above, NW.

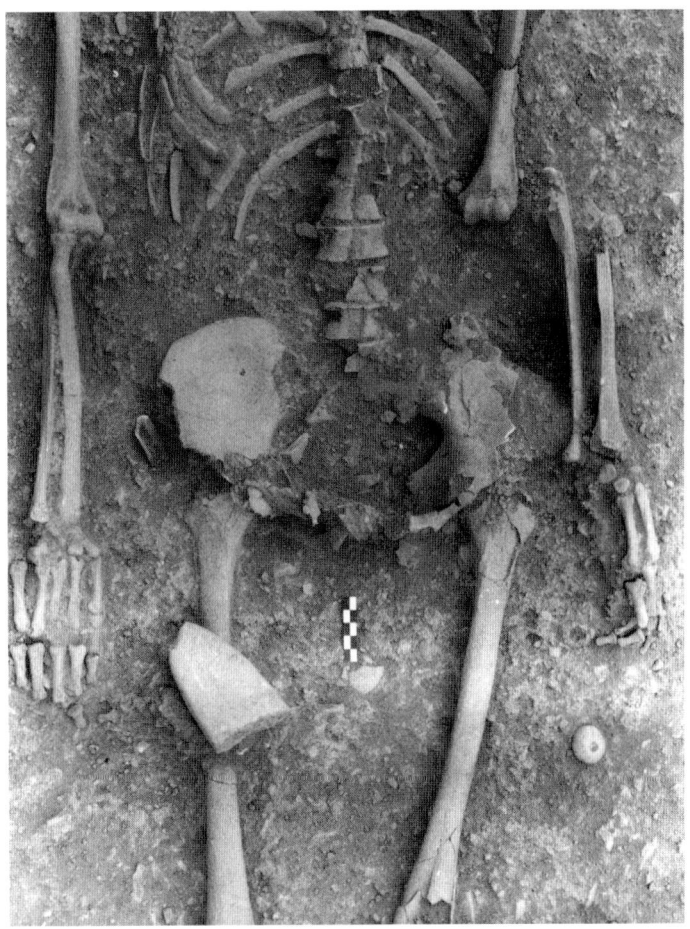

PLATE 83. Tomb 7. Detail of central torso, pelvis, and upper legs; **T7-4** and **T7-5** in situ. View from above, NW.

PLATE 84. Tomb 7. Detail of lower body; **T7-3** and the anklets **T7-7** and **T7-8** in situ. View from above, NW.

PLATE 85. Tomb 7. Detail of **T7-2** as first exposed over left arm of skeleton. View from above, SSW.

PLATE 86. Lifting Tomb 7. From right to left: Jill Carington Smith, the author, and Marian Melnyczek.

PLATE 87. Tomb 8, as preserved, from above, west (Trench 12 wall *a* to right).

PLATE 88. Tomb 9. View from SE showing cover stones as first encountered.

PLATE 89. Tomb 9. View from NW after removal of cover stones.

PLATE 90. Tomb 9. View from NW showing inhumations as preserved.
North Skull to right; West Skull at center; East Skull to left.

PLATE 91. Tomb 9. Detail from above, NE, showing lower level of human
remains after partial excavation.

PLATE 92. Tomb 9. Detail showing remains of **T9-1** as preserved near center of tomb at lower level. View from NE.

PLATE 93. Tombs 10 and 11 from NE.

PLATE 94. Tomb 10. Detail of cranium and upper body; **T10-5** in situ.
View from above, NW.

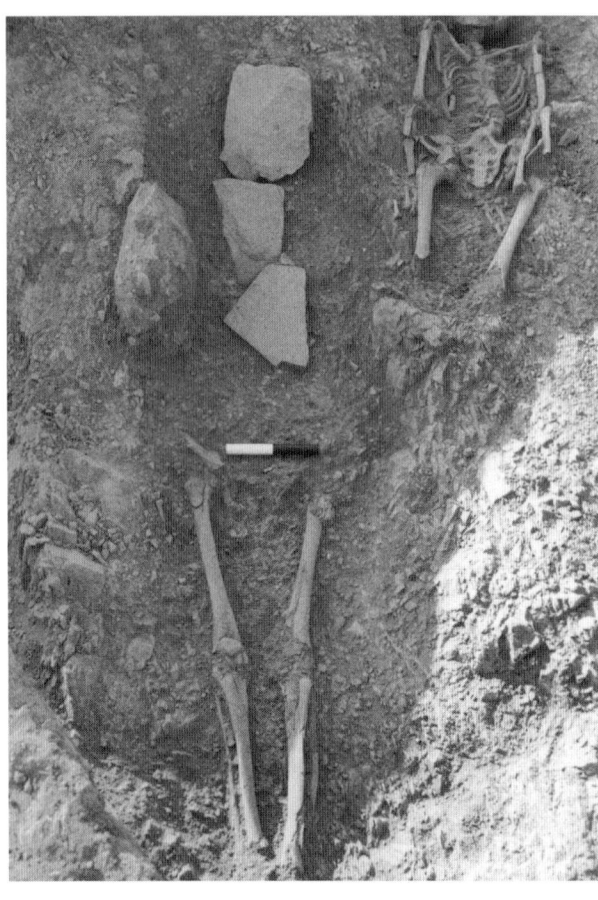

a.

PLATE 95. Tomb 10. (*a*) From above, NW, showing cover stones over upper body as found (Tomb 11 to upper right). (*b*) With cover stones removed.

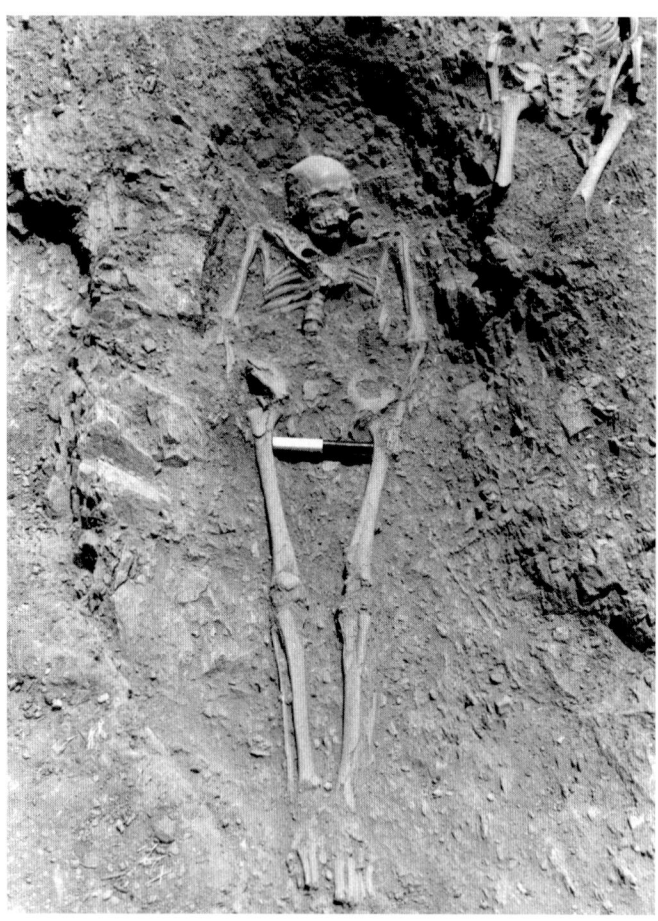

b.

a.

b.

PLATE 96. Tomb 10. Upper level as first encountered showing **T10-2**, **T10-3**, and **T10-4** in situ. (*a*) View from SW. (*b*) Detail from NE.

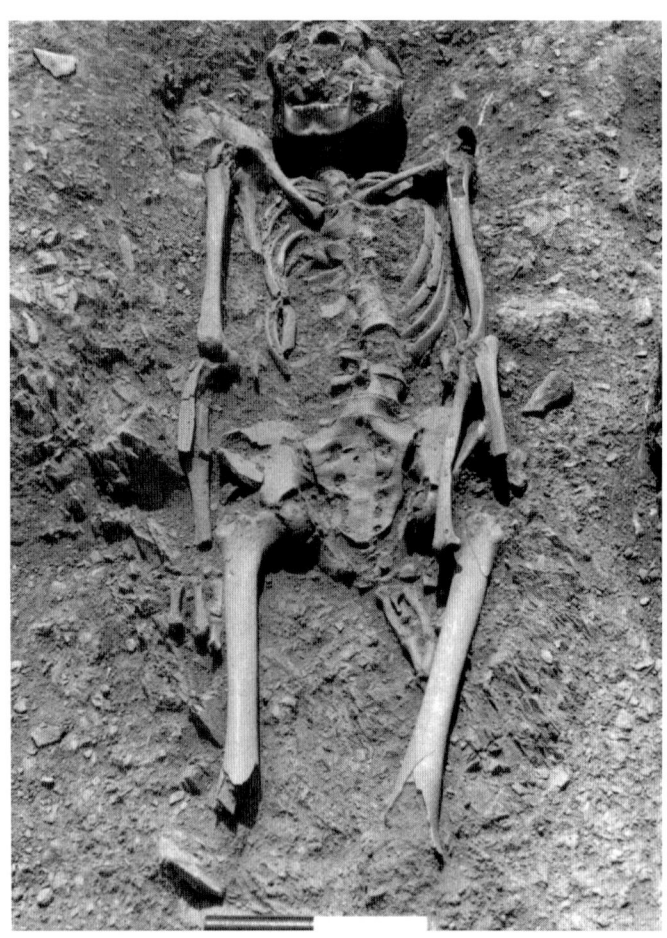

PLATE 97. Tomb 11 from NW.

PLATE 98. Tomb 11. Detail of cranium and upper body. View from NW.

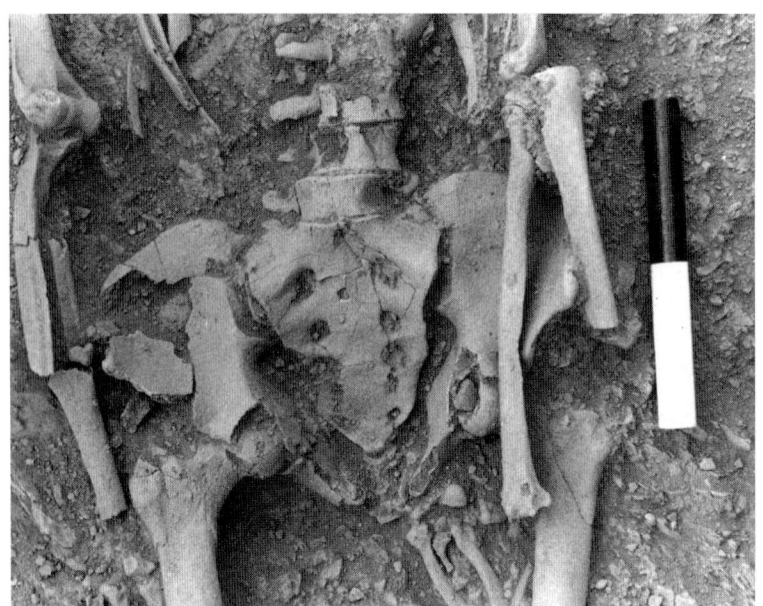

PLATE 99. Tomb 11. Detail of pelvic region. View from above, NW.

PLATE 100. Tomb 12 as encountered in Trench 25 East Baulk. View from the east.

PLATE 101. Upper level of Tomb 13 showing cover stones, **T13-1** and **T13-2** in situ, and displaced bones from Tomb 14. View from the north.

PLATE 102. Tombs 13 and 14 from above, west (note the fragments of the pithos of Tomb 12 in scarp behind).

PLATE 103. Tombs 13 and 14 from above, east. Tomb 12 in foreground as encountered in 1982.

PLATE 104. Tomb 13 from the west.

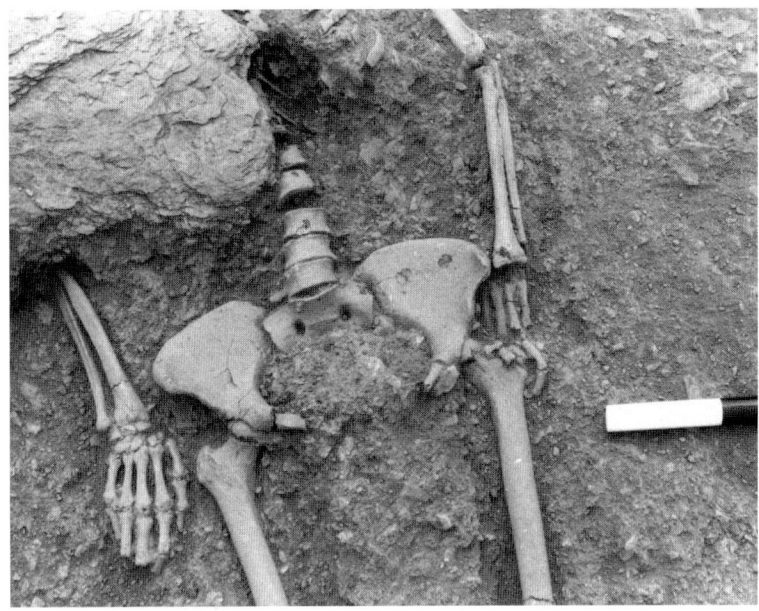

PLATE 105. Tomb 13. Detail of pelvic region (note the left hand under the hip).
View from the north.

PLATE 106. Tomb 13. Detail of feet and lower legs, from the west.

PLATE 107. Tomb 14 (covered) from above, east.

PLATE 108. Tomb 14 (uncovered) from above, NW.

PLATE 109. Detail of the jug **46** in situ from above, west.

PLATE 110. Tomb 15 as first encountered. View from NE.

PLATE 111. Tomb 15. Fragments of the krater **T102-1** removed revealing cover stones of Tomb 15. View from NE.

PLATE 112. Tomb 15 (uncovered) from NNE.

PLATE 113. The feet of Inhumation Tomb 15 resting on the ash-urn of Tomb 101. Detail from WSW.

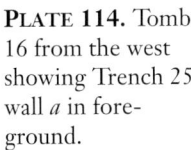

PLATE 114. Tomb 16 from the west showing Trench 25 wall *a* in foreground.

PLATE 115. Tomb 16. Detail of cranium from above, SW.

PLATE 116. Tomb 17 from the south.

PLATE 117. Tomb 18 from NW.

PLATE 118. Tomb 19 from SW.

PLATE 119. Tomb 20 (right) and Tomb 21 (left; covered) in relation to one another.
View from the north.

PLATE 120. Tomb 20 from the north.

PLATE 121. Tomb 21 (covered) from the north.

PLATE 122. Tomb 21 (ash-urn uncovered) from the south.

PLATE 123. Tomb 22 from above, NE.

PLATE 124. Tomb 23 (covered) from above, south.

PLATE 125. Tomb 23 (uncovered) from above, north.

PLATE 126. Tomb 24 from the east.

PLATE 127. Tomb 24 from above, west.

PLATE 128. Tomb 25 (covered) from SSW.

PLATE 129. Tomb 25 (uncovered) from the west.

PLATE 130. Tomb 26. View from the north before removal of stones in tomb pit.

PLATE 131. Tomb 26. Detail from above, north,
after removal of stones in tomb pit.

PLATE 132. Tomb 27 from the east.

PLATE 133. Tomb 28 (covered) from NW.

PLATE 134. Tomb 29 from above, south.

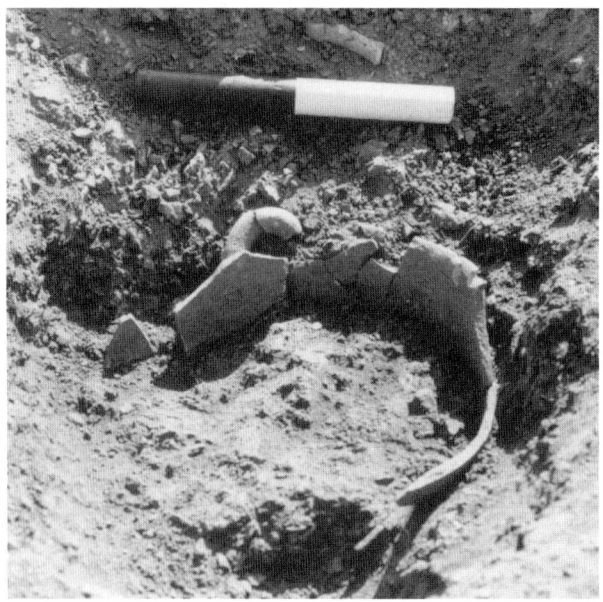

PLATE 135. Tomb 30 from SW.

PLATE 136. Tomb 31 from above, west.

PLATE 137. Tomb 33, as preserved, from NW.

PLATE 138. Tomb 35 from the north.

PLATE 139. Tomb 37 from NE.

PLATE 140. Tomb 38 from above, south.

PLATE 141. Tomb 40 from the north.

PLATE 142. Tomb 41 from the north.

PLATE 143. Tomb 42 from NNW.

PLATE 144. Tomb 43 (covered) from NW.

PLATE 145. Tomb 43 (uncovered) from NW.

PLATE 146. Tomb 44 (uncovered) from the north.

PLATE 147. Tomb 45 (top), Tomb 44, covered (bottom). View from the north.

PLATE 148. Tomb 46 (uncovered) from NW.

PLATE 149. Tomb 47 (covered) from the west.

PLATE 150. Tomb 47 (ash-urn uncovered) from NNE.

PLATE 151. Tomb 48 (covered) from the north.

PLATE 152. Tomb 48 (uncovered) from the north.

PLATE 153. Tomb 49 from the south.

PLATE 154. Tomb 50 from above, NW.

PLATE 155. Tomb 51 as first encountered (Stage 1), from NW.

PLATE 156. Tomb 51 (Stage 2) showing lekanis **T51-3** covering ash-urn. View from the west.

PLATE 157. Tomb 51 ash-urn **T51-1** uncovered (Stage 3), from NW.

PLATE 158. Tomb 52 during early stages of excavation. View from SW.

PLATE 159. Tomb 52 from NW.

PLATE 160. Tomb 53 from above, NE.

PLATE 161. Tomb 54 from the west.

PLATE 162. Tomb 55 from above, north.

PLATE 163. Tomb 56 from above, west.

PLATE 164. Tomb 57 from the north.

PLATE 165. Tomb 58 from above, WSW.

PLATE 166. Tomb 60 from above, NW.

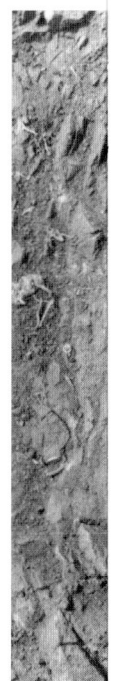

PLATE 167. Tomb 62
from above, NE.

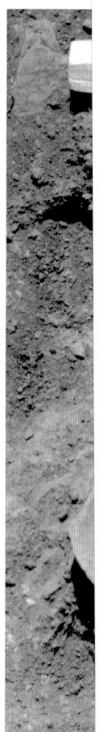

PLATE 172. Tomb 67 upper level (Stage 1) from NE.

PLATE 173. Tomb 67 (Stage 2) from SW.

PLATE 174. Tomb 67 ash-urn uncovered (Stage 3) from SW.

PLATE 175. Tomb 68 from above, north.

PLATE 176. Tomb 69 from NNE.

PLATE 177. Tomb 70 from above, NE.

PLATE 178. Tomb 70 from NE.

PLATE 179. Tomb 72 from above, south.

PLATE 180. Tomb 73 from above, north.

PLATE 181. Tomb 74 from SW.

PLATE 182. Tomb 75 from above, NNW.

PLATE 183. Tomb 76 (left) and Tomb 75 (lower right) from the north.

PLATE 184. Tomb 77 from above, south.

PLATE 185. Tomb 78 from above, NW.

PLATE 186. Tomb 79 from above, north.

PLATE 187. Tomb 80 from above, south.

PLATE 188. Tomb 81 from above, west.

PLATE 189. Tomb 82 from above, north.

PLATE 190. Tomb 83 from above, north.

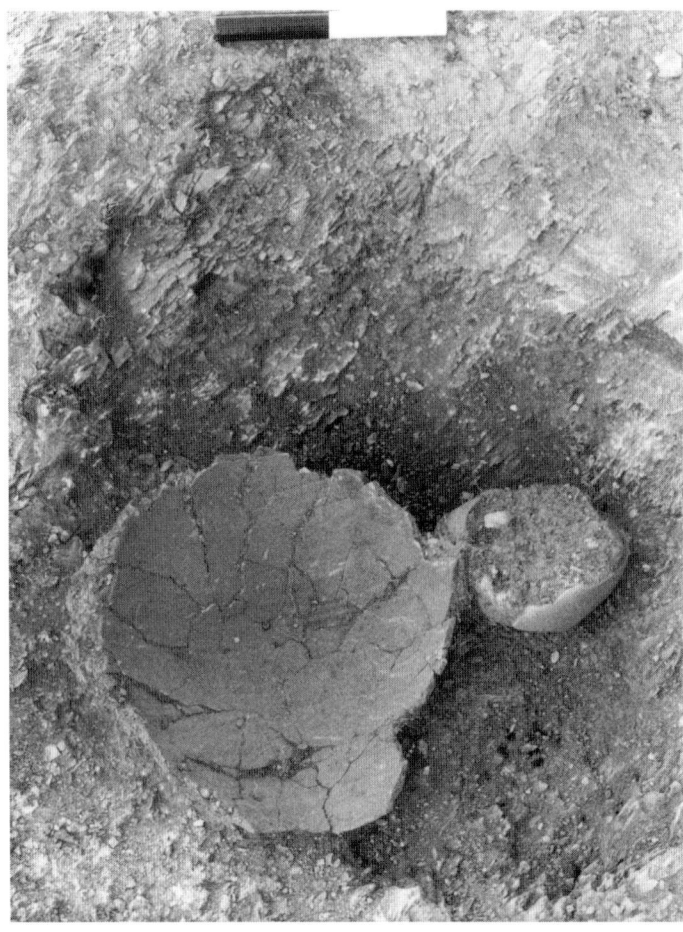

PLATE 191. Tomb 84 from the north.

PLATE 192. Tomb 85 from above, north.

PLATE 193. Tomb 86 from NW.

PLATE 194. Tomb 87 from NE.

PLATE 195. Tomb 88 from the north.

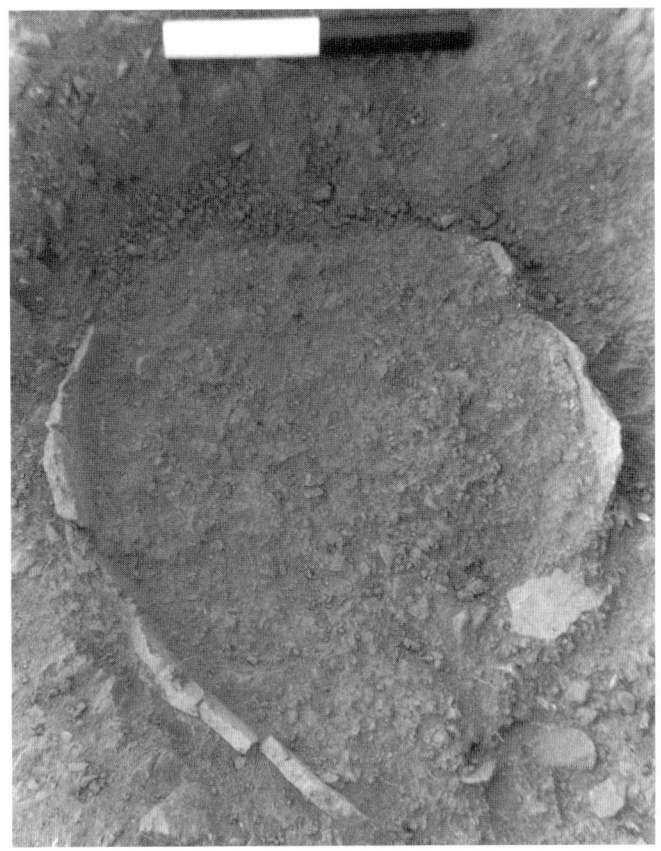

PLATE 196. Tomb 89 from above, east.

PLATE 197. Tomb 90 from above, north.

PLATE 198. Tomb 92 from the north.

PLATE 199. Tomb 94 from the north.

PLATE 200. Tomb 95 from NW.

PLATE 201. Tomb 96 from above, south.

PLATE 202. Tomb 97 from above, north.

PLATE 203. Tomb 99 (covered) from WNW.

PLATE 204. Tomb 99 (ash-urn uncovered) from the south.

PLATE 205. Tomb 100 as first encountered, with cover stones in situ. View from the west.

PLATE 206. Tomb 100 after removal of main cover stones. View from above, east.

a.

b.

PLATE 207. Tomb 102. Fragments of the ash-urn **T102-1** as found above cover slabs of Tomb 15. (*a*) View from NE. (*b*) Detail from above, WNW.

PLATE 208. Pit of Tomb 102 (as exposed below Tomb 15); Tomb 106 (covered) in background. View from the north.

PLATE 209. Tomb 103 from above, north.

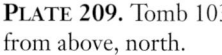

PLATE 210. Tomb 104 as first encountered from above, north (note pithos fragments in scarp behind).

PLATE 211. Tomb 104 during excavation (cover slab removed). View from SW.

a.

b.

PLATE 212. Tomb 104 with cover slab removed showing base of **T104-2** in situ. (*a*) View from the north. (*b*) View from above, NE (note additional stones and pithos fragments to the left).

PLATE 213. Tomb 104 (cover slab and broken base of **T104-2** removed) from NW.

PLATE 214. Tomb 104. Cover slab and one lateral slab removed revealing krater **T104-2** used as cover for the ash-urn. View from the north.

a.

b.

PLATE 215. Tomb 104. The ash-urn **T104-1** after removal of lateral slabs and covering krater (**T104-2**). (*a*) View from NW (note supporting fragments of pithos). (*b*) View from above, SSE.

PLATE 216. Tomb 105 (covered) from above, south.

PLATE 217. Tomb 105 (uncovered) from NW.

PLATE 218. Tomb 106 (covered) from NW.

PLATE 219. Tomb 106 (uncovered) from above, NW.

PLATE 220. Tomb 108 (covered) to right; ash-urn of Tomb 99 (uncovered) at lower left. View from the south.

PLATE 221. Tomb 108 (uncovered) from the north.

PLATE 222. Tomb 109 as first encountered. View from above, north,
showing full extent of tomb pit.

PLATE 223. Tomb 109 after further excavation. View from SW.

PLATE 224. Tomb 111 (Stage 1). View from above, NE, showing upper cover stones.

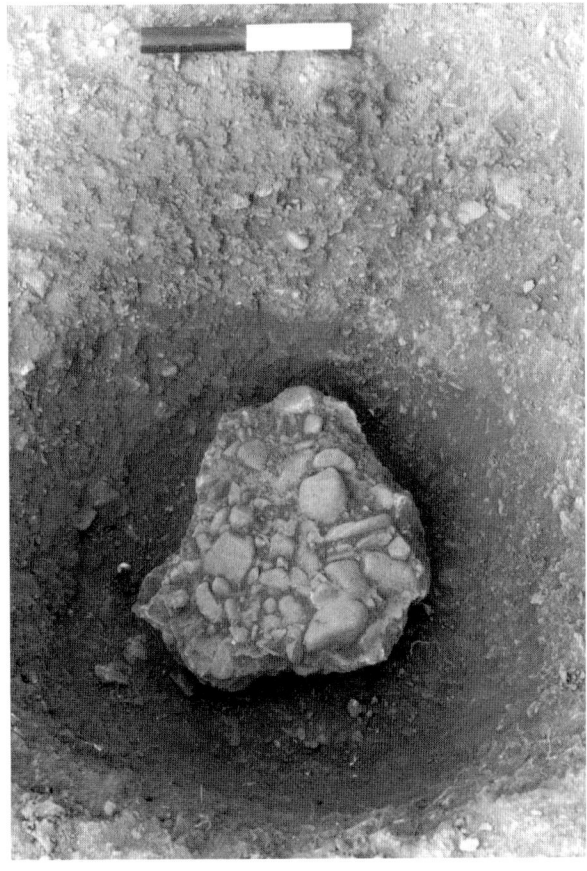

PLATE 225. Tomb 111 (Stage 2). View from above, SSE, showing lower cover stone.

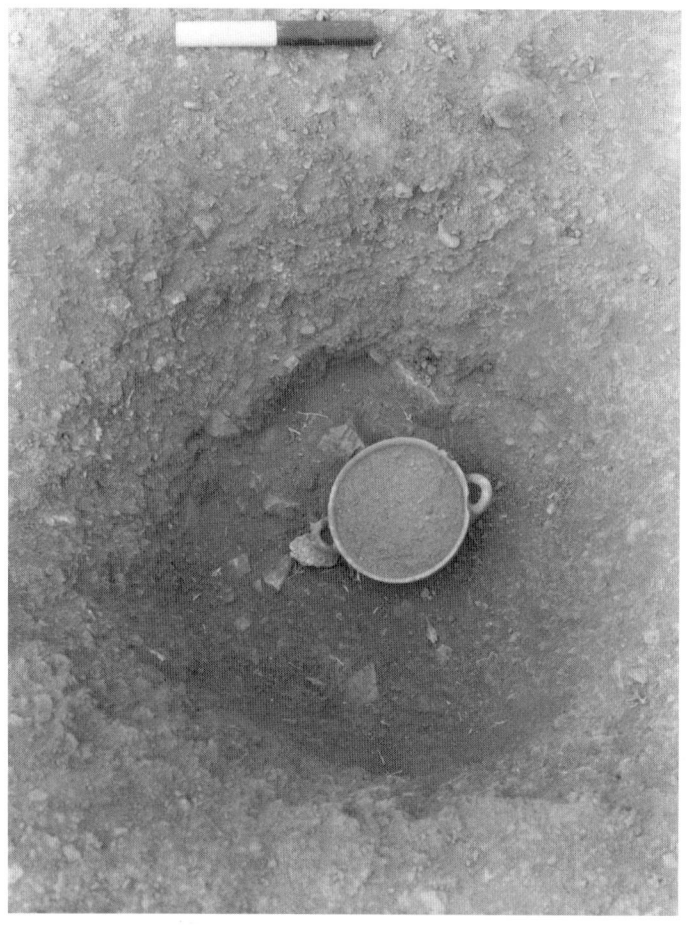

PLATE 226. Tomb 111 (Stage 3). View from above, SSE,
showing ash-urn **T111-1** after removal of cover stones.

PLATE 227. Tomb 112. View from the east showing cover stones in situ; Tomb 113 at lower right.

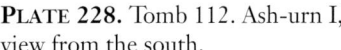

PLATE 228. Tomb 112. Ash-urn I, view from the south.

PLATE 229. Tomb 112. Ash-urn II, view from SW.

PLATE 230. Tomb 113 from above, north.

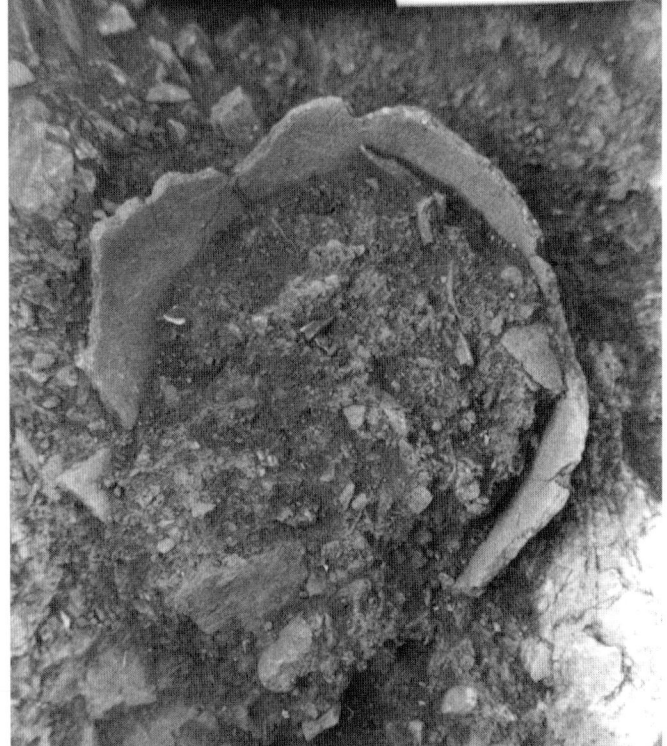

PLATE 231. Tomb 114 from NNW.

PLATE 232. Tomb 115 from above, SW (note bronze fibula **T115-2** in foreground).

PLATE 233. Tomb 116 as first encountered, view from above, south.

PLATE 234. Tomb 117 (covered) from above, north.

PLATE 235. Tomb 117 (uncovered) from above, NE.

PLATE 236. Tomb 118 from NE.

PLATE 237. Tomb 118 from above, south.

PLATE 238. Tomb 119 from above, SSW.

PLATE 239. Tomb 120 from above, SW.

PLATE 240. Tomb 122. Ash-urn **T122-1** from above, west.

PLATE 241. Tomb 122. *Kterisma* **T122-2** from above, south.

PLATE 242. Tomb 123 from above, NNE.

PLATE 243. Tomb 124. Upper level showing lekanis **T124-3** covering ash-urn.
View from the west.

a.

b.

PLATE 244. Tomb 124. Lower level showing the ash-urn **T124-1** and the jug **T124-2**. (*a*) View from above, SSE. (*b*) View from the west.

PLATE 245. Tomb 125 from above, south.

PLATE 246. Tomb 126 from the north.

PLATE 247. Tomb 127 (covered) from above, east.

PLATE 248. Tomb 127 (uncovered) from the west.

PLATE 249. Tomb 128 from NE.

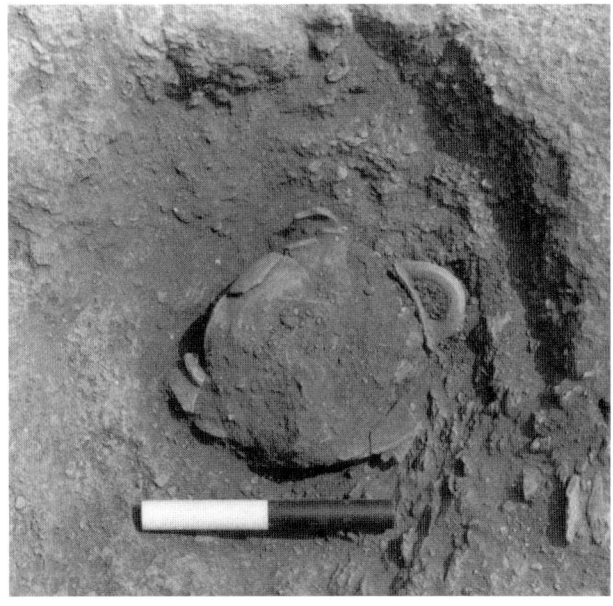

PLATE 250. Tomb 128 from above, west.

PLATE 251. Tomb 129 from the west.

PLATE 252. Tomb 130 as first encountered showing small cover stone
in situ over the mouth of the ash-urn. View from the east.

PLATE 253. Tomb 130 (uncovered) from NE.

PLATE 254. Tomb 130 (uncovered) from above, west.

PLATE 255. Tomb 131 from above, west.

PLATE 256. Tomb 132, as preserved, from SW.

PLATE 257. Tomb 133 from above, WNW.

PLATE 258. Tomb 134 from the north.

PLATE 259 (on pages 1078–1080). T52-1. WM neck-handled amphora. (*a*) Side a.

PLATE 259 (continued). T52-1. WM neck-handled amphora. (*b*) Side b.

c.

PLATE 259 (continued). T52-1. WM neck-handled amphora. (*c*) Side a/b.

a.

PLATE 260 (on pages 1081–1083). T124-1. WM neck-handled amphora. (*a*) Side a.

PLATE 260 (continued). T124-1. WM neck-handled amphora.(*b*) Side b.

PLATE 260 (continued). T124-1. WM neck-handled amphora. (*c*) Side a/b.

a.

b.

Plate 261. T41-1. Neck-handled amphora. (*a*) T41-1. (*b*) Detail of mechanically drawn circles.

PLATE 262. 8. Shoulder and handle fragments, neck-handled amphora.

PLATE 263. T73-1. Fragmentary WM neck-handled amphora.

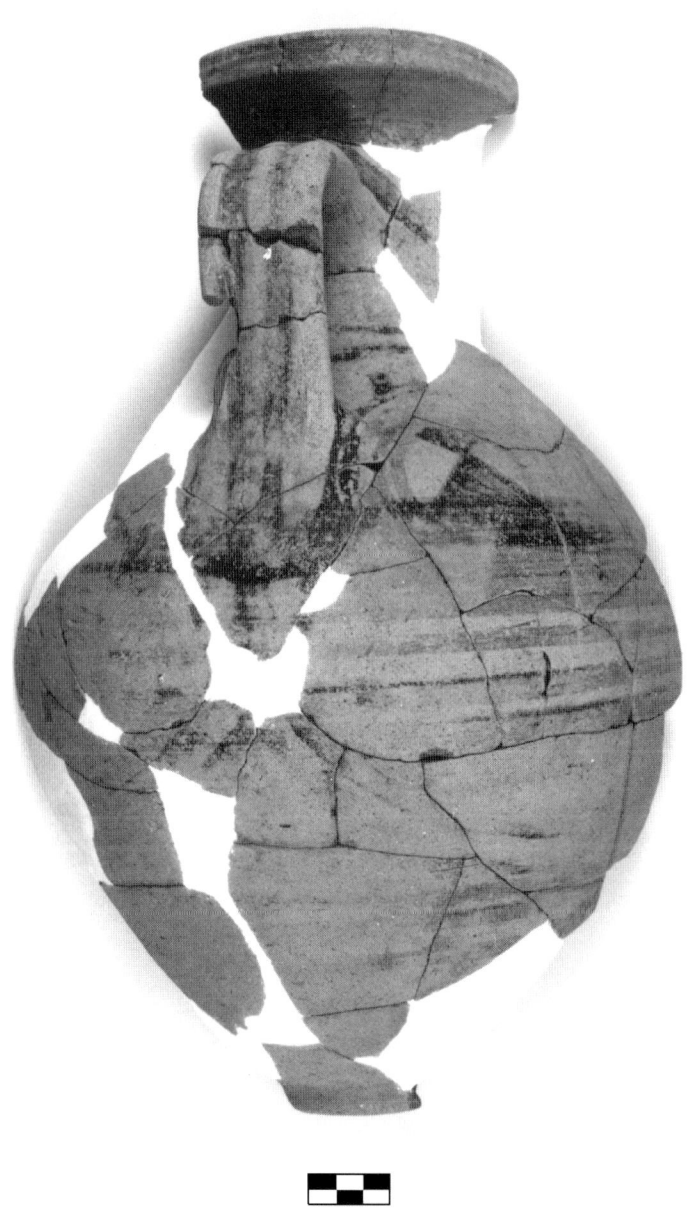

PLATE 264. T74-1. Fragmentary WM neck-handled amphora.

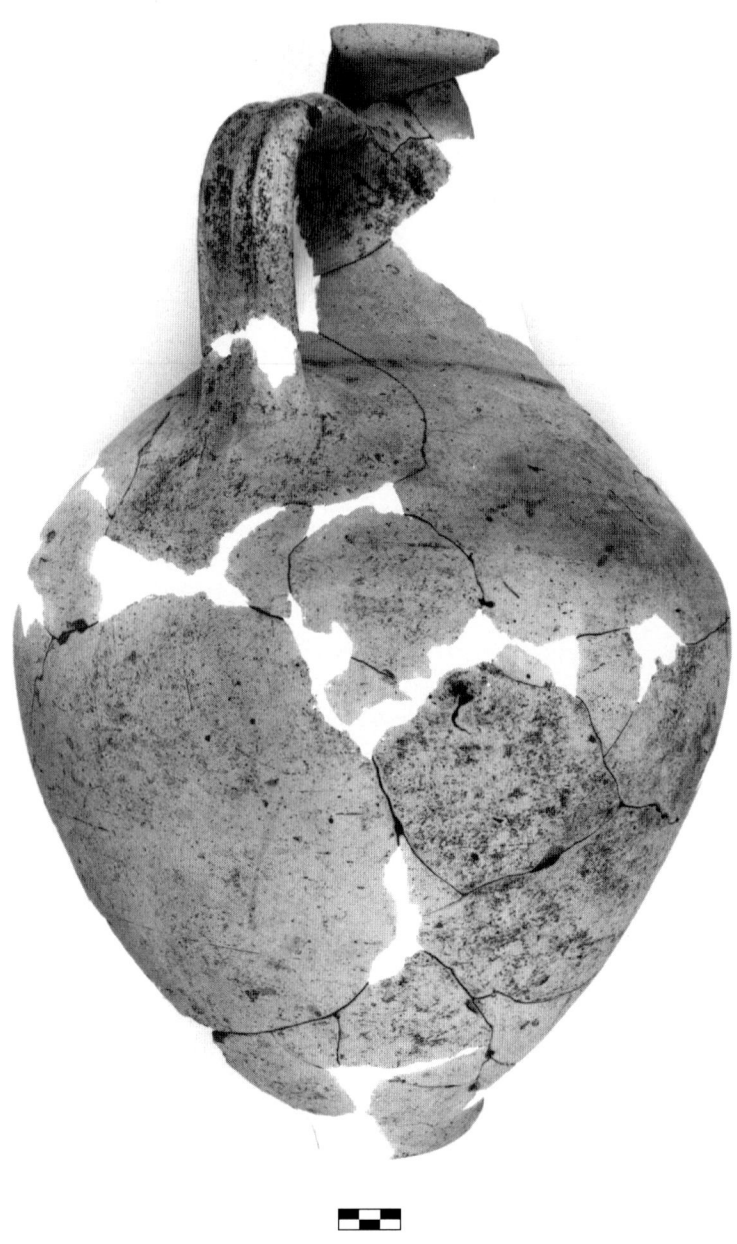

PLATE 265. T77-1. Fragmentary WM neck-handled amphora.

a.

PLATE 266 (on pages 1089–1091). T104-1. WM belly-handled amphora. (*a*) Side a.

b.

PLATE 266 (continued). T104-1. WM belly-handled amphora. (*b*) Side b.

c.

PLATE 266 (continued). T104-1. WM belly-handled amphora. (*c*) Side a/b.

PLATE 267. T75-1. Fragmentary WM belly-handled amphora.

PLATE 268. T20-1. WM belly-handled amphora.

PLATE 269. T51-1. WM belly-handled amphora.

a.

b.

PLATE 270. T95-1. Fragmentary WM belly-handled amphora. (*a*) Side a. (*b*) Showing decoration near handle before handle was attached.

PLATE 271. T115-1. WM belly-handled amphora.

PLATE 272. T60-1. WM belly-handled amphora.

PLATE 273. T24-1. WM belly-handled amphora.

PLATE 274. T134-1. Small WM belly-handled amphora (approaching amphoriskos).

PLATE 275. T120-1. WM shoulder-handled amphora.

a.

PLATE 276 (on facing page). T67-1. WM amphora with belly and shoulder handles. (*a*) Front.

b.

PLATE 276 (continued). T67-1. WM amphora with belly and shoulder handles. (*b*) Side.

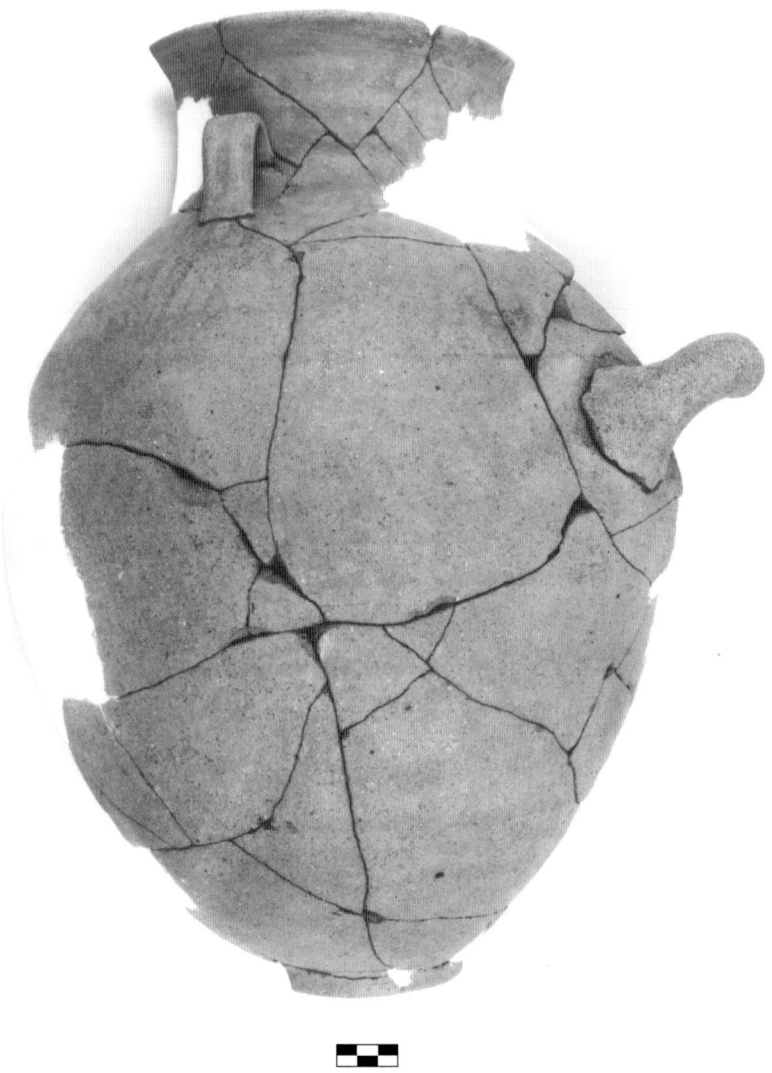

PLATE 277. T81-1. Fragmentary WM amphora with belly and shoulder handles.

PLATE 278. T82-1. Fragmentary WM amphora with belly and shoulder handles.

PLATE 279. T83-1. Fragmentary WM amphora with belly and shoulder handles.

PLATE 280. T84-1. Fragmentary WM amphora with belly and shoulder handles.

PLATE 281. 39. Belly-and-shoulder-handled amphora.

PLATE 282. T56-1. Fragmentary WM amphora, probably with belly and shoulder handles.

PLATE 283. T68-1. Fragmentary WM amphora.

PLATE 284. T122-1. Fragmentary body, WM amphora.

a.

PLATE 285 (on facing page). T26-1. WM belly-and-shoulder-handled amphora. (*a*) Front.

b.

PLATE 285 (continued). T26-1. WM belly-and-shoulder-handled amphora. (*b*) Side.

a.

b.

PLATE 286. T78-1. Small WM amphora with belly and shoulder handles. (a) Front. (b) Side.

a.

b.

PLATE 287. T86-1. WM amphora
with belly and shoulder handles.
(*a*) Front. (*b*) Side.

PLATE 288. 24. Body fragment, WM belly-and-shoulder-handled amphora.

PLATE 289. T29-1. Base and lower body, WM amphora, uncertain type.

PLATE 290. T42-1. Fragmentary WM amphora, uncertain type.

PLATE 291. T129-1. Fragmentary WM amphora.

PLATE 292. T118-2. Body fragments, WM amphora (lid/cover for **T118-1**), uncertain type.

a.

b.

PLATE 293. T96-1. WM belly-handled amphoriskos. (*a*) Side a. (*b*) Side b.

PLATE 294. T109-1. WM belly-handled amphoriskos.

PLATE 295. T101-1. WM belly-handled amphoriskos.

a.

PLATE 296 (on following page). T99-1. WM vertical-handled amphoriskos. (*a*) Side a.

b.

c.

PLATE 296 (continued). T99-1. WM vertical-handled amphoriskos. (*b*) Side b. (*c*) Side a/b.

PLATE 297. T112-2. WM
vertical-handled amphoriskos.

PLATE 298. T44-1. WM
vertical-handled amphoriskos.

a.

b.

PLATE 299. T123-1. WM vertical-handled amphoriskos. (*a*) Side a. (*b*) Side b.

Plate 300. T55-1. WM vertical-handled amphoriskos.

Plate 301. T27-1. WM vertical-handled amphoriskos.

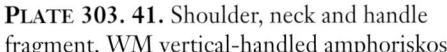

PLATE 302. T69-1. WM vertical-handled amphoriskos.

PLATE 303. 41. Shoulder, neck and handle fragment, WM vertical-handled amphoriskos.

a.

PLATE 304 (on following page). T47-1. WM vertical-handled amphoriskos (imported). (a) Side a.

b.

PLATE 304 (continued). T47-1. WM vertical-handled amphoriskos
(imported). (b) Side a/b.

a.

PLATE 305 (on pages 1127–1129). T22-2. Fragmentary WM vertical-handled amphoriskos (imported). (*a*) Side a.

b.

PLATE 305 (continued). T22-2. Fragmentary WM vertical-handled amphoriskos
(imported). (*b*) Side b.

c.

PLATE 305 (continued). T22-2. Fragmentary WM vertical-handled amphoriskos
(imported). (*c*) Side a/b.

PLATE 306. T22-1. Fragmentary WM amphoriskos with horizontal handles rising vertically and low conical foot.

PLATE 307. T23-1. WM skyphos, Type 1.

PLATE 308. T108-1. WM skyphos, Type 1.

PLATE 309. T106-1. WM skyphos, Type 1.

a.

PLATE 310 (on facing page). T105-1. WM skyphos, Type 1. (*a*) Side a.

b.

PLATE 310 (continued). T105-1. WM skyphos, Type 1. (*b*) Side b.

a.

PLATE 311 (on facing page). T103-1. WM skyphos, Type 1. (*a*) Side a.

b.

PLATE 311 (continued). T103-1. WM skyphos, Type 1. (*b*) Side a/b.

a.

b.

PLATE 312 (on facing page). **T25-1.** WM skyphos, Type 1. (*a*) Side a. (*b*) Side b.

c.

PLATE 312 (continued). T25-1. WM skyphos, Type 1. (*c*) Side a/b.

PLATE 313. T117-1. WM skyphos, Type 2.

PLATE 314. T94-1. WM skyphos, Type 2.

a.

PLATE 315 (on pages 1139–1141). T127-1 WM skyphos, Type 2 (imported). (*a*). Side a.

b.

Plate 315 (continued). T127-1 WM skyphos, Type 2 (imported). (*b*) Side b.

c.

PLATE 315 (continued). T127-1 WM skyphos, Type 2 (imported). (*c*) Side a/b.

PLATE 316. T30-1. Large WM skyphos, Type 3.

a.

b.

PLATE 317 (on following page). T28-1. WM skyphos, Type 3. (*a*) Side a. (*b*) Side b.

c.

d.

PLATE 317 (continued). T28-1. WM skyphos, Type 3. (*c*) Side a/b. (*d*) Side b/a.

a.

b.

PLATE 318. T37-1. WM skyphos, Type 3. (*a*) Side a. (*b*) Side a/b.

PLATE 319. T82-2. Fragmentary WM pendent semicircle skyphos, Type 4.

a.

b.

PLATE 320. T47-3. WM lekanis, Type 1. (*a*) Side a. (*b*) Side a/b.

a.

b.

PLATE 321 (on facing page). T124-3. WM lekanis, Type 1. (*a*) Side a. (*b*) Side a/b.

c.

PLATE 321 (continued). T124-3. WM lekanis, Type 1. (*c*) Interior.

PLATE 322. T41-2. Fragmentary WM lekanis, Type 1.

a.

b.

PLATE 323 (on facing page). T51-3. WM lekanis, Type 1A. (*a*) Side a. (*b*) Side b.

c.

d.

PLATE 323 (continued). T51-3. WM lekanis, Type 1A. (*c*) Side a/b. (*d*) Interior.

PLATE 324. T81-2. Fragmentary WM lekanis, Type 2.

PLATE 325. T102-1. WM krater, Type 1.

a.

PLATE 326 (on facing page). T116-1. WM krater, Type 1. (*a*) **T116-1**.

b.

PLATE 326 (continued). T116-1. WM krater, Type 1. (*b*) Detail of painted birds or ship.

a.

PLATE 327 (on pages 1156–1158). T48-1. WM krater, Transitional Type. (*a*) Side a.

b.

PLATE 327 (continued). T48-1. WM krater, Transitional Type. (*b*) Side b.

c.

PLATE 327 (continued). T48-1. WM krater, Transitional Type. (*c*) Side a/b.

PLATE 328. T62-1. Base and lower body, WM krater, Transitional Type.

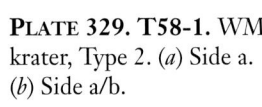

a.

PLATE 329. T58-1. WM krater, Type 2. (*a*) Side a. (*b*) Side a/b.

b.

a.

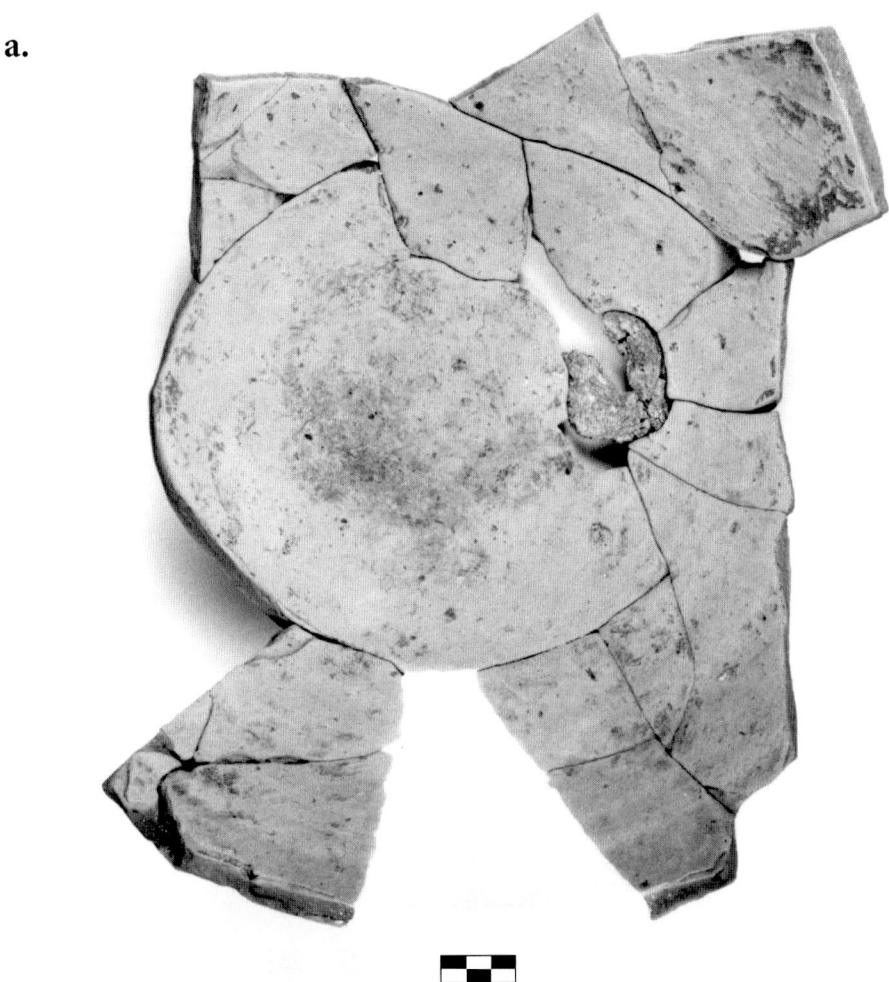

PLATE 330 (on following page). T79-1. Fragmentary WM krater, uncertain type. (*a*) Interior.

b.

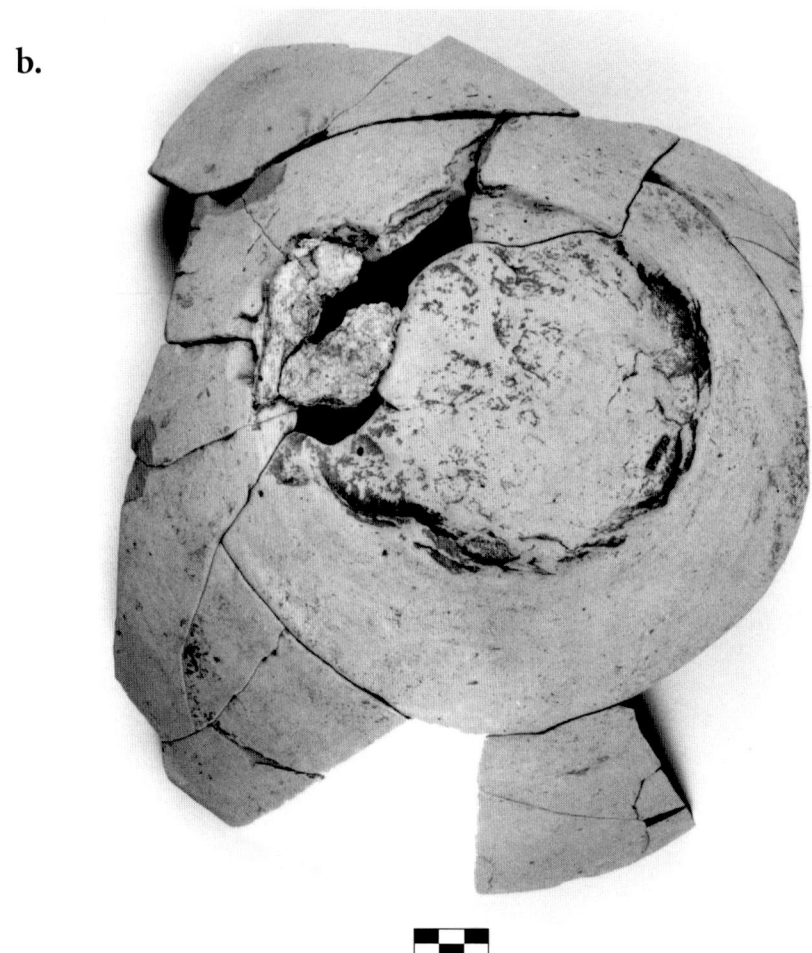

PLATE 330 (continued). T79-1. Fragmentary WM krater, uncertain type. (*b*) Exterior.

PLATE 331. T13-1. WM kantharos.

PLATE 332. 46. WM jug with cutaway neck.

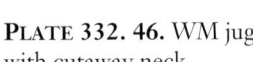

a.

b.

PLATE 333. T72-1. WM jug (imported). (*a*) Side a. (*b*) Side a/b.

PLATE 334. T45-1. WM "amphora/pyxis."

PLATE 335. T88-2. Fragmentary WM lid.

PLATE 336. T100-1. HM two-handled jar (belly-handled), Type 1.

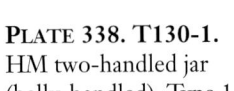

PLATE 337. T118-1.
HM two-handled jar
(belly-handled), Type 1.

PLATE 338. T130-1.
HM two-handled jar
(belly-handled), Type 1.

PLATE 339. T18-1. Fragmentary HM two-handled jar (belly-handled), Type 1.

PLATE 340. T63-1. Fragmentary HM two-handled jar (belly-handled), Type 1.

a.

PLATE 341 (on facing page). 60. Fragments of rim and upper body, HM two-handled jar, Type 1 (*a*) Exterior.

b.

PLATE 341 (continued). 60. Fragments of rim and upper body, HM two-handled jar, Type 1. (*b*) Interior.

PLATE 342. T21-1. HM two-handled jar, small variety. Type 1.

PLATE 343. T46-1. HM two-handled jar (neck-handled), Type 2.

PLATE 344. T19-1. HM two-handled jar (neck-handled), Type 2.

PLATE 345. Selection of jugs (Type 1) with cutaway necks (left to right starting at the top of): **T82-3, T41-3, T6-1, T70-2, T52-2, T67-3, T10-2.** (*a*) Lateral view. (*b*) Three-quarter view from slightly above.

a.

PLATE 346 .T6-1. HM jug, Type 1, with cutaway neck. (*a*) Side. (*b*) Front.

b.

a.

PLATE 347. T10-2. HM jug, Type 1, with cutaway neck. (*a*) Side. (*b*) Front.

b.

a.

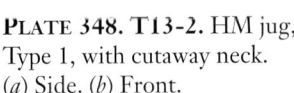

PLATE 348. T13-2. HM jug, Type 1, with cutaway neck. (*a*) Side. (*b*) Front.

b.

a.

PLATE 349. T124-2.
HM jug with cutaway
neck. (*a*) Side. (*b*) Front.

b.

a.

PLATE 350. T52-2. HM jug, Type 1, with cutaway neck. (*a*) Side. (*b*) Front.

b.

a.

PLATE 351. T67-3. HM jug, Type 1, with cutaway neck. (*a*) Side. (*b*) Front.

b.

PLATE 352. T70-2. HM jug, Type 1,
with cutaway neck. (*a*) Side. (*b*) Front.

a.

PLATE 353. T58-2. HM jug, Type 1, with cutaway neck. (*a*) Side. (*b*) Front.

b.

a.

PLATE 354 (on following page).
T41-3. HM jug, Type 1, with cutaway
neck. (*a*) Side. (*b*) Front.

b.

c.

PLATE 354 (continued).
T41-3. HM jug, Type 1,
with cutaway neck. (*c*) Back.

PLATE 355. **T74-2.** Fragmentary HM
jug, Type 1, with cutaway neck. Front.

a.

b.

PLATE 356. T75-2. Fragmentary HM jug with incised decoration. (*a*) Side. (*b*) Front. (*c*) Back.

c.

a.

PLATE 357. T86-2. Fragmentary
HM jug. (*a*) Side. (*b*) Back.

b.

PLATE 358. T38-2. HM jug, Type 1, with cutaway neck. Side.

PLATE 359. T82-3. Fragmentary HM jug. Side.

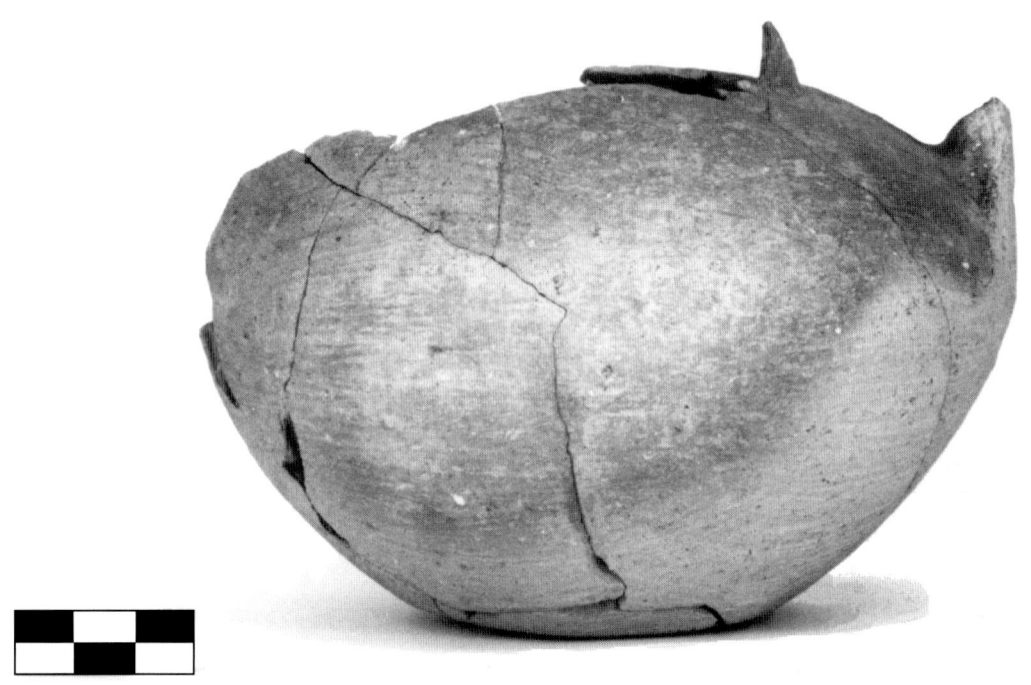

PLATE 360. T26-3. Fragmentary HM jug, Type 1, with cutaway neck. Side.

PLATE 361. T73-2. HM jug, Type 1, with cutaway neck. Side.

PLATE 362. T81-4. Fragmentary HM jug, Type 1, probably with cutaway neck. Front.

PLATE 363. T84-2. Fragmentary HM jug with cutaway neck.

PLATE 364. **T80-2.** Fragmentary HM jug.

PLATE 365. **T122-2.** Base fragments, HM jug.

PLATE 366. T81-3. Small HM jug with round mouth, Type 2. Side.

PLATE 367. T69-2. HM double vase.

a.

b.

PLATE 368. T10-3 (on facing page). HM kantharos, Type 1. (*a*) Side a. (*b*) Side b.

c.

PLATE 368. T10-3 (continued). HM kantharos, Type 1. (*c*) Side a/b.

PLATE 369. T82-5. Fragmentary HM kantharos, Type 1.

PLATE 370. T82-4. Fragmentary HM kantharos, Type 1.

PLATE 371. T75-3. Fragmentary HM kantharos, Type 1.

PLATE 372. T1-2. HM kantharos, small variety.

a.

b.

PLATE 373. 7. HM kantharos, small variety (Early Bronze Age?). (*a*) Front. (*b*) Side.

PLATE 374. T7-2. HM kantharos, Type 2.

PLATE 375. T43-1. HM cup/kyathos, Type 1.

a.

b.

PLATE 376. T57-1. HM cup/kyathos, Type 1. (*a*) Side view. (*b*) Lateral view.

PLATE 377. T10-4. Fragmentary HM cup/kyathos,
Type 2. (*a*) Side view. (*b*) Lateral view.

a.

b.

c.

PLATE 378. T67-2. HM bowl with square-cut handles. (*a*) Side a. (*b*) Side a/b. (*c*) Side a (three-quarter view).

PLATE 379. T7-1. Fragmentary rim, HM pithos.

PLATE 380. T1-1. Fragmentary body, HM pithos.

PLATE 381. T12-1. Fragmentary body, HM pithos.

PLATE 382. T27-2. Body fragment, HM pithos.

PLATE 383. T38-1. HM pitharion.

PLATE 384. T70-1. HM pitharion.

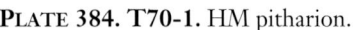

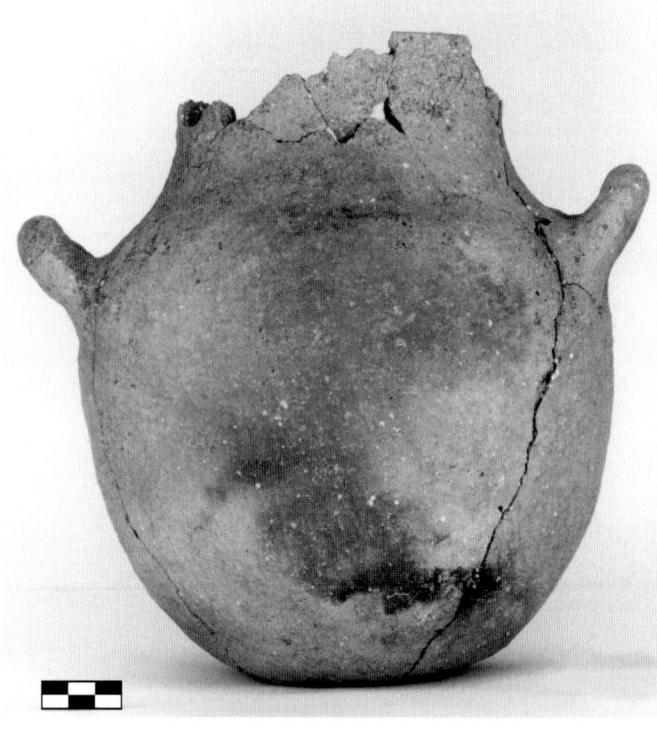

PLATE 385. T118-3. HM pitharion.

PLATE 386. T123-3. Fragmentary HM tripod cauldron.

PLATE 387. T99-3. Fragmentary HM tripod cauldron.

PLATE 388. T123-2. Fragmentary HM tripod cauldron.

PLATE 389. T123-5. Body and handle fragments, HM tripod cauldron.

PLATE 390. T123-4. Body and handle fragments, HM tripod cauldron.

PLATE 391. T7-4. Leg fragment, HM tripod cauldron.

PLATE 392. T47-4. Fragmentary HM tripod cauldron.

PLATE 393. T54-1. HM jar, imported(?).

PLATE 394. T97-1. HM two-handled jar, imported(?).

PLATE 395. T112-1. HM pyxis, imported(?).

PLATE 396. T21-3. HM bowl, imported. (*a*) Side a. (*b*) Side b. (*c*) Interior.

a.

b.

PLATE 397 (on facing page). T104-2. WM black-slip krater. (*a*) Side a. (*b*) Side b.

c.

d.

PLATE 397 (continued). T104-2. WM black-slip krater. (*c*) Side a/b. (*d*) Detail side b/a.

PLATE 398. T47-2. WM black-slip krater, reused as lid.

PLATE 399. T50-1. WM black-slip belly-handled amphoriskos.

PLATE 400. T111-1. WM red-slip stemmed kylix.

a.

b.

PLATE 401. T93-1. Fragmentary
large WM open vessel. (*a*) Underside.
(*b*) Fragments from upper body.

PLATE 402. 78. Body fragments, WM krater.

PLATE 403. T28-4. Body fragments, WM amphora.

PLATE 404. T44-2. Body fragments, WM amphora.

PLATE 405. T24-2. Body fragments, HM pithos.

PLATE 406. T114-2. Body fragments, HM pithos.

PLATE 407. T113-10. Body fragment, large WM closed vessel, probably amphora

PLATE 408. 23. Body and leg fragment, HM tripod cauldron.

PLATE 409. 27. Shoulder fragment, WM closed vessel, probably amphora.

PLATE 410. 29. Handle fragment, HM bowl with square-cut handles.

PLATE 411. 30. Rim fragment, HM pithos.

PLATE 412. 38. Rim, body, and handle fragments, WM skyphos.

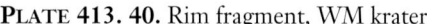

PLATE 413. 40. Rim fragment, WM krater.

PLATE 414. 44. Rim, body, and handle fragments, WM skyphos.

PLATE 415. 48. Shoulder fragment, WM amphora.

PLATE 416. 52. Rim fragment, HM open vessel.

PLATE 417. 63. Body fragment large open vessel, probably krater.

PLATE 418. 79. Rim and handle fragments, WM krater.

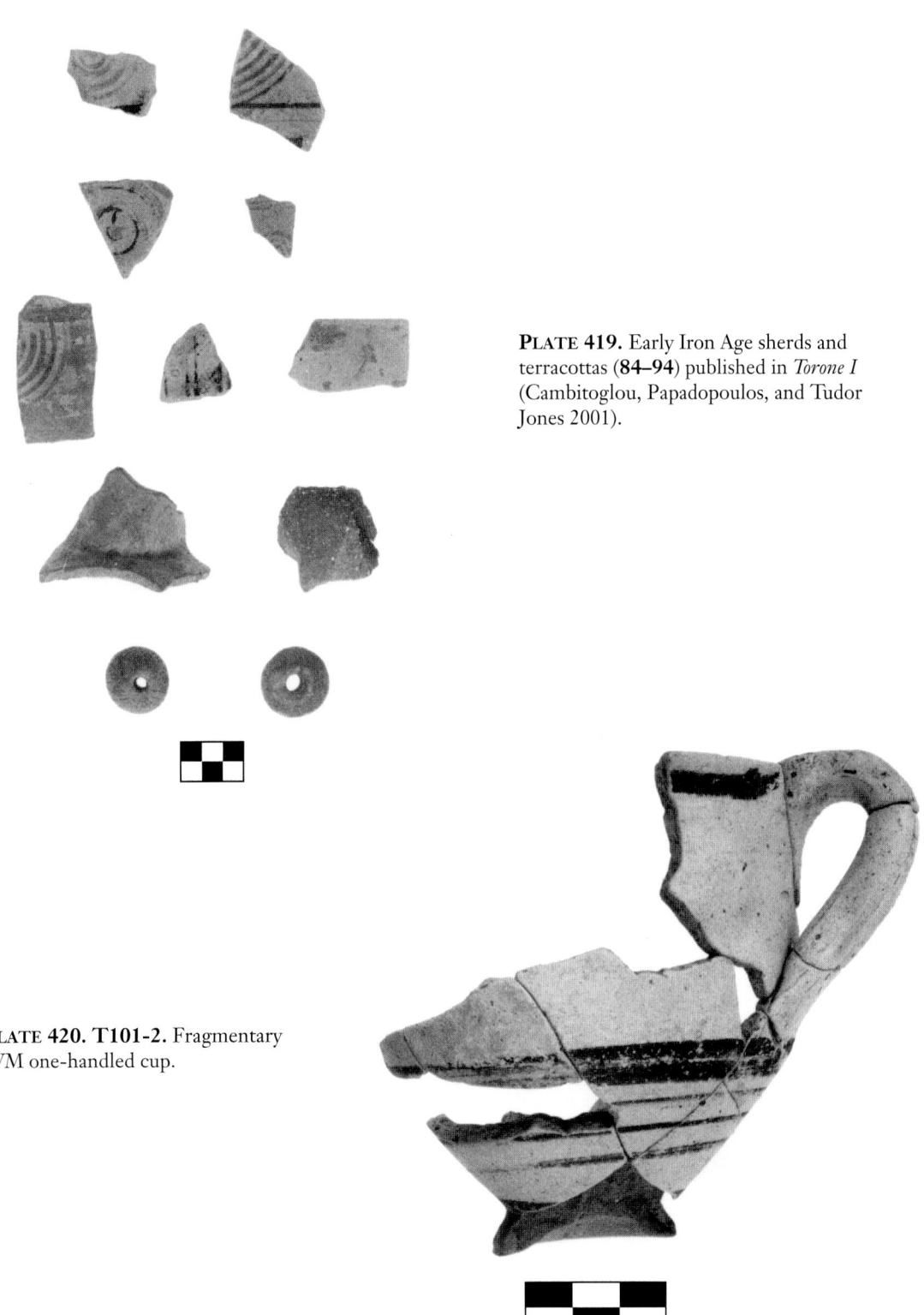

PLATE 419. Early Iron Age sherds and terracottas (**84–94**) published in *Torone I* (Cambitoglou, Papadopoulos, and Tudor Jones 2001).

PLATE 420. T101-2. Fragmentary WM one-handled cup.

PLATE 421. T101-3. Fragmentary WM one-handled cup.

a.

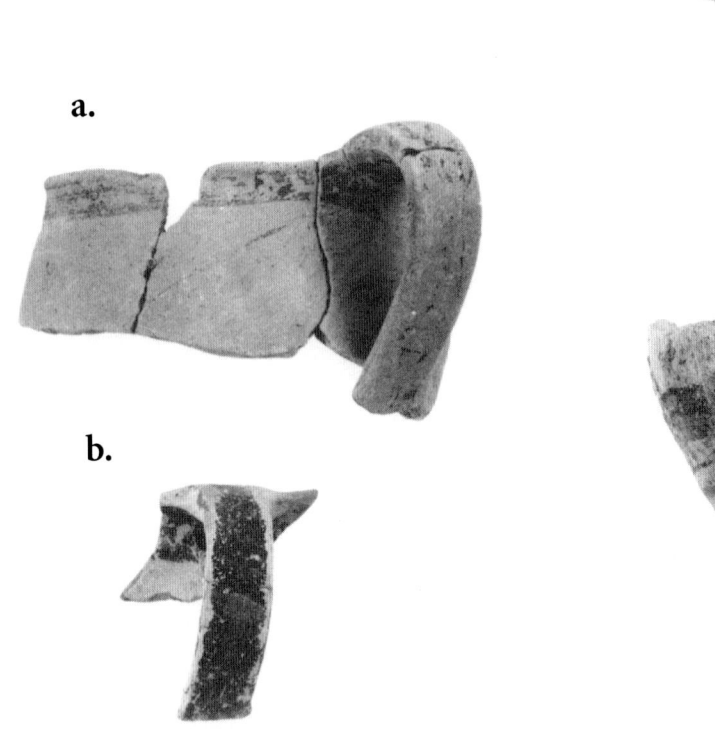

b.

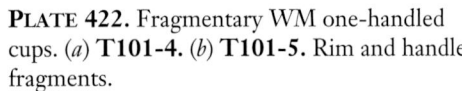

PLATE 422. Fragmentary WM one-handled cups. (*a*) **T101-4.** (*b*) **T101-5.** Rim and handle fragments.

PLATE 423. T101-6. Base and lower body fragments, WM one-handled cup.

PLATE 424. T101-7. Fragmentary WM skyphos, Type 1.

PLATE 425. T101-8. Fragmentary WM skyphos.

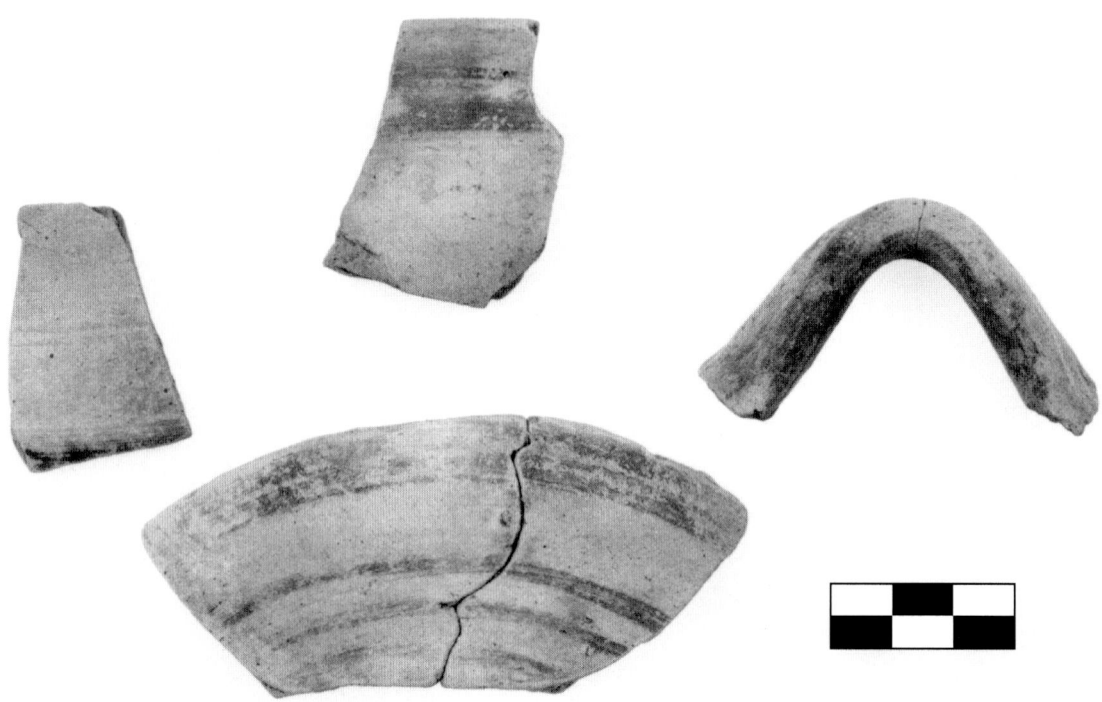

PLATE 426. T101-9. Rim and body fragments, WM open vessel (lekanis?).

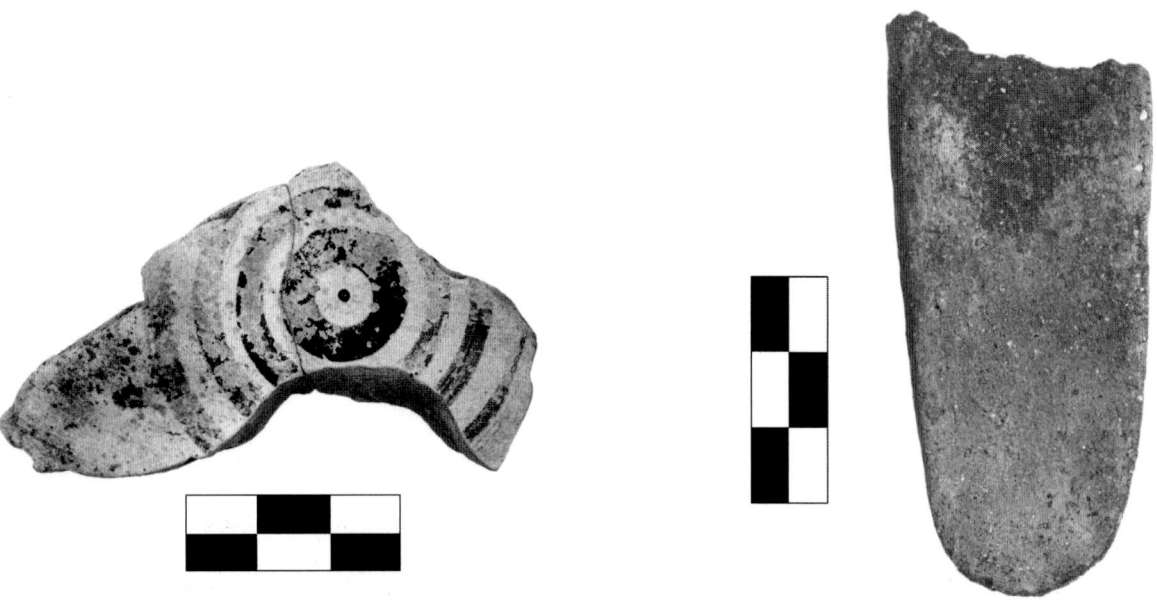

PLATE 427. T101-10. Shoulder fragments, WM amphora (before sampling).

PLATE 428. T101-11. Leg fragment, HM tripod cauldron.

PLATE 429. T101-12. HM bowl. (a) Rim fragment. (b) Handle fragment, square cut.

PLATE 430. T101-13. Handle fragment, HM vessel.

PLATE 431. T101-14. Body fragments, HM jug.

PLATE 432. T101-15. Body
fragment, WM open vessel,
probably skyphos.

PLATE 433. T104-9. Body and handle fragments, WM belly-handled
amphora.

a.

b.

c.

d.

e.

f.

PLATE 434. (*a*) T104-10. Rim fragment, WM amphora. (*b*) T104-12. Body fragment, WM skyphos.
(*c*) T104-14. Rim fragment, WM skyphos. (*d*) T104-15. Rim and handle fragment, WM lekanis.
(*e*) T104-13. Body fragment, WM open vessel, probably skyphos. (*f*) T104-11. Rim fragment, WM krater.

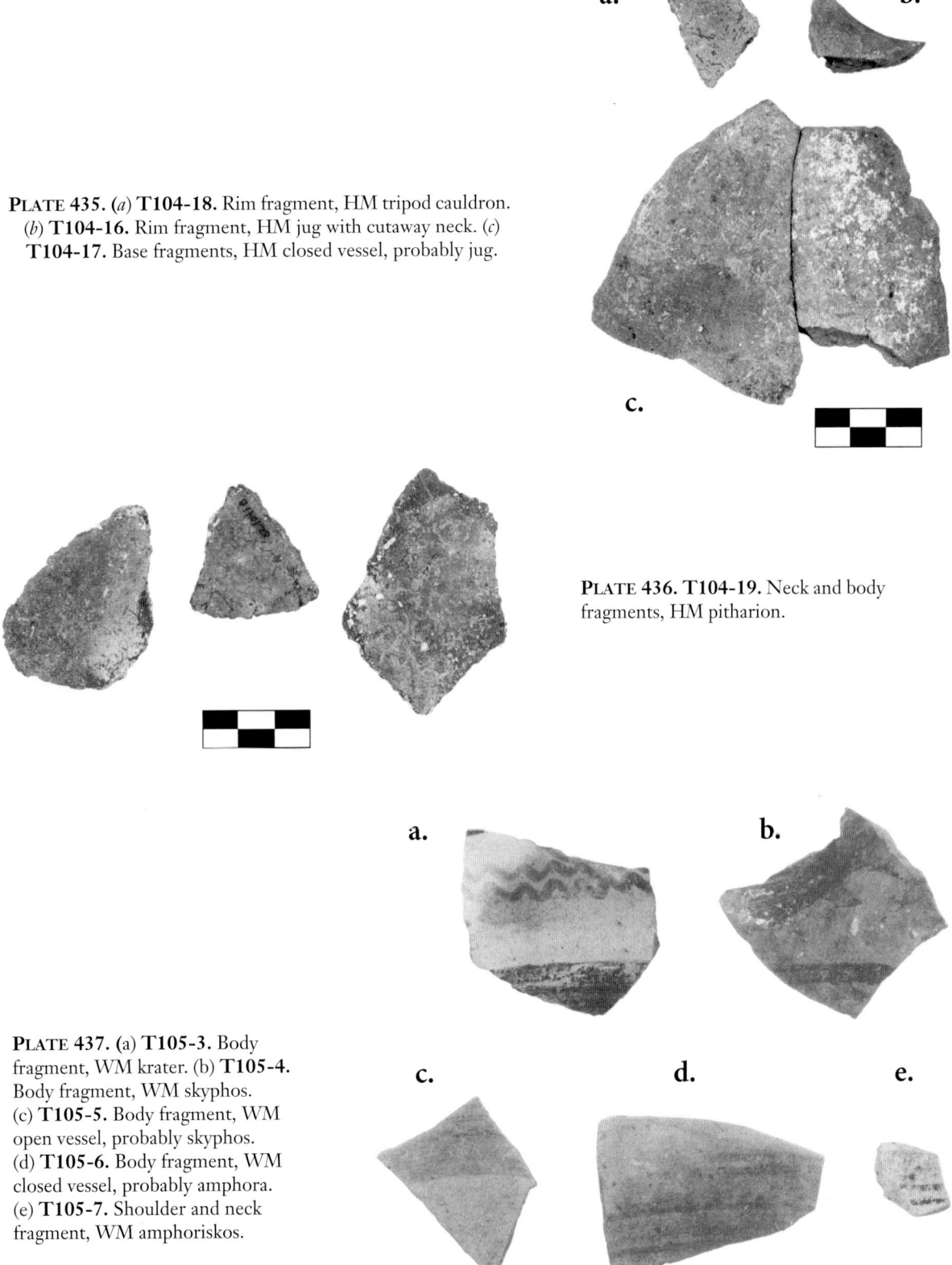

PLATE 435. (*a*) **T104-18.** Rim fragment, HM tripod cauldron. (*b*) **T104-16.** Rim fragment, HM jug with cutaway neck. (*c*) **T104-17.** Base fragments, HM closed vessel, probably jug.

PLATE 436. T104-19. Neck and body fragments, HM pitharion.

PLATE 437. (a) **T105-3.** Body fragment, WM krater. (b) **T105-4.** Body fragment, WM skyphos. (c) **T105-5.** Body fragment, WM open vessel, probably skyphos. (d) **T105-6.** Body fragment, WM closed vessel, probably amphora. (e) **T105-7.** Shoulder and neck fragment, WM amphoriskos.

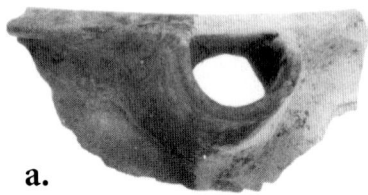

a.

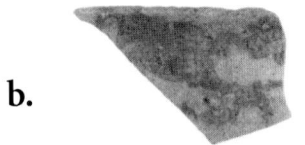

b.

PLATE 438. (*a*) **T109-2.** Rim and spout fragment, WM krater/large lekanis. (*b*) **T109-3.** Rim fragment, WM skyphos. (*c*) **T109-4.** Body and handle fragments, WM skyphos.

c.

PLATE 439 (on facing page). T109-5. Fragmentary HM jug with cutaway neck. (*a*) Miscellaneous fragments.

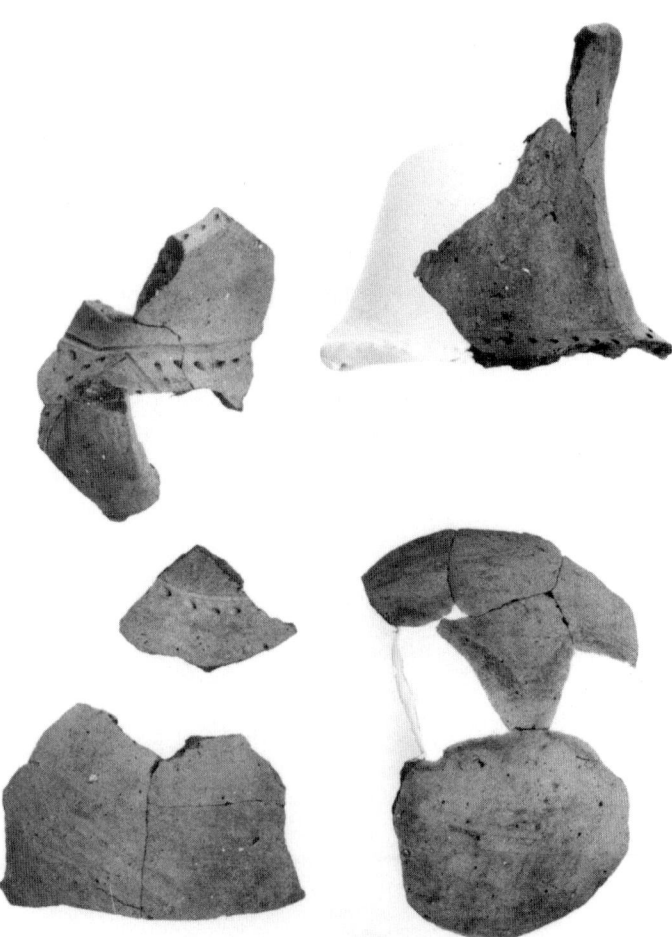

a.

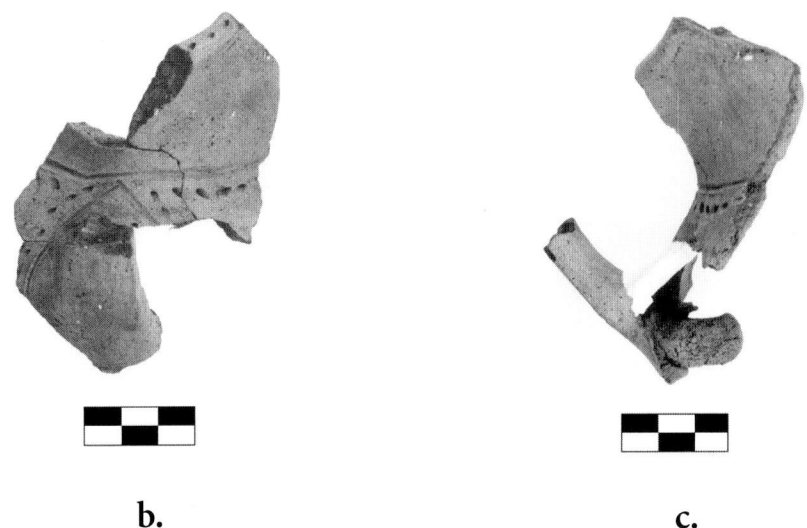

b.

c.

PLATE 439 (continued). T109-5. Fragmentary HM jug with cutaway neck. (*b*) Detail of exterior. (*c*) Detail, side.

PLATE 440. T111-2. Fragmentary WM skyphos.

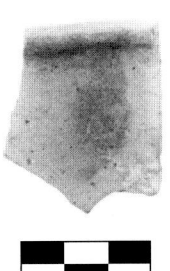

PLATE 441. T111-3. Rim fragment, WM krater/large lekanis.

PLATE 442. T111-4. Fragmentary upper body HM jug with cutaway neck.

PLATE 443. (*a*) **T112-3.** Base fragment, WM amphora. (*b*) **T112-4.** Base fragment, WM skyphos. (*c*) **T112-5.** Handle fragment, probably WM skyphos. (*d*) **T112-6.** Handle fragment, probably WM lekanis. (*e*) **T112-7.** Handle fragment HM bowl with square-cut handles.

PLATE 444. (*a*) **T113-8.** Rim fragment, WM lekanis, Type 1.(*b*) **T113-2.** Rim fragment, WM amphora. (*c*) **T113-6.** Base fragment, WM skyphos. (*d*) **T113-9.** Body fragments, small WM closed vessel. (*e*) **T113-7.** Body fragment, skyphos(?).

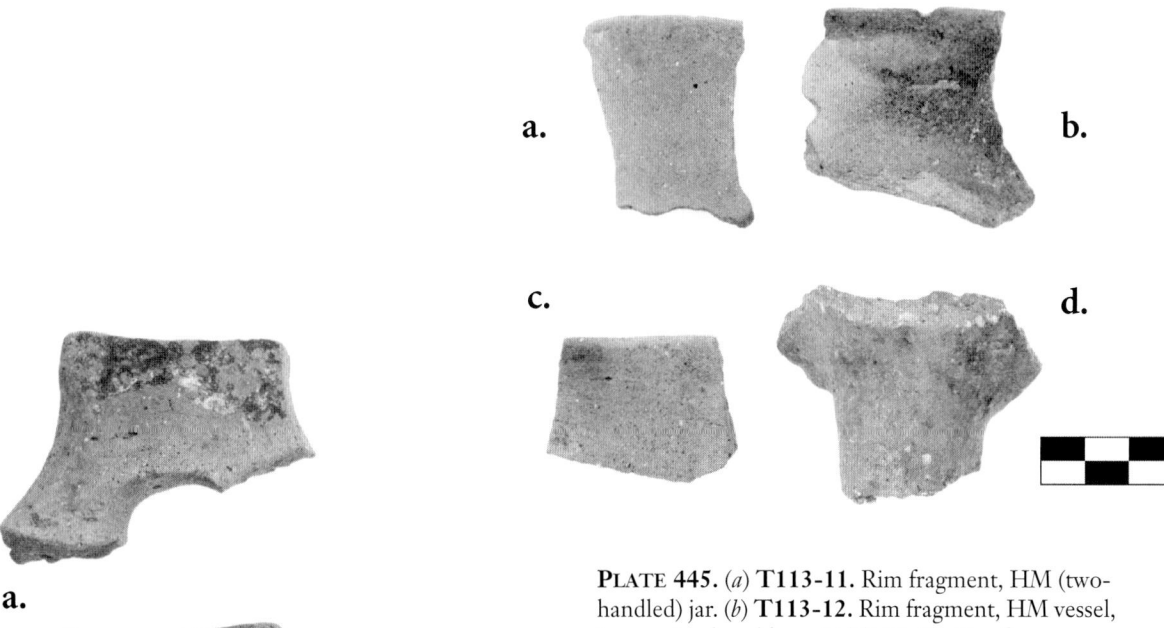

PLATE 445. (*a*) **T113-11.** Rim fragment, HM (two-handled) jar. (*b*) **T113-12.** Rim fragment, HM vessel, jar or tripod cauldron. (*c*) **T113-16.** Rim fragment, HM bowl with square-cut handles. (*d*) **T113-17.** Body and leg fragment, HM tripod cauldron.

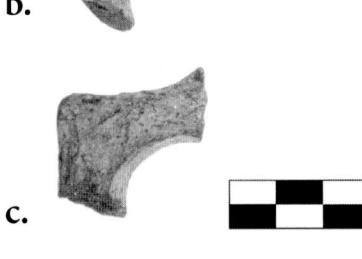

PLATE 446. (*a*) **T113-13.** Handle fragment, HM bowl with square-cut handles. (*b*) **T113-14.** Handle fragment, HM bowl with square-cut handles. (*c*) **T113-15.** Handle fragment, HM bowl with square-cut handles.

a.

b.

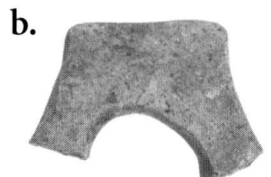

c.

PLATE 448. (*a*) **T114-5.** Base fragment, WM skyphos. (*b*) **T114-6.** Handle fragment, HM bowl with square-cut handles. (*c*) **T114-7.** Leg fragment, small HM tripod cauldron.

PLATE 447. **T114-4.** Neck, shoulder, and body fragments, small WM amphora.

PLATE 449. Tomb 117. Catalogued fire-affected sherds.

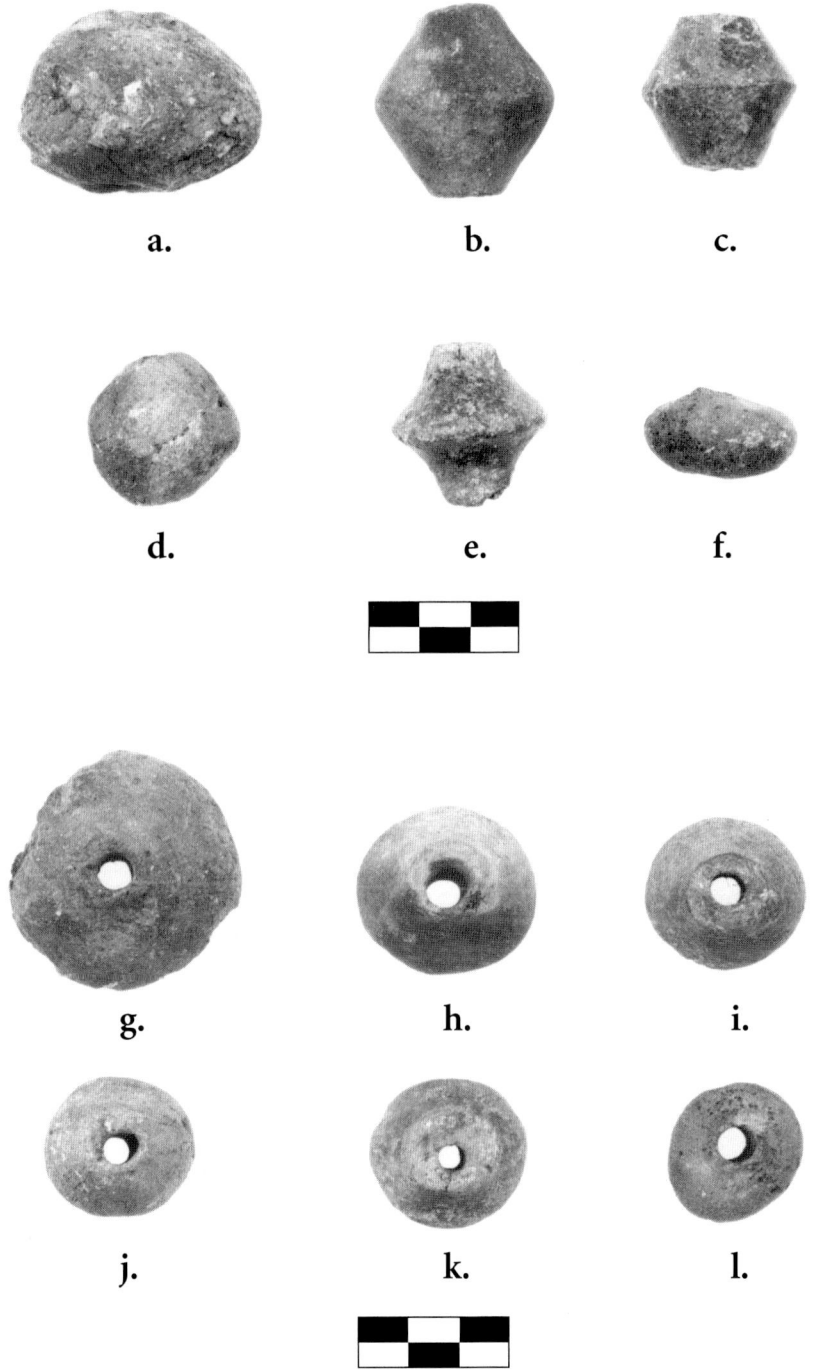

PLATE 450. Terracotta spindlewhorls, beads, or buttons. Lateral view: (*a*) **T10-5.** (*b*) **T46-3.** (*c*) **55.** (*d*) **T51-5.** (*e*) **56.** (*f*) **T7-5.** View from above: (*g*) **T10-5.** (*h*) **T46-3.** (*i*) **55.** (*j*) **T51-5.** (*k*) **56.** (*l*) **T7-5.**

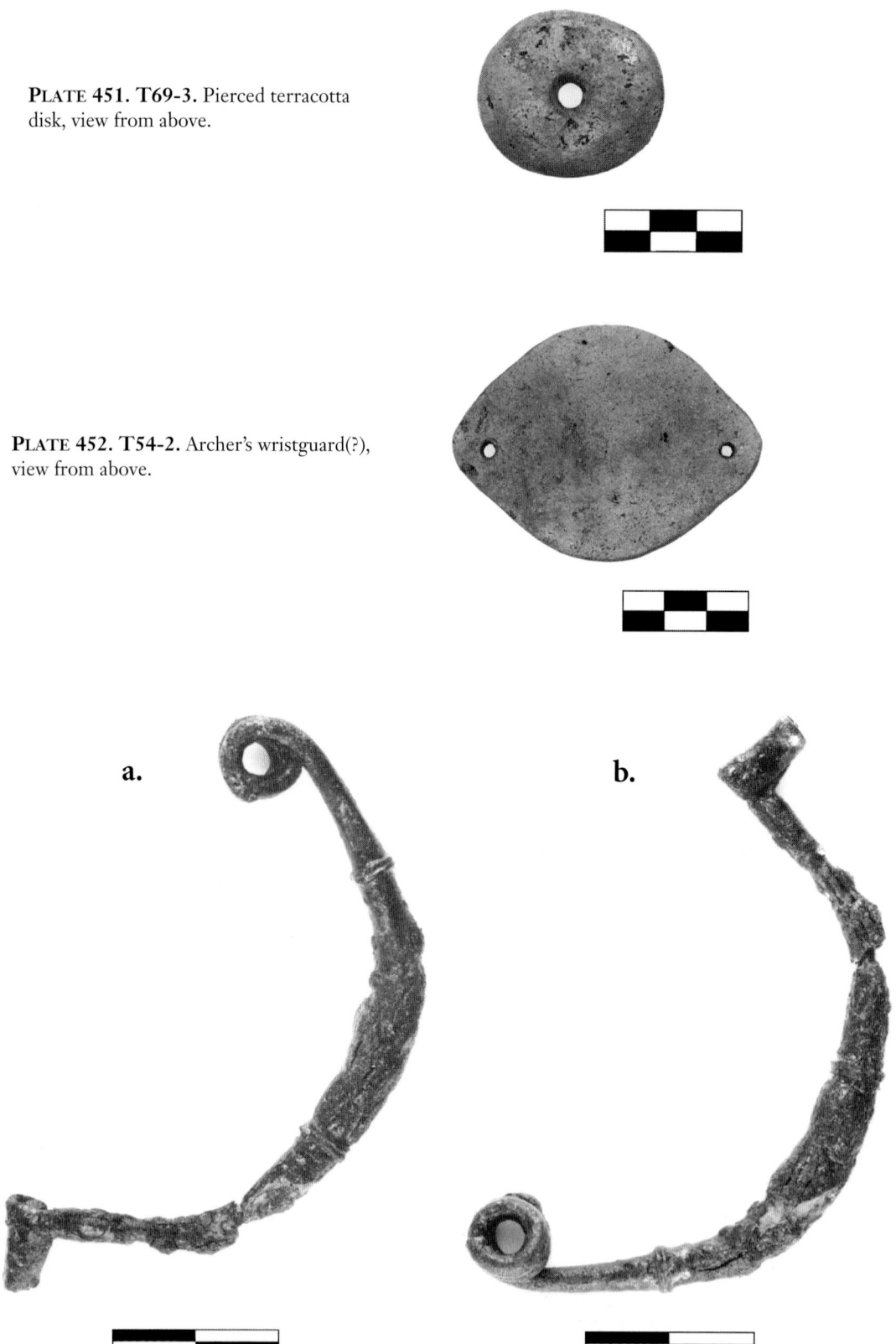

PLATE 451. T69-3. Pierced terracotta disk, view from above.

PLATE 452. T54-2. Archer's wristguard(?), view from above.

a.

b.

PLATE 453. T115-2. Bronze arched fibula. (*a*) Side a. (*b*) Side b.

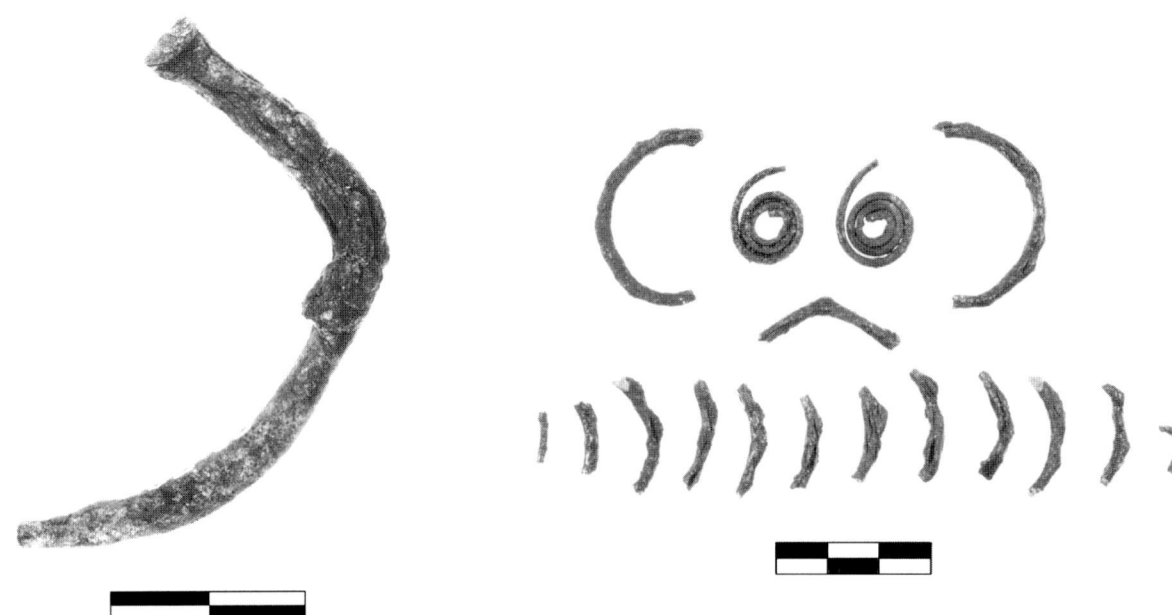

PLATE 454. T115-3. Bronze arched fibula.

PLATE 455. T16-1. Fragmentary bronze spectacle fibula.

PLATE 456. T104-8. Bronze pin shaft fragment (perhaps fibula rather than dress pin).

PLATE 457. T104-6. Bronze fragment.

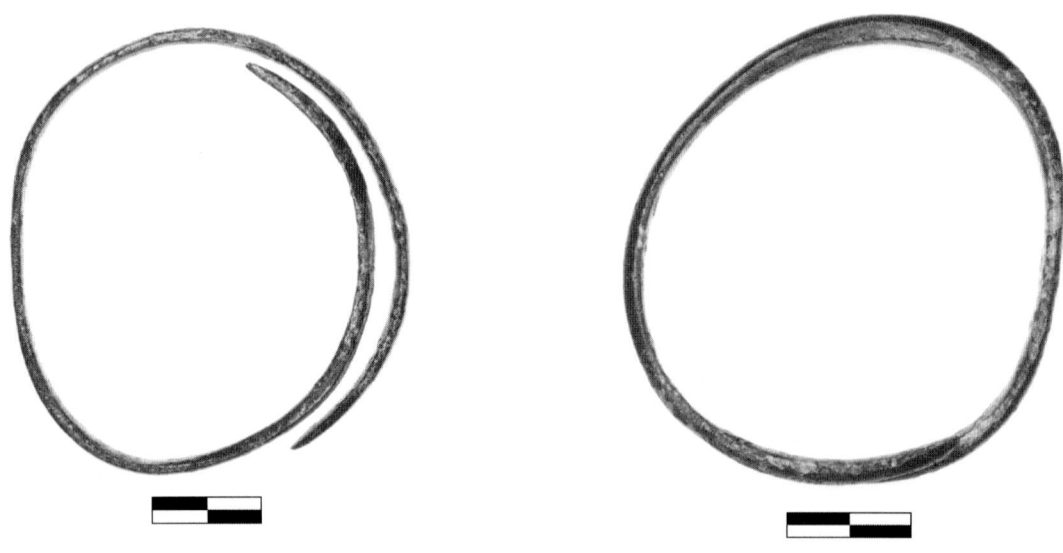

PLATE 458. T7-7. Bronze anklet, right leg.

PLATE 459. T7-8. Bronze anklet, left leg.

PLATE 460. 43. Bronze finger ring.

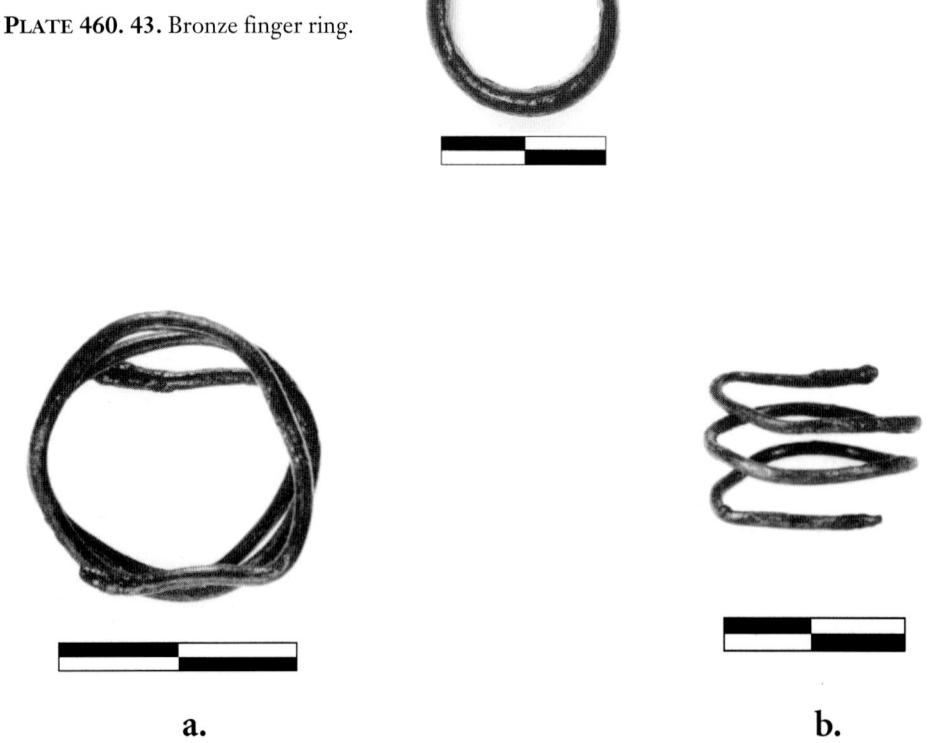

a.

b.

PLATE 461. T7-6. Bronze spiral ornament (hair ring). (*a*) From above. (*b*) Lateral view.

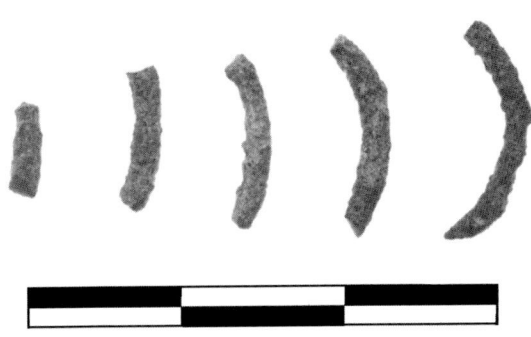

PLATE 463. T69-4. Fragments of bronze spiral ornament.

PLATE 462. T10-8. Fragments of bronze spiral ornament (hair ring?).

PLATE 464. T102-6. Fragments of bronze spiral ornament (hair ring?).

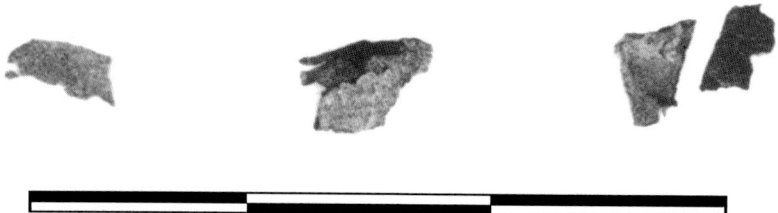

PLATE 465. T18-2. Unidentified fire-affected bronze fragments.

PLATE 466. T58-3. Unidentified fire-affected bronze fragments.

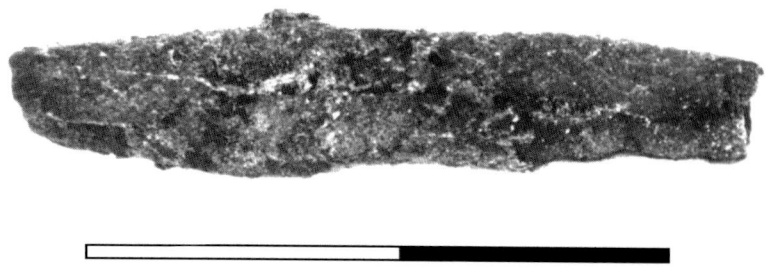

PLATE 467. T124-4. Unidentified fire-affected bronze fragment.

a.

b.

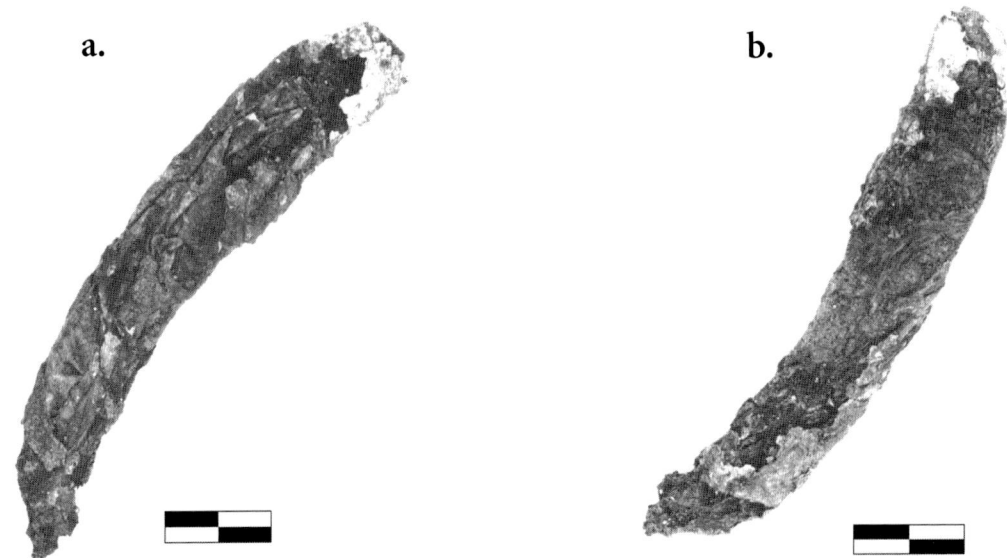

PLATE 468. T52-4. Iron knife with unriveted bone handle wrapped in leather sheath or scabbard. (*a*) Side a. (*b*) Side b.

PLATE 469. T56-4. Fragment of iron blade with possible bone handle.

PLATE 470. T38-3. Bone handle of iron knife.

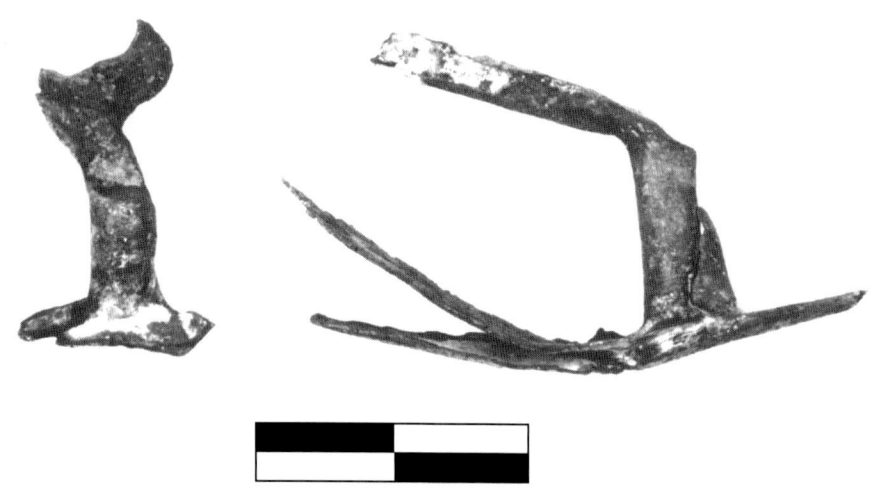

PLATE 471. T116-1. Lead clamp.

PLATE 472. T52-5. Whetstone.

PLATE 473. T104-4. Whetstone.

PLATE 474. T10-7. Bone bead.

PLATE 475. T75-4. Amber bead.

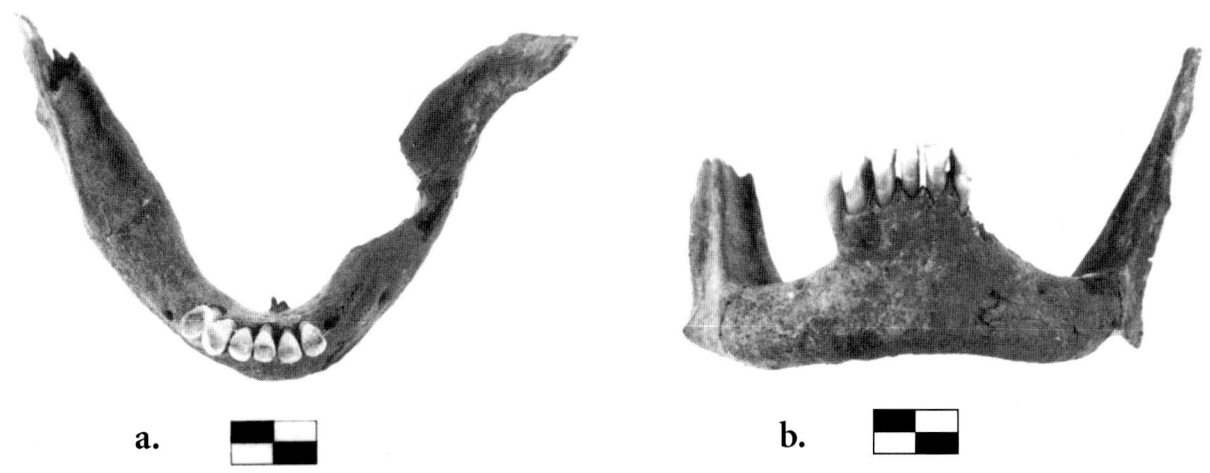

a.

b.

PLATE 476. Tomb 10. Adult male(?). (*a–b*) Details of mandible.

a.

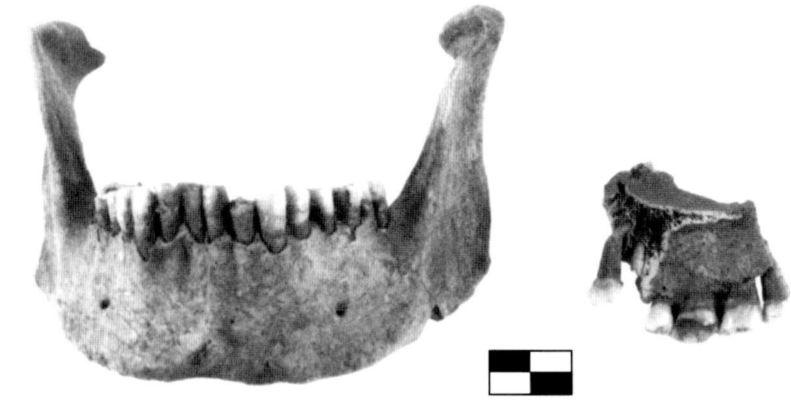

PLATE 477. Tomb 11. Adult male. (*a–b*) Details of dentition.

b.

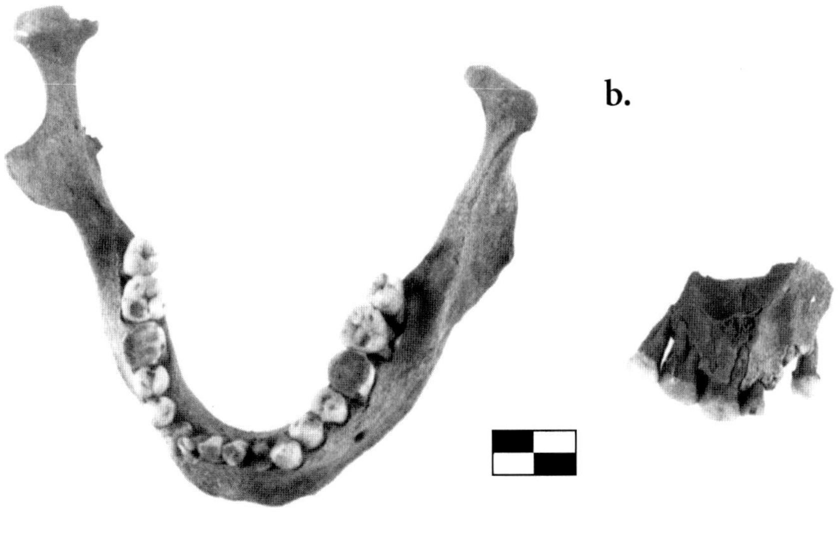

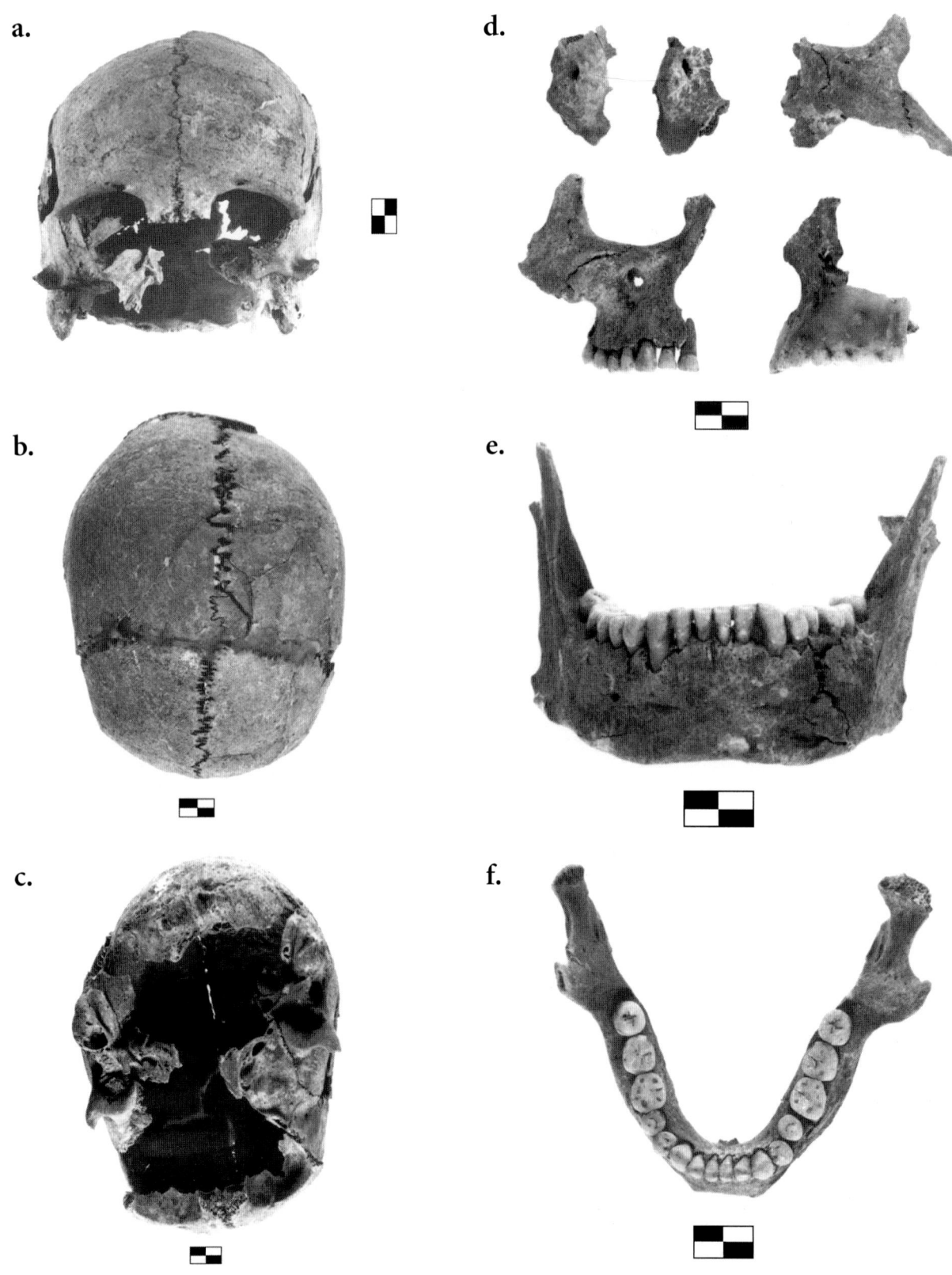

PLATE 478. TOMB 15. (*a*) Cranium, frontal view. (*b*) Cranium, from above. (*c*) Cranium, from below. (*d*) Details of dentition. (*e*) Detail of mandible. (*f*) Detail of mandible.

PLATE 479. Tomb 21.

PLATE 480.
Tomb 24.

PLATE 481. Tomb 25.

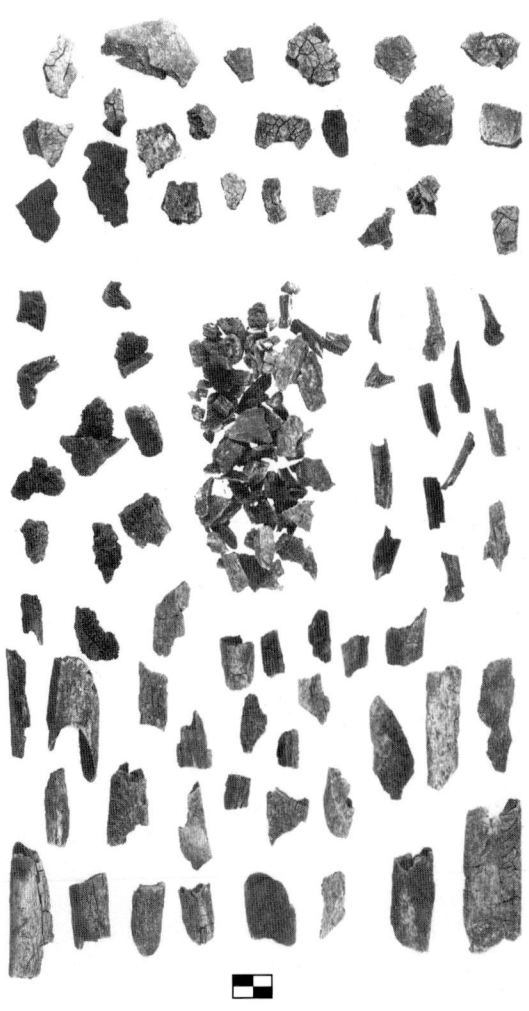

a.

PLATE 482. Tomb 26. (*a*) Cremated remains.
(*b*) Detail of some of the cremated remains.

b.

PLATE 483. Tomb 29.

PLATE 484. Tomb 37.

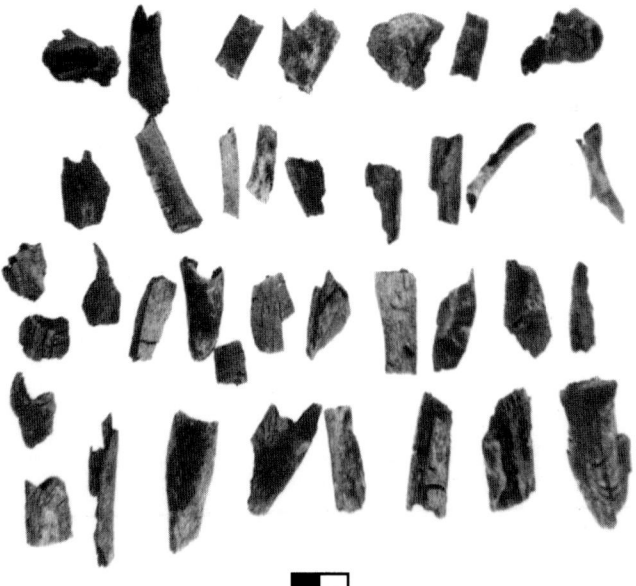

PLATE 485. Tomb 43.

PLATE 486. Tomb 44.

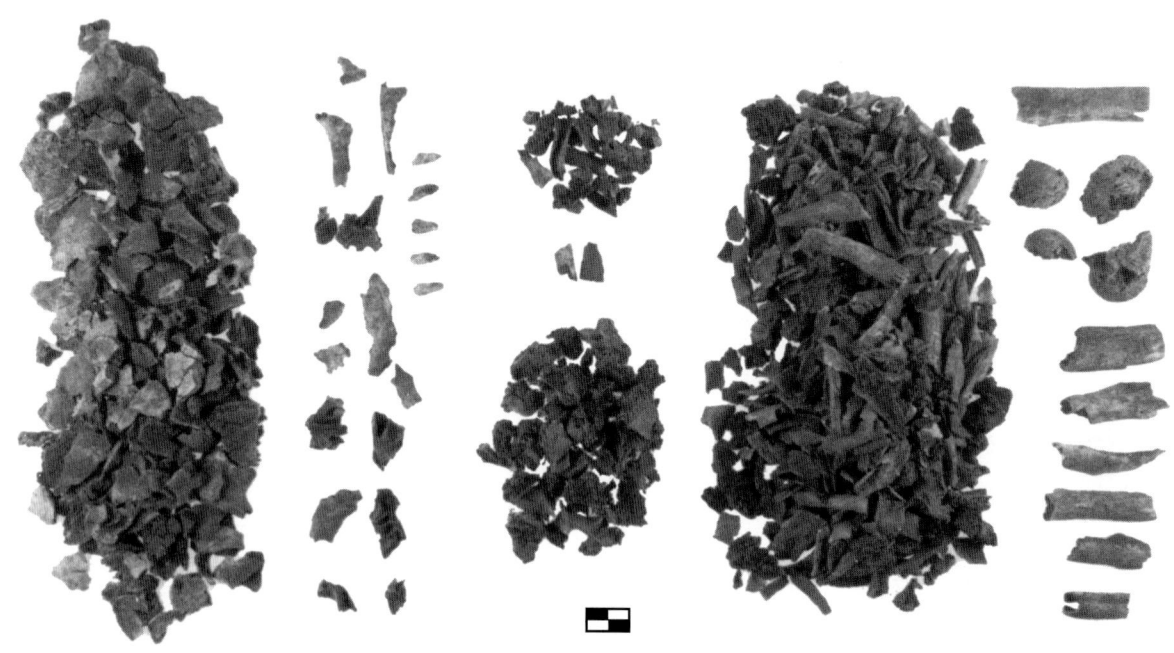

PLATE 487. Tomb 47.

PLATE 488. Tomb 48.

PLATE 489. Tomb 51.

PLATE 490. Tomb 52.

PLATE 491. Tomb 57.

PLATE 492. Tomb 58.

PLATE 493. Tomb 69.

PLATE 494. Tomb 70.

PLATE 495.
Tomb 72.

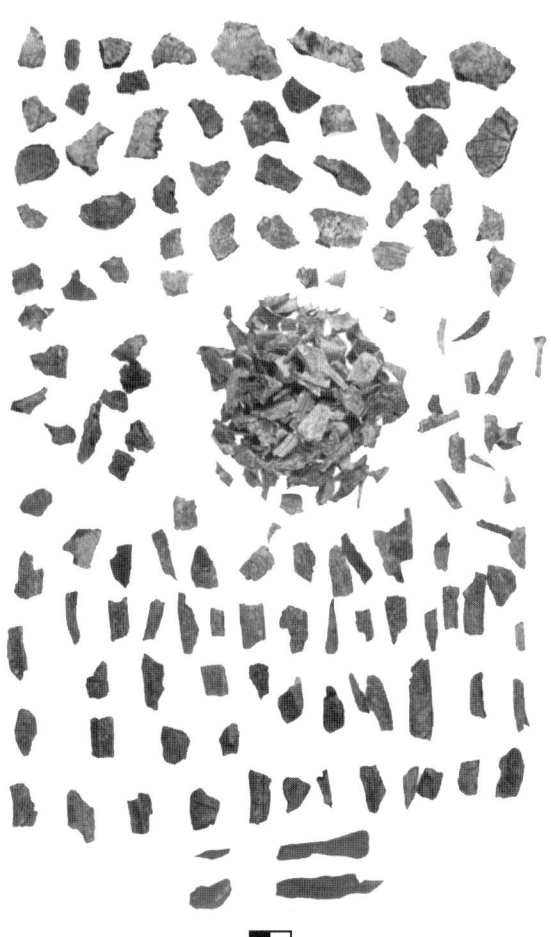

PLATE 496. Tomb 75.

a.

PLATE 497. Tomb 83.
(*a*) Adult. (*b*) Infant.

b.

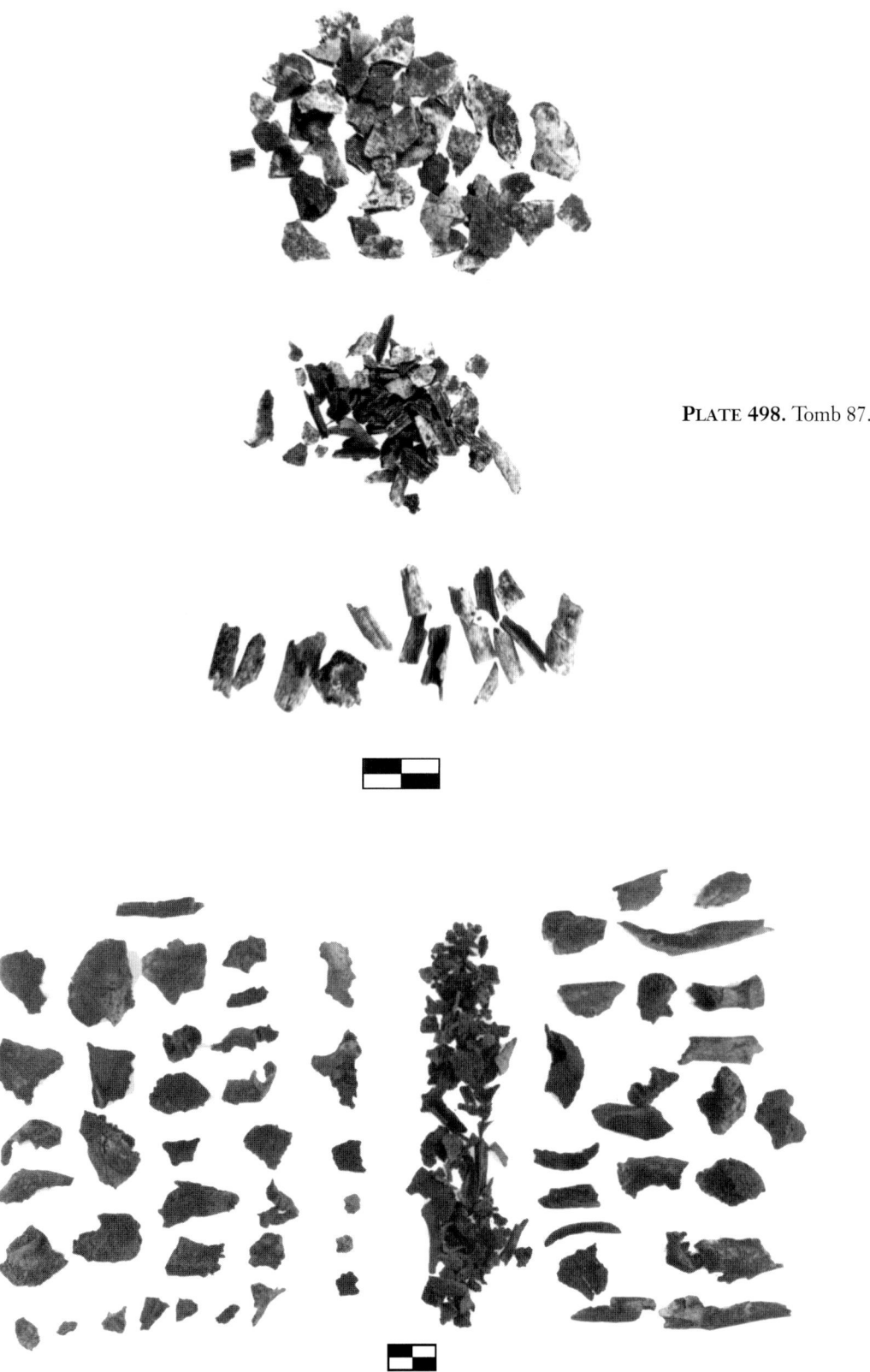

PLATE 498. Tomb 87.

PLATE 499. Tomb 96.

a.

b.

PLATE 500. Tomb 100. (*a*) Cranium.
(*b*) Postcranial bones.

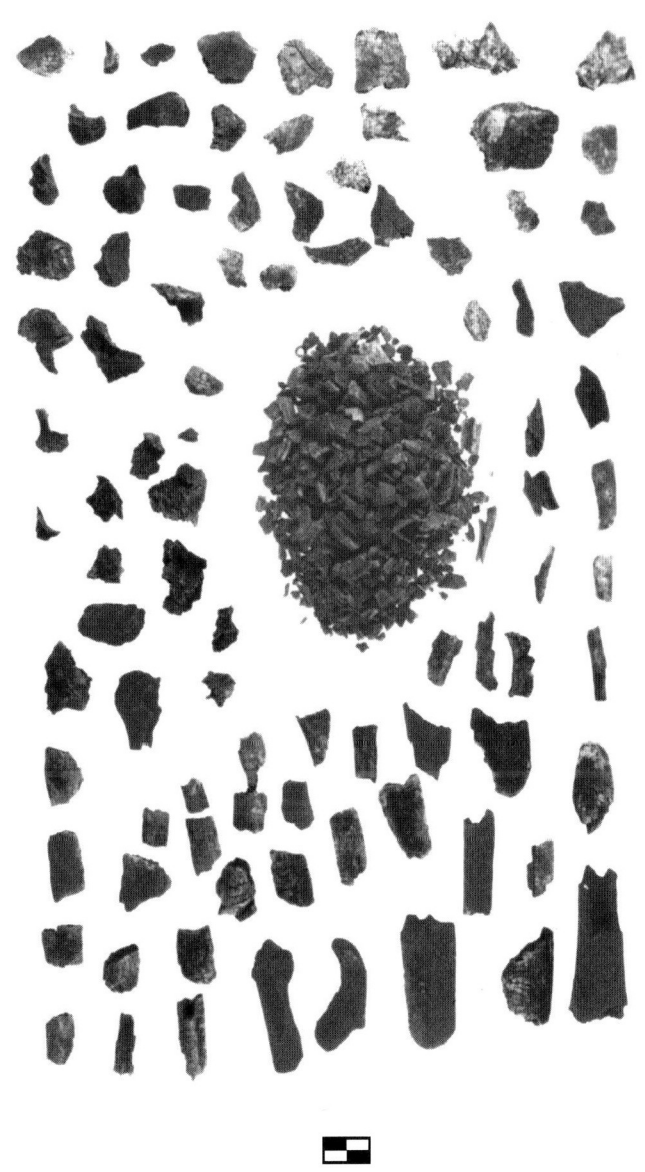

PLATE 501. Tomb 101.

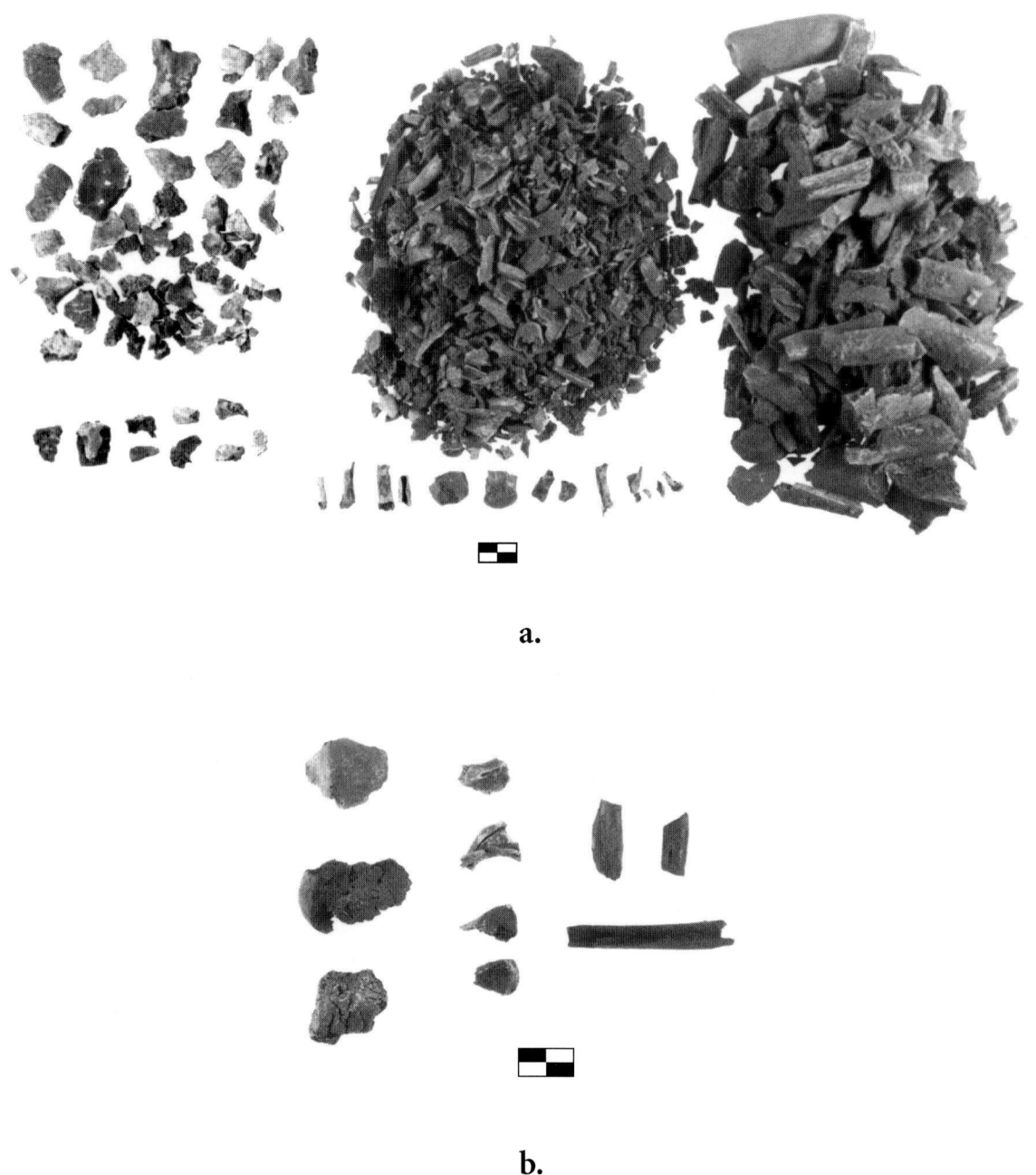

a.

b.

PLATE 502. Tomb 103. (*a*) Cremated remains. (*b*) Evidence of second individual (left), and animal bones (right).

PLATE 503. Tomb 104. Cremated remains from ash-urn (right) and pit fill (left).

PLATE 504. Tomb 106.   **PLATE 505.** Tomb 111.

a.

b.

PLATE 506. Tomb 112. (*a*) Ash-urn I. (*b*) Ash-urn II.

PLATE 507. Tomb 123. (*a*) Adult. (*b*) Fetus/neonate.

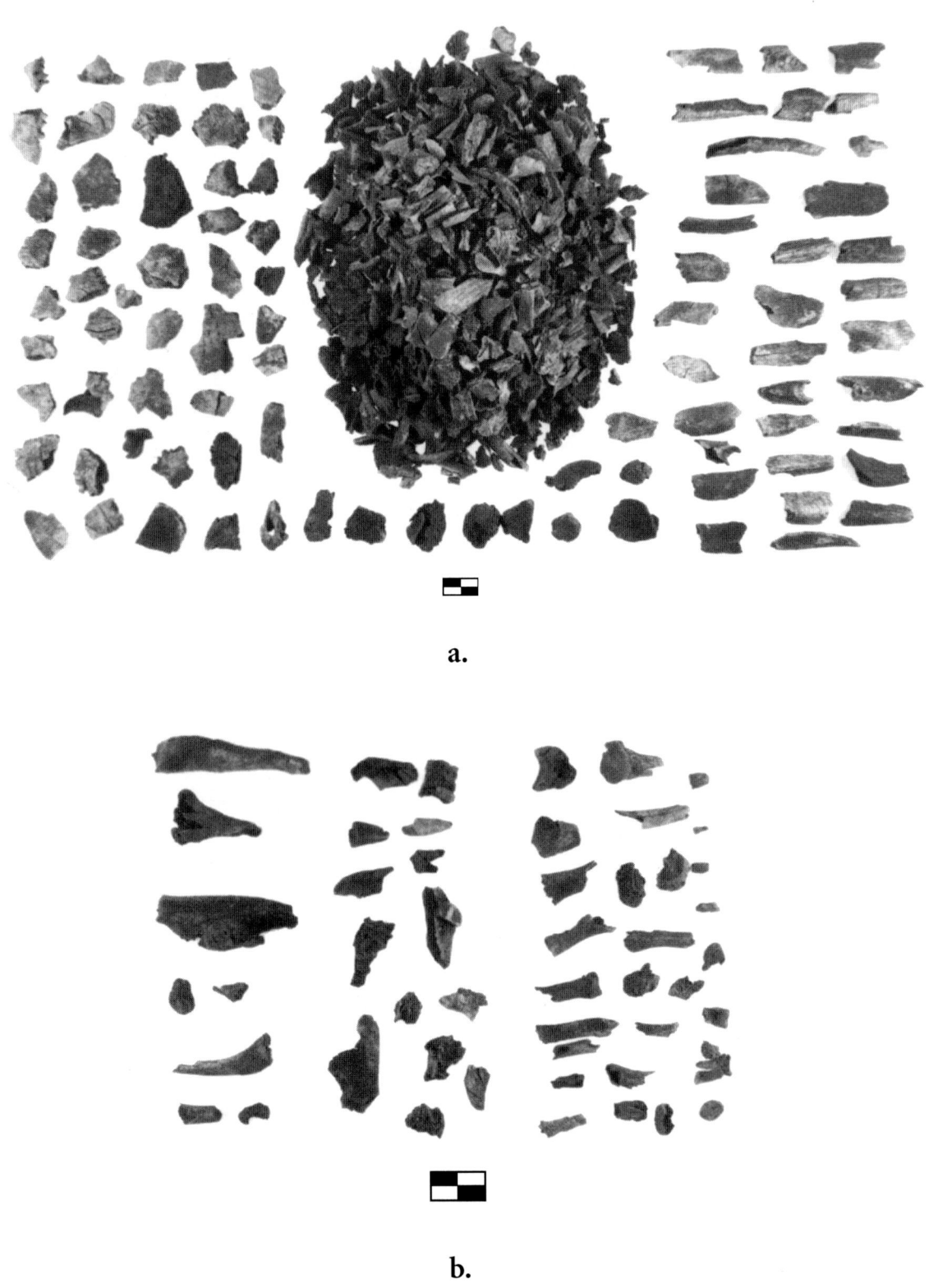

a.

b.

PLATE 508. Tomb 124. (*a*) Majority of cremated bone. (*b*) Detail of some of the bone.

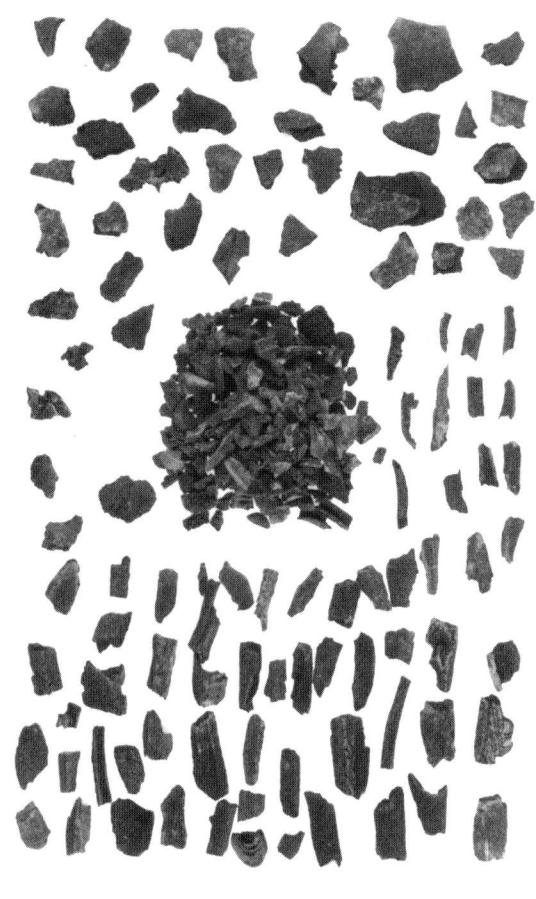

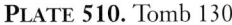

PLATE 509. Tomb 127.

PLATE 510. Tomb 130.

PLATE 511. Tomb 134.

a.

b.

PLATE 512. (a, b) Tomb 24. *Capra*: radius and ulna proximal fragment, right, adult (medial part burned to different grades of decalcination; lateral part unburned).

a.

b.

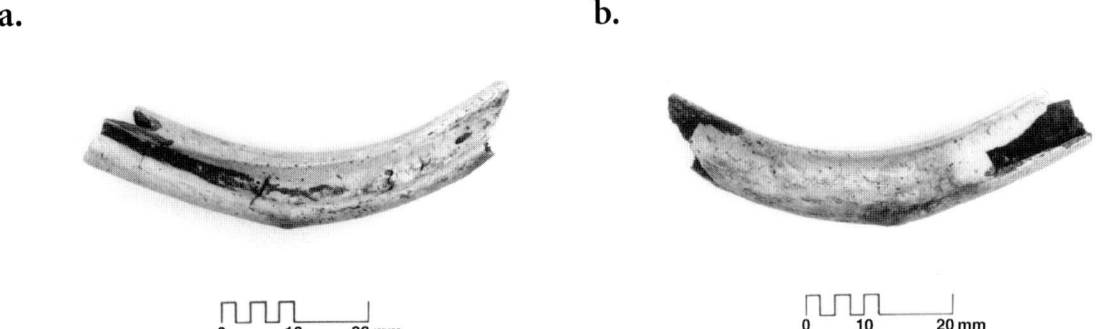

0   10   20 mm

0   10   20 mm

PLATE 513. *(a, b)* Tomb 52. *Sus domestica:* costa fragment (burned to decalcination).

PLATE 514. Tomb 103. *Ovis/Capra:* tibia diaphysis fragment (burned).

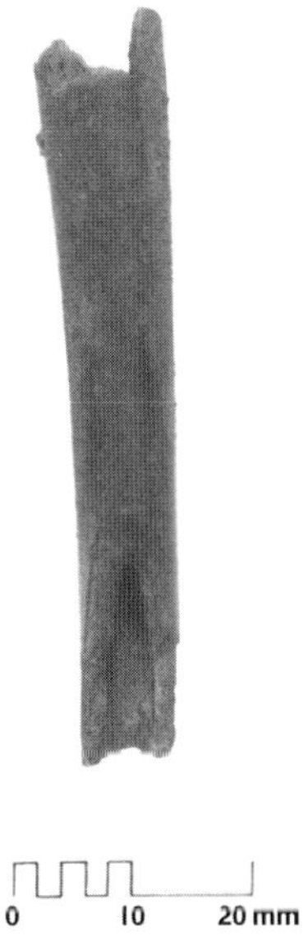

0   10   20 mm

PLATE 515. Tomb 104. Intrusive animal bones, mainly frogs (unburned).

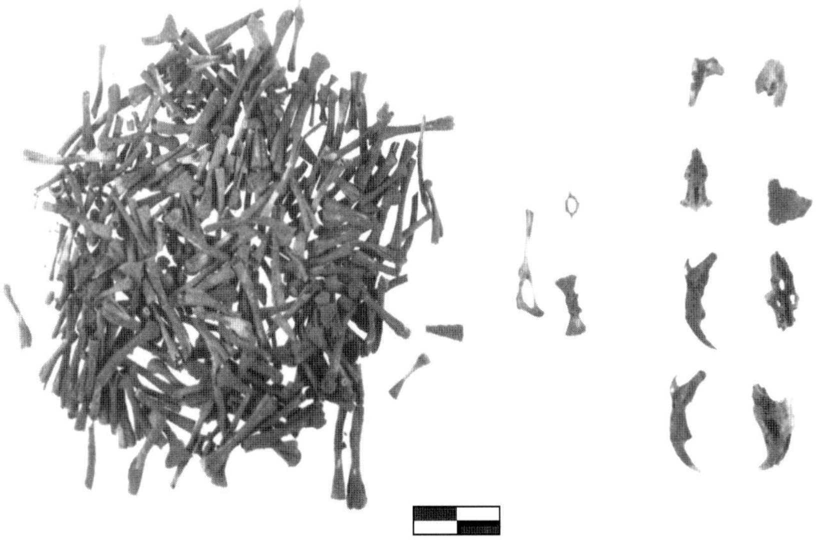

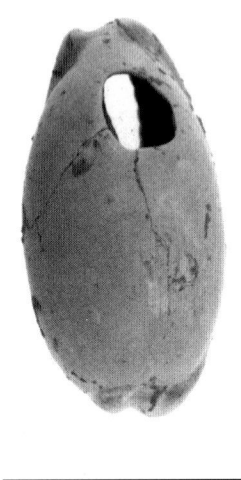

PLATE 516. Pierced cowrie shell from the Early Iron Age cutting.

PLATE 517. Tomb 115. *Spondylus* shell (**T115-4**).

PLATE 518. Assorted burned sieved shell (left) and beach pebbles (right).

PLATE 519. Water-worn and burned pieces of dove shell.

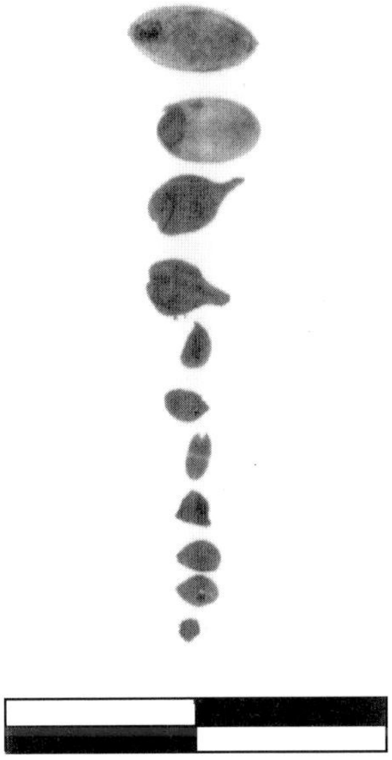

PLATE 520. Tomb 109. Various seeds including *Hordeum vulgare* and *Vitis vinifera* (carbonized), as well as various noncarbonized seeds.

PLATE 521. Tomb 114. Grape seeds (*Vitis vinifera*) and noncarbonized seeds of *Fumaria officinalis*.

PLATE 522. Detail of *prothesis* scene on an Athenian Late Geometric amphora. Athens, National Museum, inv. 804 (photo author).

PLATE 523. Detail of *ekphora* scene on an Athenian Late Geometric krater. Athens, National Museum, inv. 990 (photo author).

PLATE 524. Detail of Athenian red-figure amphora showing Kroisos of Lydia on a pyre. Paris, Louvre, inv. G 197, from Vulci (after Fürtwangler and Reichhold 1886).

LEICHENFEIER DES PATROKLOS. NEAPEL.

PLATE 525. Detail of a pyre on an Apulian red-figure krater in Naples (after Fürtwangler and Reichhold 1886).

PLATE 526. Detail showing Alkmene on the pyre. Paestan bell-krater
signed by Python. British Museum, F 149 (photo author).

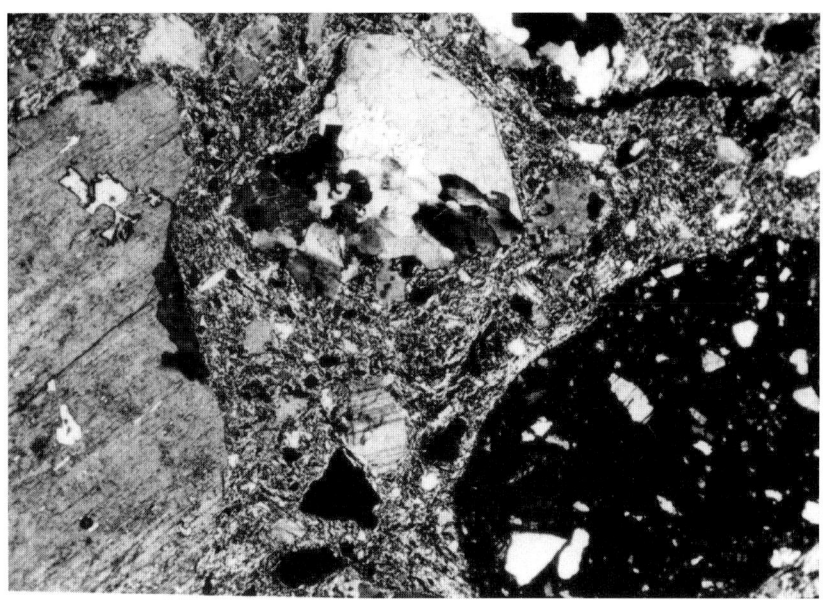

PLATE 527. Microstructure of 81.610 (**T123-2**). Granodiorite fabric with coarse-grained inclusions. Width of photograph is 3.2mm.

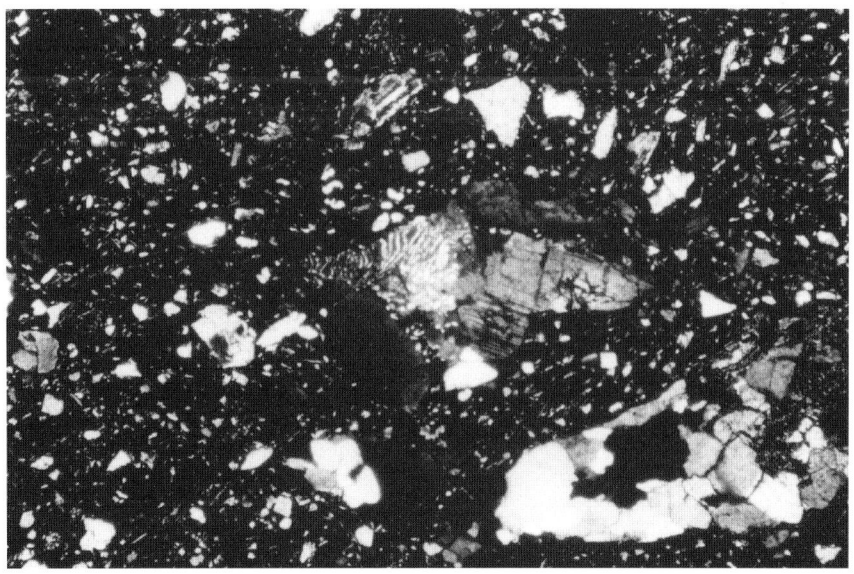

PLATE 528. Microstructure of kiln brick. Granodiorite fabric with coarse-grained inclusions, but with more micaceous (biotite) clay matrix. Width of photograph is 3.2mm.

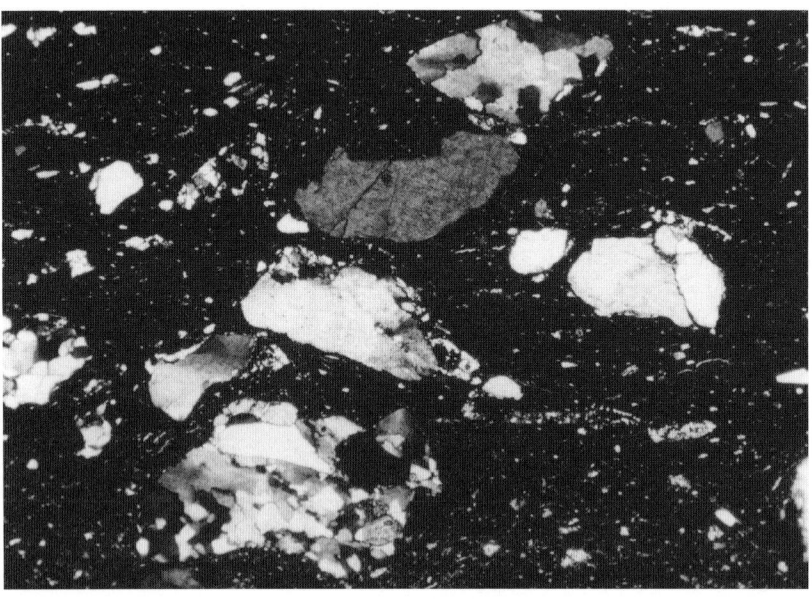

PLATE 529. Microstructure of 82.1188 (**KP-5**). Granodiorite fabric with coarse-grained inclusions; presence of quartz-muscovite schist, a distinct bimodal grain-size distribution, and a relatively fine-grained clay matrix. Width of photograph is 3.2mm.

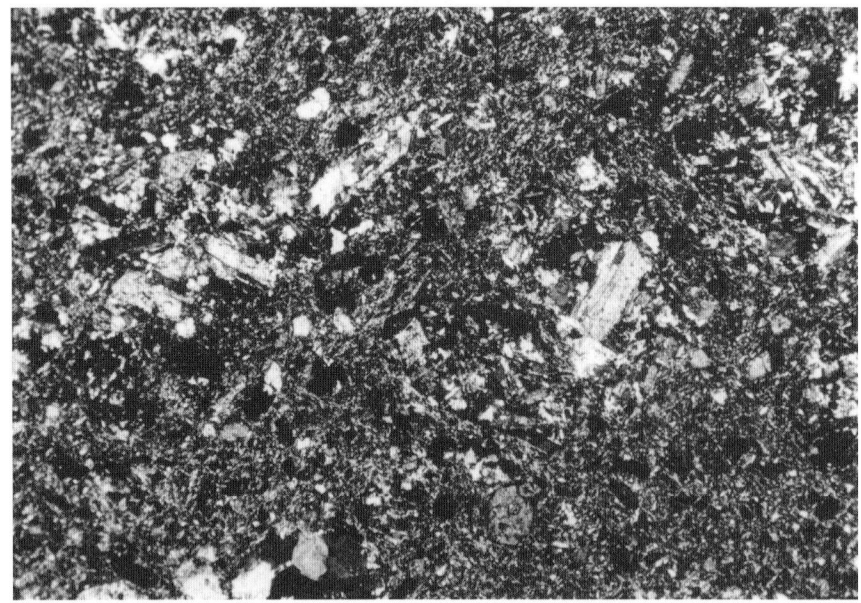

PLATE 530. Microstructure of 82.604 (**KP-1**). Metamorphic fabric.
Width of photograph is 3.2mm.

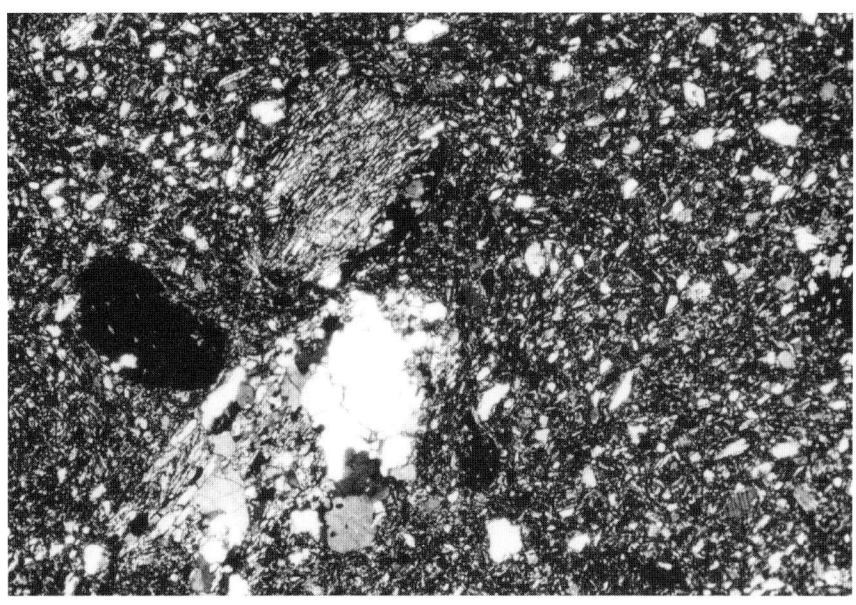

PLATE 531. Microstructure of 82.1106 (**53**). Amphibole fabric (imported handmade). Width of photograph is 3.2mm.

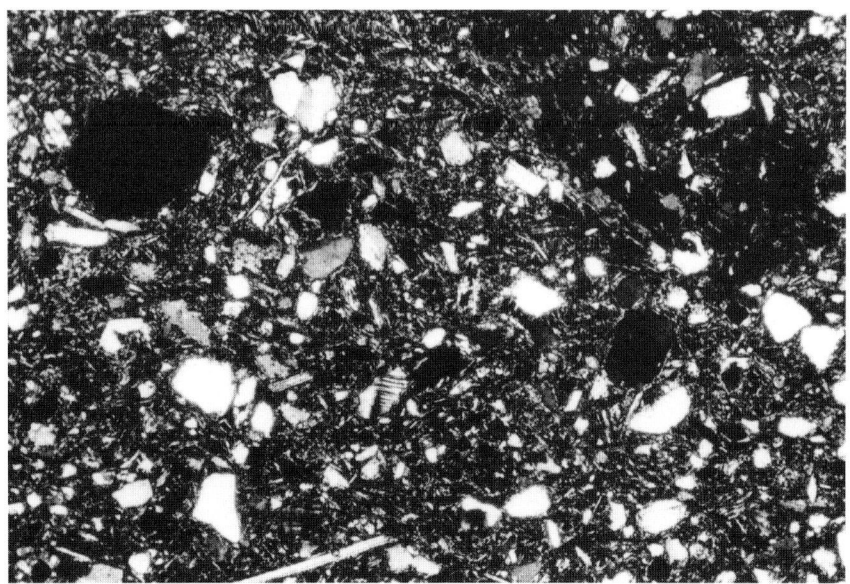

PLATE 532. Microstructure of 81.473 (**T43-1**). Fine sand fabric. Width of photograph is 3.2mm.

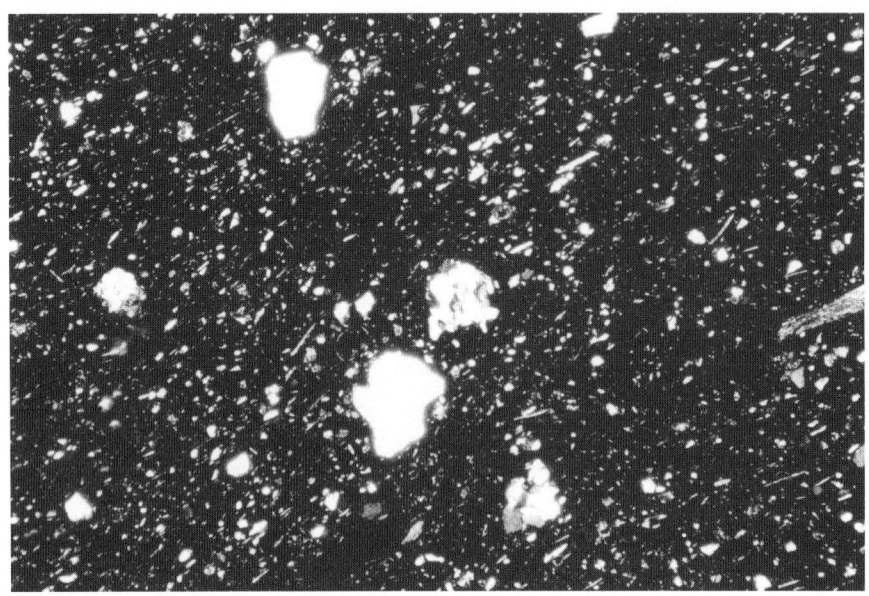

PLATE 533. Microstructure of 81.612 (**T124-3**). Very fine sand fabric.
Width of photograph is 3.2mm.

PLATE 534. Microstructure of 81.561 (**24**). Well-sorted, medium sand-grained fabric.
Width of photograph is 3.2mm.

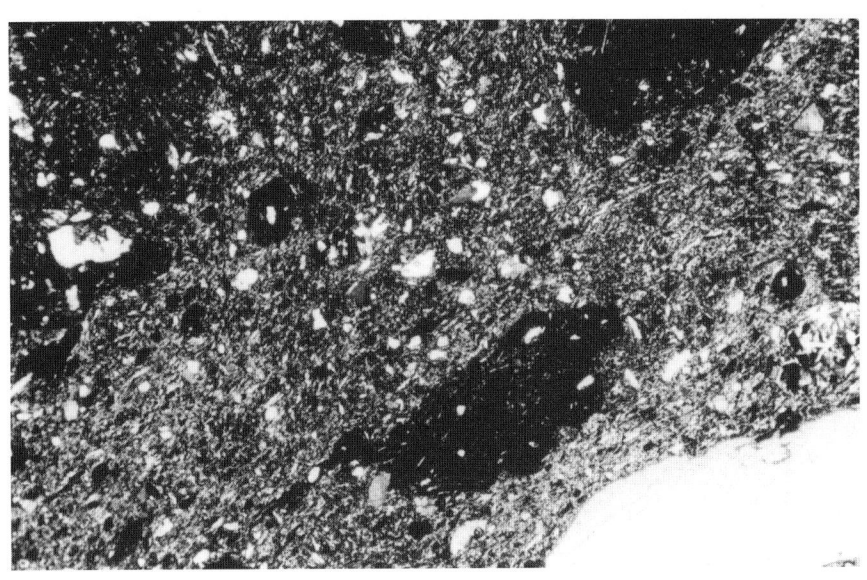

PLATE 535. Microstructure of 81.524 (**T82-4**). Large tcfs fabric.
Width of photograph is 3.2mm.

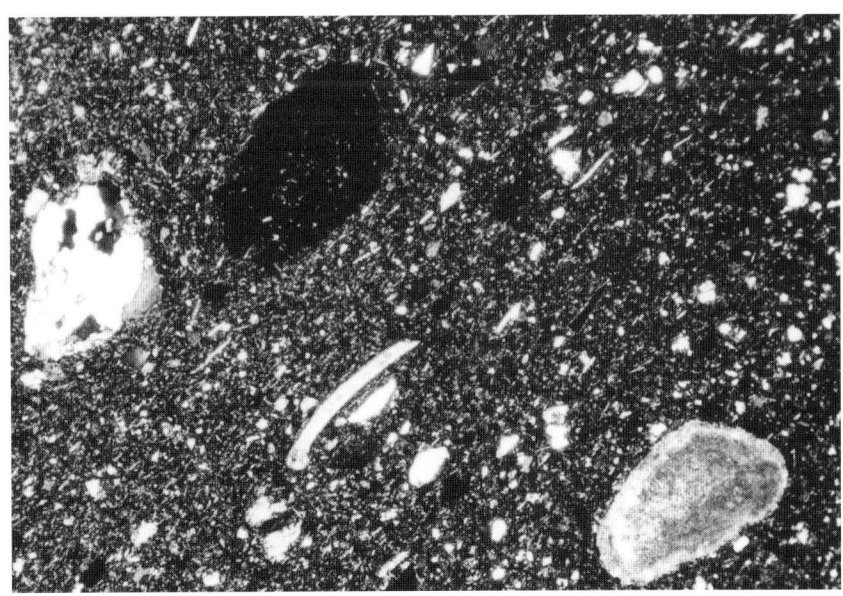

PLATE 536. Microstructure of 81.385 (**T62-1**). Calcareous fabric.
Width of photograph is 3.2mm.

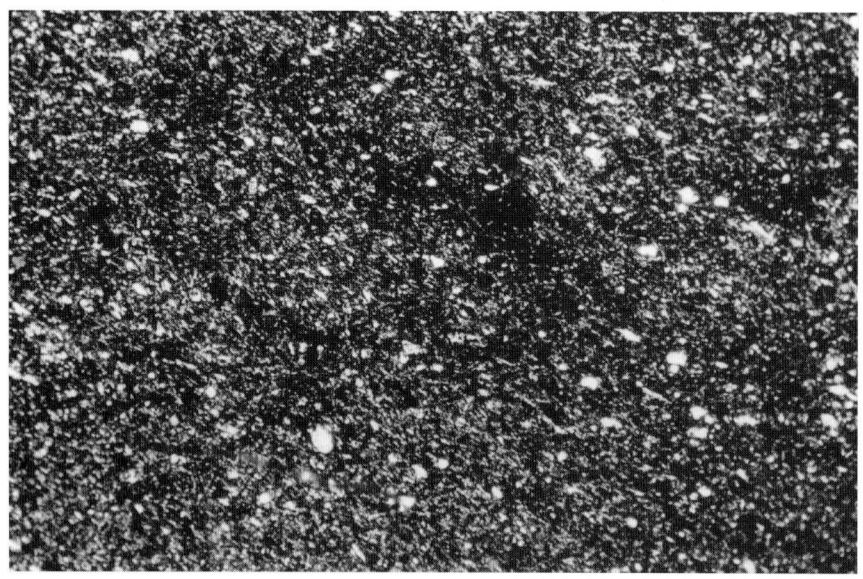

PLATE 537. Microstructure of 84.408 (T77-3). Extremely fine-grained fabric
(imported pendent semicircle skyphos). Width of photograph is 3.2mm.

PLATE 538. Microstructure of clay sample C4, from lagoon to the north
of Torone; fired at 700°C. Width of photograph is 3.2mm.

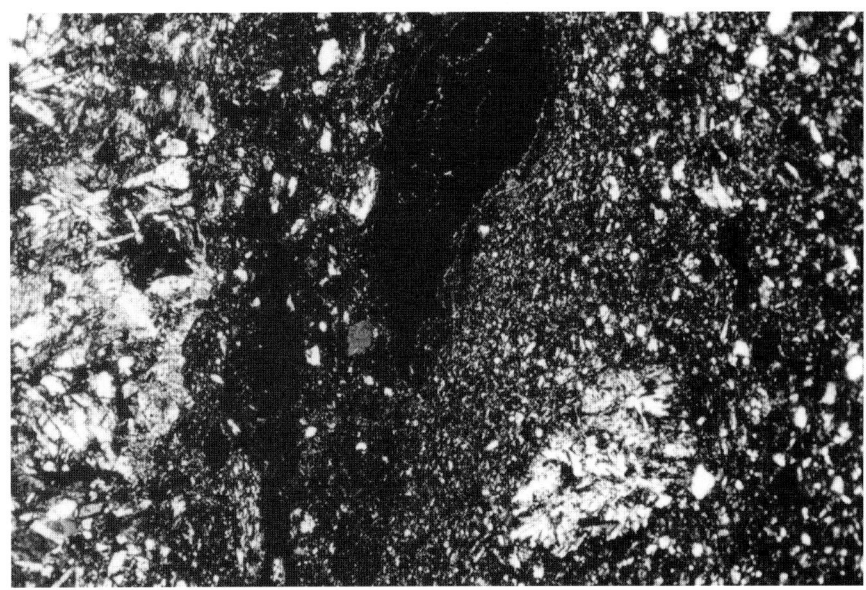

PLATE 539. Microstructure of clay sample C6, from area of amphibolite schists at the base of the NE slope of Vigla (Hill 1); fired at 900°C. Width of photograph is 3.2mm.

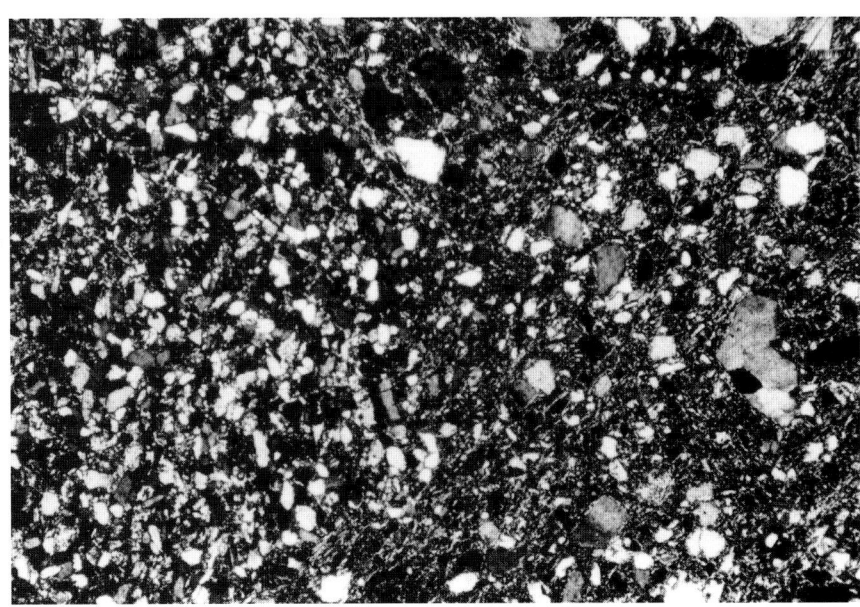

PLATE 540. Microstructure of 81.615 (**T54-1**). Sandstone fabric (imported handmade). Width of photograph is 3.2mm.

Cotsen Institute of Archaeology
Monumenta Archaeologica Series